VOLUNTARY ACTION

by Lord Beveridge

INDIA CALLED THEM

FULL EMPLOYMENT IN A FREE SOCIETY

THE PILLARS OF SECURITY

CHANGES IN FAMILY LIFE

THE EVIDENCE FOR VOLUNTARY ACTION

LORD BEVERIDGE

VOLUNTARY ACTION

A REPORT ON
METHODS OF SOCIAL ADVANCE

LONDON

GEORGE ALLEN & UNWIN LTD

PRINTED IN GREAT BRITAIN
in 11-Point Baskerville Type
BY UNWIN BROTHERS LIMITED
WOKING

CONTENTS

PART ONE

THE MUTUAL AID MOTIVE IN ACTION

PART TWO

THE PHILANTHROPIC MOTIVE IN ACTION

PART THREE

THE NEEDS THAT REMAIN IN A SOCIAL SERVICE STATE

PART FOUR

CONCLUSION AND RECOMMENDATIONS

TABLES

In addition, Section III of Appendix A contains tables of contributions and benefits in particular friendly societies.

PREFACE

"Before it is just to say that a man ought to be an independent labourer, the country ought to be in such a state that a labourer by honest industry can become independent."

WILLIAM AKROYD at dinner of Poor Law
Guardians of Stourbridge, April, 1841.

"Providence has given to no man an indemnity from affliction, disease and death; it is a duty, therefore, that every man owes to himself and family, to provide against these exigencies and that distress which inevitably attends their visitations."

Preface to original rules of Hearts of Oak
Benefit Society, June, 1842.

"Social security must be achieved by co-operation between the State and the individual. The State should offer security for service and contribution. The State in organizing security should not stifle incentive, opportunity, responsibility; in establishing a national minimum, it should leave room and encouragement for voluntary action by each individual to provide more than that minimum for himself and his family."

Report by Sir William Beveridge on Social
Insurance and Allied Services, November,
1942.

THE first two texts quoted above come practically from the same moment in time and between them define the duties of the State, that is the organized community, and the individual, in social advance. The community, through the machinery of the State, has the duty of doing those things which can only be done by the State, of so organizing itself that there is fair opportunity for all men at all times. That is the moral of the first text. This does not absolve the individual from the duty and responsibility of thinking and planning for himself. That is the moral of the second text.

The third text, a hundred years later in date than the first two, in effect repeats them both. Social advance involves action by the State and involves action by the individual. This text comes from a Report on Social Insurance and Allied Services concerned almost wholly with action by the State. It finds an appropriate sequel and completion in the present Report on Voluntary Action, which is concerned primarily with what the individual should do independently of the State, and deals with the State only for the purpose of suggesting how the State can ensure to individuals the maximum of freedom and responsibility.

The term "Voluntary Action," as used here, means private action, that is to say action not under the directions of any authority wielding the power of the State. A study of Voluntary Action, without further limitation, would be as wide as life itself, covering all the undirected activities of individual citizens in their homes as well as outside their homes. This study is confined to Voluntary Action for a public purpose—for social advance. Its theme is Voluntary Action outside each citizen's home for improving the conditions of life for him and for his fellows.

In taking as the characteristic of Voluntary Action independence from public control, I am following the same line as that taken in the valuable study of *Voluntary Social Services*, edited by Miss A. F. C. Bourdillon for the Nuffield College Social Reconstruction Survey and published in 1945. "A generation ago," as is pointed out in the Introductory chapter to that volume, " 'voluntary' was normally used to denote 'unpaid.' A 'voluntary worker' was someone who gave unpaid service to a good cause, and the group which was formed to run this good cause came to be known as a 'voluntary' organization. The group took its name, in fact, from the outstanding characteristic of the workers upon whom it depended. In recent years there has been a significant shift of meaning here. Nowadays many of the most active voluntary organizations are staffed entirely by highly trained and fairly well-paid professional workers. The distinctively 'voluntary' character of such bodies is the product, not of the kind of workers they employ, but of their mode of birth and method of government. A voluntary organization properly speaking is an organization which, whether its workers are paid or unpaid, is initiated and governed by its own members without external control."[1]

The independence of Voluntary Action does not mean lack of co-operation between it and public action. Co-operation between public and voluntary agencies, as is noted below, is one of the special features of British public life. But the term Voluntary Action does imply that the agency undertaking it has a will and a life of its own.

Within that definition this Report is concerned specifically with action inspired by one or other of two main motives—Mutual Aid and Philanthropy. The first motive has its origin in a sense of one's

[1] *Voluntary Social Services: Their Place in the Modern State.* Edited by A. F. C. Bourdillon (Methuen & Co., 1945).

own need for security against misfortune, and realization that, since one's fellows have the same need, by undertaking to help one another all may help themselves. The second motive springs from what is described in my Report on Social Insurance as social conscience, the feeling which makes men who are materially comfortable, mentally uncomfortable so long as their neighbours are materially uncomfortable: to have social conscience is to be unwilling to make a separate peace with the giant social evils of Want, Disease, Squalor, Ignorance, Idleness, escaping into personal prosperity oneself, while leaving one's fellows in their clutches.

The Mutual Aid motive has given rise in Britain to citizen associations of many types, forming the subject of Part I. One type— the Friendly Society—is dealt with more fully than the rest, for two reasons: the making of this study originated in a friendly society and this type up to the present has received less recent attention than it deserves; the last comprehensive study of this friendly society movement was made by a Royal Commission more than seventy years ago; the last book about it was published in 1891. Most of the other leading forms of Mutual Aid association— trade unions, co-operative societies, building societies and so forth have been the subject of abundant and more recent study. They also are dealt with in Part I, but more shortly.

The Philanthropic motive has given rise in Britain to an almost infinite variety of institutions, societies and agencies. No attempt can be made here to do more than describe in Part II their main types, with a few leading instances. One form of agency—the charitable trust—receives special notice, because, like the friendly societies, it has been unduly neglected hitherto. The last comprehensive study of this field was made well over a hundred years ago, by a committee under Lord Brougham, which sat from 1818 to 1837; there is no book on the subject at all, other than the admirable series of addresses given by Arthur Hobhouse (later Lord Hobhouse) between 1865 and 1879 and collected later in a small volume published in 1880 under the title of *The Dead Hand*. Examination of charitable trusts reveals many strange workings of the human mind, and the treatment of these trusts raises important issues of social policy to-day.

Besides the two main motives, of Mutual Aid and of Philanthropy, the present study illustrates the working of two other motives. One is the motive of Personal Thrift, of saving to have money at one's own command, saving for personal independence; from the combination of this more individual motive with that of Mutual

Aid spring some of the most interesting forms of voluntary association of citizens, including that particular friendly society which, as stated below, is responsible for the instigation of this Report. The other is the Business motive; the pursuit of a livelihood or of gain for oneself in meeting the needs of one's fellow-citizens; from the interplay of this motive with that of Mutual Aid or Personal Thrift have sprung organizations which are in some cases of portentous scale.

It is needless to emphasize the importance of the subject whose study is attempted here. In a totalitarian society all action outside the citizen's home, and it may be much that goes on there, is directed or controlled by the State. By contrast, vigour and abundance of Voluntary Action outside one's home, individually and in association with other citizens, for bettering one's own life and that of one's fellows, are the distinguishing marks of a free society. They have been outstanding features of British life.

The people of this small island have made several political inventions of value to the whole world—notably Representative Government and the British Commonwealth of Free Nations in lasting union. Their kindred people across the Atlantic made on an epoch-making scale the invention of Federalism. To-day fresh political inventions are needed urgently—in the international sphere to rule out war, in the domestic sphere to reconcile the responsibilities of the State with the rights and responsibilities of individuals. It is clear that the State must in future do more things than it has attempted in the past. But it is equally clear, or should be equally clear, that room, opportunity, and encouragement must be kept for Voluntary Action in seeking new ways of social advance. There is need for political invention to find new ways of fruitful co-operation between public authorities and voluntary agencies.

The Report now presented is a contribution towards this end. It shows how much all men owe to Voluntary Action for public purposes in the past. It is designed to suggest how Voluntary Action can be kept vigorous and abundant in the future, in face of the inevitable development of State action, and to outline some new forms which co-operation between the State and voluntary organization may take, now that the State has become a Social Service State.

The preparation of the Report is due to the initiative of one of the great friendly societies—the National Deposit Friendly Society—and has been made possible by their readiness to provide all the necessary funds and facilities. This Society, like other

friendly societies, being profoundly affected by the National
Insurance legislation of last year and the prospective divorce
between State insurance and voluntary insurance for friendly
society purposes, invited me to study the problem presented by
this legislation. The Society fell in cordially with my suggestion
that a Report limited to the particular problems of friendly
societies was narrower than the occasion demanded, and they
made it possible for me, with the help of a body of assessors and
with adequate staff and accommodation to cover the much wider
field, embracing the friendly societies but not confined to them,
which has been attempted in this Report.

The fact that one of the great voluntary associations typical of
British life should have made this Inquiry possible, will, I hope,
be regarded as one of the advantages resulting from the strong
development of voluntary associations of all kinds in this country.

In making the present study of Voluntary Action in a Social
Service State I have, so far as possible, repeated the methods of
my two earlier Inquiries. I began the survey of Social Insurance
and Allied Services at the request of the Government in June,
1941, simply as Chairman of a Committee of Civil Servants. In the
course of the Inquiry there was a change of responsibility. The
Committee became my technical advisers and the responsibility
for everything said in the Report became mine alone. But these
advisers functioned as a committee in examination of witnesses
and in discussion and criticism of every draft which I submitted to
them. The Report was not and could not have been prepared as
a one-man job.

My next study, of Full Employment in a Free Society, I made
not at the request of the Government, indeed with formal denial
of their co-operation. But I made it with financial resources placed
at my disposal by three friends and with the indispensable help
of a group of technical Assessors. At their own request I did not
in my Report name these assessors, but they were as indispensable
as the Civil Servants of the first study. There was rather less examination of witnesses than in the case of my first Report, but there was
even more of critical discussion of problems and drafts.

For the present Third Report I have enjoyed the help of the
Assessors named in my Acknowledgments who with me have
examined memoranda and witnesses and have seen and criticized
all my drafts. I have had the assistance of an admirable staff. I have
found in all the Government departments concerned—notably the
Registry of Friendly Societies, the Charity Commission, and the

Treasury—sympathetic readiness to give me every legitimate help. For everything written here I alone remain responsible. But what is written is as little a one-man job as were the Report on Social Insurance and Allied Services and the Report on Full Employment in a Free Society.

It has seemed convenient in this case, as it was in dealing with Social Insurance and Allied Services, to publish the results of the Inquiry in two volumes. The present volume is my Report, written by myself on Voluntary Action as a means of social advance. It is accompanied by a Supplementary Volume, to be published with it or soon after, entitled *The Evidence for Voluntary Action*. That volume will contain in whole or in part the more important memoranda submitted by organizations, or individuals not taking part in the Inquiry, the results of the two investigations put in hand through Mass Observation and Research Services, and memoranda on special topics which could not be dealt with adequately in the Report itself. By this means the Appendices in the present volume have been reduced to four in number. The Table of Contents of the Supplementary Volume, edited by myself and by Mr. A. F. Wells who assisted me throughout the Inquiry, is printed as the last of these Appendices. The present volume is complete in itself, but I hope that it will lead many to consult also *The Evidence for Voluntary Action*.

The Inquiry, by the nature of its origin, had to be compressed within a limited time, so that its results might be available for the guidance of friendly societies and others as early as possible in 1948. In the time available and despite the generous help provided by the National Deposit Friendly Society and the ready co-operation of practically all the voluntary agencies to whose notice the Inquiry was brought, the Inquiry could not be exhaustive. Indeed, any exhaustive description of voluntary activity in Britain would, by the nature of the case, be not worth making. The subject-matter of such an Inquiry alters every year or month or week, as new agencies arise and old ones decay. The essence of voluntary activity is that it should not be stereotyped.

I have dealt at some length with certain forms of Voluntary Action which have hitherto received insufficient attention. I have said relatively little about certain other forms—notably the great fields of hospital provision and of school education—not because they seem less important, but because both these services are at the moment in transition. Anything that I wrote to-day might be out of date by the time that it could be published.

To some extent this difficulty applies not only to such topics as hospitals and education, but to most of the field surveyed in this Report. Voluntary Action is being affected by a continual stream of legislation. At the date of this Preface there are two important new Bills before Parliament, one concerned with industrial assurance and friendly societies, one with children deprived of a normal home life. Both came before Parliament after what I had first written was in the hands of the printer. The final form of legislation in each case is still unsettled.

And even those forms of Voluntary Action to which I have devoted most attention are described, less for their own sakes than as illustrations of general principles. Many of them are illustrations also of the value of dynamic individuals.

The nineteenth century in Britain was a time of private enterprise, not only in pursuit of gain, but also in social reform. The interplay of these two motives of gain and service in the fields covered by this survey is one of its themes. In the nineteenth century many men made fortunes for themselves in meeting the needs of their fellows. Many others, driven by social conscience to attack want, squalor, ignorance, disease and idleness, inspired or created societies and institutions to serve their aims. The amount of unhappiness that has been put out of the world through the lives and works of such men as Lord Shaftesbury with his Ragged School Union, or Elizabeth Fry with her attack on cruel stupidity in the prisons, or Charles Booth the originator of Social Surveys, or Samuel Barnett the Founder of Toynbee Hall, or Benjamin Waugh the Founder of the National Society for the Prevention of Cruelty to Children, is beyond all calculation. Because their work was so individual, it has seemed appropriate in this Report to give a brief account of some of these pioneers, to show where they sprang from and how they were led to their service. This account of persons, like that of the institutions, is to be regarded as illustrative rather than complete. Many are not mentioned whose service to humanity was as great as that of those who are mentioned. My object in the chapter of Pioneers is not an award of honours; none of these men and women would have done their work had they cared for praise. My object is to show how some of these pioneers came to be, and to suggest the conditions for ensuring that they have successors.

The great friendly society which is responsible for the making of this Report illustrates the working of all the three motives—of Mutual Aid, of Personal Thrift, and of Philanthropy—which are the theme of this Report. The National Deposit Friendly Society—

to-day twice as large in numbers as any other Friendly Society in Britain—had its origin in Philanthropy; it is still based closely on a scheme devised 116 years ago by the clergyman of a country parish, the Honourable and Reverend Samuel Best, in seeking to promote the well-being of his neighbours in Hampshire, and adapted 79 years ago by another country clergyman—Canon Portal—to his own parish in Surrey. The National Deposit Friendly Society, born in the Rectory library at Albury, owes its amazing growth to the fact that in its structure appeals to the distinct though allied motives of Mutual Aid and of Personal Thrift were ingeniously combined by its philanthropic authors.

The other society whose earliest rules furnish one of the three texts at the head of this Preface had a different origin, also with its moral for our time. Like so many associations which ultimately spread all over the country, the Hearts of Oak began in a meeting of a handful of unknown individuals in a back room—individuals not satisfied with what they were getting from existing institutions and therefore making a new institution to meet their needs, as men always can in a free society.

The author of the first of the three texts has his place also in what is written below. William Akroyd of Stourbridge, who lived from 1804 to 1869, and made sympathetic administration of the Poor Law one of his major interests in life, was kin of an earlier William Akroyd of Marston in Yorkshire, who died in 1518, leaving land by his will for provision of scholarships at a University for his kin "to the end of the world." The way in which this foundation 250 years later, having increased greatly in value, was diverted in the main to developing education irrespective of founder's kin, is an illustration of one of the problems of Charitable Trusts discussed in this Report. Yet the intentions of the founder were not defeated. The diversion of funds was not complete. Three hundred and seventy-nine years after the founder's death I was able, as a grandson of William Akroyd of Stourbridge, to enjoy for four years a substantial scholarship at Oxford won in competition with other members of the founder's kin, two cousins, one near and one remote.

All three texts have one thing in common. They are all assertions of duty, either of the community, that is to say, its leaders, or of the individual. Emphasis on duty rather than assertion of rights presents itself to-day as the condition on which alone humanity can resume the progress in civilization which has been interrupted by two world wars and remains halted by their consequences.

February 1948   BEVERIDGE

ACKNOWLEDGMENTS

My first acknowledgments are due to those who worked with me in this Inquiry as Assessors, namely:—

THE LADY BEVERIDGE, O.B.E.
MR. D. N. CHESTER
MR. JOHN A. LINCOLN
MISS VIOLET R. MARKHAM, C.H., LL.D., J.P.
MR. J. C. MAUDE, K.C., M.P.
MRS. BARBARA WOOTTON, J.P.

They acted as a committee in interviewing representatives of organizations and individuals who came before us, and in discussions. They met formally eighteen times for these purposes. Individually the Assessors read all the chapters of my Report in draft, pointed out gaps and mistakes, and suggested innumerable improvements. I cannot overstate my debt to them for this help.

Mr. John A. Lincoln, in addition to acting as an Assessor, undertook the burden of being the honorary secretary to the Inquiry. But he was much more than a helper after the Inquiry had started. He was the originator of the Inquiry, persuasively bringing the National Deposit Friendly Society and myself together. But for him the Inquiry would not have taken place.

Nor, of course, would it have taken place without the public-spirited help of the National Deposit Friendly Society. They provided not only the necessary funds but also office accommodation and other facilities in their own building at Universal House, in Buckingham Palace Road. They did this while leaving the conduct of the Inquiry in my hands. They appeared before us simply as one friendly society among others. The smooth working of our Inquiry was helped materially by the unfailing co-operation of the Committee of the Society and its officials both present and past, including notably among the present officials Mr. D. H. Roper, now General Secretary of the Society, and among former officials Commander Longdon-Griffiths who held the same position when the Inquiry was launched.

The principal research assistants engaged for the Inquiry were Mrs. Joan S. Clarke and Mr. A. F. Wells. In finding these two to help us we were extremely fortunate. They were indefatigable, whole-hearted, able and inventive. They did not wait to be told where to research; they made each of them many valuable original suggestions. To mention no other points, Mrs. Clarke made the first suggestion of having a chapter on Pioneers, and it was she who urged the special significance, as an unduly neglected problem, of the case of the physically handicapped. Mr. Wells, while his main work was in collecting information as to friendly societies and other forms of mutual aid, insisted on my paying attention to interesting institutions such as The Trustee Savings Banks and societies for urban and rural amenities, which at first I had tended to treat as outside my scope.

It was a particular pleasure to myself to be able to obtain once more the help of my former private secretary, Mrs. Lucia Turin, as assistant secretary to the Inquiry.

All the funds necessary for the Inquiry were promised by the National Deposit Friendly Society, but when a question arose of whether we could, within the limits of our planned budget, commission investigations by each of two distinct agencies, Mass Observation and Research Services Ltd., the question was happily solved by a grant of £1,000 from the Nuffield Foundation. This grant was valuable in itself and as an encouragement to us to proceed.

The results of two other investigations have generously been placed at our disposal by those who commissioned them. I have to thank the League for Education against Gambling for giving me unrestricted access to the results of an investigation made for them by Mass Observation. I have to thank Hulton Publications Limited for giving me similar access to the results of an investigation made for them by Research Services, for the purpose of a readership survey.

The Inquiry is concerned with Voluntary Action rather than with the activity of Government departments. But there are some departments largely concerned with the encouragement or assistance of Voluntary Action, and there are others whose activity may affect Voluntary Action. At the outset of the Inquiry I wrote to the then Chancellor of the Exchequer, Mr. Hugh Dalton, to explain what I had in mind. By his kindness and that of his successor, Sir Stafford Cripps, I have been assured of a friendly and helpful reception from various Government departments and officials. Those to whom I owe a special debt are the Registrar of Friendly Societies, the Charity Commissioners, the Legal Branch of the Board of Education dealing with educational trusts, and the Treasury in obtaining for me from the departments concerned the information as to grants to voluntary agencies which is used in Chapter XI

and set out in the supplementary volume. The officials of the Registry of Friendly Societies, in particular, dealt courteously and promptly with innumerable, almost daily enquiries, both large and small, which must have imposed a considerable burden upon them. I have also had helpful statements of fact on problems of taxation from some of the departments concerned with this subject. None of this information has been confidential, and none, of course, has touched on questions of policy. It represents the kind of help which Government departments should always be ready to give, and are normally free to give to serious inquiring citizens. This help does not, of course, mean that any Government department, or any one other than myself personally is in any way responsible for anything that appears in this volume.

I have to thank finally all the societies, institutions and agencies for voluntary action in different forms who supplied me with information as to their activities, problems and needs. All this, to the limit of my time and powers and that of my fellow-workers, has been studied, and has been used up to the limit of the space available for placing it on record. I know that to some of those who have helped me with information I shall appear not to have drawn the picture in its right proportions, to have said too little of some things and too much perhaps about others. I did not attempt—I could not in any reasonable time have made—a comprehensive picture in uniform scale of all that is being done to-day by a myriad agencies to improve the material and spiritual conditions of life for our people. I shall be well repaid, and I hope that all who have helped with information will feel repaid, if what is written here helps to maintain the vigour and the inspiration of Voluntary Action.

PART ONE

THE MUTUAL AID MOTIVE
IN ACTION

I. THE FRIENDLY SOCIETIES

Friendly Societies a Natural Growth.   The Royal Commission's Picture
in 1874.   Friendly Societies Classified.   The Affiliated Orders.
Unitary Accumulating Societies.   Societies with Dividend: Dividing
Societies; Deposit Societies; Holloway Societies.   Burial Societies and
the Business Motive.   Secession the Midwife of Invention.   Friendly
Societies more than Mutual Insurance.

FRIENDLY SOCIETIES A NATURAL GROWTH

A FRIENDLY SOCIETY, in the first Act of Parliament which used that
term, was described as "a society of good fellowship for the purpose
of raising from time to time, by voluntary contributions, a stock or
fund for the mutual relief and maintenance of all and every the
members thereof, in old age, sickness, and infirmity, or for the relief
of widows and children of deceased members." This description
comes from the "Act for the Encouragement and Relief of Friendly
Societies" passed in 1793 on the initiative of George Rose, Member
for Launceston, and commonly named after its author the "Rose
Act." In its emphasis on good fellowship and the voluntary nature
of the contributions, as in its list of purposes, it gives a fair summary
of friendly societies at their best in all stages of their history.

The essence of a friendly society is that men who know one another
pay money regularly into a common fund in order to be able to
draw on that fund when they are in need. The need that has been
felt most generally as calling for this provision is the need that
arises when sickness of a wage-earner interrupts his earning. Desire
for security in sickness is the original seed from which above all
friendly societies have grown. There have been other seeds as well—
two in particular: desire to have a lump of money to spend and
desire to avoid a pauper funeral; each of these desires, as will be
noted below, has produced characteristic growths. And the growth
itself has been so varied and so great as to obscure the origin.
Common provision for sickness by men knowing one another was
the origin, and remains the staple, of friendly society work. But the
term friendly society in the course of its history has come to cover
associations which do not undertake this particular task, and in
which it is impossible for the members to know one another.

The history of friendly societies begins long before Rose's Act.
Friendly societies were and are creatures not of Parliament but of

brotherly feeling and felt need in small groups of ordinary men throughout the length and breadth of Britain. A century before Rose's Act, Daniel Defoe, writing in 1696, devoted a chapter in his *Essay on Projects* to "Friendly Societies" and used the term as something that would be well understood by his readers. The oldest society now existing in whose title the word "friendly" occurs dates from about the same epoch; it is the Goldsmiths' Friendly Society, established in Clerkenwell in 1712, and still functioning in 1945 with 74 members and funds of £4,435.

But there are considerably older associations registered and functioning to-day as friendly societies, though without that name. The Methuselah of them is the Incorporation of Carters in Leith, claiming foundation in 1555, and having 51 members and £11,007 of funds nearly 400 years later in 1945. Next to this, with foundation in 1634, comes the United General Sea Box of Borrowstouness, generally shortened to Bo'ness, another port on the Firth of Forth twenty miles west of Leith. Next, from 1670, comes the Fraternity of Dyers in Linlithgow, five miles inland from Bo'ness, with the Burgesses and Trades Poor Box of Anstruther Easter (1701), and the Ancient Society of Gardeners in and about Dunfermline (1716), both from Fife just across the Forth, following not far behind. That so many of the surviving patriarchs of the friendly society movement should all be found in this same small region may be taken as a sign of special thriftiness and persistence in the Lowland Scot.

In this, as in many other sides of British history, there is yet another un-English strain. The oldest of the surviving societies outside Scotland are Huguenot in origin, the Norman Society of 1703 and the Society of Lintot of 1708, both founded by refugees from religious persecution in France who settled in Spitalfields. A little later in the same region of London came the Protestant Refugees from High and Low Normandy Friendly Society; this has as its address to-day the University Settlement of Oxford House in Bethnal Green.[1]

[1] Two other early societies of Huguenot origin dating from 1687 and 1720, though now defunct, survived into the twentieth century. The older of them, beginning as the "Society of Parisians," changed its name and became simply the "Friendly Society" meeting in the Norfolk Arms, Ivimy Road, Bethnal Green, but retained its character as a society limited on entry to "Protestants from eighteen to forty-one years old, of undeniable character, sound in body and mind, living within three miles of Christ Church, Spitalfields," and limited to a total number of 61. More than 200 years from its foundation this society still had its full number and funds exceeding £1,200. Both these societies, with their

The oldest of the friendly societies still at work in Britain are thus either Scottish or French in origin. One of the reasons given for the Huguenot foundations is that the Huguenots found themselves as aliens excluded from relief under the Poor Law of Elizabeth; they were driven to self-help. In so far as such a motive applied to them it would apply also in Scotland, where public provision for relief of poverty long lagged behind that of England.

But though there are early strains other than English in the friendly society movement, the movement itself is more characteristically English than it is Scottish or French. The earliest Scottish societies are all associated with a particular way of earning a living; they may be trade gilds becoming societies for mutual aid. The friendly society origins in England were more general and the societies were in fact more widely spread. The table of Early Friendly Societies given in the Supplementary Volume shows hardly a county in England without a representative, while most of the Scottish counties are blank. The table shows also how in England the vast majority of these early societies were located at inns. The village inn as a social centre is more characteristically English than Scottish.

Persistence of the small local society is a feature of all parts of Britain alike. The table of early societies shows 191 societies in Britain founded before 1800 and still functioning in 1905. Seven of these were of specialized character connected with the fighting services or with churches and providing pensions for widows and orphans or annuities, or providing only for burial. But the rest appear to be ordinary friendly societies. The first World War, or probably even more, the coming of National Health Insurance in 1911, made a considerable drop in their numbers; by 1928 the 191 had been reduced to 70, but of those in spite of the second World War, 52 were still functioning in 1945, nearly all of them at least 150 years old. The average membership of the whole 52 was less than 100, but they had more than £50 a head of funds. Some of them were showing signs of age, in falling membership and rising funds, but many seemed set for another 150 years. The three female clubs of Cheddar, Wrington, and Shipham in Somersetshire, all founded in the 1790's, are typical of this persistence; they had between them 203 members in 1928 with £2,777

funds and their membership all but intact, disappeared together in 1912, presumably in view of the coming of National Insurance. The five early friendly societies of Huguenot origin, as they stood in 1897, were described in a paper by W. C. Waller printed in the *Huguenot Society Proceedings*, vol. 6, p. 201 *et seq.*

of funds, about the same as they had always had; in 1945 their membership was 199 and their funds were £3,882.

THE ROYAL COMMISSION'S PICTURE IN 1874

Organization in small units is characteristic not only of the early friendly societies but of friendly societies at all stages of their history, at least till the coming of State insurance. The very full returns published by the Registrar for the year 1905 make possible a complete survey of the field. There were at that time in Britain about 20,000 branches of the societies known as Affiliated Orders; as is shown later, each of these branches, though in federal union with others, had its own life and was for many purposes self-governing; the average membership of a branch was 133. There were in addition about 6,700 friendly societies without branches; some of these were specialized on purposes other than provision against sickness and some were large. But the great bulk were small, independent units comparable in size to the branch of an order and doing the same work of provision for sickness; half of them had less than 100 members each, and nearly another third had from 100 to 200 members each. How the friendly society movement has been affected by the coming of State insurance will be considered later. But it is still organized in the main in small local units—to-day some 18,500. The friendly societies have not been planned. They represent a local growth which has covered Britain. In all parts of Britain they have sprouted out of the soil, for the common purpose of mutual aid in meeting needs.

The luxuriance and variety of this natural growth make orderly description difficult. The Royal Commission under the Chairmanship of Sir Stafford Northcote which more than seventy years ago made the first—and the last—comprehensive study of friendly societies, classified them in a way that seems almost designed to show that they could not be classified. The Commission dealt with the registered friendly societies under twelve heads as follows:—

1. Affiliated societies or orders;
2. Ordinary, large or general societies;
3. County societies and other patronized societies not purely local;
4. Local town societies;
5. Local village and country societies;
6. Particular trade societies;
7. Dividing societies;

8. Deposit friendly societies;
9. Collecting societies and burial societies generally;
10. Annuity societies;
11. Societies of females;
12. Societies established by authority of the Secretary of State under Section 9 of the Friendly Societies Act.

The Commission's grouping of friendly societies displays as heroic a cross division as can ever have been made. The "Societies of Females," forming Class 11, must all in fact have belonged to one of the other classes as well. "Deposit Friendly Societies" and "Dividing Societies" would some of them be ordinary general, some county, some local or trade societies. Societies in most of the classes other than No. 10 might provide annuities. The sudden reference to patronage in the title of Class 3 is left hanging without explanation in the text.[1]

But this Royal Commission who thus classified in 1874 were not confused in mind. They knew their job and they did it admirably. They adopted the plan, subsequently repeated so effectively by the Poor Laws Commission of 1905–9, of appointing highly qualified Assistant Commissioners to tour the country and do anthropological field work for them. Their Report has a refreshing crispness of style:—

"Building societies do not build; they simply make advances on building."[2]

"The great bulk of collecting societies are burial societies; the great bulk of burial societies are collecting societies."[3]

"We have occasionally had to receive evidence of which we fear, none of those who heard it could doubt the deliberate falseness."[4]

The Commission's account of the Registry and the Registrar of Friendly Societies in Edinburgh is a classic deserving to be preserved. They found in the Scottish Registrar "an aged gentleman of courteous manners and evidently benevolent character who threw himself

---

[1] "Patronized" means that some local notable—usually squire or parish clergyman—was responsible for starting the society, in contrast to societies started by those who became ordinary members. The word affords another example of heroic cross division; the leading deposit friendly societies of Class 8 were "patronized," some being purely local and others not so.

[2] Second Report, para. 13.

[3] Fourth Report, para. 411.   [4] Second Report, para. 4.

open to the enquiries of our Assistant Commissioner with entire unreserve."

"But it would be idle to attempt in any way to gloss over the fact that Mr. Ritchie is now perfectly incompetent for the fulfilment of his duties. He does not in fact attempt to fulfil them, the business of the office being entirely carried on for him by another gentleman of advanced years himself, who holds no official position, is in no sense officially responsible, and has not had legal training."[1]

The Commission found that the Registrar in Dublin also had farmed out the work completely and did none of it himself, but as he employed for it, not a fellow ancient, but a competent solicitor of working age, the results were satisfactory rather than the reverse.

The Royal Commission of 1871–74 understood their material. They were describing a natural growth, and nature will not be classified tidily. To their twelve kinds of registered friendly societies, they added five more miscellaneous types falling within their terms of reference and registered by the same Registrar—building societies, cattle insurance societies and so on. When they had done with the seventeen classes of registered societies, they came on to the unregistered ones, forming "a world in themselves in England nearly co-extensive with, in Scotland far surpassing in magnitude that of the registered bodies." They did not try to classify neatly but through their Assistant Commissioners they saw and they described.

They lingered lovingly over the unregistered Old Amicable Society of Grantham, already more than 150 years old, whose Rule 2 provided that at each monthly meeting 5s. was to be spent for ale, while subsequent rules specified the benefits to be paid to each brother in sickness and on the death of a brother or his wife; a still later rule recurred to the ale and provided that it should not be consumed till the business had been transacted.[2]

[1] Second Report, para. 7.

[2] This particular society, having gone on happily without registration for 200 years, at last took the plunge of registration in 1913, and died within thirty years, in 1939, when its 26 remaining members shared out £1,304 between them. But registration made it possible for an account of the society giving many details of its history not mentioned by the Commission to be compiled by the Registrar in 1929. At that time the society was almost indecently solvent, worth on valuation 30s. in the £. In its earlier history it had entered very thoroughly into the life of its members, fining them for non-attendance at church (dissenters were rigidly excluded); admonishing them for neglect of business or disorderly behaviour; buying and distributing corn to them during scarcity (as in 1757); making loans to them without interest.

The Royal Commission dwelt with equal interest on the "four peculiar clubs" of a different type in Cheshire—the unregistered Sunday-School Dividing Societies, by which the children of the small town of Nantwich, according to their religious persuasions— Church of England, Wesleyan, Baptist, Independent—were organized into providing for their own funerals and their doctoring. The largest of the four societies—Church of England—had already lasted for nearly fifty years; it was confined to children aged one to seventeen with a contribution of 1d. a week, and a levy of 3d. on all the members for each death. This levy produced more than enough to pay all the benefits in sickness and on death, so that the society was able each year to return to the members or their parents more than their regular contribution. "There are no printed rules, and the written rules, which the Secretary found after some difficulty and which were given him when he took office 25 years ago are not the rules under which the club is now managed. According to the Secretary, the rules which really governed the society were matters of common knowledge and tradition. The Secretary's accounts are never audited, nor are the Treasurer's; no balance sheet is laid before the meeting nor is there a Committee. But the results of the yearly dividend, after allowing for the benefits, shew that the members get their full money's worth."[1] There was no 37 per cent of the contributions for administration, as in the collecting societies which came to dominate provision for funerals.

Grantham and Nantwich illustrated the two commonest foci of social endeavour in the nineteenth century—public-house and church or chapel. As the Commission said, the local village clubs fell into two groups—those meeting at a public-house and those meeting away from it. The latter were normally "patronized" by squire or clergyman, and came to be criticized for this by the democrats of the friendly society movement. On the other hand, the common connection between friendly societies and public-houses led some reformers to condemn this form of mutual aid. To meet in a public-house to encourage thrift was, in Jeremy Bentham's eyes, "like choosing a brothel for a school of continence"; he set out, as a better alternative, a scheme of "Frugality Banks" for receipt of small savings. This criticism somewhat ignored the fact that a friendly society had to be more than a mutual insurance company. It was a fellowship of men knowing and trusting and influencing one another; for that, apart from the churches, the public-house, in the early nineteenth century, provided as a rule the only social

[1] Fourth Report, para. 673.

centre. Friendly societies, as has been noticed, grew even more naturally in England than in Scotland. By contrast, savings banks, as the alternative means of encouraging thrift and escaping pauperism, took root in Scotland earlier than in England, usually under religious or philanthropic auspices.[1]

Undoubtedly the business motive of the publican entered at times into the promotion of a friendly society. Sometimes the business to the publican was more important than the good to the members. This in the days of the Royal Commission seemed sadly true of many of the "Societies of Females." The Commission reported that such societies in Bristol "appeared to be got up by the landladies of public-houses and to be conducted in their interest." They noted that "Shepherdesses" and "Oddsisters" were apt to be "greatly given to liquor." The business motive might appear also in other ways. The Commission found among burial societies an occasional connection with undertakers. The "Manchester Philanthropic Burial Society" of that day had an undertaker as its President; by the rules of the society all the coffins which it philanthropically provided had to be bought from the President. The revolutionary entry of the business motive in another form into the field of burial insurance calls for special notice later.

Above all, the Commission emphasized the natural vigour of the growth that they were studying. "The number of separate clubs," wrote one Assistant Commissioner, "that are found competing against one another in a single village is often remarkable." "Thus in Cottenham, in Cambridgeshire, I found, besides two lodges of the Manchester Unity of Oddfellows, lodges of Shepherds and Shepherdesses of the Wisbech Unity, a branch of the Cambridge Town and Country Club promoted by the clergyman, a club at the British School composed of old men attempting with the help and advice of an active resident medical gentleman to carry on an old club recently broken up, a gathering of Ancient Patriarchs with agent belonging to the London society of that name, and two ordinary public-house clubs, nine in all. . . . There are not more than 500 members in them altogether, 50 of them women."[2]

In the towns there was an equal proliferation of societies competing with one another. But by the time of the Commission's Report in 1874 the growth of mutual aid organization in most towns had

---

[1] See the very interesting *History of Savings Banks* by H. Oliver Horne (Oxford University Press, 1946) referred to again in Chapter III. I am indebted to this work for the quotation from Bentham. [2] Fourth Report, para. 227.

taken a form different from that of the country districts and from the eighteenth century. The dominant form of friendly society was that of the affiliated orders—the societies with branches, as the Registrar and the Government Actuary call them to-day.

FRIENDLY SOCIETIES CLASSIFIED

As a preliminary to describing the orders it is necessary to do what the Royal Commission deliberately declined to do, and make, so far as possible, a logical classification of the friendly societies. This is done in tabular form in Table 1, arranging all the different types of association now registered as friendly societies in two main groups A and B; dividing each group or genus into its principal species; showing for some of the species certain well-marked varieties.

The first and fundamental division is between societies which provide a sick benefit—that is to say, a cash payment in sickness on mutual aid lines—and those which do not. Those that do have in them what has been described as the first of the three seeds of the friendly society movement—the felt need for security in sickness. The provision of sick benefit remains for most of them their largest task; its administration presents problems of exceptional difficulty, whose successful solution in the past has been the outstanding contribution of the friendly society movement to social advance. The voluntary sick benefit societies of all kinds are grouped in Table 1 under the letter A. Table 2 gives the membership at various dates of some of the leading societies of this group.

The essence of a friendly society in this group is that the members fix by the rules contributions to be paid weekly, monthly or quarterly by them and weekly amounts of benefit which they are entitled to receive when sick. The rate of contribution as a rule varies with the age of entry to the society; the basic fact about sickness is that liability to it increases with age; most societies have a limit of age beyond which they will not admit. The rate of benefit is normally the same for all adult members of the same sex, but as a rule is reduced by stages if the sickness is prolonged. Most societies which pay sick benefit provide also a funeral benefit, a lump sum payable on the death of the member and perhaps half as much on the death of his wife.

In addition to the staple benefits for sickness and funerals, many friendly societies provide a variety of other benefits, sometimes covered by the over-all contribution, sometimes in return for special contributions; the commonest of these other benefits are for mater-

TABLE I

CLASSIFICATION OF SOCIETIES REGISTERED AS FRIENDLY SOCIETIES, 1945

	No.	Membership (000)	Funds £000	Leading Examples
A. SOCIETIES GIVING SICK BENEFIT—				
1. Societies with branches (Affiliated Orders)	16,017	2,687	60,250	Manchester Unity (771), Foresters (518), Rechabites (500), Shepherds (238), Grand United Oddfellows (63), Druids (41)
2. Unitary Accumulating				
(a) General				
(b) Limited by Trade, Locality, etc.	826	1,079	46,060	Hearts of Oak (429), Rational (69), Teachers' Provident (114), L.M.S. Rly. (L.N.W.) Provident and Pension (26)
3. Unitary With Dividend—				
(a) Dividing	556	311	2,105	London General Omnibus Employees (24), New Tabernacle (20), Broadway Congregational (13)
(b) Deposit				
(c) Holloway	92	2,480	46,995	National Deposit (1,600), Ideal (140), Tunbridge Wells Equitable (132)
B. SOCIETIES NOT GIVING SICK BENEFIT—				
1. Specialized Friendly Societies	1,054	2,212	37,420	See Table 22 in Appendix A.
2. Collecting Societies	138	30,033	134,685	Royal Liver, Liverpool Victoria.

Note.—Bracketed numbers give membership in 1945 in thousands.

TABLE 2

MEMBERSHIP OF SOME LEADING FRIENDLY SOCIETIES

	1872 about	1886	1899	1910	1935	1939	1945	1946
ORDERS—								
Oddfellows: Manchester Unity	426,663	597,973	713,097	759,007	745,334	758,634	770,654	764,031
Ancient Order of Foresters	388,872	582,104	666,445	620,632	547,165	546,531	518,043	510,005
Rechabites: Salford Unity	9,009	59,863	135,193	317,383	588,658	530,416	499,723	485,371
Shepherds Ashton Unity	45,517	72,000	102,933	164,188	259,039	249,717	238,119	234,033
Grand United Oddfellows	63,412	82,611	70,040	69,426	71,556	69,219	63,074	61,660
Order of Druids	57,067	60,744	55,807	69,851	52,647	46,656	41,128	43,199
Total of six Orders	990,540	1,455,295	1,743,495	2,000,507	2,264,399	2,201,153	2,130,741	2,098,299
Total for all Orders	1,260,000	2,157,765	2,397,618	2,782,953	2,904,365	2,813,595	2,686,836	2,641,502
SOCIETIES WITHOUT BRANCHES—								
Hearts of Oak	32,837	111,424	239,075	283,483	437,934	443,989	429,211	423,183
National Deposit	906	5,576	45,804	219,000	1,325,309	1,462,183	1,599,887	1,582,854
Rational Association	15,657	58,677	109,168	120,118	83,468	78,392	68,999	66,738
Ideal Benefit Society*	—	—	3,959	16,341	100,780	133,515	149,454	138,696
Tunbridge Wells Equitable†	—	209‡	3,412	19,286	103,876	122,928	131,760	132,417

* Founded 1893.   † Founded 1881.   ‡ Dec. 31, 1885.

nity, for old age (as pensions) and for lump sums at various ages by way of endowment insurance. All societies pay for the services of a doctor in sickness, both to cure the patient and to certify his disability in support of a claim to benefit; since the coming of National Health Insurance this medical attention has served the purposes both of the friendly society benefit and the State benefit that it was administering.

Many societies in Group A, in addition to their covenanted benefits, have funds for discretionary assistance of members in hardship. Several of the larger societies, including the Manchester Unity, the Foresters, the Hearts of Oak, and the National Deposit Society have established convalescent homes. Many societies now, in addition to insurance against sickness and death, offer to their members facilities for personal saving, that is to say, for putting by money through the society to be kept for those members and paid out to them with interest either at stated intervals or at a certain age or on their leaving the society.

Group A, the societies giving sick benefit, is split in Table 1 into three main species: Affiliated Orders or Societies with Branches, Unitary Accumulating Societies, and Unitary Societies with Dividend. The nature of each of these species is explained below. Here it should be noted that the distinction between the first species and both the others is one of structure. The societies with branches, commonly described as affiliated orders, are federal, with a constitutional division of powers between central, regional, and local organs. Both the other species are unitary, with single government and finance. The difference between the second and third species —Unitary Accumulating Societies and Unitary Societies with Dividend—is one of method of working. Accumulating societies are so called because they lay up funds to be paid out to their members only on the occurrence of an agreed event—sickness, maternity, death, attainment of a certain age and so forth; as the likelihood of most of such events grows greater with age, the society must accumulate reserves in respect of each member in his earlier years, in order to meet the growing liabilities of later years. Societies with dividend, in addition to making payments on the occurrence of agreed events, in one way or another allocate some part of their funds periodically for payment in cash to their members. The societies identified in Table 1 as unitary accumulating societies do not do this; they are societies without dividend. It should be added—though to this there have come to be important exceptions—that practically all the affiliated orders are also accumulating; they are federal societies without dividend.[1] The first of the three species in Group A is distinguished from both second and third in structure. The first and second together are distinguished from the third in method of working.

Societies giving sick benefit are the friendly societies *par excellence*. They are described in the rest of this report as general friendly societies. But it is possible to be registered as a friendly society without undertaking provision of sick benefit.

There are, first, the specialized friendly societies shown as B.1 in Table 1, dealing with needs other than provision of a cash benefit in sickness. They include societies for many special purposes: provision for widows and orphans; insurance against accidents; insurance against shipwreck; endowment insurance; provision of annuities and pensions; and provision of institutional treatment. They include some societies, usually on a small scale, specialized for burial insurance but not using collectors. The Registrar reckons also among specialized societies the juvenile societies, that is to say those whose membership is limited to persons under twenty-one. These may give some benefit in sickness so that strictly they do not belong in Group B.1, but it has seemed simpler to leave them there; their numbers are not important.

There are, second, the collecting societies shown as B.2 in Table 1. They began as burial societies—providing payments to cover funeral expenses from contributions gathered weekly by collectors calling at the homes of the members; insurance for sums to be paid on death remains their primary activity. They are registered under the Friendly Societies Acts, but, through their use of collectors they have special privileges and come under special legislation assimilating them to the limited liability companies which undertake the same business of industrial assurance. The historical origin of the collecting societies as friendly societies, and their rapid development into businesses run by the collectors, is a leading instance of the interplay of the Mutual Aid motive and the business motive in meeting popular needs.

[1] To this general rule there are, of course, exceptions. The list of Societies with Branches, printed in Appendix A, includes the London and Provincial Yearly Dividing Society, with 208 branches and nearly 14,000 members in 1945, and the Grand Independent Order of Loyal Caledonian Corks Friendly Sick and Dividend Society with 191 branches and 18,500 members. One of the leading orders—the Shepherds of the Ashton Unity—as stated below (p. 52), has now become a society with dividend. Other orders, including the Foresters and Druids, in addition to their general accumulating section, offer to their members a variety of insurances for endowment and other forms of personal thrift.

The specialized friendly societies illustrate the wide range and
convenience of the State's registration machinery; further information about them is given in Appendix A, Table 22. The other
main species are more important and will now be described in
turn. They are: the Affiliated Orders; the Unitary Accumulating
Societies; the Societies with Dividend, in their three well-marked
varieties of Dividing, Deposit, and Holloway Societies; and, finally,
the Burial Societies from which, under the fertilizing influence of
the business motive, have come the Collecting Societies and Industrial
Assurance.

THE AFFILIATED ORDERS

The orders are organized administratively in three tiers. The
basis is the "lodge," as it is called in the Oddfellows and Shepherds, the "court," in the Foresters, the "tent" in the Rechabites,
and the "senate" in the Ancient Romans. This has the dealings
with the individual member; the average membership of a friendly
society lodge to-day, to use for simplicity this term as applying to
all orders, is 180. Above the lodge is the district, a group of lodges
in a particular area governed by representatives from the lodges.
Above the district is the order as a whole, often described as a
unity. Thus the largest of several orders of Oddfellows is distinguished
as the Manchester Unity and the largest of the orders of Shepherds
is distinguished as the Ashton Unity. Each order is completely
separate from all the rest; the Independent Order of Oddfellows
Manchester Unity, the Nottingham Imperial Order of Oddfellows,
and the Grand United Order of Oddfellows, have nothing in common beyond one word in their titles and the fact that they are all
friendly societies with branches, making provision for sickness their
main concern.

A list of the seventy-six orders known to be in existence at the end
of 1945, with their numbers of branches and membership, is given
in Section II of Appendix A; the orders are of very different
sizes. At one end of the scale stands the Manchester Unity of Oddfellows with 771,000 members in 4,240 lodges. At the other end
to-day is the Amalgamated Order of Comical Fellows claiming
origin in the eighteenth century but reduced in the uncomical
twentieth century to thirty-nine members in three branches. In
between comes a glorious variety of nomenclature—Ancient Romans,
Ancient Britons, Anglo-Saxons, Maccabeans, Total Abstinent
Sons of the Phoenix, the Leicestershire Seraphic Order of Oddfellows, the Halifax United Order of the Peaceful Dove, St.

David's Unity of Ivorites and the Craven Unity of the Golden Fleece, to name no more.[1] Many of these orders are small; of the seventy-one orders on the Register at the end of 1945, twenty-six had less than ten branches each and in all cases but one only a few hundred members. There were practically as many large orders, each with more than fifty branches and more than 5,000 members.

As there are great differences in total size between the orders, so there are differences also in the relative numbers of lodges and districts, in the division of powers between them, and in the powers of the unity over both. But some division of powers between local lodges and larger units is of the essence of every order; in constitutional terms it is a federation, generally, in three tiers.

It is a federation in which the separate lodges retain a great deal of independence. They remain separate financial units, paying contributions for common purposes to the district or the unity. They make the primary contract with the individual member and remain in nearly all the orders responsible for the sick benefit, which is the main purpose of the society. The districts as a rule become responsible for the death benefits, re-insuring the lodges against their liabilities. The unity is responsible for general policy, and in pursuit of this is sometimes prepared to come to the rescue, on conditions, of lodges which get into financial difficulties or at least will show them what they must do to get straight.

The primary responsibility to the individual member remains with the lodge which makes the contract with him. The nature of the contract is illustrated by the following extract from the rules of one of the courts of the Ancient Order of Foresters, "Pride of the Forest," situated at Wakefield in Yorkshire.

Table 3 relating to a small court—with 74 members in 1945—shows friendly society provision for sickness and death in almost its simplest form. A few more elaborate examples from other courts of the Foresters and other orders are given in Appendix A, Section III. They show that different branches of the same order may have different benefits and contributions. In most orders each branch is given the option either of using its own special

[1] Elaborate nomenclature is not a peculiarity of the affiliated orders, as any page of the Registrar's Report for 1905 will show. Neighbouring pages of this Report yield from Yorkshire the United Order of Economists and the Yorkshire Delight Lodge, No. 245 (both founded in 1833); the Halifax Offspring of Virtue (1892); the North Yorkshire and South Durham Provident Society of Assistant Pawnbrokers (1894); and the Modern White Lamb Friendly Society (1898).

tables or of adopting some or all of the tables drawn up by the order. In a few orders, notably the Manchester Unity, all branches are required to adopt order tables. But the administrative responsibility of securing contributions and paying or withholding sick benefit remains with the branch.

TABLE 3

CONTRIBUTIONS AND BENEFITS IN A TYPICAL BRANCH

"Every adult member of the court shall pay, or cause to be paid to the funds of the court, a contribution every four weeks, or quarterly, according to the following table, as at age at entry last birthday, for the purpose of paying the sick and death benefits of members, and such amounts for the funeral expenses of members' wives and widows as are allowed by these rules . . . and for the necessary expenses of management."

TABLE

Age at Entry last Birthday	Contribution every Four Weeks	
	s.	d.
16 and under 25	2	0
25 ,, ,, 30	2	4
30 ,, ,, 35	2	6
35 ,, ,, 40	3	0

BENEFITS

10s. a week for first 26 weeks of sickness;
5s. a week for second 26 weeks of sickness.
£10 on death of member;
£7 on death of member's wife.

The affiliated order, as the Commission of 1874 pointed out, is a type of organization peculiar to Britain or countries settled from Britain. It represented a practical solution of the central problem that arises in the administration of sick benefit—that of combining the responsibility and personal contact of small units with the strength and capacity to weather storms that depend on size.

It was also a type of organization with a natural tendency to expansion. The men of a village or group of streets in a town who came together, say, at the "King's Arms" to form a sick club for Mutual Aid felt no special urge to spread outside their immediate neighbourhood or even to bring in such fellow-villagers as had the bad taste to prefer the beer or the company in the "Black Swan."[1] It was almost an accident if a club which had started locally,

[1] The eighteenth-century sick clubs often had rules fixing their maximum membership, usually at a point well below 100 (see Eden, *State of the Poor*). They were exclusive in spirit, not expansive.

developed, as the Hearts of Oak did, into a large society. But once men thought of themselves as an order—Oddfellows, Shepherds, Foresters—they became men with a mission; the first lodge sought to be parent of other lodges; it sent out missionaries to preach the gospel of Forestry or Shepherdry. The crusading spirit of the affiliated orders was as much one of their early marks as was their federal structure.

The federal structure of the orders made it possible for them to remain, in the words of Rose's Act, societies of good fellowship in spite of growth. The average membership of a Manchester Unity Lodge or Foresters' Court at the time of the Royal Commission was 114. Thirty years later, in 1905, when the total membership of these two orders had nearly doubled, the average for each lodge or court was 169. This, for two successful and growing orders, was above the average for the movement as a whole; the 20,000 branches of all orders in Britain in 1905 had 2,655,000 members or an average of 133 members each. Since that date, largely through the operation of the National Insurance Act, there has been some tendency to combine branches previously separate and this tendency has been accentuated in the Second World War, but the average member-ship of each branch remains small; the 2,687,000 members of orders in 1945 were organized in 16,000 branches, that is to say in units averaging 180 members each. Every such unit is a society with its own life, its separate rules and scale of contributions and benefits. It is a society of men who can know one another, a society which still gets from its members much unpaid service. The problem for all friendly societies is to remain, in spite of growth and of the size needed for stability, true fellowships, in place of becoming mutual insurance companies. The affiliated order was, and remains, the best solution of that problem.

The building of the federal system of the affiliated orders, like the building of the federal system of the United States of America, presented many critical problems in adjusting the balance between central authority and local independence. As in the United States, so in the friendly societies the problem of the right of secession proved the most critical of all; the question whether there should be a right of secession was answered in both cases in the nega-tive. The Manchester Unity, like most of the surviving societies to-day, and like the United States of America, was itself the child of secession, of successful revolt. But in the course of time the Manchester Unity, by argument and democratic agreement, established financial conditions which practically make secession for any branch impossible. It contrived to do this by consent, without a war.[1]

The time of the Royal Commission's Report in 1874 was the heyday of the orders.

> The affiliated societies as the clubs of highest organization among those invented by working men to meet their own wants, and at the present day greatly surpassing all others in popularity, deserve the first place which is assigned to them. . . . In some towns they have made a clean sweep of the local societies; in all they are predominant (Fourth Report, para. 94).

The Commission quoted with approval this judgment of one of their Assistant Commissioners.

They went on to emphasize the service which the leading orders were rendering in placing their finances upon a sound basis. The administration of friendly societies, like that of any other institution for voluntary insurance dealing with sickness or death, is dominated by the fact that the risk of these misfortunes increases markedly with the age of the individual. This is noted in my Report on Social Insurance and Allied Services as marking one of the two fundamental distinctions between voluntary insurance and compulsory social insurance organized by the State.

> In providing for actuarial risks such as those of death, old age or sickness, it is necessary in voluntary insurance to fund contributions paid in early life in order to provide for the increasing risks of later life and to accumulate reserves against individual liabilities. The State, with its power of compelling successive generations of citizens to become insured and its power of taxation, is not under the necessity of accumulating reserves for actuarial risks and has not, in fact, adopted this method in the past (para. 24).

The State knows that new members can always be forced to come into compulsory insurance. It can gamble, as to some extent New Zealand and Britain have both gambled, on the hope of a continually rising standard of national income to cover the cost of old age pensions and infirmity generally. A voluntary insurance agency cannot count on new members coming in; though its

[1] See *Friendly Society Finance*—Lectures given by Sir Alfred Watson at the Institute of Actuaries in 1912. "It is easy," observes the lecturer, "to criticize the equity of the measures which the Manchester Unity has adopted, but it must be recognized that if an affiliated order is to have effective control over its lodges it must have powers of a punitive order."

object is Mutual Aid, it must look always at the individual members already in the society, and set its liabilities to those members against what it expects to get from them by way of contributions. That is the essence of valuation; it means making an estimate of liabilities for the total of all the actual individual members at any moment and comparing those liabilities with the accumulated reserves held and the contributions in prospect from those individual members. Soundness requires that the assets thus calculated should be 20s. in the £ of the liabilities.

The leader in bringing valuation into the friendly society field was the Manchester Unity, with the Foresters not far behind. Before the Royal Commission sat, the Manchester Unity had already submitted themselves to penetrating expert valuation and had published the results, as for the year 1871, showing a serious deficiency. The Commission commented as follows: "It is impossible to commend too highly the frankness and courage manifested by the Manchester Unity in thus facing the facts of its position."[1] They added that there was no reason whatever to suppose that other societies would show as favourable a position.

The time of the Commission's Inquiry was a time when many people thought that friendly societies would not themselves be able to build a sound financial structure. This led to the proposal noticed in Chapter II for a great scheme of voluntary State insurance. The affiliated orders, led by the Manchester Unity, showed that the problem could be solved by the friendly societies themselves. As the Commission said, the spirit of improvement was abroad.

> The Manchester Unity may be said to have taken every step towards security except the final one of enforcing means to meet an ascertained deficiency. The Foresters have not yet got so far as to ascertain the deficiency which, it may be said, certainly exists, but they have adopted all the means necessary to enable them to do so.

In the decades that followed the Commission's report, the leading orders one by one took steps to put themselves financially in order. They showed that sickness benefit could be administered on a democratic basis by a voluntary organization.[2]

[1] Fourth Report, para. 142.
[2] The financial progress of the chief orders up to 1886 is described in Chapters VI and VIII of Mr. Frome Wilkinson's *History of the Friendly Society Movement*. An account of some of the "notable financial reforms" of a later period is given in a paper submitted to the Institute of Actuaries in 1932 by Mr. Victor Burrows, and published in the *Journal* of the Institute, Vol. LXIII, Part III, No. 307.

UNITARY ACCUMULATING SOCIETIES

The orders at the time of the Royal Commission's report had many years of expanding usefulness before them, of service which they alone could have given and which they did give in showing how Mutual Aid for sickness could be placed on a solid financial basis, and of thus making possible the later entry of the State into this field. But they were, even then, only a part of the friendly society movement, not, as some of their historians have suggested, the whole of it.[1] There remained a host of local sick clubs of every degree of solidity, the original form of friendly society. From one of these had sprung already to large stature the Hearts of Oak, a unitary general society destined to surpass in scale all but the two largest orders. There were other accumulating unitary societies with memberships reckoned by the ten thousand.

A few societies of species A.2—the unitary accumulating type—have become large. The great bulk have always been and remain very small, and till the coming of National Insurance were very numerous. Without registration the Royal Commission of 1874 could not do more than guess at the numbers or membership of such societies. Thirty years after registration had been put on a sound basis, the Registrar in 1905 recorded more than 3,700 separate accumulating societies without branches giving sick benefit.[2] An analysis for selected counties, included in the supplementary volume, shows that about four out of five of these had less than 200 members each; nearly half of them had less than 100 members.

The persistence of small societies in every part of Britain till the coming of National Insurance in 1911 is one of the most notable features of the friendly society movement. The very full Report of the Registrar in 1906, giving data for all individual societies in 1905, makes possible an interesting study of this point. In eight counties, Lancashire, Yorkshire, Cheshire, Derbyshire, Bucks, Cambridge, Devon, and Cornwall, of 2,253 societies of less than 1,000 members in 1905, 871 or nearly 40 per cent were at least fifty years old, and 253 were more than seventy-five years old. The

[1] Mr. Frome Wilkinson in 1886 confined his *History of the Friendly Society Movement* entirely to the affiliated orders.

[2] The Registrar did not till 1910 treat separately the Deposit and Holloway Societies noticed later; in 1905 he included them in his total of 3,803 sickness benefit societies which accumulated. But there were only 81 Deposit and Holloway Societies in 1910 and the number that can be identified as belonging to this class in 1905 is 67.

proportion of such survivals varied from county to county, being highest in Yorkshire among the northern counties (more than 50 per cent of the small societies being fifty years old or more), and Devon and Cornwall with corresponding percentages of nearly 80 per cent and over 60 per cent. In London, in spite of the Huguenot centenarians, the proportion of older societies among the small ones is naturally less, about 86 out of the total of 465 societies with less than 1,000 members in 1905. But it seems clear that over all at least one-third of the 6,000 small societies, with less than 1,000 members in 1905, had held their own for more than fifty years.

In contrast to these small societies, the 289 larger ones had 2,302,303 members, an average of nearly 8,000. But this high average was due largely to a few exceptional societies, and to societies not undertaking insurance against sickness. In 1905, 42 societies without branches had more than 10,000 members each and a total membership of 1,543,000. But very few of these larger societies were ordinary friendly societies providing sick benefit on the same lines as the affiliated orders. They were largely burial societies (in Lancashire, Cheshire, or Staffordshire), societies connected with mines, railways or one or two other occupations, societies of the new Deposit and Holloway types described below, or otherwise specialized. The unitary societies doing the staple business of a friendly society and having more than 10,000 members could be counted on the fingers of one hand. They were the Hearts of Oak Benefit Society in London, the Rational Association Friendly Society in Manchester, the Equalised Independent Druids Friendly Society in Sheffield, and the Twentieth Century Equitable Friendly Society in London. This statistical survey confirms what has been said above, of the advantages of the small unit in administering sick benefit, the unit standing either with others for mutual support in a federal order, or standing alone with careful selection of its members. Many of these solitary small societies are societies with a long history.

The rarity of the large unitary accumulating society makes the more notable the achievement of the largest member of this type— the Hearts of Oak Benefit Society. This started with twelve members in 1842, with expectation of remaining local, but found itself undesignedly popular; by 1856 it had 5,000 members and by 1872 32,000. The Royal Commission, with their enthusiasm for the orders, gave to the Hearts of Oak a modified blessing, as a well-managed concern for "selling insurance over the counter." The concern continued to grow rapidly, and by the outbreak of the

Second World War had reached a membership of 444,000 with funds of £16,685,000.

The Society is governed ultimately by an Assembly of Delegates representing 231 electoral areas into which for this purpose the country is divided, each area representing some two thousand members. The delegates, in annual meeting elect the President and Vice-President, Treasurer, Secretary and other officers, and an Executive Council of fifteen, paid and holding office for three years; the delegates themselves are unpaid. Since 1919 the local business is conducted mainly by local agents, about 1,300 in number, receiving a fixed salary plus commission. Prior to the National Insurance Act of 1911 an effort was made to keep local spirit alive by informal meetings of delegates and members. After 1911 this attempt appears to have diminished in vitality and it was stopped completely by the outbreak of war in 1939.

The Hearts of Oak Society offers to its members choice of a great variety of insurances to suit their wishes. Its work on the whole is rather less concerned with sick benefit and more with other forms of insurance than is that of the larger orders. In 1936 sick pay accounted for nearly 80 per cent of the benefit expenditure both of the Manchester Unity and of the Foresters, but about 66 per cent only in the Hearts of Oak. The difference is no doubt connected with the interesting change of policy made by this society in 1927 and noticed on page 52 below. In addition to these new departures, the society, since 1933, has given free legal aid to its members, and since 1938 has had its own convalescent home, as several of the larger orders have. As a centralized society, the Hearts of Oak cannot aim at the brotherly contacts of the Foresters' Court or the Oddfellows' Lodge. But it represents straightforward mutual insurance at its best.

SOCIETIES WITH DIVIDEND

The Hearts of Oak and most of the other large unitary societies at the time of the Commission's Report were like the orders in paying out money only for contractual benefits and in accumulating the money needed to pay those benefits. But even these and the host of smaller societies pursuing the same course did not exhaust the existing varieties of the friendly society movement. Still less did they include all its future forms. The inventiveness of private enterprise in mutual aid had not been exhausted by the making of local clubs, some of which became general or by the making of the orders. Some of the local clubs had made a practice of dividing regularly in cash among their members part of their funds. Just at the heyday of the orders at the time of the Royal Commission, two new models of mutual aid, with dividend in new forms, were beginning to be important. It remains to describe the third species of organization for sick benefit—the societies with dividend in their three varieties of Dividing Society, Deposit Society, and Holloway Society. The societies with dividend have in them the second as well as the first of the three seeds of the friendly society movement, desire to have a lump of money later as well as desire for security in sickness.

Dividing Societies

The dividing friendly society has at all times been extremely popular and to-day is by no means defunct. In such a society the members pay, say, a shilling a week for a year into a common fund, receive a benefit when they are sick, say, twelve shillings a week with perhaps medical attendance or funeral benefit as well; at the end of each year anything that remains in the fund, perhaps after leaving a small working balance for current expenses, is divided equally in cash among the members. The higher the contribution in relation to the claims for sickness benefit the larger will be the dividend. This type of society, with an annual share-out, has naturally always been frowned on by societies which did not divide. It has an inherent weakness: as the members grow older their claims for sickness benefit increase inevitably, and so if the contribution remains unchanged the dividend must fall, unless new young members are recruited continually, so as to keep the average age of the members as a whole from rising. If the dividend falls, the society loses in attractive power; it is unlikely to get new members, ultimately dwindles and dies. If the dividend is kept up by recruiting new blood, this means that the younger members, sharing equally with the old, will get a smaller annual dividend than they could get by forming a precisely similar new society of their own. Sooner or later the young members, or those invited to become young members, will realize this.

Dividing societies have in them the seeds of impermanence and secession. Yet there is more to be said for them than the High Priests of the friendly society movement are always ready to allow. They meet a felt need for money of one's own for unspecified emergencies, as distinct from locking up the whole of one's contribution as an insurance premium, for which one will get nothing if one is

not sick or till one dies. They are also the way to insurance without
an actuary, a form of reading without tears whose attractions are
undeniable. The members, uncertain how much sickness they are
likely to experience, put their contributions high, knowing that
what they have paid too much will come back to them in a year.
This, by the method of trial and error, cuts the Gordian knot of
valuation. The dividing society finally, while it has in it the seed of
secession, has also a natural force to check malingering. It gives
to each member a personal interest in keeping down his own claims
and keeping a friendly watchful eye upon his fellow-members.

However much actuaries and other experts may regret the fact,
dividing friendly societies in Britain have at all times been extremely popular; they show no sign as a class of disappearing.
The Reverend Mr. Portman of the remote village of Steeple Fitz-
paine in Somerset, describing such a society in his parish to the
Royal Commission of 1874, admitted that it might seem improvident
to divide the surplus each year, but "the people love to have it so."
He added from his experience as a clergyman of more than thirty-five
years standing that a little "lump" of money, though it be only twenty-
five or thirty shillings coming in now and then, is a very great boon
to the agricultural labourers. "And I have no reason to think,
speaking generally, that it is improperly and wastefully spent. It
much more often goes towards the purchase of a pig or of shoes
or of some necessary article of clothing." The whole of rural England
is or was a collection of Steeple Fitzpaines.

But dividing societies are not a country growth alone. Particularly
after the rise of the orders the dividing societies found in some
towns a fresh demand for them. Birmingham, for instance, was one
of the towns in which during the nineteenth century the orders
made a clean sweep of nearly all the ordinary sick clubs. Their
place was not taken, however, entirely by the orders. There followed
as well a great development of dividing societies. Practically all the
unitary societies shown in the Registrar's Report for 1905 as registered in Birmingham after 1877 were dividing societies or societies
for juveniles. The local clubs which merely gave sick benefit were
killed by the orders. The clubs which did something that the orders
refused to do in paying a dividend arose and multiplied. The registrations in other counties than Warwickshire—notably those for
London and Staffordshire—show a similar efflorescence of dividing
and juvenile societies from the late 'seventies onwards.

Dividing societies are not only extremely popular but also in some
cases surprisingly long-lived. The table of early societies in the Supple-

mentary Volume contains dividing societies, some of which, though born in the eighteenth century, were still going strong in the twentieth century. There were in 1945 two dividing societies, with a membership of more than 20,000 (one constituted for the employees of the London and General Omnibus Company, and one the New Tabernacle Sick and Provident Society). There were three others in the same year with membership exceeding 10,000. Two of these large dividing societies—the New Tabernacle and the Broadway Congregational Church Sick Benefit Society—are already more than forty years old and show no signs of coming to an end.

The dividing society is a form of organization which has always been popular, and which is never likely to disappear, as a combination of some provision for sickness with personal saving to have a lump of money later. In the past seventy years in Britain this combination has given rise to more highly developed forms, to Deposit societies and to Holloway societies, distinct in principle from other friendly societies and distinct from one another.

Deposit Societies

A special section of the Friendly Societies Acts[1] enables any society or branch to provide by its rules for accumulating at interest for the use of any member any surplus of his contributions which may remain after providing for any assurance in respect of which such contributions are paid. The rules naturally must specify also the times at which and the conditions under which the member may withdraw his accumulations. The Registrar describes all societies which take advantage of this section as Deposit Friendly Societies, marking them with the letter "P" in his statistical tables; there were in 1945 eighty-two societies treated by the Registrar as wholly deposit societies and ten others which had some deposit members.

As the preceding paragraph makes clear, the rules which determine the personal surplus of each member and the conditions under which he can withdraw his surplus may differ from one society to another. There is, in particular, a well-marked difference between societies like the National Deposit Friendly Society, which uses the term "Deposit" in its title, and societies on the so-called Holloway principle. Though both types are classified by the Registrar as

---

[1] Section 42 of the Friendly Societies Act of 1896. The term "accumulating" is used here, as it appears in the Act. The Registrar's use of the term "accumulating" in classifying societies means something different. He is thinking of accumulating against contractual liabilities for benefit.

deposit societies, they work on different principles, and the Holloway societies, about fifty in number, do not describe themselves, in their title or otherwise, as deposit societies. Here, in accord with the practice of the societies themselves, the term deposit society is kept for organizations resembling the National Deposit Friendly Society: the latter is so overwhelmingly the largest of its type that the system is described in terms of its particular rules.[1] The Holloway societies, as they call themselves, are dealt with in the following section of the Report.

The earliest society on the deposit principle, as that term is used in this Report, was founded in 1831 by the Honourable and Reverend Samuel Best, Rector of Abbots Ann in Hampshire. It embodied an entirely new idea which for forty years showed no sign of spreading far beyond its immediate origin. But in 1868 a society was formed at Albury in Surrey on the same principles, which began to spread and became the National Deposit Friendly Society in 1872; thenceforward it displayed a capacity for phenomenal growth, and to-day is much the largest of the friendly societies, with a membership in Britain nearly twice that of the largest affiliated order and nearly four times that of the largest rival among unitary societies. The founder of this society at Albury, like that of its forerunner at Abbots Ann, was a country clergyman—Canon Portal.[2]

The main principle of the National Deposit Friendly Society is that a contribution made by each member, after a deduction for management, goes in part to a common fund for sickness benefit, and in part to his personal account, where it grows for him at compound interest.[3] The member at entry can fix his contribution to suit his means and his needs, at any point from 2s. to 20s. a month. This determines the rate of benefit which he receives in sickness: the daily rate of benefit is the same as the monthly contribution. In addition to the contribution, he may make and is urged to make, a deposit with the society, at the rate of anything from 3d. to £30 a year, thereby increasing his personal account; this does not affect the rate of sick benefit but does affect its duration. For the benefit is drawn in part from the common fund and in part from the

[1] There are, it will be seen, about thirty societies marked "P" by the Registrar outside the National Union of Holloway Societies. Some of these work on the lines of the National Deposit Friendly Society; others have their own individual rules. Numerically they are unimportant.

[2] The original Abbots Ann Society failed to grow and was dissolved in 1931.

[3] The Society's own statement of what it offers is printed in Section III of Appendix A as one of the specimens of contributions and benefits.

personal account of the individual. If a member is fortunate enough to have little sickness, he will at the end of his working life, or on leaving the society, have a large amount in his personal account; it will have earned interest for him all the time. If, on the other hand, the individual has much sickness, his personal account may be small, indeed it may become exhausted altogether; when that happens, sick benefit ends and is replaced by "grace pay," which can be drawn for as long as sick benefit has in fact been drawn.

Each member can, within limits, make his personal account as large as he likes by his optional deposit. Thereby he increases the period for which he can draw sick benefit, and as a consequence the period for which at need he can draw grace pay. The arrangement by which the length of grace pay is made equal to that for which sick benefit has been drawn means that a member who falls sick early in his connection with the society may exhaust his personal account rapidly and so get little grace pay; but every year that a member continues with the society normally increases his personal account and so increases his claims to sick benefit and grace pay alike for his later years.

The member's personal account is fed from two sources—his original deposit, and the proportion of the monthly contribution allocated to personal account, after providing for common fund expenditure on benefits and for management. In recent years about one-third of the contributions on the average—4d. in every 1s.—has been assigned to the personal account. The fact that sick benefit comes in part from the personal account gives to every member an interest in avoiding unnecessary claims. The claims experience at the National Deposit Friendly Society is in fact very low, about half that of some other societies. This may mean that sometimes members do not claim although they really are ill, for fear of exhausting their personal account. It clearly does mean a very efficient barrier against anything like malingering.

The proportions in which sick benefit is drawn from the common account and from the personal account vary with the class in which the member is placed on entering the society, the class being determined by reference to age, sex and occupation: the classification affects also the rate of grace pay, which is treated as drawn solely from the common fund. In Class A (males joining between sixteen and thirty) one-quarter of the sick benefit comes from the personal account and three-quarters from the common fund, and grace pay is three-quarters of sick benefit. In Class B (males joining between five and sixteen or thirty and forty, and females between five and thirty) the proportions are one-third and two-thirds. In Class C (males joining between forty and fifty and females between thirty and forty-five) the proportions are half and half; that is to say in Class C half the sick benefit is drawn from the member's personal account (so that it may get exhausted more rapidly) and rate of grace pay is half the sick benefit. Classification is an ingeniously simple method of adjusting the insurance premiums to the risk, and allowing for the greater liability to sickness of older people and people in particular occupations.

Critics of the deposit principle stress the point that it represents incomplete insurance. And its authors went rather out of their way to underline the difference between their creation and the ordinary friendly societies.

> "Let the mind at the outset be divested of the idea of a common fund or club. The society is rather a savings bank than a club."[1]

So Mr. Best declared in 1831 and the rules of the Surrey Deposit Society in 1868 were equally clear:

> The club is established on the principle of a savings bank, the depositors in which agree to help each other in sickness and old age, each depositor paying something towards his own relief out of his own deposit and his fellow depositors finding the rest.

It should be added that Canon Portal and his supporters disliked not only the tendency of ordinary sick clubs to fail, but also their connection with the public-house. A fundamental rule of the National Deposit Friendly Society prohibits any meetings of the society on licensed premises.

Not unnaturally the new model was disliked by the older friendly societies. The Royal Commission quoted a violent attack made on it in the Foresters' *Miscellany* of April, 1873. Nearly twenty years later one of the historians of the friendly society movement was extremely supercilious about it. "The machinery and working of the deposit system is so complicated and intricate that in explanation of it more space will have to be given than the importance or small success which has attended this ingenious attempt to combine a savings bank and a benefit society can be said to merit. . . . There is no trace of self-evolution about it; it is a highly artificial and

---

[1] Mr. Best, as quoted in the Royal Commission's Fourth Report, paras. 370–372.

wonderfully ingenious system of provident insurance imposed on the wage-earning classes from without."[1]

The Royal Commission themselves, while seeing the advantages and ingenuity of the deposit principle, suggested that it might have been better for societies based on it to have been registered under some other provision than as friendly societies.

"They are indeed essentially savings banks rather than friendly societies. That security of provision which is of the essence of the friendly society to ensure, however it may fall short of really doing so, they do not profess to give. They are primarily individual not social. Were they certified under the Savings Banks Act all misapprehensions of their true character would cease and they would be recognized as an ingenious attempt, from the savings bank ground, to supply most of the objects which are aimed at by friendly societies."[2]

But the Commission, with all their just appreciation of the unique service rendered at that time by the affiliated orders, were far too wise to believe that there was no room for any other type of mutual aid and thrift.

The deposit societies have never set out to make full provision for sickness, however prolonged. But then neither have most of the accumulating societies done this. Full sick pay for twenty-six weeks followed by half-pay for another twenty-six weeks, and then a few shillings a week only in chronic disability was all that any but a few of the leaders could manage. The deposit system might well enable a careful man to make fuller provision for his later years of increasing risk of sickness than he could do in any other way.[3] And all the time he had the comfortable feeling that, if his deposit was not needed to support his sick pay, he would have it back with interest to spend as he wanted. The deposit system had a flexibility which the older societies did not attempt to emulate. And, as is shown by the remarkable achievement of the National Deposit Friendly Society, the deposit system met a real need.

Table 2 shows the membership of the society rushing up from under one thousand in 1872 to a few thousands in 1886, 46,000 in

---

[1] Rev. J. Frome Wilkinson in *Mutual Thrift*, pp. 54 and 58.
[2] Fourth Report, para. 400.
[3] As actual cases illustrate it is possible in the National Deposit Friendly Society to draw sick benefit followed by grace pay for many years of continuous disability. A case of eighteen years is on record, but the Society is content to name six years of continuous benefit as an example of what it can do.

1899 and 219,000 in 1910; thereafter, with the coming of National Insurance, it swiftly out-distanced all rivals in the friendly society world. All this has happened without any advertising campaign; in spite of Mr. Frome Wilkinson it has been self-evolution at an unparalleled rate. The society, moreover, in spite of its size, has remained substantially governed by its members, with large annual meetings of delegates of real power. With basic provision for sickness made by the State, the deposit principle may well prove to have an even stronger hold upon public support in future than it has had in the past.

Holloway Societies

The deposit principle was not the only new ferment in the friendly society world of seventy years ago. In the same year, 1874, in which the Royal Commission made their Report, there was founded by Mr. George Holloway at Stroud the "Working Men's Conservative Friendly Society" on a principle which two or three years later he described in an essay written for public competition. Prizes had been offered by Mr. W. E. Forster, M.P., for essays on superannuation in relation to friendly societies. Mr. Holloway entered with a description of what he was doing and planning at Stroud, and his essay won the second prize. To-day societies founded upon his principles form a distinctive element in friendly society structure. There are some fifty such societies in all, with the total membership now risen to 600,000 from small beginnings.

The Holloway societies are like the deposit societies in combining insurance against sickness with personal saving. But they make this combination in a different way, without the special features of the National Deposit Friendly Society, such as optional deposit in addition to contribution, classification and grace pay. The essential feature of a Holloway society is that the member's contribution is substantially more than enough to provide the sickness benefit to which he is entitled, but the whole of it goes in the first instance into a common fund. Each year the surplus of this fund remaining after benefit and expenses have been met is divided equally between the members, and each member's share is credited to his personal account, to be kept for him earning interest until he retires from work or leaves the society.

There are in all Holloway societies two additional features. One is that the contribution, which is the same for all ages up to thirty, increases thereafter by a small amount yearly to accord with the increased risk of sickness. The other is that individuals can adjust the extent of their insurance for themselves by taking one or more shares (up to a maximum of ten shares altogether) in the society. The surplus is divided at the end of the year in proportion to the shares held. In this and in other ways Holloway societies adjust themselves flexibly to the varying conditions of their members. But the essence of the system is the making of a contribution more than is needed for sickness benefit in order to build up an individual account for old age. The whole of the sickness benefit comes from a common fund and the member cannot run out of benefit by exhausting his personal account. There is thus also no need for the individual member to forgo claiming sickness benefit in order to avoid exhausting his provision for old age. At the same time, the fact that all the members stand to get a larger deposit if sickness claims are low gives to each member an interest in avoiding excessive claims either by himself or by his fellows.

The Holloway society is yet another ingenious idea in social provision and, like the deposit idea, has of late proved particularly successful in spite of its apparent complications. The two largest of the Holloway societies, the Ideal Benefit Society of Birmingham,[1] and the Tunbridge Wells Equitable Society, show increases in the last forty years similar in their proportions to the growth of the National Deposit Friendly Society. Table 2 shows the membership of these two multiplying more than five times between 1899 and 1910, and multiplying six times further between 1910 and 1935.

Naturally, the Holloway societies, like the deposit societies, appeared anathema to the friendly societies of the old school. One peculiar feature about them, that at their outset they had a political complexion, perhaps justified hostility. The non-political character of the friendly society movement is one of its best features. Many of the Holloway societies still carry the name "Conservative," but that has come to have little or no political implication.

The most successful of the Holloway societies present the aspect to-day rather of enterprising businesses than of associations with brotherly feeling. They have annual meetings of members, but the attendance at such meetings is apt to be similar to the attendance of any of the meetings of a collecting society, a handful of people largely nominated by the agents. Though the Holloway societies, however, have thus something of a business aspect, they are businesses undertaken not for profit but for the spreading of a very ingenious idea in meeting real needs of the British people.

[1] The prospectus of this society is printed as one of the specimens of contributions and benefits in Section III of Appendix A.

The Holloway societies, for some reason which it is not easy to understand, are not joined with the other friendly societies, including the National Deposit Society, in forming the "National Conference of Friendly Societies." They have a separate union of their own. The reason for this separation does not lie in the Holloway principle.

Indeed, one of the most important of the orders, fourth now in size, The Loyal and Ancient Order of Shepherds of the Ashton Unity, has long worked partly, and in future will work wholly, on the Holloway principle. For many years this society had two sections, one for Mutual Aid on the established lines of the other orders, one a surplus account section, in which members contributed according to their age and contributed more than was expected to be needed to provide the benefits to which they were entitled. The surplus in this section was allocated annually on the principles of a Holloway society. Experience has shown that within this order the Holloway section was more attractive than the other section. It has become predominant numerically and from 1950 onwards all new Shepherds of the Ashton Unity will be admitted only to the surplus account, that is to say, the Holloway section.

A change made in the past twenty years by the largest of the unitary accumulating societies—the Hearts of Oak—is, in another way, as notable. In 1927 this society introduced "Mutual Thrift" tables giving its members in effect the choice of going on as before, of joining an individual deposit section, and of joining a Holloway section; the choice was offered not only to new entrants but to existing members. The tables at once proved very attractive; during 1928 nearly 14,000 accounts were opened in one or other of the two sections with dividend, and less than 3,000 in the older section of accumulating insurance.

This development is of great interest for many reasons. It shows the strength of the second seed, the desire to have money at one's disposal, in combination with the first seed of having mutual aid provision for sickness.

It shows finally the impossibility of making a rigid, logical classification of the natural growth of Mutual Aid in Britain. The Shepherds of the Ashton Unity are still an order, but they have long been in part and will for all future entrants be wholly a society with dividend, of the Holloway variety. The Hearts of Oak is still in the main a unitary accumulating society, but it has two sections with dividend, one of the Holloway and one of the deposit variety, and the bulk of its new members are in one or other of these sections.

BURIAL SOCIETIES AND THE BUSINESS MOTIVE

The need to provide for special expenses at death, whether one's own death or that of a dependent, is a need as widely felt as the need for security in sickness. It has been named above as the third of the three seeds from which friendly societies have grown. From it has grown also the remarkable form of modern business, known as industrial assurance. This development has been the subject of a full-length historical and critical study by Sir Arnold Wilson and Professor Hermann Levy published ten years ago,[1] and of a lengthy appendix to my *Report on Social Insurance and Allied Services*, in 1942,[2] leading up to the proposal that the business of industrial assurance for gain should be converted into a public service. Here it is dealt with briefly, as an illustration of the interplay of social motives and business motives in meeting popular needs.

At the time when friendly societies first came under the notice of Parliament, insurance for money to be paid on the death of another person was in general illegal under an Act passed in 1774, to prevent life insurance from becoming a form of gambling. The Act made void any contract of insurance not based on "insurable interest"; this meant that the person taking out insurance against a death must be able to show that he would suffer pecuniary loss if the death occurred. The law of 1774 bore hardly upon the poorer classes in relation to funeral expenses. The rich man could out of his superfluity pay for the funeral of wife or child, parent or grandparent or any other relation for whose decent burial he felt responsibility. The poor man had no superfluity and found himself hampered in insuring against liabilities of this nature. He had certainly no "insurable interest" in his children as such or in grandparents, brothers and sisters, though he might want to pay for their funerals; throughout the nineteenth century it was doubtful whether a husband could insure to get money on the death of his wife.[3]

[1] *Industrial Assurance* (Oxford University Press, 1937).

[2] Appendix D to *Report on Social Insurance and Allied Services*, 1942 (Cmd. 6404). See also paras. 181–192 of the Report.

[3] A wife had always an insurable interest in her husband's life, since by his death she would lose the maintenance which he was bound to provide for her. But the husband had not the same claim to maintenance from his wife and it was not clear that he could insure against her death; some of the legal text-books of the nineteenth century took the view that he could not. The doubt was not set at rest till 1909 when the economic position of married women had changed. The Court of Appeal in that year, in the case of *Griffiths v. Fleming* (1909, 1, K.B.D. 805), decided that a man had an insurable interest in his wife's life just as a woman had in her husband's life.

If the poor man were to avoid contact with the Poor Law in death, as well as in life, for his family, he must be allowed to insure for funeral expenses. That the poor man wanted to do so was clear. Old Betty Higden, described by Charles Dickens as carrying "sewn in the breast of her gown the money for her burial," was and is a universal type.

> "Patiently to earn a spare, bare living and quietly to die, untouched by workhouse hands—this was her highest sub-lunary hope."[1]

To many independence in death seemed more important, not less important, than independence in life.

To meet this need, in derogation of the Act of 1774, a special privilege was given to registered friendly societies. Through them up to a limited amount a man might insure for money to be paid not only on his own death but on that of his wife or a child. By the Friendly Societies Act of 1829, the range of these societies was extended to cover any contingency whose occurrence was "susceptible of calculation by way of average"; this might have been held to cover insurance on any life whatever. By the Act of 1850, insurance through a friendly society for funeral expenses of "kindred" as well as wives and children was permitted expressly. Most of the friendly societies giving sick benefit used this privilege; they provided also a payment at the death of a member or his wife to cover funeral expenses, and many made similar provision for the death of a child. Moreover, there arose everywhere a multiplicity of societies specializing on provision for funerals.

A picturesque account of the natural origin of local burial clubs was given by one of the Assistant Commissioners, Sir George Young.

> The local burial clubs . . . have generally arisen out of the custom of sending round the hat, on the decease of a fellow-workman to collect something for his funeral and family. They thus commence in the rude form of a "levy," the con-tribution being a shilling all round which is collected by a friend of the deceased and handed over to the widow. A society in this stage has no accumulated fund, and would in no respect be benefited by registration. The first step in the way of organization is to "keep one death in hand" so as to avoid the delay of collecting the money when it is wanted and hand it over in time to meet the first necessities of bereavement. This

1 *Our Mutual Friend*, ch. 8.

involves some trouble and some responsibility in the collector and a small subscription is added sooner or later to defray expenses.

The Assistant Commissioner went on to describe how sooner or later, by extravagance either on funerals or in dividing the fund by way of bonus, the club generally came to an end.

"The burial club which survives a generation is an exception."

This, however, was written of the rural East and South-East of England. In the towns, above all in the industrial North and Midlands, the universal desire to avoid a pauper burial had been met by a response on business lines, and had brought a new way of making a living into being—the occupation of collector, paying weekly visits to the homes of the poor to collect their pennies for funeral insurance and keeping as his commission a percentage of what he collected. The dates of establishment of the three largest of this type of society to-day are 1850 (Royal Liver), 1843 (Liverpool Victoria) and 1852 (Scottish Legal). The Royal Commission noted that large burial societies were most developed in Lancashire, as were most of the affiliated orders. They were as natural a by-product of industrialization as was the smoke of the factories. Sooner or later the management of nearly all the societies came to be established in the professional hands of the collectors rather than those of the clients. But this development of collectors was practically confined to the field of burial insurance.

The Commission did not welcome this development at all. Their opinion of the collecting burial societies as a whole was in their own words "decidedly adverse." They believed that insurance of young children's lives led to increased mortality among the children, and they produced statistics in support of this belief; they went so far as to recommend that insurance of the lives of children under three years of age should be prohibited altogether. For the general problem of the collecting burial society, with its extravagance of administration and its high proportion of lapsed policies, they proposed, as is noted below, the cure of State competition.

There was at this date already another competitor with the collecting societies in the field. As the Commission observed, the privilege reserved by Parliament for friendly societies of insuring for funeral expenses "has already been assumed without authority

by joint stock companies, especially by the Prudential." They
naturally gave some attention to this development.

The Prudential, beginning its industrial assurance business in
1854, had already in 1872 more than 1,000,000 policy-holders.
At the time of the Commission's Report, the only bodies through
which legal insurances could be effected for the funeral expenses
of a wife or child were societies registered under the Friendly
Societies Acts, and the sums payable in respect of any child under
ten were rigidly limited. Friendly societies, moreover, had an apparent advantage in being exempt from Government stamp duty on
any policies issued by them. The Prudential, however, did not
wait to get legal authority for its proceedings and it turned to gain
the apparent disadvantage of having to stamp its policies. The
secretary to the company, Mr. Harben, told the Commission that,
so far from desiring to be relieved of its yearly expenditure of between
£3,000 and £4,000 on policy stamps, the Company would "unquestionably not" do so.

> "It is a very curious thing," he said farther on, "but the
> people imagine that if the policy has a government stamp
> upon it, it has some peculiar guarantee about it. We would
> not dispense with the stamp upon any consideration. . . .
> One of our great canvassing features is that we issue a stamped
> Government policy."

On this the Commission observed that "the last words clearly
admit that the stamp is actually used as an argument in canvassing
with the knowledge of the directors." They proceeded to judgment:

> "The practice of the agents of the Prudential Company in
> this respect and the advantage thus taken by the Company of
> the ignorance of its assured, are the more inexcusable because
> probably the larger number of the industrial policies of the
> Prudential, including no doubt almost the whole of those in
> the department of infant assurance, are legally worthless. . . .
> Every time that the directors of the Prudential issue a policy
> on the assurance of a wife's life by her husband, or of a child's
> by its parent, they are putting forth what they must know to
> be illegal, and by placing a stamp on it they are deliberately
> putting a semblance of legality on that which has no legality
> at all. . . . We must say that, however scrupulously companies
> doing industrial assurance may be found to fulfil engagements
> which do not legally bind them, the unchecked continuance

of this wholesale manufacture of policies without legal validity appears to us a scandal to the law and a snare to the poor, since there is nothing to prevent the most dishonest persons carrying on the same practice."

The Commission recommended that insurance on lives of children under, say, three should be prohibited altogether, and that for the future the companies should be given the same rights of insurance for funeral expenses as the societies. The first of these proposals was reduced in the legislation that followed in 1875 to the placing of a maximum limit on the amount of insurance on a child's life; not more than £6 for a child up to five, not more than £10 for a child between five and ten. Sir Stafford Northcote as leader of the House of Commons in 1875 found himself unable to take as strong a line with the collecting societies as he had taken in 1874 as chairman of the Royal Commission. The second proposal to assimilate the law in respect of friendly societies and industrial assurance companies was adopted.

The Act of 1875 was the first step on a long road of legalizing retrospectively the proceedings of industrial life offices. In 1896, when a new consolidating Friendly Societies Act was passed, an accompanying Act was passed for "Collecting Societies and Industrial Assurance Companies." This Act marked the recognition that both types of agency for burial insurance—collecting societies and collecting companies—were the same in principle, businesses rather than organizations for Mutual Aid. By that time the companies and the societies alike had already discovered a new gold mine of illegal assurance. They had begun to issue life-of-another policies, not on wife or child only, but to relations of all kinds and indeed to people who were no relations. Everyone who wanted a flutter was encouraged to have "sixpence on grandmother." By 1909, of 30,000,000 policies of industrial assurance, 10,000,000 were illegal.

The Government and Parliament of the day felt compelled to give retrospective validity to these policies. By an Act introduced by Mr. Winston Churchill as President of the Board of Trade, they validated the great bulk of the illegal policies in force and gave a carefully restricted authority for the future, extending the list of relations who might take out policies on the life of another, while limiting the purpose of insurance to "the funeral expenses." As is shown in paras. 54–57 of Appendix D to the *Report on Social Insurance*, there can be no question that the authority given by Parliament in 1909 for the future was meant to be much narrower than the white-washing of the past. Once again the industrial life offices proceeded to make their own law. They continued to press the issue of policies irrespective of actual liability for funeral expenses, exactly as before. To a committee which examined industrial assurance in 1929 they blandly proposed an amendment of the law to validate what they had been doing for twenty years. Disregard of legal niceties in pushing business among the poorest classes has been the mark of industrial life offices through most of their history.

The Royal Commission of 1874 did not like the collecting societies. They did not like much more the unauthorized rival of these societies, that is to say, the company of Prudential type doing industrial assurance. They thought that such companies should be given the same powers of insurance for funeral expenses as the collecting societies. But their real alternative to both was voluntary insurance undertaken by the State. This falls into the following chapter. The latest stage of all in the relations of Parliament and the industrial life offices—the Industrial Assurance and Friendly Societies Bill introduced in December, 1947—is noticed in Section VI of Appendix A.

SECESSION THE MIDWIFE OF INVENTION

The origins of many of the great organizations which fill the friendly society field are strikingly similar—a meeting of a dozen men or less in the evening after their work, generally in the back room of a public-house.

Thus, the Oddfellows of the Manchester Unity name as their founder Robert Naylor, who, as landlord of the "Ropemakers' Arms" in Chapel Street, Salford, started a benevolent society in 1808 from which at a larger meeting held on October 10, 1810, at the Robin Hood Hotel, Manchester, the greatest of all the orders sprang.

The Loyal and Ancient Shepherds began by a meeting of twelve men on Christmas Day, 1826, at the Friendship Inn, Ashton-under-Lyne, under the presidency of Thomas Scholfield, the host of the inn. Thomas Scholfield and his cronies were already members of a friendly society. They would have liked to get a new lodge of the Oddfellows established in their district. But the leaders of the Oddfellows refused, so Thomas Scholfield and his friends decided to start a new society, to which, on the suggestion of one of the twelve and recalling the day of its birth, they gave the name of the Ancient Shepherds.

The Hearts of Oak began a little later by another meeting of twelve men at a public-house at the "Bird-in-Hand," Long Acre, on January 20, 1842. These twelve also were already members of a provident society but dissatisfied with its administration. They decided to make a new society to fit their needs. They made one John Hadley their secretary and described him hereafter as founder, though in fact he left them in two years. They made the landlord of the inn their treasurer and made him go on as treasurer until they outgrew him altogether. The Hearts of Oak at its inception did not know whether it would be a local society or a national one. Its first rules described anyone living more than four miles from the "Bird-in-Hand" as a country member.

The back-room origin either in a public-house or in a church or chapel building applies to others than the friendly societies proper. The largest of the collecting burial societies began in 1850 by a gathering of a few thoughtful working men at the Liver Inn, St. Anne's Street, Liverpool. From this it grew into the vast business which Gladstone once held up to opprobrium and which figures largely in Appendix D of my *Report on Social Insurance and Allied Services*.

The second largest of the building societies, like nearly all the rest, had a similar insignificant origin: the meeting of a dozen men in 1874 in a room at the Abbey Road Church, in North-West London.

In most of these origins there is a similarity in a more important matter than that they began by a gathering of unknown men in a public-house or chapel. Nearly all of them began also as secessions from some earlier society. As has been stated, the original Shepherds were already Oddfellows; finding themselves forbidden by authority to establish a new lodge they made a new society. The original Hearts of Oak were all in a society with which they felt dissatisfaction; being unable to change its administration they decided to start a new society. The Ancient Order of Foresters is a break-off from the Royal Order of Foresters. The Manchester Unity of Oddfellows began by absorbing dissident Oddfellows from a Sheffield lodge of Oddfellows.

In a totalitarian State or in a field already made into a State monopoly, those dissatisfied with the institutions that they find can seek a remedy only by seeking to change the Government of the country. In a free society and a free field they have a different remedy; discontented individuals with new ideas can make a new institution to meet their needs. The field is open to experiment and success or failure; secession is the midwife of invention. The new institution may fail or may remain limited. It may grow according to the life that is in it, and growing may change the world.

FRIENDLY SOCIETIES MORE THAN MUTUAL INSURANCE

The friendly societies have been the democratic pioneers of mutual insurance. At one time the legislature was inclined to describe them as if they were nothing more. The Act of 1829, for instance, after giving a list of the misfortunes for which they might provide went on to add: "any other natural state or contingency whereof the occurrence is susceptible of computation by way of average."

But the friendly societies have been much more than agencies for dealing with averages by way of mutual insurance. They have been social clubs; they have been societies concerned with the general welfare of their members; they have been channels for the spirit of voluntary service.

The social side of the friendly society is typified by the regular "club night" forming a feature of all the affiliated orders with their branches, and of the small local societies. The club night may be monthly, fortnightly or weekly; in the early days a meeting at each full moon was common, as enabling the brethren with less difficulty to find their way there—and back after a social evening. If the meeting is that of the branch of an affiliated order, it is normally introduced by a ritual, designed to impress upon members the high aims of the society and the respect which should be accorded to these aims. There may be passwords and signs as a condition of admittance. The room will be brightened by insignia and adorned by photographs of past officers of the branch, and by other memorials testifying to the honourable antiquity and usefulness of the society. The business of every meeting, in addition to correspondence and general questions, will include the administration of individual sick benefits, the branch receiving on that occasion the reports of the "sick visitors," that is to say the individual members who have undertaken to call on sick brethren. In one of the principal orders, every meeting of every branch begins by the chairman putting three questions: first, whether any member has anything to propose that concerns the welfare of the order; second, whether he has anything to propose for the welfare of members individually; third, whether he has anything to propose that concerns the welfare of the branch. He repeats the same questions at the end, and in this way gives an opportunity for every member to make recommendations concerning organization and business, as well as proposals of a benevolent character for the help of brothers who may have fallen into misfortune.

Undoubtedly the club night bulks less in the activity of friendly societies to-day than it did in the past. It is unknown to the large unitary society, whether that works on accumulating or deposit or Holloway principles. It draws a declining attendance in the orders. A branch of 150 members may produce a dozen or fewer attenders apart from the officers, and most of them will be middle-aged. But the club night continues as an integral part of the work of the orders, and of the local societies, as distinct from the large centralized organizations.

The welfare side of the friendly society is illustrated both by the friendly individual help which may spring up naturally at a meeting, and by action on a larger scale. A friendly society does not confine itself to making a business contract with its members. It is concerned with their welfare generally.

In the Ancient Order of Foresters, for example, every branch of the order is required to establish a subsidiary benefit fund, the main object of which is to render assistance to members or their widows in distressed circumstances. The same order has other funds for assistance beyond any contract: one established in 1918 as a memorial to members who lost their lives in the First World War, and one established in the Second World War as a tribute to the memory of Stanley Duff, long the secretary of the order.

This welfare interest of friendly societies may be illustrated by two recent activities of the largest of the orders, the Manchester Unity: the Orphan Gift Fund started shortly after the end of the First World War, and the War Distress Fund, started in the early days of the Second World War.

The Orphan Gift Fund was designed to commemorate the sacrifice of serving members of the order who fell in war, but has now been extended to cover the orphans of any member. The fund is raised by a levy of a penny a year from every member, by voluntary contributions from branches and individuals, and by interest on investments. In the twenty-seven years of its activity £400,000 has been spent from this fund, and eight hundred orphans to-day are being helped by it. The gift is a gift, not a grant to which anyone has a right. The help is not confined to money; the brethren of the order help one another's children at need by advice and assistance in kind.

The War Distress Fund was started at the end of 1940, shortly after the bombing of London began, to assist members who might suffer in air raids. It was supported entirely by voluntary contributions. As the funds raised proved more than was needed for the original purpose, the balance was finally devoted to assisting members who became victims of the floods in the spring of 1947.

The friendly societies, finally, are channels for voluntary service. The larger societies must, of course, have substantial full-time staffs, but the sick visitors and other officers of branches are unpaid. The almoners of the Manchester Unity's Orphan Gift Fund must be volunteer unpaid members. The officers of all grades give service beyond any compensation that they may receive.

Friendly societies have been and are organizations for brotherly aid in misfortune and channels for the spirit of voluntary service, as well as being agencies for mutual insurance and personal saving. "Friendly Society" is a better name and means a better thing than the "Frugality Bank" by which Jeremy Bentham wanted to replace it.

II. THE STATE AND THE FRIENDLY SOCIETIES

The Issue of Encouragement or Control. The Settlement of 1875.
Present Legal Position of Friendly Societies. National Insurance Act
1911 and the Approved Society System. The Divorce of 1946 and After.
Reflections on Friendly Societies and the State.

THE ISSUE OF ENCOURAGEMENT OR CONTROL

WHEN, in the last years of the eighteenth century, the aristocratic
rulers of Britain began to concern themselves with friendly societies,
they were torn between conflicting desires. On the one hand, they
wanted working-men to get together, to make provision against the
calamities of sickness, death and old age; only if the "industrious
classes" did more to provide for themselves could the burden of
providing for them under the Poor Law be lightened for other
classes. On the other hand, with the French Revolution in full view,
there appeared to the then rulers of Britain to be obvious dangers in
causing the industrious classes to get together too much; there was
fear that they might get together to change the constitution.

The fruits of the fear of revolution were the temporary Seditious
Meetings Act of 1795, followed by a permanent Seditious Meetings
Act in 1817, the Unlawful Societies Act of 1799, and in the industrial
field the Combination Laws culminating in a practical prohibition
of trade unions in 1799-1800. The fruit of desire to encourage thrift
among the poor was Rose's Act of 1793 declaring it lawful to form
societies of good fellowship, for security against the risks of sickness,
age, infirmity and death of the breadwinner.

Rose's Act not only gave a definition of friendly societies which
is still substantially true, but laid the foundations of most later
provisions for facilitating the work of these societies. These included
registration, in the form of notification of rules to Justices at Quarter-
Sessions; exemption from taxes; ability to sue in courts; priority of
claim against officers; arbitration in accordance with the rules. The
Act added a privilege of great importance then, though now happily
out of date, in exempting friendly society members from the law of
parochial settlement.

The benefits conferred by Rose's Act were great, and no doubt
encouraged the organization of friendly societies. But the repressive
legislation of the same epoch proscribed the form of organization
which was most needed and was destined to become dominant—

the making of affiliated orders, that is to say, branches in federal union and continual correspondence with one another. As most of the orders liked to make their association by secret oaths and ceremonies and passwords, they became doubly or trebly illegal. They remained so, strictly, till the middle of the nineteenth century. Only by an Act of 1846 were the affiliated orders recognized by law and relieved, on conditions noticed below, of the stigma of being illegal societies. Fortunately being illegal did not prevent their growth. But even after 1846, for nearly thirty years, an order as such could not be registered. Every one of its branches in the eyes of the Registrar was an independent society.

This attitude of the legislature had two effects. First, the federal orders developed later than the unitary societies. The only orders claiming to have been established before 1800 are the Independent United Order of Mechanics (1756) now in process of dissolution, and the Ancient Order of Druids (1781),[1] still in existence, but losing ground to some of the other orders.

A second consequence of the repressive legislation of the later Georgian era was more important and was undoubtedly beneficial to the friendly society movement. The leading spirits of this movement were not interested in making revolutions, in changing either the structure or the policy of the Government. To make this clear, in face of the legislation which branded them as seditious because they used passwords and had branches which helped one another, they emphasized to the utmost the non-political nature of their organizations. It was not uncommon for the rules of the early friendly societies to prohibit both religious and political discussion at their meetings. The Ancient Shepherds of the Ashton Unity in 1826 added the word "Loyal" to their title, to show that though they had signs and passwords they meant no harm to the constitution of Britain. The Manchester Unity of Oddfellows a few years later went further. Having expelled some of their members for offences against the order, they found their power to expel challenged on the ground that as a society with branches they were an illegal organization; a decision was given against them. They sought the advice of the Attorney-General of the day, Sir John Campbell, and in putting the case to him in 1837 declared as a fundamental rule of the order

[1] The authority for this is the Chief Registrar's Report for 1906, p. 9. In addition to these two, a table at p. 116 of Frome Wilkinson's *History of the Friendly Society Movement* attributes an origin "before 1798" to the still existing "Grand United Order of Oddfellows" and an origin in 1796 to the "United Order of Comical Fellows," now defunct or nearly so.

that "if any member sing or give a toast or sentiment on religious or political subjects he shall pay a fine for the breach of the law." They went on to say that "the Order discountenances Trades Unions and does not allow assistance to be given to those who leave their employment in strikes or turnouts—by this means promoting good will to all men."[1] A similar attitude might not be held to promote the same result to-day.

Apart from any special provision in their rules, the conditions on which in 1846 the friendly societies were freed from the brand of sedition formally excluded them from politics. The exemption applied only to a society in which or meeting at which "no business whatever other than that of the Relief, Maintenance, or Endowment of the several persons to whom Benefits are assured by the Rules of such Society are treated of, and which is established solely for the purpose of assuring Benefits depending on the Laws of Sickness and Mortality."[2] Acts of Parliament die hard in England, even when they are obsolete.

The friendly society movement did not need this jealous care. It began as a common meeting place of men of different views for purposes transcending party differences. It has happily retained that character. One of the most valuable peculiarities of British life is the large element of public activity which by convention remains outside the sphere of party, including the churches, universities, judiciary, national and local civil servants, and, above them all as the symbol of national unity, the Crown itself. Of the three largest working class movements, trade unions, consumers' co-operation and friendly societies, the last alone retains to-day this character of transcending party differences for a common purpose, and is without any party affiliations.

Rose's Act heralded a period of great legislative interest in friendly societies. From 1793 to 1850 there were no less than eighteen Acts of Parliament dealing with these associations, which were repealed wholly or in part by a consolidating measure of 1855.[3] Several of these Acts had as their express purpose the "encouragement" of friendly societies. The question arose whether "encouragement" and the registration that went with it involved any form of public control to ensure that a society registered by the State was financially sound, and would give fair treatment to its members. This issue was fought out in the nineteenth century, with policy changing from time to time. Thus in 1819 the justices, before they registered a society,

[1] James Spry, *History of Oddfellowship* (London, 1867), p. 39.
[2] 9 and 10 Vict. c. 27, sect. 9.   [3] 18 and 19 Vict., c. 63.

E

were required to approve the scale of benefits proposed, and in 1829 this was extended to their approving the scale of contributions, while a barrister was required to approve the rules. But the need for justices' approval of benefit and contribution scales was abolished five years later, in 1834.

Public responsibility for the soundness of friendly societies was reintroduced in another form in 1846, when the barrister approving the rules received the title of Registrar of Friendly Societies and was required, before approving the rules and registering a society, to make sure that its tables of contributions and benefits had been certified by an actuary. But this lasted only four years. In 1850 societies were given the choice of being certified by an actuary or of simply being registered without certification of their tables; most of them took the latter course. In 1855 certification was abolished. The State was driven back to registration without attempting to certify soundness.

THE SETTLEMENT OF 1875

Fifteen to twenty years later the main issue fought out before the Royal Commission was whether this was enough for the State to do. There were many who wanted the State to do more. Friendly societies were felt to be socially desirable, in themselves and as a means to reducing the Poor Rate. But individual friendly societies were continuing to fail or be mismanaged, and the rising tide of burial insurance through collecting societies caused many misgivings. The real service done to the community by the Royal Commission of 1871–74 was to call attention to the achievement of the affiliated orders and of what they were doing to become actuarially solvent. In the light of what they learned of what the orders were doing and proposing to do, the commission came down definitely against any proposal that the soundness of a society's financial position should have to be certified by a Government actuary before the society was registered.

The same impression of the work and value of the affiliated orders was the basis of the Commission's treatment of another proposal made at that time for State intervention in the field of social security. One of the most remarkable documents presented to the Commission was a memorial advocating a general Government scheme of voluntary insurance through the post office, for sickness, death and old age. The memorial was signed by both archbishops, six bishops, seventeen lay peers, thirty-five Members of Parliament of all shades of political opinion, thirty-seven chairmen of Boards of Guardians, fifty-two justices of the peace, ninety clergymen, many medical men, industrialists, lawyers, etc., about five hundred men in all, "besides four ladies."[1] The argument of the memorialists was that provision by the State of a self-supporting system of insurance for all friendly society objects would (a) facilitate a strict and wholesome administration of the Poor Laws, (b) promote a good use of the advancing rate of labourers' wages, and (c) enable labourers to get sound insurance at a cost not exceeding the amount now expended by them in unsound and uncertified societies. The memorialists urged accordingly:

(1) That the provision of 27 and 28 Vict. c. 43[2] should be extended in such a manner as to offer to industrious labourers insurance suited to their requirements under the supervision of the Government and by means of the post office.

(2) That the alleged difficulties relating to sickness pay will be found . . . to have been exaggerated and are not such as to prevent the management and administration of sickness pay being undertaken and efficiently discharged by the post office.

(3) That the proposal to grant endowments through the post office should also receive the support of your commission.

(4) That . . . the certificate of the Registrar of Friendly Societies should be so amended as to make it of weight in determining the trustworthiness of friendly societies.

The Commission, while obviously impressed by this memorial, were not prepared to go the whole length advocated therein. They thought that insurance against sickness could not be undertaken safely except on a local basis; only so would there be adequate safeguards against "imposition," that is to say malingering and unjustified claims. They cited for this the views and the experience of the burial societies: "The impossibility of carrying on sick business for a burial society of extensive area is admitted by irrefragable evidence." If a centralized society could not safely undertake sickness

---

[1] The memorial, with all its signatures, is given in full in Appendix IX to the Royal Commission's Report and is discussed by them in paras. 845–53 of their Fourth Report, 1874. The four ladies admitted to the male army of 1872 were the Misses Emily Faithfull, Harriet Martineau, Jessie Boucherett and Louisa Boucherett.

[2] The Government Annuities Act of 1864, under which deferred annuities could be granted on smaller payments at more frequent intervals than under the earlier Act of 1853.

insurance throughout the country, the State could not do so either. And there was no need for the State to try. The leading societies giving sick benefit—the Manchester Unity and the rest—were respectable bodies, governed in the interests of their members and only needing help and guidance in becoming actuarially solvent.

Insurance against death was a different affair in two respects. It was simple, well within the capacity of the State. And the principal agencies now undertaking it among the poor were not, in the eyes of the Commission, people deserving any consideration. The full blast of State competition would be justified to put the collecting burial societies out of business or make them amend their ways.

"If we take the view that Burial Societies exist for the benefit of the people, and not the people for the benefit of the managers of burial societies, if we are satisfied that great abuses now exist in the management of many of these Societies, from which it is most difficult for the members to protect themselves, and which it is almost equally difficult for legislation to prevent, and if we find that the State can carry on this kind of business without involving the public in pecuniary loss and without mischievously affecting the spirit of individual independence, we shall scarcely recognize the right of the societies to object to its doing so on the ground that the competition of the Government might be prejudicial to their own interest."[1]

The Commission accordingly rejected the proposal of the memorialists as regards sickness insurance, and accepted it for insurance against death and for old age. They emphasized the simplicity of such insurance as compared with sickness. "Here the insurer pays his price, and as soon as the simple fact of death, or of the attainment of a certain age is established, the Government officers have only to pay what they have contracted to pay. But in the case of a claim on account of sickness they must exercise more or less discretion." The Commission recommended "that the existing system of Government insurance through the Post Office for death and deferred annuities be extended, so as to cover the whole ground now occupied by what is termed Industrial Assurance." What they meant by this was made plain by what they said about the practical problems of insurance among the poor. "The evidence which we have taken from all classes of witnesses shows that it is not sufficient to open an assurance book, and to insure the lives of those who take the trouble to present

[1] Fourth Report, para. 852.

themselves. The poor will not generally insure in the Burial Societies unless they are specially invited and urged to do so by personal application from collectors; nor will they keep up their payments unless the collector calls for them. There is no collector to bring them to insure at the Post Office, nor are any active measures taken to make the advantages of the Post Office insurance known to them." Obviously Sir Stafford Northcote and his colleagues seventy years ago meant that the State should go all out to get the business of the collecting societies and the Prudential, should go into the business of industrial assurance with collectors and all.

The Government accepted the recommendation of the Commission in principle, without the practical corollary necessary to make their action a success. They introduced post office insurance for death and old age; they did not establish collectors. They achieved, as the Commission had forecast, just nothing at all. The Post Office Savings Bank, exploiting the purely individual motive, has been an immense success, as of recent times the National Savings Movement has been a success. Post office insurance for old age and against death has failed to attract any custom worth mention. The more difficult task of putting over Mutual Aid for sickness has required the crusading spirit of the orders. In assurance for funerals, the State has failed to compete with the self-seeking persistence of the professional collectors. It has been driven to successive attempts to keep within bounds, by prohibitions and inspectors, the operations of the business motive in the field of industrial assurance.

But while the State has been driven to treat societies undertaking industrial assurance on altogether different lines from the societies not undertaking this, the State has done nothing to make the distinction between the two types of organization clear to the public. To the Royal Commission of 1874 the burial societies and the ordinary friendly societies were as different as chalk from cheese. It would have been reasonable to mark the difference by a distinction of name when, by the Act of 1875, registration of societies was being placed on a new permanent basis. Unfortunately this was not done. The affiliated orders which the Commission blessed and the burial societies which they damned with all the emphasis at their command and tried to put out of business were left to go on presenting themselves to the public under the same name as registered friendly societies. And even when in 1896 the substantial similarity of societies and of companies doing industrial assurance business with collectors was recognized and the term "collecting societies" was introduced, mystification of the public continued. A society established or first taking to the use of collectors after 1895 must put the word "collect-ing" in its title. But if it was a collecting society before that date it is free from this requirement, and can call itself simply a friendly society. Nearly all the more important collecting societies enjoy and use this privilege.[1] The State knows and seeks to control them as collecting societies, and as such they are described in this Report. To the public they present themselves as friendly societies.

This is the more unfortunate because the policy of increasingly stringent supervision which has been found to be necessary in respect of societies which collect, is in striking contrast to the policy for friendly societies in general. In rejecting the first proposal of the memorialists for State adventure in sickness insurance, the Commission rejected also their fourth proposal, that of making the Registrar's certificate a certificate of financial soundness. They proposed that the Registrar should be established on an adequate basis, with power to get returns from all registered societies, and to require yearly audits and periodical valuations, but also with power to exempt societies from valuation where this appeared desirable. Their recommendations here were in substance carried through by an Act of 1875. That Act has been repealed and embodied in later legislation, but its main principle remains.

Registration by the State involves a certain order and publicity in the business of friendly societies, and in return gives them privileges. Registration does not mean any guarantee by the State that the society is financially sound; that remains the responsibility of the society and its members.

PRESENT LEGAL POSITION OF FRIENDLY SOCIETIES

Apart from co-operation in the administration of National Health Insurance, begun in 1911 and due to come to an end in 1948, the relations of the State and the friendly societies to-day are governed by the Friendly Societies Act of 1896, with minor amendments made in 1898, 1904, 1908, 1909, 1924, and 1929.

The most important provision in the Act of 1896 is section 8, printed in Appendix A. This by its first sub-section defines a friendly society as one established for any or all of six purposes. By other sub-sections, (2), (3), (4), and (5), it provides for the registration of societies for certain other purposes; societies under

---

[1] Out of 138 collecting societies, 56 are in this position, including most of the larger societies, in particular the Royal Liver Friendly Society, the Liverpool Victoria Friendly Society, and the Scottish Legal Friendly Society.

these sub-sections are registered under the Friendly Societies Acts but are not called friendly societies; they are described by their appropriate names: cattle insurance societies, benevolent societies, working men's clubs, specially authorized societies, and are dealt with not here but in Chapter III.

Of the six purposes in section 8 (1) which may make a friendly society, one is of outstanding importance. It is the relief or maintenance of the members, their husbands, wives, children, fathers, mothers, brothers or sisters, nephews or nieces, or wards being orphans, in sickness, infirmity, old age or widowhood, and of orphan children of members during minority. Two other substantial purposes are provision for maternity and funeral expenses (limited to husband, wife or child of a member) and provision for endowment of members or their nominees. The remaining purposes named in section 8 (1), including insurance against shipwreck, fire or loss of tools, and maintenance on travel in search of employment are of little practical importance to-day. Societies undertaking maintenance in sickness also as a rule provide for funerals, maternity and endowment; they are the general friendly societies of Group A in Table 1. But there are many societies which undertake only a special part of the first purpose, other than maintenance in sickness, such as provision for widows and orphans, or of medical treatment or pensions, and there are other societies which undertake only insurance for funerals or endowments. All these are still friendly societies, but specialized, not general.

In relation to all friendly societies, the Registrar has five main functions—to examine the rules of the society; to obtain and examine an annual statement of accounts; to insist on or exempt from valuation; to hold a formal investigation of the affairs of a society when asked to do so; to prosecute societies or their officers where necessary for breaches of law.

Examination of the rules is directed to ensuring that they include all the provisions which the law requires and nothing contrary to the law. The most important things which by law must be provided for by the rules are the following:

(a) the conditions of membership;
(b) the conditions of benefit;
(c) the manner of governance of the society;
(d) the mode of investment of the funds;
(e) the keeping of accounts and getting them audited once a year at least;

    (*f*) the manner in which disputes between the society and its members shall be settled;

    (*g*) the right of every person having an interest in the funds to inspect the books of the society.

Examination, applied both to the original rules and to any proposed amendment to ensure that they conform to statutory requirements, is strictly the limit of the Registrar's authority in regard to the rules. In practice he has and he uses the opportunity to check inconsistencies and ambiguities; to draw attention to practical difficulties and inequities which may arise under the proposed rules; and to see that the society has made some attempt to relate the proposed benefits to the contributions. He gives friendly and generally good advice. As a guide to new societies he is prepared to supply model rules for their consideration.

The annual return with accounts is the basis of the statistics which the Registrar presents to Parliament each year. If the return sets out correctly the society's financial dealings for the year and none of these is contrary to the law, the Registrar cannot, generally speaking, take action on the ground that the society's affairs have been wastefully or negligently managed. Nor can he insist that the auditor should have any technical qualifications.

The Act includes formally, as one of the things for which the rules of a registered friendly society must provide, a valuation once at least in every five years of the assets and liabilities of the society including the estimated risks and contributions. But this is subject to a power of exemption. Under section 28 (5), the Chief Registrar may with the approval of the Treasury dispense with valuation "in respect of societies or branches to whose purpose or to the nature of whose operations he may deem these provisions inapplicable." Till recently exemption was normally given to societies and branches of the following types:—

    Those with all members under twenty-one.
    Those depending on levies.
    Those periodically dividing their funds.
    Deposit friendly societies.
    Societies limited to the purposes (*c*) and (*e*) of section 8 (1), that is to say, unemployment, shipwreck, etc., or insurance of tools.

Exemption is given in each case only for one valuation period, so that it is always subject to a change of policy. In 1935 the Registrar announced a policy of requiring valuation in suitable cases from dividing and deposit societies. Valuation for the latter (which in the Registrar's terminology includes Holloway societies) presents no great difficulties. Valuation of dividing societies often does.

Formal investigation of the affairs of a society can be made only on application from a sufficient proportion of the members, as defined in the Act, and is very rare. No such investigation was asked for in any of the ten years 1929 to 1938.

Prosecution also is a last resource. The commonest subject of prosecution is a failure to send any return. The average annual number of prosecutions for any other cause in the ten years before the war was seven.

The privileges obtained by a society through registration fall under three heads:—

(1) Exemption from taxation, including not only income tax but corporation property duty and stamp duty on documents of all kinds.

(2) Exemption from the provisions of the still existing Unlawful Societies Act of 1799 and the Seditious Meetings Act of 1817 "so long as their business and meetings are concerned with no other business than is provided for by the registered rules."

(3) Minor privileges, such as priority of claim against officers dying or bankrupt, power to give subscriptions to hospitals, and power to admit minors as members.

Of these statutory privileges those under the first head, above all for the accumulating societies whether federal or unitary, are by far the most important. In so far as they are given on condition of registration they wield a powerful incentive to becoming registered for any considerable society. Small societies may be poor enough to escape taxation even without registration; societies with an income of less than £160 a year, even though not registered, were formally exempted from income tax by the Finance Act of 1918.

The privilege of exemption from taxation has been given in part as an endowment of mutual aid, but partly also on the assumption that the members of friendly societies would in the main be themselves individuals not liable to income tax. In accord with this the maximum annuity to be given by a registered friendly society was limited in the Act of 1896 to £50 a year and the maximum gross sum payable on death or as endowment was limited to £200. By

an amending Act of 1908 these limits were raised to £52 a year and
£300 respectively. A Bill now before Parliament proposes to increase
the £300 to £500 and the £52 a year to £104. This measure—
the Industrial Assurance and Friendly Societies Bill of 1947—is
the subject of a note in Appendix A, Section VI.

NATIONAL INSURANCE ACT 1911 AND THE APPROVED SOCIETY SYSTEM

A new phase in the relation of the State to friendly societies
began in 1911, when the State embarked on social insurance,
requiring compulsory contributions from employees and their
employers, and giving statutory benefits in virtue of these contributions.[1] The Workmen's Compensation Acts of 1897 and 1906
had not taken the form of insurance; they simply imposed a new
legal liability on employers, altering the contract between employer and employee. The Old Age Pension Act of 1908 gave
pensions without contributions at the age of 70, subject to a
means test.

The National Insurance Act of 1911 represented a fundamentally
new departure, which would have been impossible without the
pioneer work of the friendly societies and the trade unions. The
actuarial calculations on which the contributions and benefits of
the State scheme were founded were based on the experience of
Manchester Unity in calculating the risks of sickness. The actuary
who made these calculations was appointed as the first Government
actuary.

More than this, the State made the fateful decision of using
existing societies to administer the new benefits and of avoiding any
direct State administration. At one time it was proposed to limit
the administration of State health insurance to accumulating
societies, whether orders or unitary, and to exclude all those classified in Table 1 above as societies with dividend. The National
Insurance Bill of 1911, as introduced, provided by section 23 (1)
that approved societies (i) must not work for profit, (ii) must be
democratically controlled by the insured members and (iii) must

[1] The National Insurance Act of 1911 was not literally the first application
of compulsory insurance in Britain. Eden, *State of the Poor,* Vol. I, pp. 605 ff.
(1797 edn.), describes two Acts of Parliament, making insurance against sickness
and other risks compulsory (with deductions from their earnings) upon coal-
heavers in London (1757) and upon skippers and keelmen employed in the coal
trade on the River Wear (1792). The underlying idea was no doubt that these
men were earning so much that they might legitimately be forced to secure
themselves against pauperism. The Acts were repealed or lapsed.

not be societies which periodically divided their funds. The first of these conditions might have been held to exclude deposit and Holloway societies, since the investment interest earned was used to increase the member's individual surplus or deposit. The third of these conditions formally excluded dividing societies and might have been held to exclude the deposit and Holloway societies. In drafting his Bill, Mr. Lloyd George naturally took first into consultation the leading friendly societies of that time. His first draft reflected the attitude of the affiliated orders and the large unitary accumulating societies; they disliked societies with dividend in any form. But between the introduction of the Bill in the spring of 1911 and the beginning of its final stages in November, there came a change of policy.

In the Committee stage of the Bill the scope of Approved Societies was widened by a proviso to section 23 (1) making it possible for societies or companies established for other purposes to set up separate sections as Approved Societies. The conditions of section 23 (1) as to not working for profit and being democratically controlled were made applicable to the separate sections and not to the sponsoring society or company; there could be no question of course of the funds of the separate section being paid out as dividend, for they were available only for purposes laid down by the Act.[1] By this means the door into administration of National Insurance was opened, not only to friendly societies of all kind, including the collecting burial societies, but also the industrial assurance companies.

The limitation originally proposed, excluding from administration of State insurance any friendly societies which were not purely accumulating, would clearly have been harmful to the friendly societies themselves. It would have shut the door to developments such as those undertaken since then by the Hearts of Oak and the Loyal and Ancient Order of Shepherds.[2] Whether it was necessary or desirable to bring into the administration of State insurance for sickness, business organizations which had never undertaken that form of insurance on their own account is another question. One can only say that the decision to bring in such business organizations was for the author of National

---

[1] Section 23 (1) itself stood unaltered in the Bill. It was left open to an accumulating friendly society itself to become an Approved Society, and many did so. The Independent Order of Oddfellows, Manchester Unity, for instance, is itself an Approved Society. It has had no need to form a separate section.

[2] See p. 52 above.

Insurance deliberate, and that subsequently he felt sure that he had acted rightly.[1]

In 1910 there were about two and three-quarter million persons in affiliated orders and nearly another two million in friendly societies of other types giving sick pay. To these figures must be added a substantial but unknown number of trade unionists entitled to sick benefit from their unions. There must then be deducted something for duplicate membership and something for persons not working under contract of service as employees. Broadly, of the twelve million employees altogether who were being swept into the net of compulsory State insurance it may be estimated that about five millions were already insured through friendly societies or trade unions. The seven millions outside included, with others, those who had thought themselves too poor to join a society, those who did not think at all, those whom for reasons of age, health or character many if not most societies would regard as unwelcome. It is arguable that, if the scope for Approved Societies had not been made as wide as it was, if the industrial life offices had not seen in this the opportunity to build up through State insurance connections for their own lines of business, a substantial proportion of those compelled to pay contributions would have failed to become members of any Approved Society. In that case the State would have had itself to undertake direct administration of sick benefit. The friendly societies feared such competition from the State, and the Government of the day wished to use voluntary agencies in preference to enlarging the Civil Service. In a letter written to the industrial assurance Approved Societies in 1933, Mr. Lloyd George expressed his appreciation of what they had done to deal with the large number of people who did not belong to the great voluntary thrift societies and who had no experience of sickness insurance. "It was only when I decided to avail myself of the services of the industrial assurance offices that I was able to feel that I had taken a long step towards the solution of this problem."

With the opening of the field for formation of Approved Soci-

---

[1] The negotiations leading up to this change of policy were described in a Memorandum submitted to the Committee on Social Insurance and Allied Services in 1942 by Mr. Percy Rockliff (Hon. Secretary to the Joint Committee of Approved Societies and Parliamentary Agent to the National Union of Holloway Friendly Societies). The Memorandum is printed at pp. 97–110 of *Memoranda from Organizations on Social Insurance and Allied Services* (Cmd. 6405). The Holloway, dividing, and deposit societies on this occasion were in the same camp as the industrial life offices against the old guard of the orders, who were not happy about the whole business of National Insurance.

eties, receipt of any benefits beyond a meagre provision for so-called deposit contributors could be made dependent on getting admission to an Approved Society. The compulsorily insured population came by 1938 to be divided between two main classes of Approved Societies attached to industrial life offices and to the friendly societies respectively, with two minor groups attached to the trade unions and to particular employers.

TABLE 4

INSURED PERSONS IN VARIOUS TYPES OF APPROVED SOCIETY IN 1938
(THOUSANDS)

	Industrial Life Offices	Friendly Society	Trade Union	Employers	Total
Men ..	5,120	5,700	1,190	50	12,060
Women ..	3,350	2,440	290	30	6,110
Totals ..	8,470	8,140	1,480	80	18,170

The industrial life offices, it will be seen, had less than half the total number of men (about 40 per cent) but more than half (over 55 per cent) of the women.

Within the friendly society movement there was a marked difference of experience as between the societies with branches, that is to say the affiliated orders, and the societies without branches. Between 1923 and 1938 the membership of Approved Societies connected with the orders declined slightly from 3,150,000 to 3,000,000. The membership of Approved Societies sponsored by societies without branches rose from 3,550,000 to 5,140,000, that is to say, by 45 per cent. The latter included the rapidly rising new models of the deposit and the Holloway societies. Table 5 below shows these figures for men and women separately.

TABLE 5

INSURED PERSONS IN APPROVED SOCIETIES CONNECTED WITH
FRIENDLY SOCIETIES IN 1923 AND 1938 (THOUSANDS)

	With Branches		Without Branches	
	1923	1938	1923	1938
Men	2,390	2,230	2,540	3,470
Women	760	770	1,010	1,670
Totals	3,150	3,000	3,550	5,140

The financial independence of every Approved Society was the essence of the Approved Society system. Under the National Insurance Act of 1911 the compulsory contributions were put high enough to provide a substantial surplus over the expected liabilities for statutory benefit in respect of insured persons' as a whole. But this surplus was not distributed among the whole body of insured persons. Every Approved Society—for this purpose each branch of an affiliated order became a separate society—was valued separately. Most of them showed surpluses, which they were then free to use for additional benefits; in practice, dental and ophthalmic benefits were those most commonly given, but many societies—notably those with a small selected *clientèle* of persons in healthy occupations—were able to make substantial additions to the cash benefits received by their members. On the other hand some societies— notably those whose members were largely engaged in dangerous or unhealthy occupations—found themselves only just able to give the bare statutory benefits. Every Approved Society had a financial interest in economical administration. It had also an interest in not admitting too many people of dangerous occupations or doubtful health or too many women. The societies which showed themselves most ready to be all-embracing were those whose sponsors had a financial interest outside insurance for sickness, that is to say, the industrial life offices.

But while the statutory Approved Societies were separate financially both from one another and from the voluntary agencies which sponsored them, whether friendly societies or industrial life offices or trade unions, for administrative purposes they were combined with these agencies. The same staff was used to administer both the statutory benefits under the National Insurance Acts and any voluntary insurance undertaken by the sponsoring body; part of the remuneration of the staff was drawn from a grant for administration made on account of State insurance. This represented a considerable economy of man-power and of salaries. It represented also, as far as the friendly societies are concerned, avoidance of duplicate administration of sick benefit. When a friendly society member fell sick, his claim for State benefit and his claim for voluntary benefit could be dealt with on the same form by the same official. One medical certificate automatically served for both services. One visitor dealt with the sick man for both purposes.

The undertaking by the friendly societies of the administration of State benefits affected of course their character. They became more official and less personal, more of insurance agencies and less of social agencies. The new responsibility affected also their numbers and their structure. This change is shown in detail in Appendix A, Tables 20 and 21. The main consequences to friendly societies of the coming of National Insurance and of two world wars may be summed up as follows:—

(1) There was pressure to concentrate in larger units, leading to disappearance of a large proportion of small societies. There were 3,117 unitary accumulating societies in 1910, but only 893 in 1939; the average membership in the earlier year was 410 and in the later year was 1,283. The dividing societies were affected in the same way but less strongly; numbering 1,335 in 1910, with an average membership of 219, they fell to 610 in 1939 while their average membership rose to 622. The orders were affected by the same tendency but, with their federal structure, showed greater resisting power. They had still in 1939 16,625 separate branches, compared with 20,580 branches in 1910. But the larger orders tended to gain on the smaller ones. As Table 2 shows, the five largest orders had 72 per cent of the membership of all orders in 1899, 1900, and 1910, and nearly 80 per cent in 1939.

(2) There was stimulus to the new models of deposit and Holloway societies combining personal saving with insurance for sickness and thus providing something which State insurance did not provide. But here too it was the large societies which grew still larger. The three largest societies of these types, shown in Table 2, had less than 70 per cent of the total membership of these types in 1910, but more than 80 per cent in 1939.

THE DIVORCE OF 1946 AND AFTER

Supersession of the system of Approved Societies giving unequal benefits for equal compulsory contributions was one of the major changes recommended in my *Report on Social Insurance and Allied Services*. The arguments set out there (in paragraphs 48–76 of that Report) need not be repeated here, because they were successful. In the first announcement of Government policy on the proposals of this report, in February, 1943, Sir John Anderson, speaking for the Coalition Government of that day, admitted with regret that the Approved Society system must go; he himself in the National

Insurance Commission had had much to do with building it up and working through it.

Abolition of the system of Approved Societies with separate finance meant that the State could no longer avoid direct administration of sick benefit. But my Report made two proposals designed to limit the field which the State must cover and to retain as fully as possible, even in that field, the services and the special experience of the staffs hitherto employed by Approved Societies.

I proposed, first, that friendly societies which gave substantial sick benefit from voluntary contributions should be used as responsible agents for administering the State benefit also to their members; this would have allowed the friendly societies of Group A in Table 1 to go on much as at present, with a continuing motive for sound administration, and would have avoided duplicating the machinery for sick pay in the home of every friendly society member.

I proposed, second, that the industrial life offices should be taken over and become a State organ of voluntary insurance, under an Industrial Assurance Board. The main reason for this proposal had nothing to do with health insurance; it was desire to cure the evils of industrial assurance as a business. But it would have had the incidental advantage of retaining for the public service the very efficient machine of health insurance built up by these offices in the Approved Societies attached to them. It would have done all that the memorialists of 1872 were after in proposing State insurance for sickness, old age, and death as a cure for the defects of the business of industrial assurance.

The Labour Government, by their two National Insurance Acts of 1946, have turned into law most of the proposals of my *Report on Social Insurance and Allied Services*, going beyond them in the speed of transition to full pensions for the existing pensionable classes; they have dealt with industrial accidents to some extent on a new basis.[1] They have accepted, as the Coalition Government before them did, the abolition of the Approved Society system. They have not accepted my proposal to take over industrial assurance, proceeding instead to an amendment of the powers of industrial life offices by a Bill introduced in December, 1947.[2] They have rejected my proposal to use the friendly societies as responsible agents for administering State benefit with their own benefit to their members. The marriage of 1911 between the State when it entered the field

[1] See Epilogue contributed by myself to the new edition of the Fabian Society study of *Social Security* (George Allen & Unwin, 1948).
[2] See Appendix A, Section VI.

of insurance against sickness and the voluntary agencies with a hundred years' experience in this field, has been followed in 1946 by complete divorce. The State, like a Roman father, has sent the friendly societies back to live in their own house. The State is now engaged in constructing a complete and exclusive administrative machine of its own.

REFLECTIONS ON FRIENDLY SOCIETIES AND THE STATE

The probable future of the friendly societies and the new tasks to which they may set their hands are considered in a later chapter. This chapter may fitly end by some general reflections on the friendly societies and the State.

Insurance of wage-earners against sickness has never in Britain presented itself to business men as in itself good business. The solution of the critical problem of combining sound finance with the sympathetic administration that is indispensable in this field has been the achievement of the friendly societies. It has been the achievement first and foremost of the affiliated orders, a typically British political invention of federalism, combining local responsibility with width of support and central guidance. It is in these orders only that provision for sickness is still the principal service. The centralized accumulating societies have depended for stability largely on other types of insurance in addition to sickness; the ingenious and useful new models of the deposit societies and the Holloway societies appeal largely to a motive different from that which leads to Mutual Aid, the motive of individual saving for emergencies.

As sickness insurance was the invention of the friendly societies, so insurance against unemployment—the other dreaded form of insecurity among wage-earners—had for its pioneer another type of working-class organization for Mutual Aid—the trade unions. The main, and for long the only type of insurance among wage-earners which appealed to the business motive of gain was burial insurance, involving payment of a single sum on an event which could be established without difficulty. Here, in the two forms of collecting society and collecting limited company, the business motive has become dominant, and gain without limit has been sought by doing the simplest possible service. The industrial life offices, before the National Health Insurance Act of 1911, never touched sickness insurance, or, if they did, they abandoned it. Even in their own field of burial insurance the industrial life offices took always the simplest line to more business, irrespective of social consequences, evading responsibility for avoiding double, treble or tenfold insurance against funeral costs, pushing business to the point where it led to a scandalous scale of lapses. Beyond funeral insurance they found their main field for development still in the relatively simple branches of life and endowment insurance. To the problems of security against sickness and unemployment they made no contribution.

In 1911 the State entered the field where no one but the friendly societies, and to less extent the trade unions, had been till then. The possibility of the State entering into competition with the industrial life offices by providing a death benefit was considered in the drafting of the National Insurance Bill of that year, but the suggestion was withdrawn in deference to threatened opposition to the whole Bill from these politically powerful organizations. Instead, the industrial life offices were given the chance, along with the friendly societies, of forming Approved Societies, and seized the chance as a means of strengthening their business connections.

By this means the State avoided setting up any machinery of its own for administering sickness insurance. It is probable that without the entry of the industrial life offices, with their large and costly organization and administrative capacity, this could not have been done. In the circumstances of 1911, the service rendered by the industrial life offices may have been indispensable and was certainly great. It was acknowledged in generous terms by the author of National Insurance a few years later. But it was a service bought at the cost of strengthening a form of gain-seeking business— industrial assurance—which has been criticized with varying degrees of severity by one impartial committee of inquiry after another.

In 1946 the State has completed what it began in 1911, providing compulsorily for all citizens benefits designed to be adequate for subsistence, and going outside the field of 1911 to provision of death benefit. In doing this the National Insurance Act gives effect to my *Report on Social Insurance and Allied Services*. In rejecting two important proposals in that Report, for the use of friendly societies to administer State benefits for sickness and allied purposes to their members, and for taking over of the industrial life offices, the Act commits the State to setting up a centralized bureaucratic machine. Whether any such machine can grapple with the fundamental problem of sickness benefit, of reconciling sound finance with sympathy and intimate local handling is uncertain. The Government of 1911 sought the maximum of co-operation between the State and voluntary agencies in the field of social insurance. The Government of 1946 has divorced the two completely.

The divorce presents problems to both sides of the dissolved alliance. The friendly societies are forced to make a difficult re-adjustment of their staff and their administrative expenditure, with their position worsened in four respects:—

    (a) Loss of income received from the State as the administrative cost of their Approved Societies;

    (b) Competition of the much higher rates of State benefits and of compulsory contributions to cover them;

    (c) Threatened increase of the rate of claims as a consequence of these higher benefits, estimated by the Government actuary at $12\frac{1}{2}$ per cent or more;

    (d) The cheap money policy of the Government which, however desirable in itself, reduces in terms of interest the reward for saving and to that extent makes provision for the future more costly in terms of present sacrifice.

As regards the first item, the National Conference of Friendly Societies put the payment received by the friendly societies in recent years for Approved Society administration as something approaching £2,000,000 a year on 8,000,000 State members. In the case of the largest of these societies—the National Deposit—the grant in 1945 in respect of 963,000 State members was £209,000. While the work for which this grant was paid will disappear with it, it will be difficult rapidly to make corresponding reductions of expenditure; it may prove impossible to make them completely. In most cases voluntary and State business have been carried on together, in the same premises and largely by the same staff. The economy of overheads made possible by this combination will now be lost to the State and to the friendly societies alike.

The friendly societies have a difficult time ahead of them, more so than the trade unions for whom sick and unemployment pay has been only a side line, more so than the industrial life offices with their armies of collectors and their development into forms of life and endowment insurance which the State is leaving untouched. The degree to which the friendly societies triumph over their difficulties will depend on the life and the spirit of service in them, on their being ready to meet new needs by new methods, in the old spirit of social advance by brotherly co-operation. That most of them will do so can be taken for certain.

The greatest danger of the present situation is not on the side of the friendly societies. They will survive; if they did not do so, their place would be taken by new forms of voluntary organization. The real danger—it is great as well as real—is on the other side of the divorce. Will the State be able to create a machine capable of doing what the affiliated orders did in the most difficult. of all forms of social insurance, of combining soundness with sympathy in administration of cash benefits to the sick? Will the State be able to avoid the evil alternatives of extravagance and of harshness? The present rulers of the State have lightheartedly taken on a task without as yet having shown understanding of its nature.

III. MUTUAL AID IN OTHER FORMS

The Registrar's Varied Field. Trade Unions. Building Societies. Housing Societies. Social Clubs. Specially Authorized Societies. Consumers' Co-operation. Trustee Savings Banks. Hospital Contributory Schemes.

THE REGISTRAR'S VARIED FIELD

THE barrister appointed to certify the rules of savings banks in 1817 and of friendly societies in 1829 proved to be a valuable political invention. He developed into the Chief Registrar of Friendly Societies. As industrialization advanced upon them, the people of Britain discovered continually new needs and new forms of association for meeting them. They were given the chance of registering their associations with the Registrar of Friendly Societies, so getting an official name and address and recognition and friendly advice without control.

A study of Mutual Aid is largely a study of the field covered by the Chief Registrar of Friendly Societies, either under that name or under some other title, held always by the same official. The field itself is immensely varied, ranging from the infinitely little of some of the societies for specially authorized purposes under the Friendly Societies Acts, such as the purpose of "promoting and encouraging the art of swimming, life-saving and resuscitation," up to the colossal figures of the industrial life offices, the co-operative societies, the trade unions and the building societies. The simplest short guide to the field of Mutual Aid is the guide to the Registry of Friendly Societies prepared by the Registrar, but it is not short. It contains now 1,779 separate paragraphs.

The Royal Commission of 1871–74, while emphasizing the variety of the functions of the Registrar of Friendly Societies, found in it all a moral unity.

"When we thus group together the various bodies of which the Registrar of Friendly Societies is the pivot, we perceive that they really form one whole, as representing the different modes in which the working spirit of self-help among what the Acts often term the 'industrious classes' has been recognized and deemed worthy of encouragement by the legislature—the various means by which that portion of the population which is most within the risk of pauperism endeavours to escape from

it. And thus although the enactments by which these bodies
have been gathered together, have been passed by the Legislature almost at haphazard, a true moral unity is to be discovered in the functions of the Registrar of Friendly Societies,
whether exercised *eo nomine* or as 'barrister to certify the rules
of savings banks.' "

The Commission went on to paint a picture of the individual
citizen always in contact with the Registrar, from the first penny
deposited by him as a school child in a penny savings bank, through
sickness and unemployment, accident and shipwreck, to old age
and his burial at last by a collecting society. They devoted an
Appendix to the making of these successive "grafts" on the friendly
society system of 1793, beginning with the appointment of a barrister
to certify the rules of savings banks in 1817, proceeding through
certification of loan societies in 1835, benefit building societies in
1836, and the scientific and literary societies which were special
protégés of the Prince Consort in 1843, to the industrial and provident
societies which in 1846, by providing opportunities for the frugal
investments of the industrious classes, found a place for "trading
friendly societies," that is to say, the co-operative stores. There
followed cattle insurance societies in 1850, trade unions in 1855,
working men's clubs, farmers' trading societies and many more.
To-day, in addition to the "grafts" named by the Royal Commission
seventy years ago, the Registrar of Friendly Societies is also the
Registrar of employers' superannuation funds, and of workmen's
compensation schemes, and since 1923 he is the Industrial Commissioner with special powers of supervision over the collecting
societies and the industrial assurance companies.

Tables 6 and 7 (pages 87 and 88) give a brief survey of this vast
and varied field of the Registrar, in 1945 and ten years before, in
1935; notes explanatory of particular entries in the tables are given
at the end of Appendix A. Altogether, even without the Trustee
Savings Banks in relation to whom his work is purely formal, and
without the two business groups at the bottom, of collecting societies
and companies conducting industrial assurance, the Registrar is
concerned with some 29,000 separate free associations, whose total
membership adds up to 30,000,000, while their funds add up to
£1,882 million. To these figures the Trustee Savings Banks add
4,438,000 depositors and £603 million of balances due to them,
while industrial assurance adds 115,000,000 separate policies and
£643 million of funds. As between the years 1935 and 1945 the

number of societies tends to fall; in many fields the large units are making life harder for the small ones. The membership figures in most cases move the other way, notably with the co-operative stores, the trade unions and the industrial assurance businesses. The funds held in various forms almost without exception go bounding up;

TABLE 6

THE REGISTRAR'S FIELD IN 1935

	No. of Societies	Membership	Funds
			£
FRIENDLY SOCIETIES[1]—			
General Friendly Societies	18,956	6,433,737	112,516,883
Specialized Friendly Societies ..	1,285	1,732,689	22,795,488
OTHER SOCIETIES REGISTERED UNDER FRIENDLY SOCIETIES ACTS—			
Cattle Insurance Societies[2]	47	1,691	10,178
Benevolent Societies[3]	101	91,444	1,181,179
Working Men's Clubs	2,191	662,843	4,915,565*
Specially Authorized Societies			
Loan, Thrift or Investment ..	222	150,300	2,371,846
Miscellaneous	(134)	(71,291)	(287,159)
Shop Clubs[4]	9	60,244	485,019
SOCIETIES, ETC., REGISTERED UNDER OTHER ACTS—			
Co-operative Stores (I.P.)	1,098	7,414,376	196,641,865*
Co-operative Wholesale and Productive Societies (I.P.) ..	115	39,129	107,931,419*
Farmers' Trading Societies (I.P.) ..	444	126,726	4,358,702*
Housing Societies (I.P.)	351	35,448	15,107,484*
Clubs (I.P.)	2,361	584,824	4,978,389*
Building Societies			
Permanent	857	1,921,091 ⎫	602,005,795*
Terminating	142	17,593 ⎭	
Trade Unions†	448	3,794,680	14,167,202
Certified Loan Societies (1840 Act)[5]	102	20,743	162,699
Literary, Scientific, and Fine Arts[6]..	?	?	?
Superannuation Funds (1927 Act)[7]..	254	—	65,673,595
Railway Savings Banks	10	160,504	23,099,961
Workmen's Compensation Schemes	10	44,788	32,604
Trustee Savings Banks	104	2,142,676	233,262,227
Collecting Societies‡	151	(22,593,703)	63,902,681
Industrial Assurance Companies‡ ..	15	(71,037,447)	296,711,958

* Total assets.

† Excluding associations of employers.

‡ Industrial assurance business only. The bracketed figures in the "membership" column represent the numbers of policies issued.

Note.—The numbers attached to certain entries in the first column refer to notes in Appendix A, Section VII. The letters I.P. mean that the Societies are registered under the Industrial and Provident Societies Acts.

the total increase in the ten years, apart from industrial assurance, is from £1,408 million to £2,485 million.

The moral unity of the Registrar's work would not to-day be expressed in quite the words of the Commission of 1874. Instead

TABLE 7

THE REGISTRAR'S FIELD IN 1945

	No. of Societies	Membership	Funds
FRIENDLY SOCIETIES[1]—			£
General Friendly Societies	17,481	6,508,444	155,409,760
Specialized Friendly Societies ..	1,054	2,211,528	37,419,545
OTHER SOCIETIES REGISTERED UNDER FRIENDLY SOCIETIES ACTS—			
Cattle Insurance Societies[2]	38	1,712	9,067
Benevolent Societies[3]	111	127,249	1,794,817
Working Men's Clubs	(2,228)*	(947,394)*	(7,264,105)*§
Specially Authorized Societies			
Loan, Thrift or Investment ..	174	106,156	2,948,957
Miscellaneous	145	142,626	502,939
Shop Clubs[4]	8	67,738	1,125,746
SOCIETIES, ETC., REGISTERED UNDER OTHER ACTS—			
Co-operative Stores (I.P.)	1,052	9,230,24	357,283,973§
Co-operative Wholesale and Productive Societies (I.P.)	161	42,765	235,961,341§
Farmers' Trading Societies (I.P.) ..	370	155,332	7,239,609§
Housing Societies (I.P.)	357	33,442	13,082,643§
Clubs (I.P.)	2,361*	860,420*	7,852,259*§
Building Societies			
Permanent	808	2,055,921	822,791,946§
Terminating	82	9,403	1,162,675§
Trade Unions†	427	6,535,938	42,417,105
Certified Loan Societies (1840 Act)[5]	76	11,399	98,324
Literary, Scientific, and Fine Arts (1843 Act)[6]	?	?	?
Superannuation Funds (1927 Act)[7]	353	—	143,315,639
Railway Savings Banks	6	224,257	44,315,924
Workmen's Compensation Schemes	6	11,963	24,461
Trustee Savings Banks	87	4,438,160	603,079,997
Collecting Societies‡	138	(29,644,895)	116,552,688
Industrial Assurance Companies‡ ..	14	(85,902,821)	526,851,101

* 1943 figures.
§ Total assets.
† Excluding associations of employers.
‡ Industrial assurance business only. The bracketed figures in the "membership" column represent the numbers of policies issued.

Note.—The numbers attached to certain entries in the first column refer to notes in Appendix A, Section VII. The letters I.P. mean that the Societies are registered under the Industrial and Provident Societies Acts.

of talking of the various means by which the portion of the population most in danger of pauperism endeavours to escape from it, we should talk of the various forms of voluntary action inspired by the motive of Mutual Aid. Nor is the unity as complete as once it seemed. In relation to industrial assurance the Registrar is concerned not with Mutual Aid but with the business motive and with keeping it from leading to harmful results. Several of the types of societies coming within the Registrar's purview are themselves businesses; broadly this is true of everything registered under the Industrial and Provident Acts (marked I.P. in the tables) and of building societies. But these are mutual businesses managed for their members.

Something is said below about each of seven of the types of association shown in Tables 6 and 7, namely, trade unions, building societies, housing societies, social clubs, specially authorized societies, co-operative stores, and trustee savings banks. For reasons stated in each case the last two types are noticed very briefly, as also is another type of association not included in Tables 6 and 7—the hospital contributory schemes; these are important and interesting forms of Mutual Aid falling outside the scope of the Registrar. Some of the other types are explained in the Notes to the Tables.

TRADE UNIONS

Trade unions have been the subject of a voluminous literature, led in Britain by the two classic works of Sidney and Beatrice Webb —*The History of Trade Unionism*, first published in 1894 with a revised edition in 1920, and *Industrial Democracy*, first published in 1897 with a new edition in 1902. But comparatively little of this literature is recent. The modern and vitally important developments of trade unionism have received insufficient notice by students of economics and politics.

Beginning as indispensable organs to secure fair terms and independence for the isolated employee, in face of the economic power of the employer, trade unions have become instruments of immense power over the lives and fortunes of individuals and the community, outside the constitutional machinery of the State, possibly strong enough to challenge the State, certainly in a position to influence and deflect its action. They remain voluntary associations in the sense given to that term here—of being independent of elected public authorities, whether national or local, but in many if not most occupations they are no longer voluntary in the sense of its being free to an individual who wishes to pursue that occupation to decide

for himself whether he will or will not join them. Trade unions are
for most wage earners as inseparable a part of their environment
as are the darkness of the country at night and the smoke of the
towns by day.

There has never been any question of the State taking responsibility for any of the activities of trade unions as there was in the
case of the friendly societies. The question has been rather as to
the extent to which trade unions should be responsible for the results
of their own actions. This issue was raised at the beginning of this
century by the Taff Vale Judgment, making the funds of the
Amalgamated Society of Railway Servants liable to damages for loss
due to a strike supported from these funds. Till then it had been sup-
posed that under the Trade Union Act of 1871 unions as such could
not be sued, and the decision led to widespread protests in the trade-
union world. The Government of the day appointed a Royal
Commission, including Sidney Webb, the philosopher and historian
of trade unions, which early in 1906 reported in favour of trade
unions accepting legal responsibility for their actions, with a recognized position within the law. But the trade unions rejected this,
and when the Liberal Government in the same year introduced a
Trade Disputes Bill on the lines of the Royal Commission's Report,
they found so many of their supporters pledged during the election
to the trade union claim for outright reversal of the Taff Vale
Judgment that they had to change the Bill and admit this claim.
Trade unionism to-day in Britain stands as an exceptional instance
of power, resting on money and organization, without financial
responsibility.

No attempt is made here to assess the importance or forecast the
future of this remarkable development—the most influential form
of Voluntary Action in Britain. The headquarters of the trade
union movement are naturally much preoccupied with the activities
of the State. The General Council of the Trades Union Congress,
when invited to co-operate in the present Inquiry, expressed themselves as unable to do so, on the ground that the Inquiry was one
that should be undertaken by the Government.

Yet the trade union movement, like every other form of getting
together in Britain, is based in the last resort on local associations
retaining independence and the capacity for revolt. And the movement has much in common, both in past history and present
activities, with the friendly society movement.

The trade unions, like the friendly societies, began the nineteenth
century under the ban of repressive legislation. In their case the

general prohibitions of societies that corresponded or had branches, and of meetings that might be seditious, were re-inforced by the Combination Laws of 1799 and 1800 directed against combinations to regulate wages and conditions of employment.

The Combination Acts were repealed in 1825, but the trade unions, unlike the friendly societies, have never been formally exempted by fresh legislation from the Unlawful Societies Act of 1799 and the Seditious Meetings Act of 1817. As late as 1912 a trade union pleaded that under these Acts it was an unlawful society, so that the courts should not concern themselves with its rules. But this Alice in Wonderland argument was rejected by the common sense of the judge. He held that, since Parliament had passed several Acts concerned with the registration and activities of trade unions, well knowing that they had branches, Parliament must be held by implication to have exempted them from the Acts of George III.[1] It is interesting to speculate as to what might have happened if the Trade Union Act of 1871 had exempted trade unions from the Unlawful Societies Act expressly, on the same strict condition as the friendly societies—that they never talked politics at their meetings.

The trade unions, like most of the large friendly societies, have been bodies with branches. The average size of a branch was much the same in the two movements. Thus at the end of 1907 the total trade union membership of 2,406,746 was divided between 1,173 unions having 18,262 branches or lodges, that is to say, an average of 131 members to each branch; this is roughly the same as the average membership of a friendly society branch at about that time. The measure of independence maintained by branches varies greatly from one union to another. It is in general less, in respect alike of trade policy and of friendly benefits, than among the affiliated orders.

The trade unions, like the friendly societies, could register themselves with the Chief Registrar, but were under no compulsion to do so, and very many of the smaller unions remain unregistered, as appears from the following figures for certain years.

[1] *Luby v. Warwickshire Miners' Association*, 1912, 2 ch. 371. The plaintiff, Mr. Luby, asked for an injunction prohibiting the union (with whose leading officials he had quarrelled) from treating him as expelled. The defending union, having failed to show that Mr. Luby had been expelled properly under their rules, put up the defence that they were an unlawful association under the Acts of George III, and that therefore the law should not concern itself with their rules. Mr. Justice Neville decided against them and gave Mr. Luby his injunction for what it was worth.

TABLE 8

TRADE UNIONS[1] IN 1907, 1912, 1932, AND 1945

	1907		1912		1932		1945	
	No.	Members (000)	No.	Members (000)	No.	Members (000)	No.	Members (000)
Registered ..	523	1,873	539	2,547	466	3,405	427	6,536
Unregistered	650	534	575	869	594	1,036	338	1,267
All Unions ..	1,173	2,407	1,114	3,416	1,060	4,441	765	7,803

It will be seen that, up to the Second World War, less than half the unions had registered, but those that did accounted for about three-quarters of the total membership. The reduction in the number of separate unions which proceeded slowly to 1944 (when the total was 952 of which 421 were registered) was accentuated in 1945, largely as a consequence of amalgamation of most coal-mining unions into the National Union of Mineworkers and of unification of a number of associations in the Civil Service. In 1945, for the first time, more than half the trade unions were registered and they accounted for 84 per cent of the total membership.

The trade unions, in addition to their primary purpose of regulating conditions of employment have always had, and still have, a large friendly benefit side, that is to say they have made systematic payments to their members in sickness, old age, unemployment and on death. After the repeal of the Combination Laws in 1825, the new model of trade unionism, the Amalgamated Society of Engineers, was organized by William Newton and William Allen largely out of two societies named respectively the "Journeymen Steam-Engine and Machine Makers and Millwrights Friendly Society" and the "Smiths' Benevolent Friendly Sick and Burial Society."[2]

Some of the provisions of the Friendly Societies Acts apply to trade unions in relation to their friendly side, others do not. Thus a registered trade union is entitled to exemption from income tax in respect of interest and dividends applicable and applied wholly for the purposes of its friendly benefits, subject to the same condition as is imposed on the friendly societies, of paying not more than £300 as a lump sum and not more than £52 a year by way of annuity. On the other hand, trade unions are not required as a condition of registration to submit to valuation, even of their friendly side. Most of them are in a position to deal with financial difficulties by means of a levy on their members.

[1] Excluding associations of employers.   [2] See Webb, op. cit., pp. 206–11.

The extent of friendly benefit provision in relation to other activities varies greatly from one union to another, and from one trade to another. Over the movement as a whole, the expenditure on such benefits is large. The 448 trade unions registered in 1935 with 3,794,680 members paid in that year over £3 million on friendly benefits, as compared with about £11 million paid by the registered friendly societies with a membership of something less than eight million. That is to say, expenditure per head on friendly benefits was nearly 16s. per head in the trade unions as compared with 28s. per head in the friendly societies.[1]

Table 9 shows how the expenditure of the registered trade unions has changed in the past thirty-three years, with friendly and dispute expenditure falling from 70 per cent of the whole in 1912 to less than 40 per cent in 1945. The "other expenditure," which has risen from 30 per cent of the whole in 1912 to more than 60 per cent in 1945 represents in the main working expenses. It amounted in 1945 to more than £6 million, of which over £5 million were working expenses; the political fund accounted for £346,000 and other outgoings, including grants to federations and other bodies, accounted for £632,000. The increase of working expenses in relation both to the membership and to the other expenditure is notable. It should

[1] Before the second World War only 1 per cent of the total membership of registered trade unions was in unions providing no friendly benefit of any kind. Since the war, the proportion has risen slightly but is still under 2 per cent. In 1945, of the total membership of 6,535,938 in 427 registered trade unions, 94,461 members were in 58 unions, mostly very small, providing no friendly benefits.

Expenditure per head by trade unions on such benefits and its distribution between different benefits have changed considerably. As appears from Table 9 overleaf, the total expenditure on friendly benefits in 1945 was £3,360,260 or little more than in 1935, though the membership had risen greatly, so that expenditure per head on such benefits was about 10s. in 1945 as compared with 16s. in 1935. Unemployment accounted for 23 per cent of the whole in 1935 and only 3 per cent in 1945. In addition to the expenditure from their own funds, as shown in Table 9, the trade unions acted as agents for paying State unemployment benefit to their members. In 1935 they paid (and recovered from the State) £1,861,641 in this way; in 1945 £263,068.

The membership of trade unions represents separate individuals. In the figures of friendly societies there is some duplication, particularly between the sick benefit societies and specialized societies such as those providing institutional treatment. The total of 8,202,000 obtained by adding up the figures for all the separate classes of friendly society in the Registrar's returns in 1935 probably represents about 7,900,000 individuals. This estimate is based on a sample investigation made by research services for the present Inquiry, whose results are given in the Supplementary Volume; the sample shows 1,195 memberships of friendly societies as representing 1,143 individuals.

be emphasized, however, that these are not the expenses of administering the friendly and dispute benefits. On these the proportionate cost of management is as low in the trade unions as in the friendly societies and may be lower. The "other expenditure" of Table 9 covers all the industrial work of the trade unions (wage and condition bargaining) as well as their political and friendly activities.

TABLE 9

EXPENDITURE OF REGISTERED TRADE UNIONS, 1912, 1935, 1939 AND 1945

	1912	1935	1939	1945
	£	£	£	£
Unemployment, Travelling, and Emigration	630,452	702,750	746,078	107,710
Sick and Accident	512,038	570,805	674,538	1,002,713
Funeral	137,156	340,541	389,221	429,711
Superannuation .. .. ⎱	523,103	1,071,188	1,200,144	1,404,365
Miscellaneous Benefits* .. ⎰		324,863	395,422	415,761
All Friendly Benefits	1,802,749	3,010,147	3,405,403	3,360,260
Disputes	1,655,163	231,936	162,812	43,481
Other Expenditure	1,077,898	3,112,331	3,977,142	6,071,141
Total Expenditure	4,535,810	6,354,414	7,545,357	9,474,882
	s. d.	s. d.	s. d.	s. d.
Per member per year				
Friendly and Dispute	20 3	17 8	14 5	10 3
Other Expenditure	11 0	17 1	16 1	17 3
	31 3	34 9	30 6	27 6

* Includes compensation for loss of tools, benevolent grants, lump sums on retirement, division of funds among members, legal expenses on behalf of member.

The trade unions, like the friendly societies and the industrial life offices, took in 1911 an active part in forming Approved Societies, which had for the most part an occupational basis, including a disproportionate number of workers from dangerous occupations like mining. These societies naturally were able to do relatively little in the way of giving additional statutory benefits, and their membership tended to decline during the period between the wars.

In one particular field—provision for unemployment—the trade unions have been pioneers. As is explained by the Webbs, to give out-of-work pay was for the unions a natural part of their policy of maintaining the rate of wages; it diminished the pressure on the men out of work to cut the union rate. There is another technical reason which in practice confined out-of-work pay to the trade unions. Before the State Labour Exchanges were established, the trade unions alone were in a position to know what jobs were available in their trade, and so to test the validity of a claim to out-of-work pay. When the State entered the field of social insurance in 1911, it had to base itself in respect of unemployment insurance on the pioneer work of the trade unions, as definitely as it based itself on the friendly societies in respect of health insurance. The value of the trade union experiment in this field was, indeed, in one respect even greater than that of the friendly societies in their field. State insurance for sickness and old age was not a new thing in the world in 1911; it had been practised successfully in Germany for nearly thirty years. But the scheme of unemployment insurance which formed Part II of the National Insurance Act of 1911 was the first of its kind; neither Germany nor any other country had attempted successfully State insurance against unemployment.

The only statistical information available in those days as to the volume and incidence of unemployment was derived from the trade unions giving out-of-work pay. Many of the details of the State's scheme, such as the requirement of signing a book in working hours as evidence of unemployment and the "waiting time" of some days at the beginning of each period of unemployment before benefit became payable, were taken from the practice of trade unions.

The trade unions giving out-of-work pay dealt with a much smaller part of the population than the friendly societies and were practically confined to skilled men. There could be no question of administering State unemployment insurance wholly through them, as health insurance was administered through Approved Societies. The State had to set up its own machinery of Labour Exchanges, but it provided also subsidies to trade union out-of-work schemes and used trade unions as agents for administering State and voluntary benefit to their members. The great changes in the nature and extent of unemployment since the First World War have made necessary a different approach to the problem, and the State scheme of insurance has been re-cast several times, but the original contribution of the trade unions in this field should be recorded, as an illustration of pioneering by voluntary action.

In addition to unemployment, the trade unions have taken special interest in provision for industrial accidents. This interest is historically the origin of the present system of social security in Britain.

A Royal Commission on Workmen's Compensation had been appointed just before the Second World War, but after receiving some evidence found itself early in 1941 unable to proceed, as the principal employers' associations declared that they were too busy with the war to prepare and give evidence. The Trade Union Congress General Council, who had already given evidence, protested. In consolation to them for the holding-up of the Royal Commission, the Government of the day set up in May, 1941, an Inter-Departmental Committee to survey the existing national scheme on Social Insurance and Allied Services including workmen's compensation. This in due course led to my Report of November, 1942, to the Coalition Government White Papers of 1944, and to the National Insurance Acts and National Health Service Act of 1946. There is seldom one road only to a place, if one really wants to go there.

BUILDING SOCIETIES

"Building Societies do not build; they simply make advances upon building." This aphorism of the Royal Commission of 1871–74 was true then as it is true to-day. But it was not true of the associations of British citizens which first called themselves building societies. The honour of being leader in this field belongs among cities to Birmingham; the date of the first society is 1781. This was a society to raise money and spend money on itself building houses for its members on a particular estate in the hamlet of Doritend. What Birmingham began London and lesser cities soon followed, still on the lines of building societies which built, sometimes with a very firm policy as to the nature of the houses. Thus, the rules of the Carlisle Society of 1824, cited by the historian of the movement, prescribed "that all the houses shall be built of one size, and as nearly as may be of one value, and as nearly alike as possible."[1] Not less than four of these identical homes were to be drawn for at any one meeting of the society. What steps were taken to secure that all the members had families "as nearly alike as possible" is not stated.

In 1836 Parliament awoke to the beginning of a new movement. "Whereas certain societies commonly called building societies have been established in different parts of the United Kingdom, principally among the industrious classes, for the purpose of raising by small

[1] *The Thrifty Three Millions*, p. 14, by Sir Harold Bellman, Managing Director of the Abbey Road Building Society (London, 1935).

periodical subscriptions a fund to assist members thereof in obtaining a small freehold or leasehold property," it appeared to Parliament expedient "to afford encouragement and protection to such societies and the property obtained therewith" and for this purpose to apply to them under the name of "Benefit Building Societies" some of the provisions of the Friendly Societies Act then in force, including the certification of their rules by a barrister. The preamble to this Act, as given above, is significant. Already the building societies are treated, not as agencies for building, but as what they have now become wholly, agencies for borrowing and lending money.

The Royal Commission of 1871–74 dealt with building societies as well as with friendly societies. They found some 2,000 societies in existence, with assets of £18 million. They found some complaints and a few mischiefs, but had no doubt as to the generally beneficial character of these associations. They made proposals for incorporating building societies, in their two types—permanent and terminating—under the wing of the Registrar. Their proposals received effect in an Act of 1874 which is still the basis of the law in this field. The purposes of a building society are defined in that Act as "raising by the subscriptions of the members a stock or fund for making advances to the members out of the funds of the society upon security of freehold or leasehold estate by way of mortgage." Building societies are thus essentially financial. They gather the savings of the public in two ways—from "share investors" who become actual members of the society, and from depositors who simply lend money to get interest on it. They use these savings to make loans on mortgage to their members for the acquisition of houses. Any surplus money in their hands must be invested in trustee securities. They are of two types—terminating or permanent. The terminating societies are based on the original purpose—of enabling each of the members to get a house, perhaps by developing a named piece of land; when the last member gets his house, the society is wound up. The permanent societies go on indefinitely, receiving share subscriptions and deposits, making loans and investing funds. They represent practically the whole of the movement to-day.

The building societies have not, like the friendly societies, been exempt from income tax and stamp duty. But by an arrangement made with the Inland Revenue authorities they have been able to offer to share investors and depositors alike the attraction of a dividend free of tax. Under this arrangement the society, before making any distribution to share investors and depositors, pays income tax at a composite rate, designed to yield the same total amount of tax as would be obtained by the normal procedure, of deduction at the source of the standard rate in all cases followed by claims to repayment by individuals not liable to pay at that rate. The assumption underlying the arrangement is that the great bulk of the members would be able to claim repayments. The arrangement is designed to avoid the trouble of a multitude of small claims for repayment; the composite rate is based on samples of their membership supplied by the societies, and is the same for all societies. The arrangement does not mean that the members of building societies, getting tax-free interest, do not pay tax on their receipts from the societies. It means that they all pay at the same composite rate; the wealthier ones pay less and the poorer ones pay more than without the arrangement; if the differences between individual members are not too wide, this loss may appear worth while to the poorer man in order to avoid the worry of taxation.

There have, of course, been occasional disputes between particular societies and their members. One of these in 1939 led to the passing of an Act designed to protect members against certain risks and to regulate arrangements between the societies and actual builders.[1] But generally speaking the movement has been little disturbed, and singularly free from parliamentary attention. There was no legislation at all during the period of most notable expansion, between 1894 and 1939.

The building society, with its tax-free interest, has offered a highly attractive opportunity for small savings. The 2,957,000 share investors and depositors of 1938 held between them £703,930,000 worth of shares and deposits, that is to say, an average of £238 each. The average advance on mortgage was also an affair of hundreds of pounds only; of the 232,294 advances made in 1938 94·3 per cent were for less than £1,000 each with an average of £465 each. In 1938 the average rate of interest paid to share investors was 3·37 per cent and to depositors 2·74 per cent, "free of tax" in each case; in 1946 these rates had fallen to 2·15 per cent and 1·70 per cent respectively. The rate charged on loans averaged 4·83 per cent in 1938 and 4·35 per cent in 1946.

The movement has shown in the past fifty years a tendency to concentrate into larger societies. From nearly 3,000 societies in 1890 the total number has come down to 874 at the end of 1946. Of these 692 were societies with assets below £1,000,000; 76 had assets between £1,000,000 and £5,000,000; 28 had assets exceeding £5,000,000. The two largest were the Halifax Society with

[1] Building Societies Act, 1939, 2 and 3 Geo. VI, c. 55.

£136,897,007 total assets and 476,057 shareholders and depositors; and the Abbey National Society with £83,980,668 of assets and 384,204 shareholders and depositors. This last is a recent amalgamation of two societies—Abbey Road, established in 1874 and National, dating from 1849. The history of the major partner in this union, the Abbey Road Society, has been told by its Managing Director, Sir Harold Bellman. Like all the rest it began locally; twelve men, for the most part workmen employed by a builder in Kilburn,

TABLE 10

BUILDING SOCIETIES, 1870–1946

(MEMBERSHIP IN THOUSANDS; AMOUNTS IN £1,000)

	c. 1870	1890	1913	1919	1929	1938	1946
Number of Societies ..	2,088	2,795	1,550	1,311	1,026	971	874
Share Investors ..	—	—	—	—	1,265	2,153	2,055
Depositors	—	—	—	—	394	804	731
Total	820	646	617	671	1,659	2,957	2,786
Advances on Mortgage during Year ..	—	—	9,131	15,841	74,719	137,019	187,392
Balance due on Mortgage	—	47,760	60,733	57,866	268,141	686,776	639,748
Investments ..	—	3,734	4,582	19,481	44,604	53,243	202,332
Other Assets ..	—					18,878	34,172
Total Assets ..	18,286	51,494	65,315	77,347	312,745	758,897	876,252

Note.—The figures for 1870 and 1890 are taken from a table at p. 31 of the *Building Societies' Yearbook* for 1945.

attendants at Abbey Road Church and members of a benefit society connected therewith, met one evening of March, 1874, in the church school-room and decided to form a society for saving with a view to house purchase; they fixed the subscription at 1s. a week per share.

The history of building societies as a whole is one of steady growth to the outbreak of the First World War followed by phenomenal expansion between the wars. A summary of this is provided in Table 10.

In the twenty-five years from 1913 to 1938 the number of individuals putting their money into building societies more than quadrupled, rising from 617,000 to 2,957,000; the sums advanced

on mortgage in the year multiplied fifteen times, rising from
£9,131,000 to £137,019,000; the total assets of the societies multiplied nearly twelve times, rising from £65,315,000 to £758,897,000.
The same period witnessed continuance of the process of the smaller
societies being driven out or taken over by the larger ones. The
total number of building societies, estimated at 2,795 in 1890, fell
to 1,550 in 1913 and to 971 in 1938.

The larger building societies between the wars conducted an
extensive advertising campaign, and no doubt this contributed to
the remarkable growth achieved. But the campaign succeeded only
because the economic conditions were favourable. These conditions
included acute housing shortage, an increase of property values,
and the desire of house owners to realize their profits by effecting
sales rather than let houses at controlled rents. Those who needed
houses to live in found it increasingly difficult to get houses otherwise
than by buying; lacking capital they found the way through a
building society. It is claimed by the societies that of the 4,000,000
odd new houses built between the wars, 3,000,000 were provided
by private builders, and that of these more than 2,000,000 were
bought for occupation by their owners with the help of building
societies.

It looks as if the exceptional growth of building societies between
the wars was in part a consequence of State policy in controlling
rents; owners of house property sold, in hope of finding a better
use for the proceeds elsewhere, in preference to continuing as rent
restricted landlords. It is possible that another action of the State
—the heavy increase of income tax—was also a contributing factor.
The composite rate arrangement made the building societies appear
attractive as a means of investment to men of higher income levels
who might have disregarded them hitherto; that this attraction
operated is suggested by the fact that the annual subscriptions rose
much more rapidly than the membership. No doubt the entry of
many such wealthier members would in due course lead to a revision
upwards of the composite rate; but even after revision the wealthier
newcomers would still be gaining something, at the cost of the older
and poorer *clientèle*. This is not said to suggest that control of rents
and high income tax were avoidable after the war. But it shows
how in a free society men find ways to escape inconvenient actions
of the State.

The objection is sometimes made to building societies that they
encourage people to buy houses beyond their means. The answer
given by the societies is that the proportion of cases in which the

borrower fails to keep up his payments is trifling. In 1938 the value of all the mortgaged properties where the societies had entered into possession was 0·16 per cent of the whole; the mortgages with payments twelve months in arrear were 0·10 per cent of the whole.

Another objection sometimes made against building societies is that in encouraging house ownership they militate against the desirable mobility of labour. But it seems doubtful whether blame for immobility of labour can rightly be placed on house ownership, as distinct from other causes. If one owns a house it is possible to sell it and go elsewhere, provided that one has another house to go to. If there is no other house available, one is no more mobile as a tenant than as an owner. In an ideal society there would be enough houses to let for those who wished to rent them, and enough houses to buy for those who wisely or unwisely wished to live in houses of their own; then the building society might enter appropriately to help on mutual lines those who had not capital of their own available.

The most vulnerable point about building societies is their name. They are doing valuable work, in their dual function of encouraging thrift and assisting home ownership, doing it cheaply and without more than inevitable minor failures. But they are not doing what their name suggests and what to-day is even more important, bringing many more new houses into being. This is the purpose of another and newer type of society also within the Registrar's ken— the housing societies.

HOUSING SOCIETIES

While building societies ceased to build and devoted themselves to the valuable but different task of enabling working and middle-class people to save and to borrow, other societies were arising to devote themselves to getting the people houses. This was the primary object of the "Society for Improving the Conditions of the Labouring Classes" which held its first public meeting in 1844 and was one of the innumerable activities over which Lord Shaftesbury (Lord Ashley as he then was) presided. This society did much to bring to public notice the appalling state of housing in London and other large cities. Apart from what it did itself to remedy the evils which it unveiled, it gave a stimulus to the formation of a number of housing trusts: Peabody (1862), Guinness (1889), Sutton (1900), and Samuel Lewis (1906). These trusts, and others like them, became officially recognized in the Housing and Town Planning

Act of 1909 as public utility societies. Now such societies are defined and governed by the Housing Act of 1936.

The State policy between the two world wars was to encourage the formation of voluntary associations for dealing with the housing shortage, in co-operation with public authorities. Under the Housing Act of 1936 a society which fulfils certain conditions may be recognized as a housing association and receives certain privileges to enable it to do its work. The main conditions are twofold:

(1) That the society shall not trade for commercial profit, any payment of dividend or interest on capital being limited to the rate prescribed for the time being by the Treasury. (This rate till recently 5 per cent, has been reduced in 1947 to 2¾ per cent.)

(2) That the objects of the society shall be to carry on the industry or trade of providing housing and any associated amenities for persons mainly of the working classes.

An organization (society, company, body of trustees) which satisfies these two conditions may be registered either under the Companies Acts or under the Industrial and Provident Societies Acts. The great bulk of them are registered under the latter Acts and thus come within the purview of the Chief Registrar of Friendly Societies. At the end of 1945 the Registrar had on his list 357 housing societies[1] with 33,442 members, and land and buildings valued at £11,728,360.

These societies have different origins and are of varying types. Some are formed by industrial firms, particularly those whose factories have been moved to isolated districts, but also by firms which take a direct interest in the housing of their employees. Some societies are fostered by local authorities, in order to supplement the work of those authorities. Some are started by groups of persons ineligible for municipal houses but wishing to provide houses for themselves. Some are formed by persons interested in the housing of particular classes, such, for example, as the aged. Some are formed particularly to carry out schemes of slum clearing and reconditioning. Some are formed on co-partnership lines requiring every member to take up

[1] The term used in the Housing Act of 1935 is "Housing Association." The term under which the bulk of these associations are registered under the Industrial and Provident Societies Acts is "Housing Society." That is also the term by which the organizations describe themselves in the "National Federation of Housing Societies." It is used here accordingly to cover all housing associations.

a certain prescribed sum in shares, but there are few of this type now in existence.

In addition to the individual societies, Section 96 of the Housing Act of 1936 provides for recognizing for consultative purposes a central association of the voluntary housing societies, and a National Federation of Housing Societies has been established and recognized as this central association. But it is not necessary for all housing societies to belong to this, and at the end of 1946 only 303 out of the 434 did so.

The chief privileges enjoyed by housing societies are three: first they can through the local authorities borrow on mortgage from the Public Works Loan Board at the same rate as local authorities, namely, 2½ per cent, but the local authority is empowered to add to this ¼ per cent to cover its own services; some authorities make this addition and some do not. The local authority, as a rule, requires that a certain proportion of the houses shall be earmarked for tenants nominated by it. Mainly for this reason housing societies sometimes prefer to borrow otherwise than through the local authority, using as their main sources either building societies or one or more of the collecting societies which have large funds available, and which are ready to lend money at lower interest to housing societies than to individual borrowers. Second, they can get an Exchequer subsidy like a local authority for houses coming within the condition of the subsidy. Third, they can get priority in respect of the supply of materials like a local authority, but this is limited to the making of new houses and not to reconditioning old ones.

Housing societies under present conditions do not find great scope for their activities. Where the houses are intended to claim the Exchequer subsidy, any house erected by a society is taken from the number allocated to the local authority in that area. The restrictions on the local authorities make them not willing as a rule to allocate houses to other bodies. If, on the other hand, the house is not subsidized, it is a private enterprise house subject to the usual ration of four public buildings to one of private enterprise building.

Apart from this general difficulty, housing societies are faced by four particular problems.

First, they cannot as a rule through a local authority borrow more than 90 per cent of the total capital required, and for that purpose must mortgage the whole of their property, so that the balance of 10 per cent must be raised without security. This in some cases may prove impossible. In the last few months the position of housing societies as borrowers has been made even harder than

before, by a ruling of the Ministry of Health that, if they want the
public subsidy on their operations they must not borrow from any
source at more than 2¾ per cent. Having covered 90 per cent of
their need by borrowing through the local authority on mortgage
security at 2¼ per cent, they must find someone to lend them the
outstanding 10 per cent at the same rate of 2¾ per cent without
any security at all. The defence of this ruling is that if subsidy is
granted steps must be taken to ensure that the benefit of the subsidy
goes to the tenant in his rent. The ruling appears to be designed
to put housing societies out of business. It would go far to block
the suggestion made below that friendly societies should invest in
housing societies with a view to securing suitable housing for their
older members.

Second, housing societies, unlike local authorities, are subject to
the Rent Restriction Acts. A claim by the societies as non-profit-
making bodies to be freed from these Acts was considered by the
Inter-departmental Committee on Rent Control, under the chairmanship of Lord Ridley, which reported in April, 1945.[1] The Committee agreed that there was a good deal to be said for the suggestion,
as many housing societies undertake housing operations for local
authorities, but they proceeded to reject the claim.

> We think . . . that it would not be practicable as a matter
> of administration to exclude only subsidized houses from con-
> trol, and we cannot recommend that all houses belonging to all
> housing associations, of which there is a great variety, should
> be excepted. We therefore recommend that there should be
> no change in the existing law on this point.

This reasoning is not altogether easy to follow, but it may be noted
that three members of the committee thought that even the local
authorities should be subject to rent restriction. What is clear is that
rent restriction now makes it financially impossible for housing
societies, as it makes it impossible for many other landlords, to
undertake the necessary repairs, the cost of which has risen greatly
and cannot be covered by raising the rents. The National Federation
of Housing Societies in October, 1947, submitted a powerfully
reasoned memorandum to the Minister of Health asking that the
exemption from the Rent Restriction Acts given to local authorities
should be extended to housing societies as non-profit-making bodies.
They urged that the increasing cost of repairs was having a disastrous effect on the ability of societies to keep their property in sound

[1] *Report of the Inter-departmental Committee on Rent Control* (Cmd. 6621), 1945.

condition for the tenants. They gave figures of local authorities making increase of rents which were forbidden to societies.

Third, housing societies can get priority and subsidy only for new houses and not for reconditioning old ones. This raises the general issue of reconditioning as against building new houses in the present difficult conditions of the country.

Fourth, the National Federation as the central consultative body which should also take the lead in stimulating fresh housing societies, if such societies are required, has never had adequate financial means.

Housing societies and their difficulties to-day raise the issue of Voluntary Action for public purposes directly and simply. The reason for having housing societies is that through them the energy and the specialist interest of public-spirited individuals can be mobilized to help in meeting urgent needs. The general argument for such societies was put in the course of our Inquiry by a representative of the National Federation in the following terms:

> "Local authorities erect and manage houses because it is their obligation; housing societies would not exist if they had not been started by small bodies of people who felt it their social duty to build or recondition houses or improve conditions."

The general argument could be illustrated by many practical examples. One recent example only need be quoted here, occurring during the Inquiry and reported in the *Observer* of September 14, 1947, under the caption of "Easing the Plight of the Elderly."

> The harder it becomes to provide comfort for the able-bodied (and a cessation of all but the most essential building is foretold), the worse will be the plight of old people. When the former Medical Officer of Health for East Sussex inspected small homes and nursing-homes for elderly people of very small means he was frequently appalled by the conditions he found. Some homes were good and the staffs did devoted work for which the monetary reward was negligible. Other homes had to be closed because of the totally inadequate standards of care and cleanliness maintained. What was then to become of the elderly women who had been paying two to, say, three and a half guineas for their keep? Alternative homes were not available; there remained the Institution.
>
> When Dr. Ashleigh Glegg, the doctor in question, retired, he made it his business to see that some homes were set up and had the support of a group of enthusiasts. Instead of saying,

"Why don't 'they' do something?" they set themselves to do it. By writing thousands of letters they raised enough money to buy and equip a first house in Withdean, at the back of Brighton, which was opened last Wednesday as a communal home for seventeen. Part of the money came as gifts, but the main part was found by subscriptions of irredeemable stock which carries a return of 3 per cent. Each woman in the house has a charming bedroom, small or large according to means, the use of lounges and a communal dining-room, a big garden, and five separate sun-houses for added privacy.

The society described in this report—the East Sussex County Association—works in full co-operation with the local authority concerned. Indeed, it cannot work otherwise. In the conditions of to-day housing societies depend on the attitude of the central Government and of local authorities. Is it or is it not worth while in meeting a desperate housing need to get the kind of help typified by the "thousands of letters," the gifts and the loans, and the personal drive in this one of many examples?

If it is worth while, then the activity of housing societies must be made more possible than it is to-day. At the moment they receive kind words and little else.[1]

SOCIAL CLUBS

Parliament has recognized that Britons may wish to meet for purposes no more serious than social intercourse, and once again has called the Registrar to their assistance. Under Section 8 (4) of the Friendly Societies Act 1896 the Registrar may register "societies (in this Act called Working Men's Clubs) for purposes of social intercourse, mutual helpfulness, mental and moral improvement, and rational recreation." He may register clubs also under a different statute, the Industrial and Provident Societies Act of 1893; societies under this Act are registered as businesses, with the word "limited" as the compulsory last word in their title. Both types alike, if they wish to sell liquor, must be registered also with the justices. There

---

[1] In a House of Lords Debate on Housing on December 3, 1947, the Government spokesman, the Earl of Listowel, beginning by expressing his personal admiration for housing societies, proceeded to reject all proposals for easing their work. *Probitas laudatur et alget.* So the satirist Juvenal expressed the attitude of the Roman world of the first century A.D. to honesty : it is praised and left to freeze. So housing societies to-day, from the Government of the day, get warm words and cold comfort.

is indeed no compulsion on any club to come to the Registrar at all. There are thus for clubs three possible relations to authority: registration under the Friendly Societies Acts, registration under the Industrial and Provident Societies Acts, and registration with the justices alone for sale of liquor. A club may also, like any other business, be a limited company under the Companies Acts, but this form of registration is rare: for the ordinary working man's club it has few advantages and excessive costs.

At the end of 1945 there were 2,270 working men's clubs with about 1,000,000[1] members registered under the Friendly Societies Acts. There were slightly more clubs, 2,370, with slightly fewer members, 860,420, registered under the Industrial and Provident Societies Acts. The substantial difference between the two classes is that clubs under the Friendly Societies Acts cannot spend money on political purposes or include political objects in their rules. As the instruction of the Working Men's Club and Institute Union on Club Formation puts it, "if the club is to be of a political or trade union character, the Industrial and Provident Societies Act is preferable, this Act giving greater power and freedom of expenditure of club funds."

The Working Men's Club and Institute Union is a national organization of clubs of both kinds, political and non-political, having affiliated to it nearly 3,000 clubs with a membership of 1,500,000. It was the creation in 1862 of the Rev. Henry Solly, a Unitarian Minister, who seven years later went on to start the Charity Organization Society. But he returned soon to his first love of the Club and Institute Union. There is also an Association of Conservative Clubs, estimated to include some 1,500 clubs with a membership of 400,000 to 500,000.

Through the Club and Institute Union a member of any affiliated club can obtain temporary membership of any other club for his convenience when travelling. The union also provides legal assistance; organizes competitions; maintains several convalescent homes, and does something to stimulate educational activities, contributing to the Workers' Educational Association and to Ruskin College, and retaining a full-time educational secretary. During 1946 almost two hundred clubs ran classes, mainly in association with the Workers' Educational Association.

But most of the clubs are purely social places—even when they have a political colour. They are the alternative to the public-house

[1] The latest year for which membership figures are available is 1943, when 2,228 clubs had 947,394 members.

for refreshment, for meeting one's friends, for playing indoor games, for the meetings of friendly societies, trade unions and the like. Naturally, the business motive applicable to the public-house enters also into the formation of clubs, as places for the selling of drink. Often a large mortgage on the premises figures among the liabilities of a club, representing a loan from a firm of brewers.

There is, as is shown below, urgent need for the development of social clubs for one large and growing class of the population, the older men. Whether the initiative in such a development could come from the Club and Institute Union or must be sought elsewhere is an open question.

SPECIALLY AUTHORIZED SOCIETIES

The drafters of Friendly Society Acts have almost from the beginning been wise enough to realize that no one could foretell in advance all the purposes for which Britons might want to get together, and might with advantage have recourse to the Registrar. The particular Act which came under the review of the Royal Commission in 1871–74, had a section 9 allowing societies to be established by authority of the Secretary of State for any purposes approved by him. This section has its successor in sub-section (5) of section 8 of the Friendly Societies Act of 1896, allowing the registration of societies for any purpose authorized by the Treasury, and extending to them some or all of the provisions of the Act; such societies are described as "specially authorized."

Under this sub-section at various dates from 1876 to 1944, a number of authorities have been given by the Treasury, of which eighteen remain in force; several of those provide different ways in which people of small means may club together to save money or invest it or borrow it. At the end of 1945 there were 174 separate specially authorized societies for purposes of loan, thrift and investment with a total membership of about 100,000 and funds of nearly £3 million. The loan societies, which bulked most largely, were limited to making loans for purposes of agriculture, arboriculture and horticulture and were declining in numbers and membership.

More significant than these small financial activities are the other purposes for which at various times it has seemed good to British citizens, with the blessing of the Treasury, to form societies. The authorities still in existence, for purposes other than loan, thrift, or investment, with the years in which they were first issued and the numbers of societies still registered under them are set out below.

TABLE 11

SPECIALLY AUTHORIZED PURPOSES AND SOCIETIES

Date of Authority	Purpose	Number of Societies on April 25, 1947
1877	Assisting members out of employment.	32
1877	Protecting and defending members of any lawful trade or calling against frivolous, vexatious, or malicious prosecutions, and, in cases of robbery or other crimes, affording them legal or other assistance for the detection and prosecution of the offenders.	2
1877	Promoting agriculture, arboriculture or horticulture.	32
1878	Guaranteeing, pursuant to the Friendly Societies Act, the performance of their duties by officers of friendly societies or branches, and guaranteeing the moneys or properties of friendly societies or branches against loss by robbery or embezzlement.	9
1878	Promoting science, literature, and the fine arts.	17
1879	Promoting a knowledge of music.	24
1883	Enabling persons of the Jewish religion to provide for the due celebration of the Passover and for the expenses incurred at Passover time.	Nil
1890	Promoting education.	12
1891	Promoting the science and art of cookery.	1
1893	Providing the members with legal and other assistance when claiming compensation under the Employers' Liability Acts.	Nil
1893	Mutually protecting and promoting the interests of friendly societies.	3
1905	Promoting and encouraging the art of swimming, life-saving, and resuscitation.	Nil
1913	Promoting lawful sports and games.	19*
1929	Carrying out, under rules approved by the Miners' Welfare Committee of the Mines Department, the objects of Section 20 (1) of the Mining Industry Act, 1920.	18
1932	Creating funds, by periodical subscriptions of the members, to be lent to members for the purpose of repairing or decorating buildings owned by them.	1
1944	Providing homes/hostels with the object of the avoidance of illness and breakdown of nurses and midwives.	1

* Includes one society registered under the Special Authority of April 6, 1878, and four societies registered under the Special Authority of June 15, 1893.

The interest of these 145 miscellaneous societies, specially authorized and averaging about 1,000 strong, lies in their variety and in the fact that, broadly speaking, they are not concerned with money. Though they come under the paternal eye of the Registrar, they do not get the friendly society privilege of exemption from taxation, and they do not have to submit to valuation. Their aim is to serve in kind rather than in cash. If, as is suggested below, meeting needs in kind by service rather than simply redistributing purchasing power, is to be of growing importance, then the avenue of the specially authorized society calls for exploration. If, for instance, a friendly society wishes to render some service to its members or any class of them which does not fall within the terms of section 8 (1), it can apply for an authority under section 8 (5), or seek to constitute a specially authorized society to render that service. For reasons given in Chapter X this facility has been little used in the past. A suitable change of law might make it important.

CONSUMERS' CO-OPERATION

Consumers' co-operation in Britain is numerically the largest of all the Mutual Aid movements, just ahead both of the friendly societies and of the trade unions; the retail co-operative stores in 1945 had 9¼ million members and funds of £357 million. Behind the retail stores stand the wholesale and productive societies with another £236 million of funds. The movement has been the subject of many books, including one by Sidney and Beatrice Webb,[1] a full-length study by three sociologists published in 1938,[2] and a historical survey by Professor G. D. H. Cole[3] published as recently as 1944. There is no need to repeat or to summarize here what is said in so many accessible volumes. It is sufficient to note five points directly relevant to the study of voluntary action in general.

First, the co-operative movement is like the other great movements studied here in the smallness and unpretentiousness of its beginnings. "All the world knows the story of the twenty-eight flannel weavers of Rochdale who, in 1844, put their pence together to buy and divide among themselves the commodities they required. What

[1] *The Consumers' Co-operative Movement*, by Sidney and Beatrice Webb (Longmans, Green, 1921).

[2] *Consumers' Co-operation in Great Britain*, by A. M. Carr-Saunders, P. Sargant Florence and Robert Peers (George Allen & Unwin, 1938).

[3] *A Century of Co-operation*, by G. D. H. Cole (George Allen & Unwin and Cooperative Union, 1944).

is of interest to us is the unselfconsciousness of their act."[1] What is specially worth noting here is that for consumers' co-operation growth was natural and advantageous. The instinct of the early friendly societies was to remain small and selective; co-operative workshops were equally unwilling to welcome all comers. The open door of the co-operative store was a distinctive feature.

Second, consumers' co-operation, providing cash dividends, had in it strongly what has been described here as the second of the three seeds of friendly society growth—the desire to have a lump of money for spending from time to time. The dividing friendly society and the co-operative store made a common appeal.

Third, consumers' co-operation exhibits strongly the tendency found in all other Mutual Aid movements to become concentrated in larger units. In 1881 there were 971 retail distributive societies with 547,212 members, an average of 564 per society. In 1903 the number of societies reached its maximum 1,455 with 1,987,423 members, or 1,366 per society. In 1945 the 9,401,927 members were in 1,070 societies, an average of 8,787 per society. The number of separate societies is nearly back at the figure of 1881; the average membership of each society has multiplied 15 times from under 600 to nearly 9,000.

Fourth, the movement illustrates the tendency of all voluntary agencies to put their strength into one particular job. As a business, consumers' co-operation has grown and grows phenomenally. Its other activities languish or are languid. In the words of the most recent authoritative study by outside observers, "in the sphere of education, after many decades of valuable achievement the movement has reached a phase where the original impetus has worked itself out." "Lack of vision and lack of drive in the development of social facilities is not unconnected with the parallel failure to attain clarity of aim in the realm of formal education."[2] The investigators of Mass Observation record the judgment that only for 1 per cent of the members is the co-operative store anything but a shop. "It is difficult to avoid the conclusion that the growth of co-operative enterprise has been accompanied by some blurring of the features which distinguish it from competitive private enterprise."[3]

Fifth, shopping is woman's sphere. It is natural that the oldest of the larger women's organizations in existence to-day should be the Women's Co-operative Guild, dating from 1883.

[1] Webb, op. cit., pp. 168–9.
[2] Consumers' Co-operation in Great Britain p. 512.   [3] Op. cit., p. 521.

"The history of the Women's Co-operative Guild illustrates the change in the status of women during the past generation. The Guild started as a sort of Co-operative 'mothers' meeting.' . . . For the first few years the leaders deprecated women 'imitating or competing with men, pushing themselves on to management committees where they should be liable to be laughing-stocks and stumbling-blocks.' But this essentially 'wives' movement' gradually grew into a virile organization, still made up almost exclusively of wives, but pushing forward on its own account women's interests, both within and without the Co-operative Movement, and taking its own distinctive line as to the right organization of the Co-operative Movement and as to industrial and political questions generally."[1]

This feminine development has not always been welcome to the predominantly male management of the movement as a whole. There have been heated controversies as to divorce reform, women's wages and other matters. In addition to all else that it has accomplished, the co-operative movement has helped women to make good their claim to citizenship, through the Co-operative Guild.

TRUSTEE SAVINGS BANKS

There are to-day eighty-seven trustee savings banks with nearly 4½ million depositors holding £600 million of balances. These institutions are part of the Registrar's field, in so far as they are registered with him, but this is now a formality. All public action in regard to the savings banks is taken by another department— the National Debt Commissioners. But the trustee savings banks have connections with the friendly society movement which make it convenient to notice them in this chapter. Their origin and development have been described excellently in a book just published by Mr. H. Oliver Horne, who from 1930 till his death in 1947 was the first full-time secretary to the Trustee Savings Banks Association. It is not necessary here to do more than emphasize a few main points, nearly all taken from this work.[2]

First, savings banks are in origin closely associated with friendly societies. They were advocated at the beginning of the nineteenth century as alternative means of enabling the poor to escape pauperism. The parent of savings banks—the bank established in 1810 at

[1] Webb, *op. cit.*, pp. 168-9.
[2] *A History of Savings Banks*, by H. Oliver Horne (Oxford University Press, 1947).

Ruthwell in Dumfriesshire by the Rev. Henry Duncan[1] was designedly given several of the characteristics of a friendly society. It had an elaborate constitution securing to the depositors a share in the management as if they were a society. It made inquiries into the suitability of would-be depositors and their morals. It imposed restrictions on withdrawals and fines on irregular savers. This was done because the savings bank was regarded not as a business but as an agency for social reform. It was done also in order to take advantage of the Rose Act of 1793 for encouragement of friendly societies. There was not at that time any specific legal place for banks.

In fact the friendly society structure did not suit the different purpose of a savings bank, and though the Ruthwell example was followed in many places, in the long run it was a simpler model of savings bank established at Edinburgh in 1813 which prevailed, without the characteristics of a society. As it is put by Mr. Horne, "the Edinburgh Savings Bank was in fact as like an ordinary bank as its founders could make it." The Rose Act of 1793 could not provide a lasting home for such institutions. Its author proceeded, as his last parliamentary achievement, to secure in 1817 a second Rose Act—for savings banks in England. Dr. Henry Duncan by his personal energy two years later secured a parallel measure for Scotland. Each provided for certification of the rules by a barrister.

Second, the savings bank, though in origin associated with friendly societies, appealed to a different motive, that of personal saving for independence rather than that of Mutual Aid. In doing so it met a real need. At the beginning of the nineteenth century there was no means by which poor men who wished to save their pennies in hope of avoiding pauperism could easily and safely do so. The ordinary banks did not cater for them; to hoard cash at home, as some of them did, was to expose themselves to risk of robbery. And the newly encouraged friendly societies did not meet all needs either; they had for the most part rigid rules of subscription for strictly limited purposes. Dr. Henry Duncan once summed up the difference when he said of friendly societies that "they provide desirable

[1] The first actual savings bank in Britain appears to have been established by the Rev. Joseph Smith at Wendover in 1798, and this was followed by one established at Tottenham in 1801 by Mrs. Priscilla Wakefield, a leading member of the Society of Friends. But neither of these set an example which spread, and Mr. Horne concludes that Ruthwell is the first parent of the savings banks of to-day, though Edinburgh also is an independent parent.

resource in sickness and old age, but they do not accommodate themselves as much as could be wished to the varying situation and abilities of their members." It was left to the Rev. Samuel Best in Abbot's Ann in 1831 to show that a savings bank and provision for sickness could be combined, and so to blaze the way for the spectacular achievement of the National Deposit Friendly Society.

Third, the savings bank movement was essentially philanthropic, even more than democratic. It was started for the people by disinterested philanthropists rather than by the people for themselves. It would fit as well into Chapter IV of this Report as into Chapter III. Many of the early savings banks contemplated charitable contributions from the rich. Not infrequently, particularly during the 1840's and 1850's, the philanthropic trustees of savings banks found themselves let in for making good the defalcations of dishonest managers.

Fourth, as with the friendly societies, so with the savings banks, there arose the question of State control and State competition, in order to prevent abuses and give real security to the depositors. State Control was in the end introduced far more definitely for the savings banks, through the requirement that the whole of the funds should be invested with the Government through the Commissioners for reduction of the National Debt, with the correlative that the State became responsible for the guaranteed rate of interest to depositors, and so was a partner in the business. In most years from 1876 to 1908 Parliament had to make up a deficiency—though usually a small one—in the income of the Trustee Savings Banks Fund. In every year since then the fund has shown an excess of income and the Exchequer has gained.

State competition also came in more effectively with the banks than with the friendly societies. The Post Office Savings Bank was started in 1861 and has proved a great success. But this has not killed the trustee savings banks, which at about the same time, 1863, were put on a new footing. The latest figures show both these organizations for saving developing rapidly. In 1905 the Post Office Savings Bank had nearly 30 million accounts totalling £150 million, while the trustee savings banks had 1,730,000 depositors with about £60 million due to them. In 1945 the Post Office Savings Bank had 21½ million accounts totalling £1,777 million; in forty years the number of accounts had doubled and their total in savings had multiplied ten times. In 1945 the trustee savings banks had 4,430,000 depositors and held for them £603 million; that is to say, in forty years the depositors had much more than doubled in number and the total amount deposited had been multiplied by ten, as with the Post Office. It may be added that the trustee savings banks show the same tendency as the building societies towards concentration in larger units. In 1861 there were as many as 645 separate banks; by 1905 these had been reduced to 224; by 1945 to 87.

HOSPITAL CONTRIBUTORY SCHEMES

Hospital contributory schemes represent one of the most remarkable growths of Mutual Aid in modern times. It is perhaps a sign of their modernity that most of them, in place of joining the large and varied collection of societies under the Registrar of Friendly Societies, are incorporated under the Companies Acts as companies limited by guarantee.[1] They are forms of Mutual Aid outside the Registrar's field.

An interesting account of the development of hospital contributory schemes was given in the *Report on the British Health Services* issued by Political and Economic Planning in 1937. The same report described also a variety of provident schemes by which persons of income classes outside the former scope of National Health Insurance contributed in advance, in order to be sure of medical treatment when they needed it, for themselves and their families. The position both of hospital contributory schemes and of provident schemes is revolutionized by the passage of the National Health Service Act. Till it is known just how that Act will operate, it is unnecessary to add to what has already been published about such schemes, more than a few paragraphs to indicate their nature and their scale.

The hospital contributory schemes are in essence schemes organized by or on behalf of the voluntary hospitals, under which persons in the lower income groups make regular contributions and are entitled, without further inquiry as to their means, to receive free hospital treatment for themselves and their dependants; in some cases the contributions of employees are supplemented by their employers. The schemes were designed to fill the gap in the provision for medical treatment under the National Insurance Act of 1911, which was limited to general practitioner service for the insured persons themselves, excluding their dependants. Most of the schemes were set on foot between 1929 and 1934; only the Hospital Fund for

---

[1] This procedure, confined to companies not seeking profits, allows the word "limited" to be left out of the title.

London had an origin prior to the First World War. They proved highly attractive of popular support.

By 1935 the 114 schemes making returns to the British Hospitals Contributory Schemes Association had an annual income of £2,722,000 derived primarily from the 2d. or 3d. weekly contributions of 5,241,000 subscribers. Eight years later, there were 191 schemes with a subscribing membership of practically 10,000,000 and an income of £6,528,000. The schemes have become a large, indeed an essential element in hospital finance. As it was put in an account of the largest of them after twenty-one years of service, the words "Hospital Saving Association" possess a double significance. To the subscribing individual they meant saving for hospital treatment. To those responsible for managing hospitals they meant associations for saving hospitals from financial disaster. They became that in practice.

Though the hospital contributory schemes proper are, with few exceptions, growths of the last twenty years, there is in the Birmingham Hospital Saturday Fund an outstanding older example of voluntary contributions from wage-earners for hospital maintenance. The first suggestion that the wage-earners of Birmingham should be asked themselves to contribute to the hospitals needed there was made by Sampson Gamgee, an eminent surgeon of the city, in connection with the building of a new hospital wing in 1869. The response was so encouraging that a few years later he followed it up with the suggestion that all should be asked to work overtime for the hospitals on a particular Saturday afternoon, to be called "Hospital Saturday." This particular method was found to be inconvenient, but the idea that the wage-earners should give continuous support to the local hospitals took root, and regular weekly contributions on pay days were established, beginning at 1d. a week and rising by 1945 to 4d. a week. The Hospital Saturday Fund may now be described as the industrial arm of the Birmingham Hospital Contributory Association. It is a standing demonstration that relatively large sums can be obtained from wage-earners in small voluntary subscriptions for a public purpose.

The hospital contributory schemes, briefly as they are dealt with here, provide a fitting conclusion to this part of the Report. They show the vitality of voluntary action on the lines of Mutual Aid, in meeting newly recognized needs even after the beginning of social insurance in 1911. Even after the extension of social insurance in 1946, many urgent needs of many citizens will remain, and, as will be argued in Chapters VIII and IX, can be met only or best by voluntary action. The original financial purpose which called the hospital contributory schemes into being will presumably come to an end within the next few years. It may be that the organizations which launched these schemes or some of them will be able to undertake new tasks of meeting human needs by citizen co-operation. It is certain that the spirit of Mutual Aid among all classes which inspired these schemes must continue in one form or another, if the Britain of the future is to be worthy of the past.

PART TWO

THE PHILANTHROPIC MOTIVE
IN ACTION

IV. THE VOLUNTARY SOCIAL SERVICES AND THEIR DEVELOPMENT

A Classification of Philanthropic Agencies. Their Changing Direction. Social Surveys. Residential Settlements. Urban and Rural Amenities. Women's Organizations. Youth Organizations. From Charity Organization to Family Welfare. Co-ordination and the Spirit of Service.

THE Philanthropic Motive—desire by one's personal action to make life happier for others—has led to the development in Britain of an immense variety of institutions and societies. Agencies inspired by this motive represent a field of human activity as extensive as the field of Mutual Aid surveyed in the first part of this Report, and even more diversified. Nor is there any official watch-tower from which a bird's-eye view of the whole country can be gained, as the field of Mutual Aid can be seen in outline through the Reports of the Chief Registrar of Friendly Societies. There is no registration of philanthropic agencies.

There is thus no possibility of making a numerical estimate of the total scale of philanthropic action. Nor indeed would much be gained by attempting this. Individual philanthropic agencies differ from one another so widely that they cannot be made the subject of useful statistical summary. They are so numerous that they cannot be described in any reasonable limit of space. They are liable to rapid change and development.

In the present chapter any attempt to give a systematic description in uniform scale of philanthropic agencies of every kind is frankly abandoned in favour of a programme more modest but, it may be hoped, as fruitful. The chapter begins with a grouping of voluntary social services under seventeen heads, with some leading agencies under each head named to illustrate its character. A brief account of each of these illustrative agencies, about eighty in number, is given in the Supplementary Volume. A complete list of all the agencies over 400 in number—which in response to an invitation furnished information about themselves, is printed in the same volume.[1]

---

[1] The Nuffield College study of *Voluntary Social Services* to which reference has been made in the preface, covers substantially the same ground as this chapter and contains valuable accounts, by different authors, of particular

A CLASSIFICATION OF PHILANTHROPIC AGENCIES

1. Agencies for the Sick and Injured, including—
   Voluntary Hospitals
   St. John Ambulance Association and Brigade
2. Agencies for Children, including—
   The National Society for Prevention of Cruelty to Children
   Dr. Barnardo's Homes
   Church of England Children's Society
   Catholic Child Welfare Society
   National Children's Home
   Nursery Schools Association
3. Agencies for Youth, including—
   National Association of Boys' Clubs
   National Association of Girls' Clubs and Mixed Clubs
   Young Men's Christian Association
   Young Women's Christian Association
   Girl Guides' Association
   Boy Scouts' Association
   Boys' Brigade
   Girls' Guildry
   Church Lads' Brigade
   Welsh League of Youth
   National Federation of Young Farmers' Clubs
   Young Christian Workers
   Association for Jewish Youth
4. Agencies for Old People, including—
   National Old People's Welfare Committee
   Old People's Homes Committee
5. Agencies for the Blind, including—
   National Institute for the Blind
   National Association of Workshops for the Blind
6. Agencies for Cripples and Other Physically Handicapped
      Persons, including—
   Central Council for the Care of Cripples
   After-Care Association
   British Council for Rehabilitation
   Invalid Children's Aid Association
   National Institute for the Deaf

types of agency, including those concerned with children, the blind, the deaf, youth, case work, and Citizens' Advice Bureaux. It contains also an historical retrospect by Professor G. D. H. Cole and studies of organizations in particular localities.

Mental After-Care Association
National Association for Mental Health
National Association for the Prevention of Tuberculosis
Papworth Settlement for Tuberculosis
7. Agencies for the Homeless, including—
S.O.S. Society
Fellowship of St. Christopher
Society for the Relief of the Houseless Poor
Rowton Houses, Ltd.
Cecil Houses
Homes for Working Boys in London, Inc.
Embankment Fellowship Centre
Morning Post Embankment Home
Wayfarers' Benevolent Association
8. Agencies for Socially Handicapped Persons, including—
National Association of Discharged Prisoners' Aid Societies
National Council for the Unmarried Mother and Her Child
9. Agencies for Family Welfare, including—
Family Welfare Association
Marriage Guidance Council
10. Agencies for Adult Education, including—
Working Men's College
Workers' Educational Association
National Council of Labour Colleges
11. Agencies for Promotion of the Arts, including
The British Drama League
The Rural Music Schools Association
12. Agencies for Physical Recreation and Holidays, including—
Central Council for Physical Recreation
National Playing Fields Association
Camping Club of Great Britain and Ireland
Ramblers' Association
Youth Hostels Association
Holiday Fellowship
Co-operative Holidays Association
Workers' Travel Association
13. Agencies for Urban and Rural Amenities, including—
Council for the Preservation of Rural England
Commons, Open Spaces and Footpaths Preservation Society
Central Council of Civic Societies
14. Women's Organizations, including—
Women's Co-operative Guild

National Council of Women
National Federation of Women's Institutes
National Union of Townswomen's Guilds
Women's Voluntary Services
Women's Group on Public Welfare
15. Service Organizations, including—
British Legion
Soldiers', Sailors' and Airmen's Help Societies
St. Dunstan's
S.S.A.F.A.
16. Residential Settlements, including—
Toynbee Hall
Mary Ward Settlement
17. General Agencies, including—
National Council of Social Service
British Red Cross Society
Shaftesbury Society
Salvation Army
Church Army
Jewish Board of Guardians

The number of heads under which the philanthropic agencies are grouped here is the same as that under which the Royal Commission of 1871–74 found it convenient to group the friendly societies and other associations with which they were concerned, and each list exhibits the same quality of cross division. As there were "Societies of Females" cutting across all the other heads in the Royal Commission's list, so there are "women's organizations" and "service organizations" in the present list. There is no heading in this list corresponding to the "affiliated orders" of the friendly society movement. But one at least of the women's organizations is as federal as any order; each Women's Institute is self-governing with independent finance. And nearly all the larger societies are organized in local branches.

Of some of the types of agency shown in the classification, very little more is said in this volume, for the reason already indicated in the Preface. Provision for the sick and injured and provision for education at all ages are in the sphere of rapidly developing State action; this does not mean that no place will be left for voluntary action, but it does mean that anything written now might be out of date by the time that it could appear under modern conditions of book production. With some other types of agency, notably those concerned with childhood, with old age, with the blind, with those physically handicapped in other ways, with the socially handicapped, as well as with agencies dealing with use of leisure and giving guidance to citizens, it is convenient to deal, not in this chapter, but in Chapters VIII and IX concerned with the needs that will remain for Voluntary Action in spite of all likely developments of public action. One particular type of agency, not included formally in the classification, namely, the endowed charitable trust, is the subject of separate examination in Chapter VI and Appendix B. It is dealt with specially because it forms an exception to the general rule of voluntary agencies. They can and do change perpetually to meet changing circumstances. The problem presented by charitable trusts is that, being tied to the views of a founder, they cannot change easily.

The list of heads under which the philanthropic agencies fall most naturally, suggests two comments. First, the grouping is in the main a grouping by needs. The Philanthropic Motive is in practice a specialist motive; it drives men to combat a particular evil or meet a particular need that arouses their interest. The general agencies noted in the last head of all are exceptional; apart from the first two, they are for the most part religious and denominational. Second, none of the heads is concerned with poverty as such. The passage of one notable agency from Charitable Organization to Family Welfare is an epitome of the change that has come over the direction of philanthropic action.

CHANGING DIRECTION OF PHILANTHROPIC EFFORT

In the first half of the nineteenth century, while industrialization of Britain was still in its early stages, the objects of philanthropy were largely those inherited from the past. There was reform of prisons and of lunatic asylums. There was relief of the aged by almshouses, of the sick and impotent by hospitals, and of the poor by doles in money and kind; there was the care of orphans, and as one of the new ferments, the interest in providing schools.

In the second half of the nineteenth century, with industrialization advancing rapidly, new problems occupied the centre of the stage and new agencies arose to meet them. Urban poverty and squalor became manifest. They led to more doles, public and private, and, as a reaction from this, to the establishment of the Charity Organisation Society in 1869. Three other movements spring from the same source of industrialization, namely, the social surveys, the residential settlements and the societies for defence of urban and rural amenities. Industrialization, with its rising material standard of life and some decrease of working hours, opened the way also for an adult education movement. One of the evils of unplanned urbanization has at last received belated recognition in the demand that large towns, lacking the natural community of village and small town life, should have community centres.

But industrialization was not the only change in the second half of the nineteenth century. There came also a social change in the position and interests of women. There had been isolated women philanthropists. Organizations of women as such for public purposes are modern and would have been impossible before. When Elizabeth Fry in February, 1818, was summoned to give evidence to a Committee of the House of Commons on the Prisons of the Metropolis, "she was the first woman other than a queen to be called into the councils of the Government in an official manner to advise on matters of public concern."[1]

Industrialization helped war to take on a different and worse aspect. War has led to the great development of agencies of two kinds, the Red Cross for mitigating so far as possible the horrors of war, and the service organizations which naturally spring out of war.

Finally, the movement for co-ordination begun by the Charity Organisation Society nearly eighty years ago has been taken up in a new form with wider reference in the National Council of Social Service.

The present chapter is devoted to illustrating this change in the content of philanthropic action, by a few leading examples: Social Surveys, Residential Settlements, Urban and Rural Amenities, Women's Organizations, Youth Organizations, Charity Organization and Family Welfare, and the National Council of Social Service.

SOCIAL SURVEYS

Discussion of poverty and of what should be done about it is as old as poverty. But in the last quarter of the nineteenth century this discussion was put on a new basis in Britain, largely as the work of one man—Charles Booth. This originator of the modern social surveys had two notable precursors at the end of the eighteenth century.

---

[1] This observation is made in an interesting account of *Elizabeth Fry, Quaker Heroine*, by Janet Whitney (George G. Harrap, 1937), available now in a cheap edition as a Guild Book.

One precursor was Sir Thomas Bernard, who having made as a conveyancer as much money as he needed, decided in his early forties, in place of making more money, to devote himself to ameliorating the lives of the labouring class. With others he founded in 1796 "The Society for Bettering the Conditions and Increasing the Comforts of the Poor" and became its mainspring. The society collected and distributed reports on social problems, with plans for their solution; one of these reports, to take a single instance, did a great deal to inspire the movement for savings banks noticed in Chapter III. Bernard described his aim in words with a singularly modern, not to say Fabian, ring: Let us make "inquiry into all that concerns the poor and the promotion of their happiness a science— let us investigate practically and upon system."[1]

The other precursor was Sir Frederick Morton Eden whose classic work on the State of the Poor[2] was finished in the same year, 1796, as saw the starting of Bernard's society. This work was based on research methods curiously prophetic of those used in obtaining some of the material for the present Report.[3] Eden drafted a questionnaire and sent an agent with it to visit as many districts as possible and collect the answers in personal interviews; he supplemented this by written enquiries of people willing to answer by letter and by personal field work of his own.

Charles Booth, following Bernard and Eden after ninety years with his Survey of London Life and Labour,[4] was like them in being a man of means who used a private fortune for the public purpose of exploring the problem of poverty. But he worked under different circumstances. By the time that Charles Booth came on the scene the problem of poverty had changed, the approach to it had changed,

[1] I owe this quotation to A History of English Philanthropy, by B. Kirkman Gray (P. S. King & Son, 1905), p. 279. This book covers the period from the dissolution of the monasteries to the taking of the first census in 1800.

[2] Published in 1797 in three quarto volumes. The author, born in 1766, was the eldest son of a baronet who had been Governor of Maryland and of a mother who was sister and co-heiress of the last Lord Baltimore. From Christ Church, Oxford, he went into business and helped to found the Globe Insurance Company. His remarkable survey was published in his thirty-first year and he died at forty-three.

[3] See notice of Research Services and Mass Observation Reports in the Supplementary Volume.

[4] Begun about 1886, the results were published between 1891 and 1903, under the general title of Life and Labour of the People in London. The earlier description of London Labour and the London Poor, by Henry Mayhew, published between 1851 and 1864, while containing much interesting information, is impressionistic rather than scientific.

and the technical possibilities of social research had improved. The problem had changed: to the misery engendered by bad harvests and high prices which were Eden's starting-point, there had succeeded the new evil of urban squalor produced by industrialization. The approach to the problem had changed: Bernard and Eden took as their subject "The Poor"; Charles Booth took as his subject "poverty," a highly significant change. The difference is not simply that to speak of "The Poor" assumed a strictly classified society; the phrase had also the implication that "The Poor" would always be with us; when Charles Booth got to work, after a hundred years of industrialization and rising productivity, the question that presented itself was why with so much wealth should there be so much poverty. Finally, the technical possibilities of social research had improved out of all recognition. Eden wrote before the first population census of Britain;[1] Booth, in addition to all the published census results, was allowed to analyse the unpublished material of the census to suit his purposes. Eden apart from his travelling investigator, had to rely for local information on the accident of finding an intelligent and sympathetic squire or clergyman; Booth found himself able to use the new army of school attendance officers as his field workers.

Charles Booth, having made, as a shipowner, enough to live on, devoted the energies of his best years to social survey. He devoted also large sums from his private fortune. He was followed a few years later by Seebohm Rowntree in York. Rowntree's studies and those undertaken by Professor Bowley at the London School of Economics in the early years of this century carried statistical techniques in social research beyond anything attempted by Charles Booth. Finally, with the development of social science departments at the universities—following the lead given by Sidney Webb in London— the practice of making social surveys a part of the work of those departments became common. Of all this, Charles Booth is the father, with his passion for dispassionate enquiry and his devotion of twenty years to social survey rather than to making more business.

This brief review of the application of impartial study to the problems of society has more than historical significance. Social

[1] Those who criticize economics and other social sciences for their inadequate present development, as compared with the natural sciences, often forget how recently the material for social science has become available. See the conclusion of my address on "The Place of the Social Sciences in Human Knowledge" given at the London School of Economics in 1937, and published in *Politica*, October, 1937.

survey has been a revolutionary agent in British history for seventy years. Charles Booth's generalization that, after a hundred years of industrial progress one-quarter of the people of East London were living in poverty, just because it was made so quietly, gave a shock to complacency and hastened social reform of many kinds. On the particular problem of old age his intervention—with the proposal in 1891 of old age pensions—was decisive in converting opinion.

The later social surveys, made by universities and others between the two world wars, have had as dramatic a consequence. They were the starting-point of the *Report on Social Insurance and Allied Services* in 1942, being used to show just how much want there was and why, and why there need be no want.

> The social surveys made by impartial investigators of living conditions in some of the main industrial centres of Britain between 1928 and 1937 have been used earlier in this Report to supply a diagnosis of want. They can be used also to show that the total resources of the community were sufficient to make want needless.[1]

From assuming with Bernard that there will always be "The Poor" to be ameliorated, from asking with Booth why there should be so much "poverty," we have come to asking whether there need be any want at all not due in the individual case to individual failure.

Knowledge and reason applied to social conditions by voluntary action have led to a great development of action by the State. This does not end voluntary action or the philanthropic motive. It sets them free for new objectives. And social survey itself—the impartial study of social conditions and informed criticism of public measures —must always be one of the subjects of Voluntary Action. The State can play a part in this field and is doing so increasingly to-day.[2] The State should never attempt to absorb the whole of it.

RESIDENTIAL SETTLEMENTS

One of the purposes for which, in the last decades of the nineteenth century, young men of enquiring mind at British universities were

---

[1] *Report on Social Insurance and Allied Services*, para. 445. See also the paragraphs following (446 and 447) and the diagnosis of want in paras. 11–16.

[2] A "social survey" organization has been maintained by the Government since 1941 and has produced many interesting statistical studies. One of these— on the occupations of old people—is referred to in Chapter VIII, and another— on cinema attendance—is referred to in Chapter IX.

advised to live at Toynbee Hall or some other residential settlement, was that they might look for the answer to the question named in the last section: Why, with so much and increasing wealth, does so much poverty persist? Some took this advice. The institutions known as residential settlements have been, among other things, places where the residents might learn;[1] many of them have been used for social surveys; many to-day act as the clinics where students of social science in the universities go for their practical experience. It is important to realize that a settlement is not in essence a place for doing these things or, indeed, a place for doing any one particular thing.

"Toynbee Hall seems to its visitors to be a centre of education, a mission, a centre of social effort. It may be so; but the visitors miss the truth that the place is a club-house in Whitechapel, occupied by men who do citizens' duty in the neighbourhood."[2] In these words Canon Barnett, the founder of Toynbee Hall and thus the originator of settlements, made plain just what he meant. No community can be well managed unless there are in it sufficient people with the taste, the training and the leisure to undertake essential civic duties. The development of great centres of population in which all the wealth and leisure were in one region, while the poverty and the squalor were in other regions, meant that these latter regions were without their proper complement of responsible public-spirited and leisured citizens. The settlement movement was an attempt by voluntary action to counteract the break-up of cities into preserves of the rich and leisured, and warrens of the poor and labouring.

A settlement as it was conceived by Canon Barnett, and established in Whitechapel in 1884, was to be first and foremost a residential club in which all residents paid for their board and lodging, and of which the condition of membership should be that they took sufficient part in the life of the district to justify their living there. Just what part they took would depend on their interests and aptitudes. One resident might be interested in adult education, another in board schools, a third in social clubs, a fourth in local government, others in charity organization, or co-operation, or relief of unemployment, or music and the arts. The club character of Toynbee Hall in its early days was well marked; admission to the club depended on the vote of the existing members who, after

[1] Toynbee Hall I described once as "a school of humanity in Whitechapel for those who have done *Literae Humaniores* in Oxford."

[2] *Towards Social Reform*, pp. 262-3.

a probationary period, would decide whether any candidate for admission showed sign of doing sufficient civic duty in his new community. Most of the residents in the early days had their own professions, the Civil Service, in teaching and the law; some were people of private means who devoted themselves wholly to what they were doing in East London; one or two held official posts in the settlements and lived by them, as warden, sub-warden or secretary or the like. Toynbee Hall was a centre of social activities, adult education, social clubs, organization of children's country holidays, conferences, debates, concerts and art exhibitions. But these were a consequence rather than the essence of the settlement.

The essence of a settlement lies in the individual lives of the residents, as they are affected by the special experience of living in that particular place. Any full account of a settlement and any estimate of its significance would have to bring in the biographies of the residents and note all the movements which directly or indirectly emanated from their stay there.[1]

To-day there are in Britain some forty-eight settlements altogether affiliated to the British Association of Residential Settlements. A brief account of them is given in the Supplementary Volume, as an annex to the Memorandum from their Association. As will be seen from this, each settlement has its individual character and special interests. Some are denominational and others not. Some, indeed most, are associated with a university, a college or a school and derive strength from this. Like all institutions, settlements tend with time to become more professional. Like all philanthropic institutions they are in difficulties of finance. Like all good causes they have suffered from the war. With part of its premises damaged in air-raids and another part let for urgent public purposes, Toynbee Hall itself is far less of a residential club than it was, less so than some of the other settlements. But this, it may be hoped, is only a passing phase.

Settlements have not accomplished—no one can have imagined that they would accomplish directly—the objective of putting an end to social and economic segregation. That needs the strong arm of the State and is beyond the power of Voluntary Action. The settle-

[1] One of my earliest evenings at the London School of Economics and Political Science, in 1904, when I was sub-warden of Toynbee Hall, was devoted to reading a paper to the Students' Union on "The Influence of University Settlements." Only gradually did it appear that the paper was concerned with the effects of these institutions not on their surroundings but on their inmates. The paper was a foolish leg-pull which long after I showed with great trepidation to Canon Barnett, but it was not wholly without point.

ments have been centres where or from which much admirable philanthropic work has been done, in care of particular classes in need, in promoting social intercourse, in adult education, and increasingly now in spreading the amenities of civilized life to all who can enjoy them. They have become invaluable adjuncts of the universities in the development of social science. They have ensured, in communities which otherwise would have lacked them, citizens of public spirit to undertake civic tasks. They have been indispensable centres of criticism and unveiling of social evils. This perhaps has been their greatest contribution, and it represents a continuing need.

Of course a man or a woman who from philanthropic interest wishes to live in the poor part of a city rather than in a rich part can do so without a residential club. He can settle individually, as Edward Dennison and one or two others did before the founding of Toynbee Hall. Or after a period in a settlement, he and others can hive off elsewhere. But the club solves his residential difficulties. And the community life of a settlement, with the older members guiding and helping the new ones, is of importance. Few who have passed through a settlement will question the value of Canon Barnett's social invention.

Ultimately, when all towns have been rebuilt as mixed communities, there may be no need for settlements, but until that happens the need will continue. The settlements to-day are not only essential centres for civic work but means of conducting a continual survey of economic and social conditions through the eyes of those who live there.

URBAN AND RURAL AMENITIES

The endless growth of great cities which led to the settlement movement as one reaction, led at about the same time or a little earlier to another reaction, in defence of urban and rural amenities. "When I first began to work," Octavia Hill remarked to her sister, "people would say, 'I'll give you money for necessaries for the poor, but I don't see what they want with recreation'; then after a few years they said, 'I can understand poor people wanting amusement, but what good will open spaces do them?' and now everybody recognizes the importance of open spaces."[1]

This observation, reported by the biographer of Octavia Hill, shows how voluntary action may confer public benefits which would

[1] *Life of Octavia Hill,* by E. Moberly Bell (Constable, 1938), ch. xviii.

not have come otherwise. In the eighteen-sixties the spreading of
London outwards began to raise acutely the question of the commons
on its borders; more and more land was needed for building; each
lord of a manor on the outskirts of London saw that this need could
be met with personal gain to himself, if he were able to enclose the
common and use it in part at least as a building estate. To resist
such measures, in the same year, 1865, in which Octavia Hill began
her housing management in the heart of London, there was set up
the Commons Society, now the Commons Open Spaces and Footpaths Preservation Society. Its first chairman was G. J. Shaw
Lefevre, afterwards Lord Eversley, who later wrote the history of
the society. Among other original members were John Stuart Mill,
T. H. Huxley, James Bryce, T. Fowell Buxton, Leslie Stephen,
Octavia Hill and Robert Hunter. This society was instrumental in
saving, among other open spaces, Hampstead Heath, Berkhamstead
Common, Plumstead Common, Wandsworth Common, and Epping
Forest—an achievement of Voluntary Action for Londoners which
very few of them realize sufficiently. London owes its lungs to
Voluntary Action.

A fuller account of the Commons Society and of other voluntary
organizations which have followed it, in defence of urban and rural
amenities of various kinds, is given in the Supplementary Volume.
They include, among others, the following:

The Society for Protection of Ancient Buildings, founded in
1877 by William Morris to stop vandal restorations, and continuing to give technical advice on problems of restoration and
preservation;

The Scapa Society (1893) for Checking Abuses of Public
Advertising;

The National Trust for Preservation of Places of Historic
Interest and Natural Beauty, with Octavia Hill, Robert Hunter
and Canon Rawnsley as its moving spirits, incorporated as a
company in 1895 and now with statutory powers for acquiring
and preserving land and buildings for the benefit of the nation;

The Council for Preservation of Rural England (1926), concerned, as its title suggests, with rural amenities.

The Central Council of Civic Societies (1939), concerned to
stimulate public interest in urban amenities, and having
affiliated to it about sixty local societies.

The Georgian Group (1937), concerned specially to defend
buildings erected in the Georgian style.

In addition to these societies, national in scope, there are societies concerned with particular localities—Oxford, Cambridge, Coventry, the Peak District, the Lake District, and so on. And there are societies whose purposes—of rambling, camping, natural history, architecture—lead them to defence of country amenities of one kind or another. Most of these specialized societies are affiliated to the Council for the Preservation of Rural England.

It is noteworthy that several of these agencies are of recent origin. Some, indeed, have come into being after the damage of industrialization, which may prove to be irretrievable as well as needless, has been done. This is sadly true of the Oxford Preservation Trust; as a place where the minds of the young may be moulded by beauty and calm, the "home of lost causes" has become an all but lost cause itself.[1] The price of preservation of amenities is eternal vigilance, to-day even more than in the past.

Defence of urban and rural amenities has always been the work of far-sighted individuals, advancing continually into new fields where public opinion was not for some time ready to follow them. The preservation of commons from the landlord without public spirit; the preservation of buildings from destructive restoration; the preservation of scenery in trust for the nation; the control of unsightly advertisement; the preservation of special and at the time unfashionable classes of building; the ideas of regional planning and of national parks—all these germinated in the minds of individuals,

---

[1] The needless destruction of amenities in Oxford is a classic example of unintentional vandalism. The turning of the incomparable High Street—in which old pictures show dons holding their academic discussions *off* the pavement—into a torrent channel for thundering motors with drifting foam of bicycles—is not the result of through traffic; the normal congestion disappears largely once a week on early closing day in Oxford and will be practically unrelieved at other times by the laboriously constructed by-passes. The normal state of the High Street is due to the new industrial city of Cowley having been built on the east of Oxford, while the railway is on the west and the shopping and entertainment centres for the new population have been allowed to develop in the west-centre. Nothing like the present disaster would have happened if the Nuffield Works had been placed in empty ground west of the station, as rational town-planning would have placed them. Granted their present situation, the palliative is not by-passes for through traffic but deliberate development of a new civic centre—town hall, shops, cinemas, etc., in Cowley, prohibition of any such development west of Magdalen Bridge, removal of much that has come there, and some new railway connection. The academic centre of Oxford might then be closed practically to motor traffic. Such a programme would not deprive the University in any way of its new advantage of contact with an industrial community. It would show that industry can be reconciled with amenity and with respect for irreplaceable beauty.

were fought for by voluntary groups, and at length were accepted by the public and the State.

WOMEN'S ORGANIZATIONS

Of the six organizations named under this head three—the Women's Co-operative Guild (1883), the National Council of Women (1895) and the Women's Group on Public Welfare (1940)— are in the main bodies for forming public opinion, watching and promoting public action, and making any distinctive point of view of women felt on political and administrative issues. The three others are essentially agencies for organizing Voluntary Action, as it is defined in this volume. All of them are twentieth-century developments.

The oldest of the three is the organization of Women's Institutes, the first of which was established in Anglesey in 1915 following an example set eighteen years before in Canada. To-day there are more than 6,500 Women's Institutes with a membership of 350,000. The movement is essentially rural, having as its principal named purpose "to improve and develop conditions of rural life." All country women are eligible for membership, no matter what their views on religion or politics may be. In general, Women's Institutes are confined to communities of less than 4,000 inhabitants. Each institute is self-governing and has its separate finance; the movement represents a federation with power mainly in the separate units.

The movement began in Britain in the First World War, as a means, among other things, of getting necessary national work done, in food production and food preservation. In the Second World War it has served the same purposes, and has received Government grants for particular activities of this kind. Its lasting peace-time purpose is to emphasize the new character of country women as citizens with interests outside their homes.

The work of the institutes is first and foremost social intercourse, the bringing together of the women of a village and the encouragement of friendliness and neighbourliness, with a monthly meeting as the focus of social activities. Education and social service are two other purposes; the extent to which these take place varies greatly from one institute to another. The movement is democratic; the starting of an institute depends upon a movement in the village itself, and the government rests in the hands of the members. But, as in other democracies, what any particular institute does depends upon its leaders. And in the past the leaders have naturally been those whose economic and domestic circumstances gave them leisure. Now leisure is available only in much smaller individual quantities.

The urban counterpart to the Women's Institutes is found in the Townswomen's Guilds, with some interesting differences. This movement began later—with a National Union of Townswomen's Guilds established only in 1929, and is far less extensive. At the end of 1946 it counted about 12,000 members in 800 guilds, and had a programme of adding 250 guilds during 1947. The stated objects of a Townswomen's Guild are:

> To encourage the education of women to enable them as citizens to make their best contribution to the common good.
>
> To serve as a common meeting-ground for women, irrespective of creed and party, for their wider education, including social intercourse.

The emphasis is thus on education for citizenship, with social intercourse coming last and without the practical activities of the country woman. This leads to a difference of attitude on subjects for addresses or debates at meetings. The Women's Institutes, with their proper determination to stand clear of party politics, are apt to shy at any discussion of controversial issues. The Townswomen's Guilds see that education for citizenship means learning to settle controversial issues rightly after debate. "There is a growing realization," states the Annual Report for 1946, "of the value of being able to discuss highly controversial subjects, including party political questions; and of how this is made possible by the fact that the Guild itself cannot, because of its objects, undertake propagandist action as a corporate body."

Another difference between the urban and the rural movements is that the former has to consider the problem of numbers in each guild. All the women in a village can join an organization without making it unwieldy; the average membership of a Women's Institute is little over fifty. For a Townswomen's Guild the last Annual Report suggests 150 as the optimum number. "A large membership of 200–250 and even, in some cases, 300 and over, means that there is need in the neighbourhood for another Guild or Guilds." The figure of 150 is much the same as that of the average friendly society branch. It may be hoped that the Townswomen's Guilds will grow, as affiliated orders grew, by multiplying their separate cells and keeping each down to a manageable size. Education for citizenship is one of the most vital conditions of success in democracy, and education is not a mass product.

The latest and largest of the women's organizations has a special character. The "Women's Voluntary Services," universally shortened to W.V.S. came into being in 1938 at the request of the Government of the day, as part of preparation for possible war. The immediate problem at that moment was to secure enrolment of sufficient volunteers for Air-Raid Precautions. Once established the W.V.S. has taken as its aim assistance of statutory authorities in the discharge of their obligations. It has held itself ready to do anything that it was asked to do, has become auxiliary to more than twenty Government departments and has co-operated with local authorities in more than 100 different operations. It had at one time more than 1,000,000 enrolled members and still has some 900,000.

In one sense the W.V.S. is not a voluntary agency, that is to say, it is not independent of public authority in deciding what it shall do and how.[1] The Chairman of the W.V.S., the Dowager Marchioness of Reading, was appointed to that position by the Home Secretary; the necessary expenses are met by the Government or by local authorities; initiative and instructions come from the centre. In the words of Lady Reading, the W.V.S. is not a policy-making body at all. It receives its drive and its policy from the top rather than from its members. And in contrast to most voluntary agencies the W.V.S. is not specialist—not interested more in old people than in children, in cripples than in exports.

In another sense, on the other hand, the W.V.S. is more voluntary than most agencies described in this volume—in the sense of having in relation to the whole a smaller paid staff than most. In its total enrolled membership of 900,000 about 200 are paid, and about 5,000 wear uniforms. The W.V.S. is a means by which individual women can give such service as they have time for, to do work prescribed for them; on enrolment each member undertakes "to serve as a volunteer in the Women's Voluntary Services, to take any necessary instructions or training, and to serve under the directions of the officers of the services." To the statutory authorities, on the other hand, the W.V.S. has been and is the means of getting things done and getting services rendered, which often

[1] In the Nuffield College study of *Voluntary Social Services* the W.V.S. is formally excluded from the category of voluntary organizations for social service, as defined in that volume. But fortunately that does not prevent the editor of the volume, Miss Bourdillon, from including a brief account of the W.V.S. in the chapter dealing with the "Needs of the Countryman" or from "paying tribute to the heroic contribution of many individual W.V.S. members."

could not be got for payment. That there will continue to be needs of this kind to be met in peace, as in war, is certain. It seems likely also that there will be room and need for at least one general body with no specialty save that of giving service. The W.V.S. may be compared to the general agencies in the seventeenth group. As most of them are channels for a religious inspiration, so the W.V.S. is a channel for the desire of women to serve some object outside their homes.

YOUTH ORGANIZATIONS

Utilization of the additional resources and leisure of adolescence presents itself as one of the most important problems of the present and of the immediate future. Upon the formation of the right attitude to life of those who are now adolescent depends the prospect of having a democracy capable of rising to its responsibilities, both national and international. The importance of the adolescent period in life has been recognized by public authorities and by the voluntary agencies alike. The problem and some of the organizations attempting to deal with it are the subject of a memorandum in the Supplementary Volume. Here it need be dealt with in outline only.

A circular issued by the Ministry of Education in November, 1939, under the title "The Service of Youth," urged all Local Authorities for Higher Education to set up youth committees, and emphasized the importance of associating voluntary effort with the public system. A second circular in June, 1940, on "The Challenge of Youth" described the response of Local Authorities to the first circular as "almost universal." There has followed the Education Act of 1944, designed in due course to raise the school age for all to sixteen, introducing compulsory part-time education up to eighteen, and making it the duty of Local Education Authorities, under Section 41 (b), to provide not only for education but for "leisure time occupation, any such cultural training and recreative activities as are suited to their requirements, for any persons over compulsory school age who are able and willing to profit by the facilities provided for that purpose." By Section 53 the Education Authorities are given the further duty of providing "adequate facilities for recreation and social and physical training." In doing so they "shall have regard to the expediency of co-operating with any voluntary societies or bodies whose objects include the provision of facilities or the organization of activities of a similar character." There is now in being everywhere a Youth Committee of the Local Education Authority, with secretary and staff.

Facing these statutory authorities are a number of voluntary organizations. The membership covered and other data as to twenty-one of these organizations are set out in Table 12 attached; nineteen of them are now members of a Standing Conference of National Voluntary Youth Organizations, and meet for consultation while retaining their freedom of action. The youth organizations fall very roughly into three groups—those whose primary aim is association of young people for social intercourse or personal improvement or for some common interest of their own; those that emphasize service to others; and those that have a definitely religious purpose or association. The first six organizations shown in Table 12 are of the first type; the next five of the second type; and the last ten are in varying degrees religious or denominational. Missionary fervour is perhaps most marked in the last two of them.

Finally, to supplement the resources of these organizations is the King George's Jubilee Trust, with an invested capital of one million pounds and large income coming in annually, whose stated object is "to advance the spiritual, mental and general welfare of the younger generation and especially of young persons who are aged fourteen and upwards." With a view to obtaining guidance as to how the purposes for which it was founded can best be furthered in the post-war period, the Jubilee Trust commissioned the making of a survey of a particular area (the county of Nottingham was chosen for this purpose), and from this survey written by Mr. L. J. Barnes of the University of Liverpool, many interesting facts as to the needs of young people and the provision made for them emerge.

The task before the youth organizations is formidable. The membership figures in Table 12, reckoned by tens or occasionally hundreds of thousands, make a poor show against the millions of young people who go weekly or twice weekly to the cinema. Nor, of course, do the figures in Table 12 represent separate individuals; sociable or service-minded young people often belong to more than one association. On the other hand, the figures do not cover everything; they omit the pre-service organizations and many school associations. But, taking all these into account, the registration statistics for October, 1944, quoted in Mr. Barnes' Report on Nottingham, suggest that barely half the boys of fourteen to eighteen and less than half the girls can claim to be members of any youth organization; only a proportion of these would be active members.

The task of the youth organizations is beset by practical difficulties.

TABLE 12

YOUTH ORGANIZATIONS

	Organization	Date of Establish- ment	Membership, Grouping, Age
1.	National Association of Boys' Clubs (C)	1925	170,000 (72 per cent 14–18), in 2,147 clubs.
2.	National Association of Girls' Clubs and Mixed Clubs (C)	1880	117,000 in 1,900 clubs. "Mixed Clubs" added in 1944.
3.	Welsh League of Youth (C)	1922	107,400 in 426 clubs (46,800 under 14; 27,600 14–20; 33,000 over 20).
4.	National Federation of Young Farmers' Clubs (C)	1932	65,000 in 1,300 clubs (10–25).
5.	Scottish Association of Young Farmers' Clubs	1938	7,500 in 120 clubs (14–25).
6.	Co-operative Youth Move- ment (C)	1924	40,000 in 380 groups (15–29).
7.	Boy Scouts' Association (C)	1908	471,000, of whom 156,511 Wolf Cubs, and 219,391 Scouts of various kinds.
8.	Girl Guides' Association (C)	1910	465,000.
9.	British Red Cross Society— Youth Department (C) Junior Department	1942 1923	16,400 15–20 (15,155 girls); 21,600 11–16.
10.	St. John Ambulance Brigade Cadets (C)	1923	50,800 in 2,300 divisions (11–17).
11.	Girls' Guildry (C)	1900	(8,000).
12.	Boys' Brigade (C)	1883	81,000 in 2,400 companies (12–18).
13.	Girls' Friendly Society (C)	1875	(9,500, 11–25).
14.	Church Lads' Brigade (C)	1891	(30,000, 10–18).
15.	Girls' Life Brigade (C)	1902	33,000 10 upwards, and 15,000 cadets 6–10.
16.	Young Men's Christian Associ- ation (C)	1849	75,000 in 500 local associations in 1939.
17.	Young Women's Christian Association (C)	1851	(51,000 over 15).
18.	Catholic Young Men's So- ciety (C)	1849	30,000 in 423 branches in 1939 (16 +).
19.	Association for Jewish Youth	1927	(7,000 over 14).
20.	Salvation Army Youth Department (C)	1896	
21.	Young Christian Workers	1937	

Notes to Table 12

Organizations marked (C) are members of the Standing Conference of Voluntary Youth Organizations.

The statements as to membership, grouping, and age (if not printed in brackets) are taken from the articles descriptive of each organization in *Youth Organizations of Great Britain*, edited by Douglas Cooke (Jordan & Sons, 1946, 2nd issue). The figures, except where the contrary is stated, relate to some date in 1945. For a few organizations no membership figures are given in the work cited, but figures from other sources have been inserted in brackets. In addition to the organizations which are actually members

There is acute shortage of persons capable of being youth leaders. There is paralysing lack of accommodation. Mr. Barnes describes the premises available for club purposes as "the weakest feature of the youth service at present." The Youth Advisory Council of the Ministry of Education, reporting in 1943 on the youth service after the war, went out of their way to stress the same point:

> "We know that thousands of young people have to live in surroundings which make it almost impossible for them to grow up into decent citizens. Until these physical conditions are radically changed much of what is done for young people can be no more than tinkering. We therefore make it our first recommendation that at the earliest possible moment this scandal be removed and healthy conditions of living be guaranteed for all."

They put as their first recommendation: "That at the earliest possible moment a building programme be carried out which will guarantee healthy conditions of living for all young people." This, of course, is one aspect only of the general housing shortage, working out badly for young as for old.

In the last resort the success of youth organizations will depend less on material conditions than on the right choice of objectives and agencies. On this the following suggestions may be made.

First, service *of* youth should be diverted consciously into service *by* youth. Here lies the secret of the success of the Boy Scouts and Girl Guides. Here has lain the appeal of the Cadet Organizations during the years of war. Mr. L. J. Barnes, in his Report on Nottinghamshire, has some just comments on the suggestion that the joining of these organizations by so many boys was due to unwise persuasion by their elders:

> "The cadet units had no need to 'run after boys'; the boys offered themselves in numbers greater than the units could absorb. There are lessons here from which the non-uniformed organizations may profit when the pre-Service star is no longer in the ascendant.
>
> The basis of the cadet units' success appears to have been

Notes to Table 12—*continued*]
of the Standing Conference there are a number of other bodies associated with it as follows: Air Training Corps, Association for Jewish Youth, British Council of Churches, British National Cadet Association, Central Council of Physical Recreation, Ministry of Education, National Association of Training Corps for Girls, National Catholic Youth Association, Sea Cadet Corps, Toc H.

a wideawake appreciation on the part of the boys themselves of the urgency of the nation's need. The prime impulse was a clear youthful patriotism sharply conscious of the ardours and endurance of fathers and elder brothers in the field, and proudly eager to steel itself for the same testing. To his amazement the young patriot found that the adult world had for the moment stopped trying to do him good and was asking for his help. For the first time in his life he was publicly wanted; he was actually invited to put his powers at full stretch on behalf of the community.

He had been accustomed to think of the usual youth club as a glorified play-centre—a roping-off for children for purposes of recreation. By contrast his cadet work was a real initiation into adult life. True, it required him to study—and study hard; but it bore little resemblance to school. For he found in it an atmosphere where there was both mutuality and seriousness; the teachers wanted to teach and the pupils wanted to learn. In a word, he found conditions which offered some satisfaction to at least three of his primary psychological needs—needs which the world as he had hitherto known it appeared to go out of its way to thwart.[1]

Youth clubs and other organizations should be presented to young people not as a means of enjoyment which the elders think better for them than the cinema, the dance hall, or the street corner, not as a means of enjoyment at all, so much as a means of learning to be useful in the world. And one need not be old to be useful. Elizabeth Gurney began her career of social service at eighteen, by teaching her neighbours' children in the country, though she never learned to spell correctly herself. Quintin Hogg began at nineteen, starting his own Ragged School in London while working as a junior clerk in an office.

Second, the example of Germany shows the vital necessity of not allowing youth organization to become a function of the State, so that it can be used to further a particular policy of the State. Here above all there must be free action by diverse voluntary agencies.

Third, the ultimate purpose is preparation of young people for their duties as citizens, which means understanding of public problems at home and also understanding of international problems. The youth organizations must regard themselves as training-ground for adult education of every kind.

[1] *Youth Service in an English County*, by L. J. Barnes (p. 72).

FROM CHARITY ORGANIZATION TO FAMILY WELFARE

The philanthropic society now known as the Family Welfare Association began in 1869 as the "Society for Organising Charitable Relief and Repressing Mendicity." A year later, in April, 1870, while keeping this full title, it took a short name, "Charity Organisation Society." Forty years later, in April, 1910, it changed its long title, dropped the repression of mendicity, and became the "Society for Organising Charitable Effort and Improving the Condition of the Poor." Thirty-five years later still, after seventy-five years of charity organization, it became the Family Welfare Association. These changes of name are an epitome of the times and of the way in which voluntary activity adapts itself to changing circumstances.

At the time when the Society began, urban squalor and poverty were forcing themselves on public attention and were being dealt with largely by doles of money, from the public purse in the form of out-relief by the Guardians, from charitable trusts, from private citizens giving a shilling to a beggar to keep him quiet or in response to a begging letter. In 1867 one of the recurrent depressions of trade had had its normal consequence in London of a Mansion House Fund. In the following year a Unitarian Minister, the Rev. Henry Solly, read a paper to the Society of Arts on "How to Deal with the Unemployed Poor of London, and with its 'Roughs' and Criminal Classes." This led to the formation of what became the Charity Organisation Society, with Mr. Solly, for a short time as its first honorary secretary, and John Ruskin as a large financial supporter.[1]

"The founders of the Association had in view the reduction of the beggary and the pauperism then rife in London. There was much unemployment; of the many families evicted from their homes by the construction of the railways, only twenty thousand had been rehoused, and it was estimated that over a hundred thousand children were homeless. Inadequate out-relief was supplemented by coal and bread funds, free dormitories, soup kitchens, free refuges, etc., but these only relieved the immediate distress. Boards of Guardians gave inadequate relief because they knew it would be supplemented by indiscriminate charity; the charities gave because the Guardians' relief was inadequate.

"From the first the Association held that gifts of food and

[1] See Chapter I of *Social Work in London 1869 to 1912, a History of the Charity Organisation Society*, by Helen Bosanquet (John Murray, 1914).

money, however necessary, were by themselves insufficient and that people in distress could only be helped constructively through the careful study of each individual problem."

As this historical statement from one of its latest publications suggests, the Charity Organisation Society was based on a clear view as to the nature of money and as to the responsibilities attaching to all laying out of money. Money is not itself wealth, but it is the means of directing human activity. If paid as a wage, it can be used to induce human beings to make one thing rather than another. If it is given as public relief or private charity, it affects equally the attitude and actions of the recipient. All passing of money influences actions, for good or ill. To give money to a man because he writes a moving begging letter is to pay him for doing so, and if the gift is repeated, sooner or later it makes the writing of such letters an occupation like any other. To give money to a person because he shows his wounds is to encourage the showing of wounds. To feed the starving on condition that they will present themselves in all weathers in the middle of the night on the Thames Embankment is to make misery a condition of relief, and exhibition of misery a theatrical gesture. The central doctrine on which the Charity Organisation Society was founded was the immense responsibility which attached to any spending of money whether charitable or otherwise, and the need to accompany any transfer of money by personal care.

Early in its history the Society found a secretary—who became its guiding spirit—Charles Stewart Loch. As a young barrister fresh from Oxford he had become the honorary secretary of one of the local committees of the Society. When in 1875 the Society was looking for a secretary it appointed him, from many competitors, at the age of twenty-six. He stayed there for forty years, and when his obituary notice came to be published, it said of him justly, "The Charity Organisation Society was he and he was the Charity Organisation Society." An idealist with a critical intellect he did indeed represent the Society as a whole.

Naturally the Charity Organisation Society with its definite point of view found itself often engaged in controversies. It set up an enquiry department to which anyone might refer for information about an applicant for relief, or a charitable agency. This led to the unmasking of many professional beggars and fraudulent charities. It led also to controversy with agencies of standing comparable to its own. Thus at one time Dr. Barnardo's Homes for Children were on the cautionary list which the Charity Organisation Society on request gave to charitably minded persons; the society were not satisfied as to the method of management of these homes. At another time the Charity Organisation Society launched into public criticism of the National Society for the Prevention of Cruelty to Children in respect of its finance and administration. Keeping expenditure within income was never a strong suit of Mr. Benjamin Waugh, the moving spirit of that organization, but he had other strengths more needed for his task. Two more important issues, affecting not administration but principle, were raised by the Charity Organisation Society in relation to the Royal Home for Incurables and its voting system, and the Salvation Army and its *Darkest London* scheme.

Voting charities are now rare, but were at one time common. During the earlier part of the nineteenth century a number of philanthropic institutions—orphanages, almshouses, homes for incurables and so on—adopted the practice of making admission to them dependent upon an election, in which subscriptions and donations gave voting rights. This was both a means of deciding between candidates—when as was common there were more candidates than places to be filled—and a means of encouraging subscriptions. The Charity Organisation Society in 1872 launched a campaign against this procedure, which was taken up by a Charity Voting Reform Association, formed a year or two later. The enquiries of this reform association showed some truly remarkable results from the application of electoral methods to the administration of charity.[1]

For a popular institution with a large body of subscribers, canvassing for votes might reach formidable proportions. One philanthropic lady described how she had spent six years getting another old lady into a home, sending out in one year 10,000 letters, with reply paid envelopes at a cost approaching £100: "during the six years I was canvassing I spent so much money . . . that at last in desperation my husband bought £50 of votes and assured the election, but it would have been cheaper to us to have allowed her a small annuity from the beginning."

There might be exchange of votes, illustrated by the following advertisement from *The Times* of May 10, 1872.

"TWENTY EIGHT VOTES for the ensuing ELECTION of the ROYAL MEDICAL BENEVOLENT COLLEGE, Epsom, would gladly be EXCHANGED for ROYAL INCURABLES, Address, E. H., Post Office, Carshalton, Surrey."

[1] These illustrations of by-gone charity elections are taken from a bound volume of pamphlets on "Charity Voting Reform," in the library of the Family Welfare Association.

As the reporter of this observed, "The quotations of the relative value of 'Royal Incurables' and 'Royal Benevolents' would be a curiosity."

There might be still more elaborate election deals. Thus the friends of one Emily Chitty made eleven unsuccessful attempts in five and a half years to get her voted into a home. After the eleventh failure they thought of a better plan. "An effort is now to be made to transfer the votes promised to her at the next election to another candidate: and when this last is elected her friends are bound to vote for Emily Chitty."

The road from such electoral bargains to business traffic in votes was short. There were well-known dealers in votes. Persons describing themselves as charitable ladies and gentlemen interested in getting people into homes, to whom votes might be entrusted, made a living out of this business. There were professional canvassers for votes who would offer to procure any quantity of votes for any institution at 2s. 6d. a vote.

The traffic thus revealed was remarkable and regrettable, but it was not the main evil. The main evil was the miserable waiting for years and years of the candidates, sometimes to succeed when success came too late. The Charity Organisation Society were clearly in the right in attacking this method of financing institutions. The Charity Reform Association were able to report in 1912 that no institution established in the past forty years had adopted the voting system. By most, though not all, of those who had it before, it has now been abandoned. Charity means giving without seeking power for oneself.

The Charity Organisation Society's polemic against the Salvation Army lasted several years following the publication of *Darkest London and the Way Out*. In the words of the historian of the Charity Organisation Society it appeared that the Salvation Army Social Scheme of 1891, "combined most of the methods of wholesale charity against which the Charity Organisation Society had been striking."[1] In this controversy there was right on both sides. Undoubtedly it was not the best thing to do for the vagrants of London to feed them at midnight on the Embankment. But since many of them were genuinely without shelter, it was necessary that their existence should be brought home in some way to the conscience of the public.

But the Charity Organisation Society, though critical, has been far from merely negative. Its own positive job was case-work, dealing through the district committees with tens of thousands of individuals,

[1] Helen Bosanquet, *op. cit.*, p. 341.

in such a way as to restore their independence. As the historical memorandum already cited points out, "it combined this system of case-work with an active campaign for the improvement of social conditions."

> It co-operated with Miss Octavia Hill in all her housing reforms; it worked ceaselessly for better housing conditions, and organized a body of over five hundred voluntary health visitors. In 1886 it inaugurated the work of visiting the sick and crippled children out of which grew the Invalid Children's Aid Association. For many years it urged the appointment of Hospital Almoners, and in 1894 a Charity Organisation Society Secretary (paid jointly by the Hospital and the Charity Organisation Society) became the first Almoner at the Royal Free Hospital. The first school children Care Committee was formed by the Society in 1893, and in 1907 the work was taken over by the L.C.C. The first Tuberculosis Dispensaries and Care Committees were organized in 1908 and were later taken over by the local authority.

To this list of positive activities named by the Society itself may be added its setting up in 1906 of a Special Committee on Unskilled Labour, which helped to bring to light many of the characteristics of casual employment in London.[1]

It was not possible for intelligent humane people, as the leaders and the workers of the Charity Organisation Society were, to see London poverty and squalor at first hand without wishing to make many changes. Nor can any just person doubt that one of the changes most needed was the change whose advocacy made the Society unpopular—abandonment of the giving of doles to keep beggars quiet.[2]

The early fathers of the Charity Organisation Society, however, were not content to criticize charitable doles. They had definite views also as to action by the State. They waged a campaign against outdoor relief by the Guardians. They opposed municipal hospitals and old age pensions and were severely critical of most plans for State action in regard to the unemployed. As late as 1912 the his-

[1] This Charity Organisation Society Committee on Unskilled Labour, of which I was secretary, provided much of the material used by me in the chapter on "The Reserve of Labour" in my book on *Unemployment: a Problem of Industry*.

[2] A vivid account of Whitechapel under doles in 1872 is given by Dame Henrietta Barnett in describing the beginnings of Toynbee Hall. *Towards Social Reform*, pp. 241–4 (T. Fisher Unwin, 1909).

torian of the Society, in speaking of the old-age pensions movement, declared that: "The Charity Organisation Society has always been opposed to it, as it has to all plans for granting a stereotyped form of relief to large numbers of persons whose needs are very varying and only capable of being met by individual attention."

Here, of course, the Charity Organisation Society found itself fighting a losing battle. Here to-day its attitude is different. While it was still the Charity Organisation Society, it welcomed instead of opposing the main proposals of the Beveridge Report.

> The society is of opinion that in the post-war world the community must accept responsibility for supplying the basic needs of its citizens, and that this must include the provision of adequate housing, adequate health services, and adequate maintenance, when the citizen is unable, through no fault of his own, to provide these services for himself and his family. The society believes, with Sir William Beveridge, that the scope of social insurance should be extended to a degree that will supply, when circumstances make this necessary, a benefit sufficient for the maintenance of a decent standard of living for the family.[1]

The Society went on to support the proposals of my Report on Industrial Assurance: "As a Family Case Work Agency, it has had much experience of the abuses of the present systems of industrial insurance and it believes that such a scheme as that envisaged by Sir William Beveridge would be a social improvement of the first order." The fighting spirit of the "C.O.S. militant," as its biographer calls it, had not left it in 1943, in spite of conversion to social security.

But it was already describing itself as what it has now become in set terms—a family case-work agency. The need for charitable gifts of all kinds has become less, but the need for personal service is as great as it ever was and is being rendered by the society as before. The modern activities of the Family Welfare Association still include case-work, helping tens of thousands of individuals in a difficulty to get out of it into independence. They include as a new development the Citizens' Advice Bureaux described in a later chapter. They include many valuable publications. And they include an indispensable emphasis on the importance of training for dealing with human problems.

[1] *Statement on the Beveridge Report*, issued by the Charity Organisation Society on January 28, 1943.

The old argument of the Charity Organisation Society that all passing of money affects human actions has not lost all application to-day. If money is paid on any condition it tends to bring that condition about; if it is paid or given on degrading conditions sooner or later it degrades. If, on the other hand, money sufficient for subsistence is assured to all at all times without any conditions, it does not degrade, but the question arises whether this may sap effort. The question whether or not this will happen depends upon whether those who are guaranteed a minimum for subsistence at all times can be persuaded to feel wants above that minimum, which will call for continuing effort from them. To propose that freedom from want should be secured by State action implies a belief in human nature, belief that men can be led by hope and idealism and ambition in place of being driven by fear.

CO-ORDINATION AND THE SPIRIT OF SERVICE

The change of name of the Charity Organisation Society had two implications. It meant not only the passing over from charity in the sense of giving money to the giving of constructive help and guidance apart from money. It meant also passing from being an agency with general interests to being one with special interests. "Organization" has gone from the title as well as "Charity."

The Society continues its enquiry department, which still receives some 2,000 queries every year, but with the passing of the House to House Collections Act of 1939, the worst of the evils of fraudulent charity with which the society once went to war, have disappeared. More important is the disappearance of the need for charitable giving of money, food and clothing, as the standard of income security guaranteed by State action rises steadily.

Co-ordination of philanthropic effort in giving direct relief is less important than it was. Does this mean that there is no need for co-ordination among philanthropic agencies undertaking the newer and more difficult tasks of to-day? In the First World War the principal philanthropic agencies certainly did not think so. They met in conference in 1916 on measures of war relief and personal service, to discuss how, in dealing with the many new problems then facing them, they could avert "confusion, chaos, overlapping and indiscriminate begging." The conference led to a Standing Joint Committee of the principal organizations, which in turn led to the setting up in 1919 of the National Council of Social Service, incorporated in 1924.

The structure, methods of working, and relation to other voluntary agencies and to public authorities of this new body, as well as some of its achievements, are described in a memorandum printed in the Supplementary Volume. That such a body is needed and can serve useful purposes seems clear. The purposes which it may serve include the following:

> To provide for the systematic pooling of ideas between different agencies.
>
> To diminish overlapping by free consultation between different agencies.
>
> To be perpetually on the watch to unveil new evils, to discover new needs and to promote ways of dealing with them.
>
> To give advice and help if desired in promoting local developments.
>
> To improve the technical efficiency of voluntary action by pressing for adequate standards of training of those who undertake it.

All these things the National Council of Social Service has set itself to do.

Of course, the way of co-ordination of the spirit of service is hard. Any organization which attempts it will run into storms. It will appear from time to time as the critic as well as the friend of other organizations, as an additional hurdle to be surmounted on the way to some cherished aim. It will be accused of being more interested in co-ordination than in getting anything done. Its officers will be told that they are becoming another bureaucracy, indistinguishable from the civil servants with whom they deal. If, in addition to promoting co-ordination, it undertakes directly any work of its own, it will appear as the competitor instead of the friend and ally of the other agencies.

The nature of Voluntary Action is to be free and independent. Enterprise in this field, as in most others, comes before co-ordination. No central body should be established to break or weaken the connection between voluntary agencies for special purposes and the Government departments or local authorities which wish to use them. Co-ordination and consultation must be free, not forced.

Yet it should come freely in growing measure, for the need for self-criticism among voluntary agencies is even greater to-day than in the past. As material standards rise and security of subsistence income is achieved, the relatively simple task of meeting needs for money falls into the background. The new tasks of voluntary agencies then become more difficult, not less difficult: they are concerned with such tasks as the formation of the right outlook in youth, or helping to adjust personal relationships, or rescuing the handicapped physically or socially. All these things and many other things that have still to be done to make a good society need knowledge as well as goodwill in the doers. The spirit of service is a wind that bloweth where it listeth. But if it is a true spirit it implies readiness to learn how to serve as well as desire to serve.

That there is this spirit in Britain to-day as in the past should not be doubted. The last and largest of the three organizations of women noticed above, with its 900,000 members, has shown for women how widespread is desire to serve, when it is clear that service is needed. The largest of the organizations for boys and for girls are those which put first in their aims service through fellowship, learning how to be useful and doing good turns. The call to service in the cadet corps has proved in the war years to be the strongest magnet for youth. Two famous organizations—the Red Cross Society and the Order of St. John of Jerusalem—described in memoranda in the Supplementary Volume, have shown the same thing for many years, in peace as in war; each to-day has still something like 140,000 men or women or young people seeking to serve. These are examples only. The same thing is shown by innumerable smaller organizations of every kind.

The spirit of service is in our people. It is true that only a minority give any service outside their homes to-day. "No matter in what sort of area they lived, whether in the East End of London, in the industrial north, or in a small village, only a minority, less than a third, of the people with whom investigators come into contact, were found to be giving any sort of fairly regular voluntary help to people outside their families." This is the first generalization from the investigation of voluntary services undertaken for the purpose of this Report by Mass Observation. It is confirmed with notable agreement by the sample enquiry conducted statistically by Research Services. But the Mass Observation investigators go on to say that those who do not help others commonly feel that they should do so, and make excuses of lack of time and means. "Most of those who do not go out of their way to help their neighbours—this being especially true of women, are somewhat guiltily conscious of the fact that they do not do so. . . . There is a reserve of willingness to be drawn upon if ways and means of dealing with people's more immediate material needs can be devised."

The spirit of service is in our people. But only in the few is it a driving force which makes them pioneers, not to be stayed by difficulties. There is always need for the few—dynamic individuals wholly possessed by this spirit. They call it forth in others; they create the institutions and societies through which it acts; they lead by their example. Voluntary Action depends on its pioneers.

V. A CHAPTER OF PIONEERS

Shaftesbury	1801–1885	Ragged Schools, etc.
Some Forerunners of Shaftesbury:		
John Pounds	1766–1839	
Thomas Cranfield	1766–1838	
Samuel Robert Starey	c. 1820–1904	
Henry Duncan	1774–1846	Savings Banks.
Elizabeth Fry	1780–1845	Prisoners' Aid.
Andrew Reed	1787–1862	Homes for Orphans and for Incurables, etc.
Frederic Denison Maurice	1805–1872	Working Men's College.
Henry Solly	1813–1903	Club and Institute Union, and Charity Organisation Society.
George Williams	1821–1905	Y.M.C.A.
William Newton	1822–1876	Amalgamated Society of Engineers.
Thomas Rhodes Armitage	1824–1890	National Institute for the Blind.
George Holloway	1825–1892	Holloway Friendly Societies.
William Booth	1829–1912	Salvation Army.
Octavia Hill	1838–1912	Housing Management, etc.
Emma Cons	1838–1912	The Old Vic.
Benjamin Waugh	1839–1908	N.S.P.C.C.
Charles Booth	1840–1916	Social Surveys.
Samuel Augustus Barnett }	1844–1913	Toynbee Hall
Henrietta Barnett }	1851–1936	Garden Suburb, etc.
Robert Hunter	1844–1913	Commons Preservation.
Thomas James Barnardo	1845–1905	Dr. Barnardo's Homes
Quintin Hogg	1845–1903	Polytechnics.
Mary Augusta Ward	1851–1920	Mary Ward Settlement.
Baden-Powell	1857–1941	Boy Scouts.
Beatrice Webb }	1858–1943	London School of Economics
Sidney Webb }	1859–1947	and Political Science.

ONE day in the autumn of 1903, when I was working as sub-warden at Toynbee Hall, a young man came to talk to Canon Barnett and myself about a new plan for the development of adult education among wage-earners. The main ideas underlying the plan were that education depended on the co-operation of the pupil, and that for adult education, accordingly, the first thing to do was to discover and create a demand for teaching, among groups of men and women who would pledge themselves to regular attendance and study. The young man was the son of a mechanic, and had come to know Canon Barnett through his mother, who was a member of the Women's Co-operative Guild; he was without resources or influential friends, working as an employee in the Co-operative Depot at Leman Street, close to Toynbee Hall. As soon as Albert Mansbridge had left us, after expounding his dreams, the Canon turned to me and said: "That young man has fire in his belly." From that fire has come the Workers' Educational Association and other kindred movements.

No study of voluntary action as a means of social advance would be complete which did not describe, however briefly, some of the individuals who had fire in their bellies, show their origins and how they came to their tasks. Emergence and freedom of action of pioneers are the conditions of progress.

In this chapter, accordingly, a brief account is given of some of the pioneers of social advance who marked the nineteenth century in Britain. After Lord Shaftesbury and his forerunners the pioneers are given in the order of their birth. Most of these men have left institutions and abiding organizations which look back to them as founders. But one can also be a pioneer who does his work and blazes a trail but leaves nothing but his example behind him; such were John Pounds and Thomas Cranfield, noted here among the forerunners of Shaftesbury. The latter himself is dealt with at more length than the others, partly because he represents almost every variety of philanthropic effort, but still more because he was so interesting a character.

Those noticed in this chapter are a selection only. There are others more famous than most of them: Florence Nightingale is so obvious that it seemed better to look for others less known. There are others whom it has proved convenient to mention in dealing with their institutions rather than here; Charles Stewart Loch who made, though he did not found, the Charity Organisation Society, and Morton Eden and Thomas Bernard who preceded Charles Booth in social surveys, are illustrations of this procedure.

Those noticed here are described as pioneers of direct Voluntary Action rather than of action designed to influence parliaments and governments. Many of them, notably Shaftesbury, the Webbs, and Benjamin Waugh, were active in this latter way also. The purpose of this study is to illustrate not so much how changes are brought about in the law and in the actions of the State, as how they are brought about in the field still left for private action.

It is common, of course, to all these men and women that they set out to do things without asking what they would get thereby for themselves. Three other points stand out from this review. One is the significance of the middle class, that is to say, people who have to work for a living but do not as a rule work under direction of another or to fixed hours. A second point is the significance of the religious motive. The third point is the need for material resources to put new ideas into practice; some of the pioneers had fortunes of their own; others had the fortunes of friends at call.

The list of pioneers includes as its most prominent figure one aristocrat (Shaftesbury), but few could be found from his particular stratum to set beside him. The list consists predominantly of people of the middle class, with family traditions, or with a background which made it possible for them to choose their vocations. Among the best-known Victorian philanthropists, the one who next to Shaftesbury began with the greatest economic and social advantages was Quintin Hogg. He was the son of James Hogg who made a fortune as a barrister in India and became a baronet; he went himself to Eton; his family connections gave him the chance of starting early in a business of sugar wholesaling in which he made a fortune of his own; from this fortune he spent largely on his philanthropic purposes.

The manual workers are as sparsely represented in my list of pioneers as are the aristocrats. Even the founder of the Amalgamated Society of Engineers, though he started as an operative and was born the son of an operative, came of stock which had been middle class. This does not mean that dynamic personalities are not to be found everywhere in British society. They can be found if they are given a chance, but in the past they have in fact largely found their chance of social service through not having to work to fixed hours as parts of a great machine in earning their livings. Moreover, most of the pioneers, so far as anything is known of their opinions, were moved by a religious motive or came from a home where religion was a reality.

To-day both the first two conditions: of opportunity for independent earning and of religion as a living force, are less present than they were. It is important in one way or another to ensure in future the continuance of the conditions which led to progress in the past. There must be opportunity for independence; there must be something either to revive the religious motive or to do what it did in the minds and hearts of men. Granted this, the third condition also becomes important; there must be surpluses of money available for social experiment.

There is also at times the intervention of what some will call

happy chance, and others will call Providence, guiding men to
their appointed tasks. Shaftesbury, Maurice, Barnardo, Quintin
Hogg and others in this chapter, all set out to do something other
than what in the end they did. One or two—Robert Hunter and
George Holloway—found the road blazed for them by the typical
Victorian accident of winning prizes in public essay competitions.
The outstanding example of this route to a vocation falls too early
for inclusion in this chapter and is concerned with political change
rather than with Voluntary Action. But it is worth putting on record
again. It is the case of Anti-Slavery Clarkson. Having as an under-
graduate at Cambridge won a junior prize for a Latin essay one year,
Thomas Clarkson incurred a moral obligation to compete in the
following year—1785—for a senior prize. He found set as the subject:
Anne licet invitos in servitutem dare? (Is it permissible to make men slaves
against their will?) The subject was unfamiliar to Clarkson, but he
hurriedly collected his material and gained the prize. By this his
whole life was changed, and innumerable other lives were changed.
With Clarkson the prize essay, and the classics, scored a bull.

The men and women described here are the pioneers of Philanthropy rather than the pioneers of Mutual Aid. One or two of the
newer types of friendly society have individual inventors. Thus
the deposit societies are based on an idea first put into force in his
own parish, by a country clergyman of aristocratic origin—the
Honourable and Reverend Samuel Best. Another group of societies
combining Mutual Aid with personal saving in a somewhat different
way are also the invention of one man, and describe themselves as
Holloway societies to mark this; George Holloway is included
here, though unfortunately not enough is known about him. The
foundation of one of the pioneering trade unions of the nineteenth
century is sufficiently associated with one man—William Newton—
for him to appear in this chapter of biographies.

But Mutual Aid movements generally have more often and more
appropriately been the creation of a group of men, sometimes with
no clearly marked leader, than of one man. This is true above all
of the friendly societies of which Eden wrote in 1796: "These
societies do not owe their origin to parliamentary interference;
nor to private benevolence; nor even to the recommendations of
men of acknowledged abilities or to professed politicians."

Thus the Loyal Order of Ancient Shepherds sprang from "twelve
good men of Ashton" of whom one, Thomas Scholfield, took the
lead chiefly because he was landlord of the Friendship Inn at
which the meeting took place. As such he naturally officiated as

treasurer, and in the centenary volume of the society is pictured as "Founder," with Philip Buckley, of whose occupation nothing is stated, as godfather, because he suggested the name. The Hearts of Oak Benefit Society, also beginning as a meeting of twelve men in an inn, in their centenary volume describe as founder John Hadley, who was appointed the first secretary to the society, but of him no further biographical particulars are given except that after two years he resigned his post in order to undertake a coach builder's business. The honour of founding the Manchester Unity of Oddfellows is sometimes disputed, but the leader seems clearly to have been Robert Naylor, landlord of the "Ropemakers' Arms" in Salford, who gathered there a group of men to follow him into secession.

It is important that the road should always be open for gifted individuals to blaze new trails. It is as important that there should remain the liberty of simple men to associate for action, in new forms for new purposes, free of prohibition either by the State or by associations already established.

SHAFTESBURY (1801–85)

In any study of social reform during the nineteenth century one name almost inevitably comes first, that of Anthony Ashley Cooper, Earl of Shaftesbury, born in 1801 and living to 1885. The list of 200 religious and philanthropic institutions represented by deputations at the memorial service to him, held in Westminster Abbey on October 8, 1885, reads like the contents table of a Report on Nineteenth-century Agencies for Social Service. With all these agencies Shaftesbury was more or less directly connected.[1]

Shaftesbury was an aristocrat of aristocrats, connected in one way or another with many ruling families. He himself was the seventh earl of his line, his mother being daughter of the third Duke of Marlborough. He married a daughter of the fifth Earl Cowper whose mother later married Lord Palmerston as her second husband. Very early in his career he won the friendship and patronage of the Duke of Wellington. During his father's life he held the courtesy title of Lord Ashley. Here he is referred to always as Shaftesbury, though he did not succeed to this title till he was fifty.

[1] The list is printed as an Appendix in Vol. 3 of *The Life and Work of the Seventh Earl of Shaftesbury, K.G.*, by Edwin Hodder (Cassell & Company, 1886). Many quotations here are taken from this work, noted as *op. cit.*

After an unhappy childhood at home, having passed through Harrow and Christ Church, Oxford, he was at the age of twenty-five, when still Lord Ashley, returned to Parliament in 1826 for the pocket borough of Woodstock, and was in Parliament for nearly all the rest of his life either in the House of Commons or, from 1851 onwards, in the House of Lords. He was out of Parliament only for two years from 1846 to 1848.

Shaftesbury was continuously associated with legislative action for the improvement of the conditions of the working classes, most notably with the Factory Acts, but also with many other Acts of Parliament such as those for safety in coal mines, for protection of chimney-sweeping boys and for dealing with lunatics. The latter of these was the subject of his first public speech and he became and remained for fifty-seven years Chairman of the Lunacy Commissioners.

The present study is concerned with Voluntary Action rather than with legislation. Activity through voluntary agencies was for Lord Shaftesbury as important as activity in Parliament and proved a complete alternative for it when for a moment that activity was cut off. In January, 1846, he resigned his seat in Parliament because he had become convinced that opposition to the repeal of the Corn Laws must be abandoned, but felt at the same time that he was pledged to his agricultural supporters in Dorset to maintain the Corn Laws. He thought that Cobden and Bright, who were and remained among the bitterest opponents of his own campaign for factory legislation, had made out their case against the Corn Laws. At the time he felt that, in resigning, he was giving up all hope of usefulness.

> "I shall resign my seat, and throw up all my beloved projects; all for which I have sacrificed everything that a public man values; all that I had begun, and all that I have designed. Nearly my whole means of doing any good will cease with my membership of Parliament." (*op. cit.*, ii, 27.)

Shaftesbury was wrong; he found in fact that temporary release from parliamentary duties became the beginning of new interest in Voluntary Action. He used his leisure to see for himself the conditions of life in the slums of London, and was led by this to throw himself heart and soul into the activities of the newly formed "Society for Improving the Conditions of the Labouring Classes," mainly by improving their housing.

Shaftesbury is interesting to-day even more through his character than for his achievements. He came to social reform not as his first choice but because the times called for it.

"In early life I was passionately devoted to science, so much so, that I was almost disposed to pursue science to the exclusion of everything else. It passed away and I betook myself to literature, hoping that I should not only equal, but that I should rival many in mental accomplishments. Other things were before me, and other things passed away, because, do what I would, I was called to another career, and now I find myself at the end of a long life, not a philosopher, not an author, but simply an old man who has endeavoured to do his duty in that state of life to which it has pleased God to call him."[1]

When he realized that he would shortly have to leave the House of Commons for the House of Lords, in a review of his career and what he had attempted and what he had accomplished, he said that naturally he had always wanted power and patronage but "I have obtained neither; have *never* held any post in which I could act on my own authority; nor ever have I had the disposal of a single place, either ecclesiastical or civil." (*op. cit.* ii, 358).

Shaftesbury was not so much an inventor of movements as a tremendous force for giving impetus to movements started by others, using for that purpose the power which his position as an aristocrat gave him in a world not yet democratic. Thus, the Ten Hours Bill for factories had been introduced by Michael Thomas Sadler in the unreformed Parliament of 1832, but Sadler lost his seat through the abolition of his constituency by the Reform Act. In 1833, at the request of the Rev. G. S. Bull, Shaftesbury, being still in the House of Commons as Lord Ashley, took up the Bill in Sadler's place, commenting in his diary as follows:—

"I have only zeal and good intentions to bring to this work; I can have no merit in it—that must all belong to Mr. Sadler. It seems no one else will undertake it so I will—I believe it is my duty to God and to the poor and I trust He will support me. Talk of trouble! What do we come to Parliament for?" (*op. cit.*, i, 148.)

In regard to the blind, he was approached in 1834 by a Mr. Harman. The result of that interview was the formation of the

[1] *Op. cit.*, i, 89. The particular science interesting Shaftesbury was astronomy in which, under the guidance of Sir James South, he was for a time completely absorbed, thinking "that at last his object in life had been found."

"Indigent Blind Visiting Society" of which Shaftesbury became president for fifty years. (*op. cit.*, i, 273.)

The Ragged Schools are, next to the Factory Acts, the movement with which Shaftesbury is most associated. On them he made the often-quoted remark:—

> "You must keep your Ragged Schools down to one mark . . . in the mire and the gutter; so long as the mire and the gutter exist. So long as this class exists you must keep the schools adapted to their wants, their feelings, their tastes and their level. I feel that my business lies in the gutter and I have not the least intention to get out of it." (*op. cit.*, ii, 410.)

Shaftesbury became the perpetual President of the Ragged School Union, personally presiding over nearly every meeting and "for many years the ragged children of London were rarely out of his thoughts waking or sleeping" (*op. cit.*, ii, 152). Yet Shaftesbury "was not the founder of Ragged Schools nor was he the founder of the Ragged School Union" (*op. cit.*, ii, 146). He first learnt of the ragged school idea in a letter of appeal for help from Field Lane Ragged School appearing in *The Times* of February, 1843, and he welcomed this as the idea for which he had been looking. The actual originators of the Ragged School Union were three unknown simple men, S. R. Starey, W. Locke, and J. G. Gent, meeting in April, 1846. Six months after that meeting Shaftesbury was asked to become their president (*op. cit.*, ii, 146). So with the London City Mission. That had been founded by David Nasmith and two others in 1835.[1] Shaftesbury appears first in its activities in 1845.

It is important to note both how Shaftesbury came by his social conscience and how he came by the material resources which were needed for his work. His social conscience sprang from his religious convictions. He was an Evangelical of the Evangelicals, believing almost in the verbal inspiration of the scriptures. His religious views made him very unhappy about one side of national education in 1870. They made him hostile to one only of the movements for social regeneration in his time, the Salvation Army of William Booth.

Shaftesbury was not himself a rich man as aristocrats went in his time. When as Lord Ashley he stood for Dorset in 1831 he did so on the understanding that the election expenses would be borne

[1] See Dr. John Campbell's *Memoirs of David Nasmith*, Chambers's *Eminent Scotsmen*, and the *D.N.B.* Nasmith was born in 1799 and died in 1839.

by the Anti-Reform Party at whose request he was standing. When the election expenses worked out at £15,600 5s. 7d. and Shaftesbury found himself landed with paying the greater part and threatened with a petition against his return, he told the Anti-Reform Party that he could not afford to oppose the petition; it was for them to do that if they wanted him to keep the seat.[1] For his philanthropic work later he had to draw on friends and "fans" and was able to do so. One lady, Miss Portal, gave him year after year £1,000 to spend as he liked and gave more for any special purpose. In April, 1885, a Mrs. Douglas died and two months later Shaftesbury learned for the first time that she had left him £60,000 for distribution among the charities of London.

Shaftesbury was not an inventor of new movements, but without him few of the movements which he took up could have had their wonderful success. He was not a figure-head, but a worker. He could not see suffering in any form without wanting to end it. He was a man with a social conscience who happened to have been born in the purple. He represents the aristocratic tradition at its best. He would not have done what he did if he had not been religious. He could not have done it without wealthy friends.

SOME FORERUNNERS OF SHAFTESBURY

John Pounds (1766–1839)[2] like Thomas Rhodes Armitage (noticed later) is an instance of a man turning his own misfortunes to means of good for others. Beginning life as a shipwright in Portsmouth dockyard, at the age of twelve, he fell into a dry dock and became a hopeless cripple. He made himself a cobbler, earned his living as such, and at the age of fifty-two turned himself to trying to cure a crippled child, his nephew. From this came a collection of children around him and he started to teach them. He is thus often described as the originator of Ragged Schools, but in actually setting out to teach he seems to have been anticipated by the man named next below.

Thomas Cranfield (1766–1838)[2] was a soldier who suddenly found religion, and having opened a tailor's shop started a Sunday School

---

[1] *Op. cit.*, i, pp. 119–20. The table of expenses, as recorded by Shaftesbury himself to the last penny, presents a striking picture of elections before the Corrupt Practices Acts. Most of the money was spent at nineteen public-houses in Dorchester and its neighbourhood.

[2] See *Harvest*, by Hugh Redwood, a centenary record of the Shaftesbury Society, published by the society in 1944.

for "slum-ridden children who are too ragged to attend Sunday School." It was in fact in 1791 the first Ragged School.

Samuel Robert Starey appears to have been the leader or at least the convener of those who founded the Ragged School Union; it was in his room that they met. The account of him given below is taken from *Ninety—Not Out*, by David Williamson.[1] It will be seen that those named by this authority as Starey's first associates are not identical with those named above from Edwin Hodder's *Life of Shaftesbury*.

Starey, by Williamson's account, came of an old English family and was born in the former palace of the Archbishops of Canterbury in Croydon, where his parents and ancestors had resided for a century. After leaving school he served in a lawyer's office for ten years, and as a young man began to help in the school in Field Lane, to which he had been invited by a devout carpenter. Gradually, his interests widened until he was connected with three other schools—the Colonnade Sunday School, Smith Buildings Ragged School, and Britannia Ragged School in Gray's Inn Road. His father had moved from Croydon to 17, Ampton Street, and it was there, on April 11, 1844, that Samuel Starey met with three like-minded friends—Messrs. Locke, Moulton, and Morrison—and passed a resolution, confirmed in Bloomsbury on April 26th, forming these four schools, with sixteen Sunday Schools, into a union. The advertisement in a London newspaper appealing for sympathy with the new movement attracted the attention of Lord Ashley. He put himself into communication with Messrs. Starey, Locke, Moulton, and Morrison, and was soon heart and soul concerned with their excellent scheme. It is an example of the far-reaching effect of a small advertisement and of the readiness of one man to join others in a benevolent enterprise. Thus was called into being what has grown into the Shaftesbury Society and Ragged School Union. It was Samuel Starey who had the happy inspiration to suggest "Ragged School Union" as the title of the new organization, and Lord Shaftesbury designated him, in consequence, "The God-father of the 'Ragged School.' " Starey's arduous work broke down his frail health, and he left London in 1845 to join his brother in

---

[1] The title of this book, published by Hodder & Stoughton in 1934, refers to the period covered since the foundation of the Ragged School Union. The book gives the date of Starey's death in 1904. It has not proved possible to ascertain when he was born, but since he had been active in ragged school work for some time in 1844, something like 1820 appears the most probable date. This would make him well over eighty at death in spite of his "frail health."

carriage manufacture at Nottingham. Several years later, having retired from business, he returned to the Metropolis and did excellent service as Chairman of the St. Pancras Board Schools.

HENRY DUNCAN (1774–1846)

Henry Duncan was a son of the manse, born in 1774, at Loch-rutton, Kirkcudbright. He was descended on both sides of his family from a clerical ancestry which went back to the time of the Covenanters; both his sons in due course entered the ministry and his only daughter married a minister.[1] He combined education at no fewer than three Scottish universities (St. Andrews, Edinburgh, and Glasgow) with a period of work in a Liverpool bank, where he showed few signs of making a good banker. Having decided to enter the ministry, he received the offer at twenty-five of a choice of parishes, and chose the smaller and poorer one, Ruthwell in Dumfriesshire. "This was but another example of his 'distressing lack of ambition,' for neither then nor later did his own financial position or prospect of advancement influence his decisions in the least."[2] The point of Ruthwell was that even though the stipend would at first be less than £100 a year, Henry Duncan there would have opportunity to experiment, to test his theories, and to write. He was not ambitious for money, but he was far from having no ambition to get things done. He became convinced that the poor must be given opportunities of saving and encouragement to use them, but it was not enough to write this. He must prove his case by example. He established accordingly in May, 1810, the Ruthwell Savings Bank with an elaborate constitution. Another savings bank of a simpler type was established at Edinburgh three years later, and from these two examples the new institution spread rapidly throughout Scotland.

Henry Duncan proved himself a dynamic creature and a doughty controversialist. He disposed of the claims made by his Edinburgh rivals to be the real authors of savings banks. He secured almost by his own unaided exertions the passage of a Bill in 1819 under which savings banks were established in Scotland and no longer needed to be registered as friendly societies. He regarded indepen-

---

[1] These clerical particulars are taken from the biography of *Dr. Duncan of Ruthwell*, by his great-granddaughter, Sophy Hall (Oliphant, Anderson, and Ferrier, 1910). Most of the other items in this account come from Mr. Oliver Horne's *History of Savings Banks*, noticed in Chapter III.

[2] Horne, *op. cit.*, p. 41.

dence of character as God's greatest gift to men, and thought that every new scheme must be judged by whether it contributed to the making of independent men and women.

ELIZABETH FRY (1780–1845)[1]

Elizabeth Fry was born at Earlham Hall, near Norwich, the fourth out of twelve children of John Gurney, wool stapler and banker, and of Catherine Bell who, like John Gurney, belonged to a well-established and highly considered Quaker family. Though Quakers, the Gurneys were not "plain Quakers." They attended Meeting, but they did not wear the distinctive dress or abjure plays, dancing, or music. As the result of religious influence, in particular the visit of an American preacher, William Savery, Elizabeth decided at seventeen to become "a plain Quaker." She had not till then been studious and she never managed to spell very well; when already world-famous she expressed alarm at the prospect of meeting Harriet Martineau as one who was "realy clever." But lack of spelling appeared to young Elizabeth no reason why she should not start a school; at eighteen she began teaching village children round her home. At twenty she married Joseph Fry, a member of one of the richest Quaker families, also a banker, and from 1801–22 had eleven children, the last of whom was born on the same day as her first grandchild, born to her second daughter.

In her thirty-third year Elizabeth Fry visited Newgate prison for the first time and found it as it was then currently described, a "hell upon earth." Four years later she returned to start visiting it in earnest. She was enabled to do so by the fact that through financial difficulties she had found it necessary to send four of her older children away to stay with uncles and aunts. This gave her unexpected leisure. By a combination of diplomacy and obstinacy she persuaded the prison authorities to let her start a school for the children in the prison, making one of the women prisoners the teacher. She went on to find employment for the women themselves in knitting and other work, and by this brought about an almost instant revolution in their way of life; in three months "already from being wild beasts they appear harmless and kind." Within a year the Grand Jury of the City of London officially appreciated

---

[1] This account is based largely on *Elizabeth Fry, Quaker Heroine*, by Janet Whitney (George G. Harrap, 1937), with some references to the *Memoirs of Elizabeth Fry*, edited by two of her daughters (John Hatchard, revised edition, 2 volumes, 1846).

the important service rendered by Mrs. Fry and her friends "and the habits of religion, order, industry, and cleanliness which her humane, benevolent and praiseworthy efforts have introduced among the female prisoners." They added that if the principle governing her regulations were adopted towards the males as well it would be the means of converting the prison into a school of reform. Thereafter Elizabeth Fry became established as one of the powers in the land, dining with royalty (often to the scandal of her Quaker meeting), being summoned to give evidence before a House of Commons Committee—"the first woman other than a queen to be called into the councils of the Government in an official manner to advise on matters of public concern."[1] "The American Ambassador wrote home to say that he had now seen the two greatest sights of London—St. Paul's Cathedral and Mrs. Fry reading to the prisoners in Newgate."[2]

At sixty she launched a new venture, for training nurses, a thing she had in mind from time to time for thirteen years. Hers "was the first attempt in England to train and standardize nurses and nursing on a professional basis." Florence Nightingale took some of the "Fry Nurses" with her in the first band that went to the Crimea.[3]

Like Shaftesbury, Elizabeth Fry started with an established social position and had kinsmen in governing circles. Her husband could and did ask the Governor of Newgate to dinner in order to get assent to her experiments.

Elizabeth Fry's life illustrates the oddly interfering nature of the Quaker congregation. They thought she was not strict enough; even in her time of greatness she was "eldered" by them for variation from the narrow line. Her husband, on the other hand—who loved music—thought her too strict, since he had to visit concerts almost by stealth.

Elizabeth Fry's philanthropic service was combined with family responsibilities far exceeding those undertaken by most women. Her bringing up of eleven children depended, of course, upon her having sufficient service to help her, but her memoirs show how much anxiety went to the management of this family. In the months when she was beginning her serious work in Newgate she was also nursing one of her children.

Elizabeth Fry illustrates nearly all the points made in regard to philanthropic pioneers in this volume.

(1) Her philanthropic action sprang from religious influence. "I can say one thing—since my heart was touched, at the age of

---

[1] Whitney, *op. cit.*, p. 215.   [2] *Ibid.*, p. 235.   [3] *Ibid.*, pp. 297–8.

seventeen, I believe I never have wakened from sleep, in sickness or in health, by day or by night, without my first waking thought being how best I might serve my Lord."[1]

(2) By Voluntary Action she broke in on official routine which was cruel because it was dull. The evils of Newgate were not deliberate and they were unnecessary, but it needed a philanthropist from outside to show this.

(3) She brought about her reforms, not by giving money, but by giving the prisoners something useful to do. In answer to a question she declared her belief that no reformation could be accomplished without employment. "We may instruct as we will but if we allow them their time and they have nothing to do, they naturally must return to their evil practices."[2] Reform by education without employment and hope would have been idle in Newgate, as it is being idle in Germany to-day.

(4) The bringing about of reforms called for untiring personal service. One of the worst moments in the lives of the prisoners was when they were on the point of being transported to Australia. The night before habitually became pandemonium. Elizabeth Fry got permission to spend the day before with some of the women prisoners known to her who were due for transport, and she made arrangements for their humaner treatment on board. Thereafter for twenty-five years she "visited and organized every convict ship that carried women prisoners to the colonies until her final illness in 1843. A total of 106 ships and 12,000 convicts came under her hands."[3]

(5) Elizabeth Fry, like Shaftesbury, is an example of turning adversity to advantage. Just as his direct study of London slums was occasioned by loss of his seat in Parliament, so her time for taking Newgate in earnest came through financial difficulties and parting for a while with her elder children.

ANDREW REED (1787–1862)[4]

Andrew Reed was born in St. Clement Danes, London, the fourth son of a watchmaker and of a mother who before and for some time after her marriage taught in a dames' school, but sub-

---

[1] *Memoirs*, vol. 1, vii.   [2] Whitney, *op. cit.*, p. 219.
[3] Rev. Timson, *Memoirs of Elizabeth Fry*, p. 138, quoted by Whitney, *op. cit.*, p. 223.
[4] This account is based almost wholly on a pamphlet on the Royal Hospital and Homes for Incurables written by L. French and published in 1936.

sequently exchanged her school for a very successful china shop in Clerkenwell. Young Andrew was brought up in a home atmosphere of deep piety, his father when not engaged in his trade acting as lay evangelist and itinerant preacher, his mother devoted to visiting the sick. Apprenticed at the age of fifteen to his father's trade of watchmaking, Andrew found this uncongenial and decided to enter the Congregational ministry. After studying at Hackney College for four years, he was at the age of twenty-four ordained a pastor of New Road Congregational Chapel in the East End of London, and held that charge for fifty years till within a year of his death. He was a highly successful pastor, but his main activity was in the founding of a succession of public institutions to which he gave both his time and his money. Within a few years of beginning his pastorate his salary was doubled. He recorded at the time three resolutions: not to lay by a shilling of his salary, to live as economically as was suitable to his state and character, to devote any surplus to objects of benevolence.

The institutions founded by him included the East London Orphan Asylum in 1813, now become the Watford and Royal British Orphan School with an income of over £24,000 a year; the Infant Orphan Asylum, with foundation-stone laid by the Prince Consort in 1841; the Asylum for Fatherless Children in 1843, now become the Royal Infant Orphanage at Wanstead with an annual income of £20,000; the Asylum for Fatherless Children in 1843, now become the Reedham Orphanage housing 300 children with an annual income of £19,000; the Asylum for Idiots in 1855, now become the Royal Earlswood Institution for Mental Defectives; and in the same year, 1855, an Incurables' Hospital which has now become the Royal Hospital and Home for Incurables at Putney.

Reed was occasionally a difficult colleague; he had a powerful mind wanting always its own way and moving more rapidly than the minds of others. The history of the Incurables' Hospital was marked by crises of disagreement on policy. But in the end every one of the great charities founded by him is recorded as a triumphant success.

FREDERICK DENISON MAURICE (1805–72)[1]

Frederick Denison Maurice was born at Normanston near Lowestoft, the fourth of eight children of a Unitarian Minister, and, through his mother, grandson of a Yarmouth merchant.

[1] The brief notice of Maurice given here is taken from the *D.N.B.*

Revolting against Unitarianism he went to Cambridge with a view to becoming a barrister, but decided to take orders in the Church of England, went to Oxford for the purpose, and at twenty-five was baptized. Among his religious activities and controversies he interspersed at forty-three the founding of Queen's College for Women, and at forty-nine, of the Working Men's College (partly based on a "People's College" started in Sheffield in 1842), of which he became first Principal. Deeply impressed by the economic consequences and human degradation of unemployment, sweating wages and the struggle between man and man for jobs, Maurice about 1851 had organized a "Society for Promoting Working Men's Association," a combination of co-operation and trade unionism. But very soon he came to the conclusion that it was of little value to have an "association" if the people in the association did not understand what it was all about. This led him to starting some evening classes, and very rapidly to the Working Men's College. Maurice was, in Kingsley's judgment, "the most beautiful soul he had known." He suffered from severe illnesses, partly due to overwork, but behaved like a man in strong health. He was absolutely unworldly, shrinking from preferment when it was within reach, as in previous days he had frankly uttered the convictions which then made preferment possible.

HENRY SOLLY (1813–1903)

Henry Solly, a leading figure in the history of working men's clubs, closely concerned also with the beginnings of the Charity Organisation Society and a prophet of "industrial villages" or garden cities, was born in the City of London in 1813. He was the son of a merchant in the Baltic timber trade and was descended from Daniel Neal who wrote the History of the Puritans. Solly, after leaving school, entered the newly opened University of London in 1829, and remained there for several years planning a literary and scholastic career, but, his father wishing him to follow in his own trade, he was taken away from the university and put into an office in the City. To this career it seems he bent himself dutifully but showed little aptitude; he varied it in his spare time by literary pursuits and such pastimes as debating societies.

After some years in City offices he became the assistant to a shady and intemperate chemist who was desirous of inventing marketable substances and taking out patents for them. In this pursuit it appears that Solly narrowly missed stumbling upon the discovery of what is now known as Reckitt's Blue, but he lacked the knowledge to perfect it. His affairs were complicated at this time by the collapse of his father's business. Solly thereafter took various posts as a clerk in branches of the London and County Bank. This rather aimless and unsettled period appears to have been terminated about 1840 when he entered the Congregational ministry. His first pulpit was in Yeovil where he, having recently married, lived on the modest stipend of £65 a year. It was followed by Shepton Mallet, Cheltenham (where in 1850 he founded the first working man's club with which he was concerned), Carter Lane in London (1851), and Lancaster.

In all these places Solly was brought for the first time into direct and dramatic contact with the condition of life of the working class. As a consequence he became much concerned with possible means of alleviating their lot. He became actively sympathetic to Chartism and an ardent temperance reformer and educationist. He took some part in the movement initiated by Frederick Denison Maurice for the formation of working men's colleges. At the same time, however, he felt that in his own words "Their long hours of work, want of early education, miserably limited dwelling-space, and incessant ubiquitous temptations of public-house and beer-shop, all combine to make something other than education and temperance appliances necessary."[1] Thus began his connection with the movement for which he is best known, the working men's clubs.

At an inaugural meeting under the chairmanship of Lord Brougham in 1862 the Working Men's Club and Institute Union was set up. Solly became its first secretary and thereupon gave up his Congregational ministry and took up his home in London. He resigned the secretaryship, however, in 1867, owing to various differences between himself and the Board.

Whilst still being active in the working men's club world, he then turned his attention also to doing, for the large and disorganized stratum which lay below the working class, something of the healing which the clubs had done for the latter. This idea led him in 1868 to propose what others had already independently thought of, the formation of a "Society for the Prevention of Pauperism and Crime." Of this society, which became the Charity Organisation Society, Solly was the first honorary secretary, but held this post only for a few months. His departure may have been occasioned by disagreements with colleagues, but was in the main due to his interest in movements of a different kind. In words quoted by Mrs.

[1] *These Eighty Years*, ii, p. 161. This is an autobiographical work published by Solly in 1893.

Bosanquet, "his supreme devotion was given to movements like the Working Men's Club and Institute Union, which seemed to him to aim more directly at the realization of his dream of social regeneration by the fellowship of class with class."[1] He stayed, however, with the Charity Organisation Society long enough to defeat a determined, and all but successful, effort to turn it into a "Back to the Land" Society.

In 1873 Solly's interest in the betterment of the working class led him to the formation of a "Trade Guild of Learning," apparently the germ of adult educational classes of a vocational cast. From this, however, he once again quickly resigned: he followed this scheme with that of an Artisan's Institute. This had its headquarters in Castle Street, Upper St. Martin's Lane, and combined a liberal and a technical education—Solly himself providing much of the former. It preceded the foundation of the City and Guilds Institute, and Solly claims that it helped to form a pattern for the latter.

In 1884 he read a paper on "Industrial Villages" as a remedy for overcrowding in towns, for rural desolation, and for the prevalent destitution and poverty. The suggestion was essentially one for the setting up of new village communities, containing their own industries and means of livelihood, and also their own social centres. In this, he appears to have preceded Ebenezer Howard. But although, in 1884, a Society for the Promotion of Industrial Villages was formed, it had unhappily soon to be wound up, owing partly, Solly says, to its having secured for secretary a man who was not only intemperate but a forger!

Solly, who was father-in-law of Philip H. Wicksteed, died in 1903. Passages in his autobiography, and in contemporary tributes, suggest not only that he possessed rather more zeal than prudence, but that, though a charming man, he had a certain vein of autocracy which made him difficult to work with. Perhaps this is why, though he started so many good things he left no institution to carry on his memory. He has no mention in the *D.N.B.* and *The Times* obituary notice when he died at ninety was very meagre. Fortunately he left an autobiography, already cited, and a second edition of his book on *Working Men's Clubs*, published in 1904 after his death, contains some notices of him. He was a restless, inventive, constructive spirit, part author of at least three large living movements: charity organization, working men's clubs, and garden cities.

[1] *Op. cit.*, p. 347.

GEORGE WILLIAMS (1821–1905)

George Williams was born near Dulverton in Somerset, the youngest of eight sons of a Devonshire farmer. Brought up in the Established Church he left it for Congregationalism at sixteen. He came to London at nineteen to work in drapery and in due course married the daughter of his employer (George Hitchcock). On June 6, 1844, when George Williams was twenty-three, twelve men, all but one being employees of Hitchcock, met in Williams' bedroom and established a society to which at their second meeting they gave the name of the Young Men's Christian Association. The aim of the society was definitely religious, "the winning of young men for Christ." It was as definitely undenominational or inter-denominational; "of the first twelve members, three were Anglicans, three Congregationalists, three Baptists, and three Methodists." Beginning with this religious aim the movement was led step by step to provide for the educational, social and physical needs of young men and boys, as well as for their spiritual needs. It achieved phenomenal growth not only in Britain but elsewhere. Its founder was knighted on the occasion of its Jubilee in 1894 when 2,000 delegates attended from all parts of the world.

George Williams, coming to London without interest or capital, amassed a fortune. But evangelical religion remained his dominant interest. According to his biographer, "all who came to him, on whatever errand, were spoken to of their soul's salvation."[1] In his business room hung a framed card illuminated with the words "God First."

WILLIAM NEWTON (1822–76)

William Newton is described by the Webbs as the most prominent personality in the movement which led in 1851 to the setting up of the Amalgamated Society of Engineers. His biography is given as follows:—

William Newton was born at Congleton in 1822, his father, who had once occupied a superior position, being then a journeyman machinist. The boy went to work in engine shops at the age of fourteen, joined the Hanley Branch of the Journeymen Steam-Engine Makers' Society in 1842, soon afterwards moving to London (where he worked in the same shop as Henry James, afterwards Lord James of Hereford,

[1] *The Life of Sir George Williams*, by J. E. Hodder Williams, p. 247 (Hodder & Stoughton, 1906).

then an engineer pupil, and later noted for his knowledge of trade unionism), and rose to be foreman. After his dismissal in 1848 for his trade-union activity he took a public-house at Ratcliffe, and devoted himself largely to the promotion of the amalgamation of the engineering societies. In 1852 he became, for a short period, secretary to a small insurance company. At the General Election of 1852 he became a candidate for the Tower Hamlets. He was opposed by both the great political parties, but the show of hands at the hustings was in his favour. At the poll he was unsuccessful, receiving, however, 1,095 votes. In 1860 he was presented with a testimonial (including a sum of £300) from his A.S.E. fellow-members. In later years he became the proprietor of a prosperous local newspaper and was elected by Stepney Vestry as its chairman and also as its representative on the Metropolitan Board of Works. He became one of the leading members of that body, on which he served from 1862 to 1876, filling the important office of deputy chairman to the Parliamentary, Fire Brigade, and other influential Committees. In 1868 he again contested the Tower Hamlets against both Liberals and Conservatives, receiving 2,890 votes; and in 1875 he unsuccessfully fought a by-election at Ipswich. He died March 9, 1876, when his funeral, in which the Metropolitan Board of Works took part, assumed a public character.[1]

It will be noted that though William Newton's father at the time of his birth was a machinist he had come to that "from a superior position." And though Newton himself began life as an operative, he became a foreman in his early twenties and later branched out into middle-class activities. He never apparently at any time held a full-time salaried post as a trade union official. His achievement depended on his gifts and his sacrifices.

> Gifted with remarkable eloquence, astute and conciliatory in his methods, he was equally successful in inspiring masses of men with a large idea and in persuading the representatives and officials of rival societies to agree with the details of his scheme. His influence was augmented by his tried devotion to the cause of trade unionism. In 1848 he was dismissed from a first-rate position as foreman in a large establishment owing to his activity in trade matters and in the following years his business as a publican was seriously damaged by his constant absence on society business.[2]

[1] Webb, *History of Trade Unionism*, pp. 206–7.   [2] Webb, *op. cit.*, p. 207.

THOMAS RHODES ARMITAGE (1824–90)

Thomas Rhodes Armitage was born in 1824 in Sussex, the sixth of seven brothers. It has not been possible to obtain particulars of his parents but they were clearly people of means and of cosmopolitan interests. Thomas' childhood was spent largely in France or Germany, and at eleven he spoke German as fluently as English; part of his later education was at the Sorbonne. At sixteen he became a medical student in London, qualified as surgeon, served in the Crimea and returned to medical practice. But at thirty-six his sight, which had given trouble before, failed completely. He was, however, a man of deep religious faith and soon saw one direction in which his practical experience as a doctor, his private fortune, and even his blindness could be turned to good account. "I cannot conceive," he wrote, "any occupation so congenial to a blind man of education and leisure as the attempt to advance the education and improve the condition of his fellow-sufferers."

Accompanying one of the missioners of the Indigent Blind Visiting Society which had been founded by Shaftesbury, Armitage came quickly to two conclusions: that what the blind needed above all was education, and that the people best fitted to decide what system of reading and writing was most likely to suit the needs of the blind were the blind themselves. He formed in 1868 the British and Foreign Blind Association for Promoting the Education of the Blind, each member of whose executive committee must be a man obliged on account of defective sight to read by touch, with a knowledge of at least three systems of embossed type and having no financial interest in any. This Committee—Armitage, who had been a doctor, W. Fenn, who had been an artist, James Gale and Daniel Conolly—spent two years examining thoroughly all the alternative methods of making books for the blind, before they came down unanimously in favour of Braille as best for the intelligent blind of all ages, though for the illiterate and those with work-toughened fingers Armitage always favoured Moon.[1]

The introduction of Braille was the first contribution of Armitage and his association to the welfare of the blind. But it was the first contribution only. The "Blind World was Dr. Armitage's parish"; the association became in due course the National Institute for the Blind, carried on by him and after his death in 1890 by his wife till

---

[1] Braille and Moon are the only methods in substantial use to-day. But the committee of 1868 had to examine at least half a dozen other methods, at that time as strongly or more strongly supported.

her death in 1901. His personal activities included a visit to Dresden to study methods of providing employment for the blind, and he became a strong advocate of the "Saxon system" which he saw there.

Armitage is an outstanding example of turning his own handicap to the means of overcoming it for others. In doing this he was in a fine tradition, for the earliest of all known British institutions for the blind, the School for the Indigent Blind established in 1791 at Liverpool, was itself the creation of a blind man—Edward Rushton.

Armitage, blind for thirty years, hunted all his life, seeing or not seeing, and died at sixty-six as the result of a hunting accident.[1]

GEORGE HOLLOWAY (1825–92)

George Holloway was born at Stratfield Turgess in Hampshire. His father was engaged in agriculture and may have been an agricultural labourer; of his mother, only her name—Fanny Cane—is known. He came very young and in very modest circumstances to Stroud, but had a grammar school education, and at twenty-four, with his brother, founded a ready-to-wear clothing firm, which claimed to be the "first to introduce power sewing-machines into England." Business success led to his becoming a prominent local citizen, and from 1886 to 1892 Conservative Member of Parliament for Stroud. He was always trying new ideas—a profit-sharing scheme for the labourers on his farm, a housing society which had no practical success, and the highly successful new model of friendly societies associated with his name and described in Chapter I. The winning of a prize in a competition called attention to this model, but success came through its intrinsic merits. Critics of the Holloway system point out that it was only a second prize that he won. The motto of the Stroud Society which he founded was: "God helps those who help themselves."

WILLIAM BOOTH (1829–1912)

William Booth was the son of a speculative builder in Nottingham and a Jewish mother. The father sometimes had money; he described himself as "gentleman" in registering his son's birth and prepared

[1] There appears to be no biography of T. R. Armitage. The account given here is based on an article prepared in the National Institute for the Blind, with one or two particulars added from the Institute's *Annual Report* for 1946.

the son to be a gentleman after him. But the money was lost, and through family poverty William at thirteen was apprenticed to a pawnbroker. He seems to have imbibed no religion from his parents, but at fifteen became "converted" and in his own phrase decided to "go in for God." At twenty he came to London, still working as a pawnbroker's assistant but preaching in his spare time; at twenty-three he became a whole-time preacher of the Methodist New Connection, but broke with this and at thirty-six began an independent Christian Mission in Whitechapel, living from collections, sale of pamphlets and songs and the help of a few prosperous sympathizers. After thirteen years, the name of this was changed, almost accidentally, to "Salvation Army."[1] The new name worked like an electric stimulant of growth.

William Booth was as far as possible from being an intellectual; he was ignorant of theology and is described as entertaining "an almost savage prejudice against science and philosophy." His motive power was a religious feeling as simple as Shaftesbury's though different in its manifestations. His aim was and remained primarily religious rather than philanthropic. He often said that "you cannot make a man clean by washing his shirt," and the social work of the Salvation Army was for him chiefly an excuse for getting at the souls of men. But it was not easy to spend one's life in the East End of London without feeling the need for improving social conditions and there was one characteristic of William Booth which made this interest inevitable. He was of very delicate constitution and of almost exceptional sensitiveness to squalor in his surroundings. It was this "which made him so effective in unveiling the dark places of civilization. He saw sharply what others scarcely saw at all, and he felt as an outrage what others considered to be natural." (*D.N.B.*)

OCTAVIA HILL (1838–1912)

Octavia Hill was the youngest daughter of James Hill, corn-merchant and banker of Wisbech (noted for municipal and educational reform) and through her mother was grand-daughter of

[1] William Booth, walking about his room, was discussing plans for the mission with his son Bramwell (then twenty-one) and an assistant who from a proposed article read out the phrase "We are a Volunteer Army." Young Bramwell exclaimed, "Volunteer! Here, I'm not a volunteer. I'm a regular or nothing." William Booth stopped walking, looked at his son for a moment, took the pen from the assistant's hand, scratched out "Volunteer" and wrote in its place "Salvation." This is the story as told in the *Life of William Booth*, by Harold Begbie, vol. 1, p. 439.

Dr. Thomas Southwood Smith (authority on fever and sanitation). After her father's death, she lived with her mother and three sisters in Marylebone, all five supporting themselves by keeping a girls' school, and at the same time doing various forms of social service. Octavia Hill to-day is most individually associated with the improvement of housing management by a new type of rent collector; she was enabled to make her first practical experiment in this in 1865 by financial help from Ruskin; more than thirty years after, looking back she said: "There has never been a time when the extension of our work has been delayed by want of money." She was also associated from their beginnings with several other new forms of Voluntary Action, in particular the Charity Organisation Society, whose first local committee was formed in Marylebone in 1869,[1] the Commons Preservation Society founded in 1865, and the National Trust for the Preservation of Places of Historic Interest or Natural Beauty founded in 1894 (see Sir Robert Hunter below).

EMMA CONS (1838–1912)

Emma Cons was born in London, the daughter of Frederick Cons, whose father had emigrated from the Rhineland to England, and of Esther Goodair, daughter of a mill owner and cotton spinner in Stockport, who was one of the first manufacturers to instal machinery in place of hand labour. Emma was one of seven children and made her start in life as an illuminator of books and manuscripts, and then took up watch engraving, learning in six months what it usually took seven years for a man to learn. She was driven out of this work by the opposition of men already in the trade, and took to painting on glass. While making art her profession, she devoted herself to a succession of public causes: housing (with Octavia Hill), hostels for girls, the Horticultural College at Swanley, the establishment of coffee taverns. She threw herself naturally into the agitation for women's suffrage, and was one of the three women members of the first London County Council, which led to a prolonged dispute as to the right of women to sit there. But her main task was the establishment of the Old Vic as a place of entertainment, where the best could be brought within reach of the poorest person.

---

[1] The parts played by Octavia Hill and others in 1869 are described by Dame Henrietta Barnett in her *Life of Canon Barnett*, vol. 1, pp. 27–9. The future Canon Barnett was then curate at St. Mary's, Bryanston Square, the parish in which the Hills lived, and his future wife, Henrietta Rowland, as a girl of eighteen, was enrolled to work under Octavia Hill.

Very often in its early days the Old Vic was in danger of coming to an end through lack of finance, but always by one way or another it was rescued.

BENJAMIN WAUGH (1839–1908)

Benjamin Waugh was born at Seattle, a small town in Yorkshire, the son of a saddler of Scottish descent and of a mother of Yorkshire yeoman stock. His mother died when he was eight and his father married again; a son by this second marriage became a successful lawyer and K.C. Benjamin at fourteen was apprenticed to a draper in Southport, but after serving his time felt a call to religion; became a theological student at twenty-three, was ordained as Independent Minister at twenty-six and became pastor at Newbury, in the same year marrying the daughter of his Southport master. At Newbury he showed his interest in the treatment of children by a speech of protest to the Newbury justices against imprisonment of boys for stealing, and on transfer to a pastorate at Greenwich was in 1870 elected with T. H. Huxley a member of the first London School Board. He published at thirty-four in 1873 an attack on the criminal laws affecting children, *The Gaol Cradle: Who Rocks It*, and in the year after became editor of the *Sunday School Magazine*, giving up the ministry finally and completely at forty-six. He was not the originator of the idea of a Society for Prevention of Cruelty to Children, but when such a society was being formed in London he became its driving force, first in an honorary capacity, later when his own financial circumstances worsened, as its salaried managing director. He above all was responsible for making the society national in scope and is regarded as its founder.[1]

He was a combative creature, often on the "Waugh-path" as the tired civil servants whom he harried used to say. He was a man

[1] The first society for the prevention of cruelty to children was established in the United States, in Philadelphia. Thence it spread to New York, where in 1881 a Liverpool business man, Mr. T. F. A. Agnew, saw a sign with its name, made enquiries, and came home determined to copy it in his native town. In the same part of England others, in particular a Cheshire Vicar, Rev. George Staite, had independently been urging the same proposal. A Liverpool society was duly formed. There followed a move in London, and at a meeting convened by the Lord Mayor at the Mansion House on July 8th, with eighty-three-year-old Lord Shaftesbury moving the main resolution, and with an immensely distin-guished platform of supporters, a London society was formed, under the driving power of Benjamin Waugh, to become five years later the present National Society for the Prevention of Cruelty to Children.

M

of ferociously independent mind; when once approached by Canon
Barnett as to a project of Church reform uniting the various Christian
communities in Britain he answered that there was little in the
doctrine of the Established Church that caused him difficulty:
"I am a dissenter chiefly because a minister's legitimate liberty is
above all things precious to me."

CHARLES BOOTH (1840–1916)

Charles Booth was born at Liverpool, the fourth of five children
of Charles Booth, a corn merchant, and Emily Fletcher, both parents
coming from well-established business and professional families,
and both being strong Unitarians. Charles the younger, according
to the memoir written of him by his wife, "was not considered one
of the clever ones," did only respectably at school, and in early
manhood was often in poor health; throughout life he had to limit
himself to a diet of trying abstemiousness. At twenty-two he became
partner in a firm of shipowners and at twenty-six he and a brother
invested practically the whole of their capital in the purchase of
two ships, which grew into the Booth Steamship Company, of which
in due course Charles was the Chairman. But his attention was
caught by the problem of poverty and from the age of forty onwards he devoted much of his time and his money to research
into social conditions, producing over a period of sixteen years—
1887–1903—a study of London life and labour in eighteen volumes
This was the first of the large-scale social surveys based on scientific
collection of facts rather than on impressions and had great influence
on public opinion; the idea of using the School Board Attendance
Officers as means of studying the condition of the people, came to
him through his wife's cousin, Beatrice Potter (later Mrs. Sidney
Webb), from Joseph Chamberlain. The latter had been struck by
the immense amount of information as to the lives of the people
which must be possessed by these School Board visitors, and observed
that anyone who could tap this source of knowledge could reap a
rich reward.

One specific reform to which Charles Booth was led by his re
searches was the provision of old age pensions, which he advocated
first in a paper read to the Royal Statistical Society in 1891. This
paper met a very hostile reception among the statisticians, and
Booth followed it by other books which eventually made his case
But he never claimed to be the first advocate of old age pensions
This credit he gave to Mr. R. P. Hookham, of Islip, of whose work

in 1879 Charles Booth had been unaware when he read his paper in 1891, but to whom he dedicated his book on the subject in its revised form of 1899.

SAMUEL AUGUSTUS BARNETT[1] (1844–1913) and HENRIETTA BARNETT (1851–1936)

Samuel Augustus Barnett was born at Bristol, the son of a manufacturer on a large scale of iron bedsteads, and through his mother grandson of a shipowner with many vessels. He was sent to Oxford and after taking a respectable degree there, taught for two years in Oxford and at Winchester, visited America and returned to be ordained as deacon when nearly twenty-four. How he came to choose a clerical career is unknown: he was not particularly religious at Oxford. The critical decision of his life was acceptance, when nearly twenty-nine, of the post of Vicar of St. Jude's, Whitechapel, which was described by the Bishop of London in making the offer as "the worst parish in my diocese, inhabited mainly by a criminal population, and one which has I fear been much corrupted by doles." This decision was evidence both of his courage and of that of twenty-one year-old Henrietta Rowland, to whom he had just become engaged to be married.

Samuel Barnett's Oxford connection brought him from Whitechapel often to Oxford, and led to his inviting young men to visit him in Whitechapel and so to the invention of Toynbee Hall—not a mission but "a club-house in Whitechapel occupied by men who do citizen's duty in the neighbourhood" while pursuing their own occupations. Dame Henrietta Barnett has described how this idea was first formulated by her husband in 1883, while seated on the railway bank during a train breakdown on a journey from London to Oxford, in response to a letter from a Cambridge don telling him that some men at St. John's College, Cambridge, wished to do something for the poor, but were not quite prepared to start an ordinary college mission.[2] The letter to St. John's, Cambridge, was expanded to a paper read at a College meeting held in St. John's, Oxford, in November of the same year. There had been individual settlers before Toynbee Hall. Dame Henrietta names Edward Dennison as the first in 1869 followed by Edmund Hollond;

---

[1] This account is based mainly on *Canon Barnett: His Life, Work, and Friends*, by His Wife (2 vols., John Murray, 1918), and on *Towards Social Reform*, by Canon and Mrs. Barnett (T. Fisher Unwin, 1909). The first of these is cited below as *Life*.   [2] *Towards Social Reform*, pp. 239–54.

and one of the ideas underlying Toynbee Hall was that after making their contacts and discovering their special interests men might hive off in twos or threes into houses of their own. But the settlement was an indispensable bridgehead for this movement. The decision of the Barnetts to undertake the wardenship, when after ten strenuous years in Whitechapel possibilities of a life with more amenities elsewhere were opening was not reached easily, and was another test of courage. The settlement was named for Arnold Toynbee, after his death.

Henrietta Barnett was both the indispensable colleague of her husband in all his work, and an independent driving force. Born in May 1851, she was the daughter of Alexander Rowland who made a considerable fortune in business ("Rowland's Macassar Oil") and was brought up in comfort and to country pursuits. She came, however, to do social work in Marylebone with Octavia Hill; there she met Samuel Barnett, then one of the curates at St. Mary's, Bryanston Square, and after some hesitation accepted his written proposal of marriage. Thus his fine mind and sensitive nature were joined to her limitless energy and assertive personality. In the many new things which the two of them created, he was relatively more prominent in regard to Toynbee Hall, she in regard to the State Children's Association (founded in 1896 to work for improvement of conditions for children in workhouses), and the Garden Suburb at Hampstead. Each of them was active in starting the Children's Country Holiday Fund in 1878, and the Whitechapel Art Gallery, established in 1898 (with subscriptions from Passmore Edwards and others) after temporary exhibitions in their own house, since 1891, had proved attractive.[1]

Samuel and Henrietta Barnett were different in many ways but alike in two essentials—of inventiveness and of fearlessness. The text which adorned their hearth in Whitechapel was a clue to both their characters: "Fear not to sow because of the birds."

ROBERT HUNTER (1844–1913)

Robert Hunter was the only son of Robert Lachlan Hunter educated privately and at the University of London. He was admit

[1] For the beginnings of the Children's Country Holidays Fund see *Life*, i, 177 *et seq.*, and for the art exhibitions see *Life*, ii, chapters xl and xli. Dam Henrietta states that the first exhibition "arose out of the suggestion of Mr Stockham, an old soldier, who lived with and drilled the boys in the Shoeblacks Home." (*Life*, ii, 151.)

ted as a solicitor at twenty-three and in the same year won a prize offered in a competition for essays on methods of preventing enclosure of metropolitan commons. This led to his becoming a partner in the firm of Fawcett, Horne, & Hunter, who had become solicitors to the Commons Preservation Society, founded in 1865. At thirty-eight Robert Hunter was appointed by Henry Fawcett, then Post-master-General, to be Solicitor to the General Post Office and he remained there till within a few months of his death at sixty-nine. While working in the Post Office he continued his interest in preser-vation of amenities and in 1894 was associated with Octavia Hill and Canon Rawnsley in founding the National Trust for Preserva-tion of Places of Historic Interest or Natural Beauty, incorporated in 1907 under the National Trust Act.

DR. BARNARDO (1845–1905)

Thomas John Barnardo came of a Spanish Protestant family which in the eighteenth century settled in Germany to escape religious persecution. His father, born in Hamburg, settled in Dublin as a wholesale furrier and became a British subject. His mother was of Quaker family. He began work at ten as clerk in a wine merchant's office, but experienced religious conversion at sixteen, and at twenty came to London and qualified as a doctor with a view to going to China as a medical missionary. While in London he became a ragged school superintendent, saw the slums, and at twenty-two founded in 1867 an "East End Juvenile Mission for Care of Friendless and Destitute Children." In 1870 he estab-lished a boys' home at Stepney Causeway, the germ of "Dr. Barnardo's Homes" now spread throughout the country with an income, entirely from voluntary sources, of £196,287 in 1905, and more than £1,000,000 in 1946.

QUINTIN HOGG (1845–1903)

Quintin Hogg was born in Grosvenor Street, London, the four-teenth son of James Hogg (who made a fortune in India as a barrister and returned to England to become M.P. and a baronet) and of a mother from a propertied family in Durham. From Eton he went direct into the City for commerce, first working for a firm of tea-brokers, then joining a brother-in-law in sugar wholesaling. He began almost at once to interest himself in ragged schools, hiring with Arthur Kinnaird (later Lord Kinnaird) a room in "Of Alley" near Charing Cross, from which in due course the Polytechnic sprang. On the Polytechnic later, before charitable trust and public money became available, Quintin Hogg from his own fortune made in commerce spent £100,000. The second home of the Ragged School in Endell Street carried as its sign "Youths' Christian Institute." The secrets of Quintin Hogg's achievement were exuberant vitality both of body and of mind and religious fervour. He was an all-round man; "what we wanted to develop our institute into was a place which should recognize that God had given man more than one side to his character, and where he could gratify any reasonable taste, athletic, intellectual, spiritual or social." This statement from a letter is quoted by Charles Booth in vol. vii, p. 393, of his survey of Religious Influence in London, with the following footnote: "Mr. Hogg is at least the sixth great man whose influence on the social conditions and religious life of London has been cut short by death while I have been trying to record it. The others I would mention are Archbishop Temple, Bishop Creighton, Father Dolling, Mr. Hugh Price Hughes and Dr. Parker; each (as was Mr. Quintin Hogg also) a master man. It would indeed be difficult to point among the living to any six equal to those who are gone." But the wonder workers for youth were not at an end with Quintin Hogg.

MARY AUGUSTA WARD (1851–1920)

Mary Augusta Arnold was born at Hobart Town, Tasmania, the eldest of eight children of Thomas Arnold (son of Dr. Arnold of Rugby), Inspector of Schools (later Professor of English Literature), and through her mother grand-daughter of a civil servant in Tasmania. She married at twenty-one Thomas Humphry Ward, then fellow and tutor of Brasenose College, Oxford, and was the first secretary of Somerville College, Oxford. Most widely known by her novels, she was also a social inventor, and founded in 1897, with the help of money from Passmore Edwards, the settlement now known by her name in which was instituted the first children's play centre, the first non-resident school for crippled children, and the first vacation school. She was the foundress both of the Women's National Anti-Suffrage League (1908) and of the Joint Advisory Council of Members of Parliament and Women Social Workers, for bringing the views of women to bear on Parliament without the vote.

BADEN-POWELL (1857–1941)

Robert Stephenson Smyth Baden-Powell was born in London, one of ten children of a Savilian Professor of Geometry at Oxford, by his third marriage to the daughter of an Admiral who was also a prolific writer. The Professor of Geometry, who was elected a F.R.S. at twenty-eight, was also a clergyman of broad church opinions, and a contributor to the *Essays and Reviews* which caused a storm in 1860. The future B.-P. had brains from both sides of the family, and artistic gifts on his mother's side. For his future work of founding a new and immensely successful organization for youth he had the first-hand preparation of being brought up in a family of ten—seven of his own mother's children who survived infancy, two half-sisters and one half-brother; he had opportunities of understanding boys which are relatively rare to-day. At his public school he was not particularly distinguished and he astonished his friends by coming out near the top of an examination for army commissions.

B.-P. was an intellectual by birth, whom the accident of competitive examination swept into the Army. Till this happened, as his biographer says, there had been nothing to determine his career: "There was no family tradition to help; the Powells for centuries had been small landowners, merchants or lawyers, with occasional clergymen and army and naval officers."[1] His army career lasted thirty-four years, including service in India, Ashanti, South Africa, Malta, and Matabeleland, and South Africa again in 1899–1901. He wrote a first book on *Reconnaissance and Scouting* at twenty-seven and another on *Aids to Scouting* at forty-two. Then at fifty-one he wrote *Scouting for Boys*, and by its immense success discovered his lifework, and left the army at fifty-three to become the founder of the Boy Scouts and, with his sister's help, of the Girl Guides. The "Good Turn" idea first saw the light in a letter of advice written by him some ten years before to a boys' club. The distinctive features of his movement were that it meant learning how to do things with a view to being useful, and that it substituted self-education for drill. From a visit to Russia in 1924 B.-P. drew the moral: "Don't trust to military training as the best preparation for modern citizenship. For up-to-date self-government up-to-date self-education seems the right preparatory stage."

---

[1] *Baden-Powell*, by E. E. Reynolds (Oxford University Press, 1942), p. 167. The account here is based entirely upon this biography.

SIDNEY WEBB (1859–1947), *and* BEATRICE WEBB (1858–1943)

Sidney Webb was born in London, second of three children of an accountant in a small way, and a mother whose family were small working property owners; she herself before and after marriage kept a hairdresser's shop, which at all times was the main source of the family income. Intellectual interests and a desire to do public service rather than make money Sidney could get from his father; energy and industry from his mother; his exceptional intelligence seems to have been a freak.

Beatrice was born in the Cotswolds, the eighth of nine daughters of Richard Potter, highly successful business undertaker and railway magnate, who began as Radical and Unitarian to end Conservative and Anglican, and of Lawrencina Heyworth of a similar capitalist, nonconformist, radical family.

Their decision on marriage that Sidney should give up the Civil Service, and that the two should become a studying and writing partnership on our public problems was made possible by Beatrice's assured income—they made it sufficient by having no extravagances except secretaries.

Most of their achievements—they were two of the most influential minds of this or any generation—fall outside the sphere of this Report, being concerned with promoting public action. Directly within its scope is the invention and founding of the London School of Economics and Political Science, made possible by Sidney's influential position in technical education and an unexpected legacy for "the promotion of socialism" bequeathed by an admirer previously unknown to him. Sidney got friendly legal advice that if he believed that impartial scientific study of economic problems must lead to Socialism, he could use the legacy to found an institution which should be devoted to impartial scientific study. His attitude to the school, which remained always his dearest child, was characterized by outstanding generosity. Of the first four directors, all of whom in substance he selected, two were Conservatives who became members of Parliament, and only one was in any sense a Socialist. More than this, while untiringly ready to give any help he could to the School, and continually thinking out ways to advance it, he never interfered in any way with the direction of the School. He was as generous as he was industrious.

Sidney Webb is the latest of the great Victorians to go. One of them who is still a living and inspiring voice—Gilbert Murray—

looked back recently in a broadcast address[1] on the "bad old world" before 1914, and expressed his dislike for a way of describing the present and future that has become habitual: "I am rather sick of being told that this is to be the century of the common man. If that only means that the under-privileged are to receive their share of privilege, if it means that the plain man with his conscience and common sense is to be given full consideration in diplomacy and politics, of course I am all for it. But it is always the exceptional people who make good leaders in time of trouble, and if they speak out the common man likes to accept their guidance."

This is a chapter about exceptional people, of widely different types and origins, and different experiences in life. Some found themselves reaching one objective after another in steady progress. Others—the first of them, Shaftesbury, is a notable instance—had moments when all that they had fought for, and the chance of continuing their work, seemed to be lost. But there is one thing common to them all. No one who studies their stories and reads their own words can doubt that their lives were happy lives—happy in struggle and achievement, happy in being lives with purpose, happy in the love and respect of those whom they helped and those who worked with them. "Who is the Happy Warrior?" Wordsworth asked once and gave the Happy Warrior's character, in phrases which recall much of what has been said in this chapter.

> 'Tis, finally, the man, who, lifted high,
> Conspicuous object in a nation's eye,
> Or left unthought-of in obscurity—
> Who, with a toward or untoward lot,
> Prosperous or adverse, to his wish or not—
> Plays, in the many games of life, that one
> Where what he most doth value must be won:
> Whom neither shape of danger can dismay,
> Nor thought of tender happiness betray;
> Who, not content that former worth stand fast,
> Looks forward, persevering to the last,
> From well to better, daily self-surpast:
> Who, whether praise of him must walk the earth
> For ever, and to noble deeds give birth,
> Or he must fall, to sleep without his fame,
> And leave a dead unprofitable name,

[1] "A Victorian Looks Back on Twenty-five Years," printed in *The Listener* of November 13, 1947.

Finds comfort in himself and in his cause;
And, while the mortal mist is gathering, draws
His breath in confidence of Heaven's applause:
This is the happy warrior; this is he
That every man in arms should wish to be.

These pioneers, one and all, were Happy Warriors. Their fame walks the earth; it should be for ever the exemplar and spur to noble needs.

VI. CHARITABLE TRUSTS

The Statute of Elizabeth. The Doctrine of *Cy Près*. The Testator
Challenged and Defended. Endowed Schools Commission and Act.
City of London Parochial Charities Act. Some Major Modern Trusts.
Continuing Rule of the Testator.

THE STATUTE OF ELIZABETH

THE Elizabethan Poor Law of 1601 was described in my first Report
as the starting-point of State provision for social security; it remained
for 233 years the basis of public provision for the poor. There was
passed in the same year another Statute destined to remain for an
even longer period the basis of State treatment for one of the subjects
of my present Report; it was entitled, "An Act to redress the Mis-
employment of Lands Goods and Stocks of Money heretofore given
to Charitable Uses." This Elizabethan Statute of Charitable Uses
was not formally repealed till 1888, even then it was not
repealed wholly. The preamble was expressly kept alive—as a
definition of charity. It is to the words of this Elizabethan Statute,
or to interpretations of these words given by earlier judges, that
our judges to-day may still refer, to decide whether a gift of
money is charitable, and should enjoy the privileges reserved for
such gifts.

The Elizabethan Statute on Charitable Uses is a starting-point
because it marks a turning-point in national policy. Till the Reformation was felt to be secure there had been a division of views as
to charitable endowments. Parliament had feared such endowments
as tending to get land into the dead hand of institutions, some of
which might be openly or secretly devoted to "superstitious," that
is to say Catholic, uses. The Ecclesiastical Courts, on the other hand,
which then dealt with wills, favoured bequests for charitable objects,
which in many cases put money into the hands of religious foundations. By the forty-third year of Elizabeth the Reformation was felt
to be safe. At the same time the great economic and social changes
of the sixteenth century and the threats of war from abroad
made it desirable to encourage charity. The Statute of Elizabeth
on Charitable Uses was passed at practically the same moment
as the Statute for Relief of the Poor and formed part of a con-
certed social programme for dealing with urgent problems of

transition.[1] The rich in future were to be encouraged to give of their superfluity, and so to relieve the payers of rates and taxes. The gifts already made for charitable purposes must be rightly used.

The Statute of Elizabeth provided accordingly for the appointment by the Lord Chancellor of commissioners to enquire and ensure that gifts for charitable uses were used for the purposes for which they were given by the donors. It was a sign of the privileged position already won for themselves by the universities of Oxford and Cambridge that they and their colleges, as well as the colleges of Westminster, Eton, and Winchester were exempted from this inquisition. The authorities of these favoured institutions were to be left free of Government interference, to use their endowments according to their consciences.

How much these first Charity Commissioners of Elizabeth did is uncertain; they did not become a permanent institution. The lasting influence of the Statute lay in another direction. In the words of a modern authority: "The effect of this Act was out of all proportion to its terms, for the Courts, supposing that the Legislature intended thereby to cure all defects and omissions in point of form in instruments whereby property was given to charitable objects construed it in the most liberal spirit."[2] That is to say, if it appeared that the general intention of a testator was charitable, however badly the intention might be expressed, the Courts in any dispute would do their best to ensure that the gift was used for some charitable purpose within the preamble of Elizabeth's Statute, and as near as possible to the testator's intention. The policy was to encourage charity, even at the cost of the next of kin. And once a gift was held to be charitable, it was exempt from the legal rules against perpetuities, preventing the tying up of property for more than a limited period. For a charitable purpose property could be tied up for ever.

A charitable purpose, moreover, meant something different from the ordinary implication of charity—the relieving of the necessities of one's neighbour out of the kindness of one's heart. It came to mean in essence a public rather than a private use, almost any giving of land or money or otherwise than for the benefit of specified

[1] The Poor Law is cited officially as 43 Eliz., c. 2; the Statute on Charitable Uses is 43 Eliz., c. 4. The one intervening Statute, 43 Eliz., c. 3, was part of the same programme. It provided for the necessary relief of soldiers and mariners left stranded out of the wars.

[2] Tudor on *Charities*, p. 2.

individuals.[1] A gift did not cease to be charitable however mean or base or vain the motive for which it was made. And a gift did not cease to be charitable by being limited to inhabitants of a particular parish or members of a trade or even to the kindred of the donor. The Founder's Kin scholarships established by William of Wykeham in founding Winchester and New College in the fourteenth century, and those established in 1518 by William Akroyd of York continue. There is in Yorkshire to-day a charity with an income of more than £1,000 a year dating from 1638 and devoted wholly to relieving the descendants of the sister of the founder, and part of Henry Smith's very wealthy foundation of 1627 is also reserved for the relief of poor kindred of Henry Smith.[2]

Of course there were some bequests which the Courts declined to treat as charitable. They boggled at a trust for keeping the testator's house shut up for twenty years, as the Scottish Courts boggled at a trust for disfiguring the Highlands with statues of the testator and his family.[3] They turned down flat a bequest of £5,000 by one John Collett in 1849 to be used during the next five years in paying the fines or securing the discharges of persons convicted under the Game Laws: "Looking at this bequest in a plain common-sense point of view, it is obviously calculated to encourage offences prohibited by the legislature."[4] At about the same date they rejected a bequest of £1,000 "towards the political restoration of the Jews to their own land," on the ground that, if "political restoration" meant anything, it meant promoting a revolution in a friendly country; recognition of such an object would not be consistent with "our amicable relations with the Sublime Porte."[5]

[1] Quite recently a bequest to establish prizes for chess in Portsmouth has been upheld as a valid charity on the ground that chess is educational. (*In re Dupree's Deed Trusts*, 1945, Ch. 16). The judge in this case realized that he might be starting on a slippery slope—proceeding through bridge to games more and more of chance while offering something to skill.

[2] Founder's Kin charities have been the subject of an important legal decision in 1945. See Appendix B, Section II, on Anti-Vivisection and Founder's Kin as Subjects of Charity.

[3] See Appendix B, Section III, for a Note on Charitable Trusts in Scotland. Though Scottish law is in origin distinct from English law, and knows nothing of the Statute of Elizabeth, the law of charitable trusts has come to be practically the same in both countries. The administration is different.

[4] *Thrupp v. Collett* (No. 1), (1858). 26 Beavan, 125.

[5] *Habershon v. Vardon* (1851), 4 de C. and Sm. 467. In more recent times the Courts have rejected the claim of an association for settling Jews in Palestine as not charitable, and therefore as not entitled to exemption from income tax. *Kerin Kayemeth Le Jisroel Ltd.* v. *Inland Revenue Commissioners* (1931), 2 K.B.D. 465.

Broadly speaking associations for enforcing the law are charities, but associations for encouraging disregard of law or whose main purpose is to bring about a change of the law are not charities. The Royal Society for the Prevention of Cruelty to Animals is a charity. The National Anti-Vivisection Society, by a decision given as lately as July, 1947, is not a charity.[1]

THE DOCTRINE OF CY PRÈS

The policy of the Statute of Elizabeth as interpreted by the Courts was to encourage the application of wealth to public rather than to private uses. But they were to be public uses, according to the intention of the man who had given the money or, more often, had left it by will and gone to his rest. The Statute named as the main evil to be combated disregard of the wishes of the founder. The Courts of Equity applying this Statute followed this rule. They were concerned not with the needs of the time or with the views of living men. They were there to do the best they could to meet the wishes of the dead.

Of course in carrying out this policy difficulties were often encountered. The founder might have expressed himself badly, so that it was impossible to understand what he meant or to do what he said. The circumstances might change, so that the objects named by him no longer existed. The value of the endowment might grow, so as to become out of all proportion to the objects named; this was particularly likely when the gift consisted of a bit of land on which a town came to be built perhaps hundreds of years later. To deal with such problems the Courts developed the famous legal principle of *cy près*.

Cy près is Norman French for "as near as possible." The *cy près* principle is that when a testator manifests a general intention of charity, but the particular object of his bounty cannot be carried out literally, it must be carried into effect as nearly as possible. Failure of a particular mode proposed by a testator should not be allowed to destroy the charity; the law will substitute another mode of devoting the property to charitable purposes, in place of handing it back to the next of kin for their private enjoyment.

---

[1] *The National Anti-Vivisection Society* v. *The Commissioners of Inland Revenue* (not yet in official reports). The decision in this case, given by a majority of the law lords against strongly argued dissent of one of them, settles several important points and raises interesting issues of public policy. See Appendix B, Section (II), on "Anti-Vivisection and Founder's Kin as Subjects of Charity."

Occasionally the desire of the Courts to keep charitable money for charitable purposes and away from the next of kin went to the length of paying scant attention to the desires of the testator. Thus in the case of *De Costa* v. *de Pas*,[1] Lord Hardwicke applied a bequest for instructing people in the Jewish religion for the benefit of the Foundling Hospital; the only apparent connection is that teaching Jewish religion and foundlings were at that time equally illegitimate. But this freedom of handling by the Courts was unusual. Generally they made laborious and ingenious attempts to do something at least to please the testator. The nature of their problems and efforts can be shown best by one or two examples.

The Elizabethan Statute named specifically as a charitable object the "relief or redemption of prisoners or captives" and the rescuing of British citizens taken captive by the pirates of Turkey or Barbary became a favourite object of testamentary disposition in the eighteenth century. Thus in 1723 Thomas Betton, a member of the Ironmongers' Company, left his residuary estate, as to one-half for the redemption of British slaves in Turkey or Barbary, as to one-quarter for charity schools in London and suburbs where education should be according to the Church of England, as to one-quarter for a sermon and for necessitous decayed freemen of the Ironmongers' Company and their families. He provided expressly that the capital was to be kept intact. In course of time there came happily to be no British slaves in Turkey or Barbary, but the trustees duly saved the money in case there should be, till by 1840 the income available for this non-existent purpose had risen to about £3,500 a year. When the case came before the House of Lords, the Ironmongers' Company argued that this £3,500 a year should be divided equally between the two other purposes named in the will, namely, Church of England Charity Schools in London, and necessitous decayed ironmongers and their families. But the House of Lords pointed out that the bequest had been made for redemption of all British slaves, not only for those who came from London and its suburbs or had been ironmongers. They assigned the £3,500 a year, in accordance with the testator's obvious fondness for schools, to schools in all parts of England with Church of England education.[2]

In this case the Court had something to go on as to what the testator might have done if he had realized that there would at some time be no British slaves in Turkey. In another case a little later they were without such guidance. There, Mrs. Ashton, dying in

---

[1] Ambler, p. 228 (1753).
[2] *Ironmongers' Company* v. *Attorney-General* (1844), 10 Clark and Finelly, p. 108.

the same year as Thomas Betton, left her estate on trust to build
six almshouses in Dunstable, to pay £6 a year each to the six almswomen living in them, to distribute bread to constant poor church-
goers, to repair a public clock, and finally to be divided as to any
surplus between the six almswomen in the six almshouses which
she erected at Dunstable. The terms of the will made it clear that
she was not sure if there would be a surplus; that would depend,
among other things, on the behaviour of the clock, and how often
it needed repair. But some of Mrs. Ashton's estate consisted of land
on which the town of Luton came to be built and produced thus
in due course a large surplus, about £6,000. The Court held, not
unreasonably, that to divide this surplus among the six almswomen
would make them no longer almswomen, and thus would defeat
instead of carrying out the objects of the bequest. The Court then
said, without giving any reason, "the best thing that can be done
with this charity is to apply it to the purposes of a school at Dunstable which shall be conducted on Church of England principles
but shall be open to Dissenters."[1]

It is a little difficult to see how the foundation of a school on
these precise terms, or any terms came in. But, granted the school,
the influence of the testator was decisive as to its location; the school
had to be where Mrs. Ashton had lived and died 136 years before,
in Dunstable, not where the new wealth to found it had been
created and where, presumably, it was most needed—in Luton.
The Courts had sometimes to interpret the words of the dead-and-
gone founder with considerable freedom. But they were ruled by
these wishes of the past, not by what might appear the best use
of the funds in the present:

> "This Court . . . is not at liberty to speculate upon whether
> it would have been more expedient or beneficial for the com-
> munity that a different application of the funds in charity
> should have occurred to the testator . . . accordingly instances
> of charities of the most useless description have come before the
> Court, but which it has considered it is bound to carry into
> effect."

So saying in 1859, the same year as that of Ashton's case, the Court
turned down a suggestion to provide for old people the hospital
treatment which they needed as well as the almshouses which were
all that had occurred to the testator.[2]

[1] *Re Ashton's Charity* (1859), 27 Beavan, 117.
[2] *Philpott* v. *St. George's Hospital* (1859), 27 Beavan, 107.

The immobility of the dead testator's mind has to be seen against a background of endless economic and social change. Neither resources nor needs remain through centuries as they appeared to the testator when making his will. The change of resources through appreciation in the value of land has sometimes been fantastic. The change of needs cannot be illustrated better than by reviewing the preamble of Elizabeth's Statute in the light of to-day.

> Whereas Lands, Tenements, Rents, Annuities, Profits, Hereditaments, Goods, Chattels, Money and Stocks of Money have been heretofore given, limited, appointed and assigned as well by the Queen's most Excellent Majesty, and her most noble Progenitors, as by sundry other well disposed Persons, some for Relief of aged, impotent and poor People; some for the Maintenance of sick and maimed Soldiers and Mariners, Schools of Learning, free Schools and Scholars of Universities; some for the Repair of Bridges, Ports, Havens, Causeways, Churches, Sea-Banks, and Highways; some for the Education and Preferment of Orphans; some for the Relief, Stock or Maintenance for Houses of Correction; some for Marriages of poor Maids; some for Supportation, Aid and Help of young Tradesmen, Handicraftmen, and Persons decayed; and others for Relief or Redemption of Prisoners or Captives; and for Aid or Ease of any poor Inhabitants concerning payment of Fifteens, setting out of Soldiers, and other Taxes.

Some of the headings named here have become superfluous. Such is relief or redemption of prisoners or captives in the way in which the Elizabethans would have understood those terms. Private relief of prisoners condemned for breaches of the law has to wait in the main till they cease to be prisoners. Relief from imprisonment for debt—a not infrequent subject of early Victorian charities—is also in the past.

Some of the headings represent tasks now wholly or mainly taken over by public authorities, at the cost of rates or taxes. Such is the repair of bridges and all that follows down to highways, except the "churches" oddly spatchcocked between "causeways" and "sea-banks." Such is the maintenance and stock of houses of correction. Such in another way is the aid or ease of any poor inhabitants in the payment of taxes. By developed fiscal technique in graduating taxation and granting relief the State gives this ease—or should do so—at its own cost.

There is one heading, the "Maintenance of Schools of Learning, free Schools and Scholars of Universities" in regard to which the State has taken over more responsibility stage by stage. But this is not likely to leave, and should not be allowed to leave, no place for voluntary action and endowment.

There are, on the other hand, important present-day subjects of charitable gifts which do not figure directly in Elizabeth's list, though they have been accepted as within its spirit. Such are hospitals, convalescent homes, maternity homes and ante-natal care; provision for children deprived of normal home life and for the unmarried mother; youth service, adult education and provision for holidays; settlements in great cities; preservation and extension of rural amenities.

The preamble to Elizabeth's Statute is still formally part of our law to-day.[1] But being interpreted by the judges as living men, in the spirit rather than by the letter, it never prevented the Courts from recognizing for new gifts new needs of which Elizabeth never dreamt. For old gifts the courts were bound and, as will be shown, they are still bound to-day, by what the long-dead giver said. And he has no chance of correcting himself or of saying that his mind has changed.

THE TESTATOR CHALLENGED AND DEFENDED

In the early part of the nineteenth century, there was an exhaustive enquiry into charitable endowments, by a Commission under the chairmanship of Lord Brougham which sat for eighteen years, from 1819 to 1837. The Commission was set up, in the spirit of Elizabeth's Statute, to inquire into misapplication of funds and to find some means of dealing with charitable trusts less costly and dilatory than litigation in the Courts of Equity. It threw light for the first time on the scale of the problem and the complexities arising through change of conditions. Its enquiry, after another sixteen years

[1] For a modern recourse to the Statute of Elizabeth, reference may be made to the case *In re Macduff* (1896), 2 Ch. 451, and particularly to the remarks made then by Lord Justice Lindley (at p. 467). In this case the Court of Appeal held that there might be philanthropic purposes which would not be charitable within the meaning of the Statute of Elizabeth; they decided accordingly that a bequest by a clergyman of his whole fortune for "charitable or philanthropic purposes" was not valid. In practice the courts do not often get back to the Statute of Elizabeth in so many words. They go back to a famous classification of charitable trusts by Lord Macnaghten in *Pemsel's Case* (1891), A.C. 531, which in turn was an adaptation of a classification by Sir Samuel Romilly as counsel, in giving an interpretation of the Statute of Elizabeth.

of incubation, led to the setting up in 1853 of a permanent Charity Commission. Experience on the Commission led one of its members, Arthur Hobhouse, later Lord Hobhouse, to challenge the policy of allowing testators to dictate for ever the use of the money which they left behind.

The Commissioners were given extensive legal powers of enquiring into the administration of charities, including the summoning of trustees and examining them on oath, and the right to receive and audit the accounts of all charities. The Commissioners were empowered in various ways to secure the safe custody and due investment of the property of charities and to diminish the cost of legal proceedings. Finally, they were authorized to do what the Courts had done hitherto in framing schemes, to adapt the use of charities to altered circumstances according to the principle of *cy près*. Thus the heavy costs of litigation would be saved and charitable funds would be kept for charitable purposes. The Commissioners did not and do not make any charge for their services.

These measures and others which followed, and will be noticed below, for dealing with endowed schools, gave many people the impression that the treatment of charitable trusts had been altered fundamentally. They gave this impression, among others, to John Stuart Mill, who in an article in the *Fortnightly Review* of April, 1869, wrote as follows:

> We have well nigh seen the last of the superstition which allowed the man who owned a piece of land or a sum of money five hundred years ago, to make a binding disposition determining what should be done with it as long as time or the British nation should last; which, after limiting an owner's power we tie up his property in favour of individuals to the term of a single generation, thinks it spoliation to disobey his orders after the lapse of centuries, when their apparent purpose is connected with religion or charity. . . . There is, as on all other great questions, a minority behind the age. . . . But with the bulk of the nation the indefeasibility of endowments is a chimera of the past.

Mill went on to urge that the danger was now on the other side, of excessive interference with the rights of testators.

Mill's article was attacked vigorously by Arthur Hobhouse who had been a Charity Commissioner and was at the time a member of the Endowed Schools Commission. He argued that the law and practice had not been changed materially and that they needed drastic change. He gave a series of addresses between 1869 and 1879 on the subject of charitable endowments which were collected later in a volume entitled *The Dead Hand*. This book and the whole debate are well worth reading still, for they raise permanent issues of policy. And the law and practice of charitable trusts other than those for education, is to-day substantially as Arthur Hobhouse described it seventy years ago, and is in need of the kind of changes that he proposed then.

Against some of his opponents Mill was on strong ground. There was, for instance, Joshua Fitch, an able and devoted educationist of the nineteenth century, whose deprecation of private enterprise in public affairs has an odd twentieth-century ring. Thus Mill quoted with damaging effect an article by Joshua Fitch in *Fraser's Magazine* for January, 1869, proposing that it should be made illegal to devote any money by will to public objects except through the agency of some recognized body which was amenable to public control.

> "Is it too much to expect," asks Mr. Fitch, "that we shall soon see the wisdom of restraining the power of private persons to tamper with any one of those great national interests such as education and the relief of the poor, which demand organization and fixed principles, and which still more imperatively demand complete readjustment from time to time, in accordance with the supreme intelligence and will of the nation, as represented in Parliament?"

This, said Mill, is "a doctrine breathing the very spirit, and expressed in almost the words, of the apologies made in the over-centralized governments of the Continent for not permitting anyone to perform the smallest act connected with public interests." In opposition to this, Mill proceeded:

> "The truth needs re-asserting, and needs it every day more and more that what the improvement of mankind and of all their works most imperatively demands is variety, not uniformity. What is called tampering by private persons with great public interests, as if it meant obstructing the Government in what it thinks fit to do for public uses with the funds at its disposal, means trying to do with money of their own something that shall promote the same objects better. It is tampering as those tamper with the religion of the country who build nonconformist chapels."

As against Joshua Fitch, Mill was in the right. It is desirable, so long as any testamentary power remains, that individuals should be able to endow experiments in the use of money after their deaths —for a limited time according to their ideas, and thereafter according to the judgment of living persons other than the Government of the day. Mill himself proposed that after a term of years—fifty years or a hundred—it should be made possible to divert endowments to new purposes. He proposed also that, even within that period, there should be power of diverting to other uses money which, if spent as directed, would be positively mischievous, as in the case of doles.

As against Arthur Hobhouse, Mill was in the wrong. When he suggested that the danger was now of too much interference with the wishes of testators, he was at the disadvantage of not knowing the ground. Hobhouse knew it at first hand. From his experience both as Charity Commissioner from 1866 to 1872 and as member of the Endowed Schools Commission of 1869, he was able to make a collection of cases illustrating strikingly the vagaries of founders, their mean and vulgar motives in some cases, and the harm done by them in many more cases even when the motive was good. The cases of George Jarvis, Christopher Tancred, Henry Smith and Archbishop Abbott, to which reference is made below, are all from this collection, exhibited in the Charities' Chamber of Horrors.[1]

Hobhouse, starting from the view that all property is the property of the dead, not of the living, laid down two fundamental principles in regard to charitable foundations. The first is that the public shall not be compelled to take whatever is offered to it but shall here, as in other countries, have the right of considering whether that particular use which the founder has fancied shall take effect, or whether the property shall be turned to some other public use or given back to private uses. The second principle is that the grasp of the dead hand shall be shaken off absolutely and finally; in other words, that there shall always be a living and reasonable owner of property to manage it according to the wants of mankind.

Hobhouse's argument is in accord with modern economic views of the nature of wealth. Endowments do not produce anything; they determine the command of the goods and services, which can be produced only by the labour of hand and brain of living people applied to the equipment which has come down to them or which they have made. The advantage of placing command in one hand rather than in another depends on which of the two commands is

[1] Appendix B, Section I.

likely to lead to the best use in the common interest of mankind. From this point of view Hobhouse's doctrine that the command of resources should always be in the hands of a living and reasonable owner of property is irrefragable.

But to this the gloss should be added: that it is important that there should be command of resources for social purposes in the hands of some living body other than the Government or the State. Hobhouse himself fully realized this. He differed as much from those who, like Robert Lowe, wanted practically to abolish all charitable endowments, as from Mill who thought that the dead hand was no longer a danger. He urged that "there should be an authority constantly at work to adjust these foundations to the wants of the age." But subject to this he held that "it might be very useful to have a public fund always available for objects for which it might be difficult to raise taxes."

The particular cases cited by Hobhouse in support of his argument against the dead hand have been set out in Appendix B, Section I, as a Charities' Chamber of Horrors; notes have been added showing, so far as possible, what has happened to these foundations since his day. It can be questioned whether these cases justify the thesis which Hobhouse advanced at one stage of the debate: that most charitable endowments had done more harm than good. It cannot be questioned by any reasonable person that they and the accompanying argument made a case for further reform. Yet while the case for reform is clear, it is necessary to see these examples in due proportion and not to be unfairly critical, either of the judges laying down the law, or of the law itself, or of the motives which have led to charitable gifts.

First, the judges laying down the law are not themselves responsible for the law. Their duty is to declare the law as they find it, as it has been laid down by precedents which they are bound to follow. Often in maintaining charitable trusts the judges have gone out of their way to show that they thought the purposes of the testator unwise or useless or even mischievous, but they would have been wrong to give any decision other than that which they did give. It has not been unknown in other fields that judges, applying a bad law as they found it, have taken steps to make its badness patent, as a means to reform. There is a famous judgment given by Mr. Justice Maule in 1843, when there was no Divorce Court, sentencing a poor man to prison for bigamy, because, his wife having left him in wretched circumstances, he had gone through another ceremony of marriage to get a mother's care for his children. In sentencing the prisoner, the judge explained to him just how he should have acted to keep within the law; first, he should have brought an action in a Civil Court against the other man for *criminal conversation* with his wife and obtained damages; second, if successful, he should have gone to the Ecclesiastical Court, and got them to repeat what appeared to have been decided already; third, he should have gone to the House of Lords and proving his case and all the preliminary proceedings he could have obtained a full and complete divorce, after which he might if he liked have married again. "The prisoner might perhaps object to this that he had not the money to pay the expenses, which would amount to about five hundred or six hundred pounds—but this did not exempt him from paying the penalty for committing a felony of which he had been convicted." "The law was the same for him as it was for a rich man and it was equally open for him through its aid to obtain relief." Some of the judgments given by judges in applying the law of charitable trusts were, as clearly as with Mr. Justice Maule in this case of bigamy, inspired by desire to suggest how much the law needed amendment.

Second, in so far as the law which has made some bad charitable trusts possible in the past is a bad law, its badness is part of the general evil of unrestricted testamentary disposition. The law of most civilized countries, including all those based on Roman law, has always limited the right of a testator to disinherit all his dependents, and has given indefeasible claims to his widow and children. Unrestricted power of willing away property has only recently been abolished in England. It was not the Statute of Elizabeth that made possible George Jarvis' disinheriting of his descendants. He could have done that by giving the money to his butler or to a total stranger.

Third, though the motives which lead to a charitable gift may in some cases be despicable, and in many cases are no better than a desire to exercise power though one is dead, this is not true generally. Christopher Tancred and George Jarvis were thoroughly unpleasant people who figure deservedly in the Charities' Chamber of Horrors. But most givers to charitable uses are not like this. Mrs. Ashton was obviously seeking to continue after death her pleasant relations with her neighbours in life, in providing six almshouses for six old women, and in planning to keep always a public clock in repair for her fellow citizens in Dunstable; she could not know that the land which she gave for this purpose would become so valuable that the money could not wisely be used just as she intended. So, too, Archbishop Abbott, desiring to benefit his native town of Guildford, had obviously a kindly human motive; he could not

know that in time to come the citizens of Guildford would not wish
to have the stocking trade re-established there. Henry Smith never
dreamt that the £60 a year which he wished in 1627 to guarantee
for relief of the poorest of his sister's descendants would become
£60,000 a year in 1947, because his trustees had bought eighty-four
acres of land in Kensington.

It is a fair guess that Mrs. Ashton and Archbishop Abbott and
any number of testators like them, whose good intentions have been
defeated by change of circumstance, would have been only too
happy to make a different disposition had they been able to foresee
the future. In other words, all charitable gifts that are really given
in the spirit of charity are gifts which the donors would want used,
perhaps for choice for one type of need rather than another, or for
one loved place rather than another, but which they would certainly not wish tied to uses which had become unsuitable or impossible. They would welcome a sympathetic living hand to make their
gifts always a cause of happiness, however conditions might change.

"Defer not charities till death; for certainly if a man weigh it
rightly, he that doth so is rather liberal of another's money than
of his own." This saying of Francis Bacon is true of those who give
nothing till they are dead. But much giving after death is but a
continuance of neighbourly acts and human kindness during life.
The great bulk of charitable gifts still come from a feeling of charity.
In so far as they do, they will continue, even though the State takes
power to use the testator's gift according to his charitable desires
rather than in accord with the particular way which seemed best
to him at the time.

ENDOWED SCHOOLS ACT OF 1869

Hobhouse did not suggest that nothing at all had been done to
improve matters. One great breach in the absolute sanctity of the
dead founder's assumed wishes had been made by the passing of
the Endowed Schools Act of 1869. Another was made just after the
time when Hobhouse was writing, in the passage of the City of
London Parochial Charities Act of 1883.

The Endowed Schools Act, 1869, followed on an elaborate inquiry
by Royal Commission which from 1864 to 1868 examined not only
the state of secondary education but the nature of many charitable
endowments. It set up a body of Endowed Schools' Commissioners
(of whom Hobhouse became one) with special powers of investigating
and regulating educational endowments and of adding to them from

endowments for other purposes which had become less important. For this latter purpose Section 30 of the Act provided as follows:

"In the case of any endowment which is not an educational endowment as defined in this Act, but the income of which is applicable wholly or partially to any one or more of the following purposes; namely,

Doles in money or kind;

Marriage portions;

Redemption of Prisoners and Captives;

Relief of Poor Prisoners for debt;

Loans;

Apprenticeship fees;

Advancement in life, or

Any purposes which have failed altogether or have become insignificant, in comparison with the magnitude of the endowment, if originally given to charitable uses in or before the year of our Lord one thousand eight hundred,

the Commissioners, with the consent of the governing body, may by Scheme under the Act treat in whole or part as an educational endowment."

Section 30 was far from drastic. An endowment could not be touched under it merely on the ground that its purposes had failed altogether or become insignificant, unless it was also at least seventy years old. No endowment could be touched under it except with the consent of the governing body, who often would be constituted specially as guardians of the views of the founder. But Section 30 did represent a new departure and set a precedent which might well be followed to-day, in revising whole classes of endowments.

Apart from Section 30 of the Act of 1869, for transferring to education gifts originally devoted to other purposes, the setting up of a special body of Endowed Schools Commissioners with a vigorous policy of initiative and enquiry brought many valuable reforms in regard to endowments which were already educational. This side of the Act has changed completely the treatment of educational endowments; broadly they are in living hands, not dead ones. Its use in making more money available for education can be illustrated by an example in which I have a personal interest.

William Akroyd, Rector of Marston and a priest in the Cathedral Church of York, making his will in 1518 "an old man weak in body but sound in mind," left certain lands to two of his nephews first to maintain them at Oxford or Cambridge, thereafter to them with others as trustees "to keep one scholar at Oxford or Cambridge to the end of the world." The trustees were to choose as scholar one near to the founder in blood and bearing his name; failing such, one near in blood though not of his name; failing that an inhabitant of Marston or Hooton. The early history of this foundation is obscure, but certain members of the Akroyd family certainly did go to Oxford or Cambridge in the sixteenth and seventeenth centuries, presumably as scholars, and in 1699 the foundation was placed on a definite basis by a decree of Chancery, as a means of giving scholarships for ever to Founder's Kin, which came to mean descendants of the nephews or uncle of the founder; the trust estate at that time comprised lands at Grimethorpe, Brierly and Batley. Two of these three pieces of land became lost or diverted to other uses during the centuries, but the third of them remained and on it in the middle of the nineteenth century part of the rising town of Batley came to be built. The annual income of the foundation rose from about £150 to about £1,500 a year (it is now £1,700 odd). The Endowed Schools' Commissioners learned of this and in 1871 swooped down with a suggestion that this new wealth should be used to establish a college in the West Riding. They were fortunate in finding as chairman of the trustees one who was not only of Founder's Kin, as all the trustees had to be up to 1871, but a man in public life, Lt.-Col. Edward Akroyd, M.P. for Halifax. He had already used the foundation to help three of his nephews to the university. He now persuaded his somewhat reluctant fellow-trustees to agree to a scheme, made in 1874, whereby about £175 a year was retained for scholarships reserved for Founder's Kin, and additional scholarships were made available for boys from Yorkshire schools, while the bulk of the money was divided between Batley Grammar School and a College of Science which was one of the two origins of the University of Leeds.

The adoption of the scheme of 1874 was regarded by some of the Founder's Kin as an invasion of their rights. But it undoubtedly turned the windfalls of William Akroyd's foundation to admirable use, and it did not interfere with his desire to have one scholar of his blood always at Oxford or Cambridge.[1]

[1] Somewhat oddly William Akroyd has seldom been able to have a scholar of his name as well as his blood; the blood seems to run most persistently in the female line. In the year 1897 when as grandson of William Akroyd of Stourbridge (whose father's real name was Bates) I competed for a Founder's Kin scholarship and won it, my rivals were named Mowatt and Collins. In the complete list of nearly forty persons who have held William Akroyd Founder's Kin scholarships since 1875 the name Akroyd does not appear. I owe many of the facts

It is important to note the special circumstances which in 1874 made possible this new scheme for a foundation already 350 years old. It required the consent of the trustees, which might not have been forthcoming, for they all then had to be Founder's Kin. It depended on the existence and initiative of the Endowed Schools' Commissioners who had the traditional vigour of new brooms.

The powers granted to the Endowed Schools' Commissioners in 1869 were in the first instance temporary, to come to an end in 1875 unless the Act were renewed. The Act was renewed in 1873, but in 1874 the newly returned Conservative Government, in renewing the Act for another five years, abolished the special commissioners, and re-united the educational and non-educational trusts in the hands of the less turbulent Charity Commission. There they remained, with the Act of 1869 renewed year by year, till the Board of Education took over in 1899. Since then educational endowments have been dealt with by the living hands of an educational department. The detailed rule of the dead in education has ended. Two comments are needed, to complete the story of the Endowed Schools' Act, and draw its morals.

First, section 30 for turning obsolete charities to educational purposes, though still formally in existence, is no longer of practical use. The endowments to be dealt with under this section are non-educational, and the preparation of schemes under the section is the function of the Charity Commissioners rather than of the Ministry of Education; in practice no action has been taken under this section for many years. The new purposes, on the other hand, to which endowments can be diverted under this section are limited to educational purposes; to-day with the great extension of public activity and public expenditure in the educational field, diversion of charitable money to educational purposes has not nearly the urgency which it seemed to have seventy years ago.[1] But Section 30 set a precedent which should be revived. Though it is no longer important to divert non-educational endowments to educational

given here to the *History of the Family of Aykroyd in the County of York*, written by the Rev. F. Palliser Costobadie and privately printed in 1934. Mr. Costobadie is himself of Founder's Kin and there were several scholars of his name in the eighteenth century.

[1] One of the charitable purposes which the legislators of 1869 thought obsolete was the provision of marriage grants. To-day, with the threatened decline of population, provision of such grants to facilitate early marriage without the burden of hire-purchase agreements, presents itself as an excellent subject for voluntary action on mutual aid lines.

purposes, it is as important as ever to see that non-educational endowments are used to advantage. This can be illustrated by an up-to-date example. A favourite object of charity in the past was the provision of money pensions to the aged. To-day the State has undertaken provision of pensions for all old people, designed to ensure them enough money to buy the necessaries of life. In so far as the State pensions are given subject to a means test, a charitable pension may serve merely or mainly to reduce the charge to the State, in place of bettering the condition of the old. Even where the State pension, being contributory, is paid without regard to the other resources, a money addition from a charitable trust may be far less important to him than something in kind—a place to live, home service, a club for companionship. All the charitable gifts made for old age in the past should now come under a review, tied not by the doctrine of *cy près* but directed by the spirit of the giver— of doing for the old what they need most in the changed conditions of to-day.

Second, the freedom from the rule of the testator in the educational field that is given by the Endowed Schools Act is limited by the words of the Act itself. Educational endowment in that Act means providing "education at school of boys and girls or exhibitions tenable at a school or university or elsewhere." The State, by the Education Act of 1944, has taken on for itself and for local authorities full financial responsibility in this field. If educational endowments are kept to this field, they may appear mainly to be serving the purpose of keeping down rates and taxes, rather than of advancing education. The function of Voluntary Action and charitable endowment is to pioneer. It would be reasonable now to make possible the diversion of endowments which, as the law stands, must be kept for boys and girls, to promoting education irrespective of age and to activities ancillary to formal education.

CITY PAROCHIAL CHARITIES ACT, 1883

The City Parochial Charities Act of 1883, like the Endowed Schools Act of 1869, was the child of a Royal Commission, under the chairmanship of the Duke of Northumberland. The Commission, sitting from 1878 to 1880, not only took evidence from all the City parishes, but had the benefit of detailed reports made on their charities over many years by Mr. Hare, one of the officers of the Charity Commission, who became later an assistant commissioner. Their report, the minutes of evidence, and Mr. Hare's reports, all published in full,[1] are a treasure-house of oddities illustrating the waste that may occur through leaving charities perpetual while the world around them changes. Three examples out of many—St. Christopher-le-Stock in the Bank of England, the Cemetery without any Dead at St. Michael's, Crooked Lane, and the Love Feast of St. Clement's, Eastcheap—are included in the Charities' Chamber of Horrors forming Section I of Appendix B. The general picture presented by the Royal Commission is of charities meant to lighten the lot of the poor by doles of money or bread or coals in days when there was no Poor Law, having their largely increased incomes used to pay vestry officials or to keep down the cost of poor relief to the ratepayers. Of one parish where this was happening, one of the commissioners observed that the charity was really going to the wealthy parishioners. "They would not like to be told that," answered the vestry clerk. "But it is so, is it not?" persisted the commissioner.

The Royal Commission had no difficulty in showing that many hundreds of endowments in the hundred odd parishes of the City of London had outgrown the purposes for which they had been given perhaps hundreds of years before. They made a plan for combining these under one body of trustees and this plan has in substance been carried out. Under the Act of 1883, the Charity Commissioners were empowered to make a scheme or schemes vesting the property of all the endowed charities of the City of London in official trustees. Subject to certain savings as to ecclesiastical charities, the purposes for which the schemes might provide were named in order as education, libraries, open spaces, provident institutions and working men's and women's institutes, and finally "physical, moral and social improvement of the poorer inhabitants and other persons." Subject to a few exceptions for particular parishes, the benefit of all the endowments could be made available for the whole of London, that is to say, the Metropolitan Police District.

The Charity Commissioners, presented with these drastic powers, took plenty of time for deliberation, producing a scheme finally in 1889, and the new trustees, known officially as "The Trustees of the London Parochial Charities," began work in 1891. The income of the Trustees when they began was about £80,000 a year; it had grown in 1945 to about £160,000. This large stream of money gathered together from so many separate

[1] Vol. XX of the Parliamentary Papers of 1880, c. 2522. The Minutes of Oral Evidence are in Appendix II and Mr. Hare's reports in Appendix III in the same volume.

streams was turned at first in three principal directions: the
promotion of higher education notably in the Polytechnics, the
provision of open spaces, and the strengthening of the resources of
the Ecclesiastical Commissioners. But the hands of the Trustees were
fortunately not tied. They can, and do, change the direction of their
expenditure to fit changing times; in a later chapter note will be
made of an interesting experiment which the Trustees are making,
in meeting the needs of the old. The £3 which, under the will
made by Anthony Death in 1679, was being paid two hundred years
later to one "poor honest ancient washerwoman" selected each year
from her fellows in a particular parish is now part of the great fund
which is being used to show by example how life can be made
happier for all old people. The City Parochial Fund to-day stands
as one of a group of half a dozen modern foundations, each with large
resources and large powers. To complete the picture of charitable
trusts it is necessary to describe these modern foundations.

SOME MAJOR MODERN TRUSTS

The charitable trusts described hitherto have for the most part
been small local trusts, and devoted by their founders to definite
purposes. The problems that have arisen in regard to them have
turned largely on the question of how, as circumstances changed,
they could be made most useful, without disregarding completely the
instructions of the founder. Within the past fifty or sixty years a new
type of charitable trust has developed in Britain: large, not tied to
specific purposes, administered by trustees with a liberal measure of
freedom. These trusts represent money in living hands independent
of the Government of the day. They include five foundations of a
general character, namely, the City Parochial Foundation of 1891,
the Carnegie United Kingdom Trust of 1913, the Pilgrim Trust
of 1930, the King George Jubilee Trust of 1935, and the Nuffield
Foundation of 1943. The origin of the first of these and some of
the modern purposes to which its trustees have devoted and are
devoting the great resources now in their hands, have been noted
already. About each of the four others something will be said in
turn briefly. In addition to these, reference must be made to two
foundations of a slightly different character—the King Edward's
Hospital Fund for London dating from 1897 and the Royal Commission for the Great Exhibition of 1851. Both of these represent
substantial funds, available in the one case for medical purposes
and in the other for educational purposes. In regard to each of

them an interesting problem arises as to their best use in future, in view of the developments of State action.

The City Parochial Fund, beginning work in 1891, represented charitable giving from the past. The first of a new type of foundation on this side of the Atlantic was the Carnegie United Kingdom Trust, established in 1913 with an endowment of ten million dollars by Andrew Carnegie as one of his many benefactions. Its annual income to-day is about £135,000. The trustees were given great freedom by the founder. "The purpose of the trust is to assist pioneer projects of national scope by such means as come under the category of 'charitable' according to Scottish or English law," and the trustees are enjoined to bear in mind that the needs of the community are constantly changing as the masses advance. Subject to this direction the trustees have the maximum elasticity consistent with legal form and direction. The trust made in the early days grants for a great development of libraries. It is now working in quinquennial cycles, and planning for the coming quinquennium grants for music and drama, for village halls and for education and youth services. The spirit of the Carnegie Endowment was expressed in the founder's letter, supplementary to the Deed of Trust of the Carnegie Hero Fund: "While I only give money, many of you are giving yourselves freely to service for your fellows without compensation other than that all-sufficient reward of knowing you are thus performing a holy duty, since the highest worship of God is service to man."

The Pilgrim Trust was founded in 1930 with a gift of £2,000,000 sterling by an American citizen, Edward Stephen Harkness of New York. The founder desired "to show his admiration for what Great Britain has done by a gift to be used for some of her more urgent needs." The Trustees, five in number, are empowered to apply both capital and income for such charitable purposes within Great Britain and Northern Ireland as they may from time to time determine. There is no restriction, except that the money must be spent in the United Kingdom and for purposes within the legal definition of charitable. The income of the fund in 1946 was about £112,000. Until 1939 grants were divided mainly between social welfare, particularly schemes for the benefit of the unemployed and the preservation and restoration of objects of beauty or historical interest. During 1939–45 assistance was given temporarily to war services. Since 1945, with the great extension of social legislation, the trustees have withdrawn from the social welfare field and are concentrating most of their resources on preservation of buildings and amenities, and on the encouragement of art and learning. They do not make grants to established charities, such as hospitals or individuals, and they have not used hitherto the power given to them by the founder of spending capital.

King George's Jubilee Trust was established in 1935 in commemoration of the Silver Jubilee of King George V, having as its object "the advancement of the physical, mental and spiritual welfare of the younger generation." The trust is therefore more limited in purpose than the Carnegie United Kingdom Trust and the Pilgrim Trust. It differs also in that, though it has a capital endowment of about £1,000,000, it continues to collect and appeal for funds. Its purpose of helping the younger generation is so general that it consults informally with the four other great trusts mentioned here for co-operation in spheres of interest common to more than one of them.

The Nuffield Foundation was established in 1943 by Lord Nuffield, with an endowment of £10,000,000 in ordinary stock units of Morris Motors, Ltd. The three main objects of the Foundation in the words of the Trust Deed are:

(i) the advancement of health and the prevention and relief of sickness . . . in particular . . . by medical research and teaching and by the organization and development of medical and health service . . .

(ii) the advancement of social well-being . . . in particular . . . by scientific research and the organization, development and improvement of technical and commercial education, including the training of teachers and provision of scholarships and prizes;

(iii) the care and comfort of the aged poor.

These objects, it will be seen, give a large measure of freedom and initiative to the trustees, who have expressed their attitude in the following terms: "The widening obligations of Government and the spread of State subvention impose a healthy duty on those responsible for the disposal of private funds, to accept risks which cannot be proper to those accountable for the taxpayer's money. They should venture those free funds for experiments about whose success there may be some measure of doubt. . . . The challenge to seek out opportunities is accepted by this foundation." The Nuffield Foundation had an income in 1946–47 of nearly £400,000, so that it is the largest of all the foundations. Like the other trusts named, it plans its work over periods of five years. Its programme for the current five years covers five main fields: the medical, the natural, the social

sciences, fellowships and similar awards for Great Britain and the
Dominions, and the care of the aged poor. For the latter purpose
the Foundation has just set on foot a corporation with an endowment
of £500,000.

The King Edward Hospital Fund for London was founded in
1897 as a national memorial to Queen Victoria's Diamond Jubilee,
and took its present title in 1902. Incorporated by Act of Parliament
in 1907, its object was defined as "the support, benefit or expansion
of the hospitals of London." The trustees of the fund, however, have
never taken a narrow view of its functions, holding that these include
medical education and the advancement of medical science, as well
as grants for hospital maintenance. The fund has an endowment
of more than £4,000,000, and its total income in 1945 (including
the results of appeals and legacies) approaches £350,000. Its
primary original purpose, of supporting and maintaining hospitals, has now become a State responsibility. The administrators
of the fund look forward to this, not as the end of the fund, but as
the setting free of resources for purposes other than those to which
they have been devoted in the past. They plan to ensure that those
responsible for the day-to-day maintenance of the hospitals are as
far as may be free from the restrictive regulations which are almost
inseparable from the expenditure of monies derived from the national
exchequer.

It remains at the end to mention one more foundation, much
older than any of those named above. It plans to celebrate its
centenary in a few years. This is the Royal Commission for the
Great Exhibition of 1851. The exhibition left a surplus which was
devoted to "promoting the knowledge of science and art and their
application in productive industries." It has given scholarships,
established museums, and done many things of this kind. It has
helped science and research outside the United Kingdom. Its income
is something like £24,000 a year. Like King Edward's Hospital Fund
it is faced by the problem of finding a new sphere of activity in view
of the great extension of the responsibilities of the State.

The five general trusts—City Parochial Foundation, Carnegie
United Kingdom Trust, Pilgrim Trust, King George's Jubilee Trust,
Nuffield Foundation—have between them an endowed income of
something like £750,000 a year. The King Edward's Hospital Fund
and the Royal Commission of 1851 bring the total well above
£900,000; the first of these, like the King George's Jubilee Trust,
plans and hopes to continue to receive gifts and legacies in addition.

All this money is money just as Arthur Hobhouse wanted it, in living hands not dead hands, in private hands not those of the State, but for public purposes. It is money for experiment and pioneering by Voluntary Action. All of it and much more can be well used for such a purpose.

CONTINUING RULE OF THE TESTATOR

Foundations such as those described above are a modern addition of great importance to our agencies for social advance by voluntary action. Their existence does not diminish the need for a complete overhaul of the charitable trusts that have come down from the past, and of the law under which trusts may be created in the future.

The Endowed Schools of 1869 and the City of London Parochial Charities of 1883 were notable victories over the dead hand of the testator. They remained isolated achievements which did not decide the campaign. In relation to all trusts other than educational and outside the City of London victory has remained with the testator, not with Hobhouse and his fellow reformers. Neither Hobhouse's proposals nor the lesser remedies suggested by Mill—for a time limit and for rejection by some authority of mischievous endowments— have been adopted. The wide power of adjusting charitable endowments of every kind in Scotland which once was given to the Home Secretary came to an end in 1881; the Endowed Institutions (Scotland) Act of 1878 was a salient which could not be held. The Endowed Schools Act in England does not apply to any endowment even for educational purposes if it was made after 1869. In England and in Scotland alike the law of charitable trusts to-day is substantially the same as it was 70 or 370 years ago.

Forty-one years after Mill's article, the Court of Appeal, in rejecting a scheme by the Charity Commissioners for administering a sum of £100,000, laid down the law in the following terms:

> The function and duty of the Court is to give effect to the testator's will . . . nor is there any jurisdiction to apply *cy près* so long as any lawful charitable object of the testator's bounty is available, however inexpedient such object may appear to the court as compared with other objects. . . . I, of course, give the Commissioners and the trustees full credit for desiring to do their best, but it is contrary to principle that a testator's wishes should be set aside . . . and his bounty administered not accord-

ing to the view of the Commissioners, and if it is wished that testators should continue to become "pious founders" it is eminently desirable that no doubt should be cast on the security and permanency of their bequests. One of the strongest inducements to gifts of this nature is that desire for posthumous remembrance which has inspired similar gifts for centuries. . . .

It was no part of the Commissioners' duty to consider whether cottage hospitals are or are not desirable.[1]

Thus in 1910 did Mr. Justice Farwell, in dealing with Weir Hospital, echo what had been said in 1867 by Lord Cairns in rejecting a scheme by the Charity Commissioners of that date for Thomas Brown's Animal Sanatory Institution, and denying the right of the commissioners "to make a new will for the testator."

For the majority of the nation, as Mill had said in 1869, the indefeasibility of testamentary dispositions might be a chimera of the past. But the minority who held a contrary view included then and in 1910 and to-day, the people who mattered—the judges bound to apply the law as they found it. Hobhouse once asked the question: "Why should a man whose opinion no one regarded in life, be able to dictate how posterity shall use part of the wealth they make centuries after he is dead?" In the teeth of this question, the decision on Weir Hospital, given in 1910, is still the law.

The judgments given in 1947 in the case of the National Anti-Vivisection Society show greater readiness than has been shown always in the past to question the dictates of testators. But the courts cannot go far on this road without becoming arbiters of public policy and usurping the functions of Parliament. And however far they go their power is insufficient. They may reject as not charitable the purpose for which a testator leaves money; the result is not that the money gets diverted to some better public purpose, but that it goes into the private hands of the next of kin. The courts, again, can do nothing to secure that existing charities are directed to good purpose in accord with new conditions. That, in relation to existing charities in England, is the function of the Charity Commissioners and the continuing legal powers of the Charity Commissioners for making schemes are as completely tied to the assumed intentions of the Founders as were those of the Courts of Equity in the eighteenth century. The particular absurdities and evils pilloried by Hobhouse in his Chamber of Horrors have for the most part, after long delay, been abolished or reduced. But there is nothing to prevent fresh

[1] In *re Weir Hospital* (1910), 2 Ch. 124.

absurdities being created to-day, and no power to bring them to an end.

The administrative position of the Charity Commissioners to-day is as weak as their legal one. All charitable foundations are formally required to send to the commissioners annual accounts of their revenues, but in practice it is impossible for the commissioners to ensure that this is done. Many bodies of trustees may be unaware of this legal obligation. The commissioners have no automatic means of learning about new trusts. They can and do take steps to learn about trusts created by will, studying the public Press and the register of wills at Somerset House. But if a trust is created by deed during the lifetime of the donor, the commissioners may get no notice of it at all.

Of such accounts as are sent in the commissioners make no use for the preparation of a survey; in contrast to the wealth of statistical material as to friendly societies and other agencies compiled by the Chief Registrar, there is for the neighbouring field of charitable trusts—all equally privileged in taxation—almost no information at all. The Brougham Commission of 1818–37 reported on 29,000 charitable foundations and put their total income at £1,200,000. The General Digest of Charitable Trusts completed by the Charity Commissioners in 1876 recorded 36,000 foundations with an income of £2,200,000. To-day the Charity Commission put the number of charities from which accounts are expected by them at a little over 56,000. This is exclusive of the trusts—nearly 30,000 in number—which, being educational, are dealt with by the Ministry of Education.[1]

The Charity Commissioners' figure, for the reasons given above, may well be below the mark. And they cannot give even a guess at the total income involved. It is certain, however, that the total income must be much greater than in any of the earlier estimates. The recent survey made by the Nuffield Foundation of charitable trusts for relief of the aged put the income of something under 5,000 trusts of this nature at £5,000,000 a year, with endowments and property exceeding £80,000,000. These 5,000 trusts are in number less than one-tenth of the whole number with which the Charity Commissioners are concerned. The six modern foundations described in the preceding section of this chapter, with others like them, may

---

[1] In response to an enquiry made by the Social Study Department of Birmingham University, the Ministry of Education in 1937 gave the number of educational foundations known to them as 29,355, but could not state the total income. This figure excludes Scotland, with its separate Department of Education.

have an annual income of a million or so. The 56,000 charitable trusts of the older type have an income which may be ten or twenty or fifty times greater than that.[1]

The Charity Commissioners finally are confined to England. There are charitable trusts in Scotland with the same privileges of perpetuity and of tax exemption, but there is no body which even formally is responsible for knowing about them. Any adjustment of them to meet changing conditions requires a judicial decree as it did in England till 1853. The case for a complete overhaul of the law and administration of charitable trusts in all parts of Britain is not open to question.

[1] The Inland Revenue accounts give a figure of £53,960,000 in 1944-45 as the income *assessed under Schedules A, C and D and exempted*, as accruing to Charities, Colleges, Hospitals, Schools, Friendly Societies, Trade Unions, Queen Anne's Bounty and Savings Banks (Schedule B exemptions are negligible). The Inland Revenue authorities cannot distinguish the proportion of this income received by Charities.

There is a further unknown sum received by Charities as income which is paid in full and not assessed, mainly in the case of Schedule C (pensions, grants, etc., from public funds) and Schedule A (income from property). Not being assessed, this income is not included in the £53,960,000. The assessment having been discharged, the Inland Revenue authorities make no inquiries about income received in Schedule A cases.

Some charities also receive income which is assessed under Schedule D (profits) but which is not exempted because the conditions are not satisfied. The total figure under this head is not ascertainable.

Finally, the Inland Revenue figures omit payments to Charities under the "Seven Year Covenant." A reliable estimate puts the total of these payments at about £4,500,000, "Most of which relates to Charities."

THE NEEDS THAT REMAIN IN A SOCIAL SERVICE STATE

PART THREE

THE NEEDS THAT REMAIN IN A
SOCIAL SERVICES STATE

VII. THE CHANGING ENVIRONMENT OF VOLUNTARY ACTION

To describe completely and in precise terms the changes of the environment in which Voluntary Action has proceeded in any period would mean writing the economic, social and political history of that period. That for Britain in the past hundred and fifty years would fill many books. It is sufficient, as it is necessary, in this chapter to notice those major changes and tendencies in Britain which are most relevant to the subject of this study. They are the rise of the general standard of living since the early part of the nineteenth century; the movement to greater equality in the distribution of incomes in the past thirty or forty years; the parallel movement to greater equality in the distribution of leisure; and the coming in the same period of the Social Service State.

RISING STANDARD OF LIVING

The rise in the general standard of living in Britain, as measured by wages and what they could buy, up to the outbreak of the First World War is a commonplace. The continuing rise to the outbreak of the Second World War was emphasized in my Report of 1942 in advocating abolition of want as a practicable post-war aim:

> The real wages of labour, what the wage-earner could buy with his earnings just before the present war, were in general about one-third higher than in 1900 for about an hour's less work each day.[1]

From this continuing rise in the general standard of living two morals were drawn in 1942:

> First, growing general prosperity and rising wages diminished want, but did not reduce want to insignificance. The moral is that new measures to spread prosperity are needed. . . . Second, the period covered by the comparisons between, say, 1900 and 1936 covers the First World War. The moral is the encouraging

[1] *Report on Social Insurance and Allied Services*, para. 446.

one, that it is wrong to assume that the present war must bring economic progress for Britain, or for the rest of the world, to an end. After four years of open warfare and diversion of effort from useful production to the means of destruction in 1914–18, there followed an aftermath of economic conflict; international trade was given no chance to recover from the war, and Britain entered into a period of mass unemployment in her staple industries. Yet, across this waste period of destruction and dislocation, the permanent forces making for material progress —technical progress and the capacity of human society to adjust itself to new conditions—continued to operate; the real wealth per head in a Britain of shrunken oversea investments and lost export markets, counting in all her unemployed, was materially higher in 1938 than in 1913.

The note in 1942 after three years of a second war was one of belief in continuing progress. On what terms the same note can be wisely sounded in 1948 after three years' experience of war's aftermath, will be considered in the final chapter. In this chapter the influence of a generally rising standard of living on Voluntary Action will be noted, after account has been taken of other economic and social changes.

REDISTRIBUTION OF INCOMES

The rise in the general level of wealth per head during the nineteenth century was not accompanied by any marked change in the distribution of wealth. Stability of the proportions in which, under an economic system governed by the price mechanism, the total product of industry is divided between the principal factors in production—as profits, interest, wages and so forth—is a well-recognized economic phenomenon. Till the Social Service State began to come into being in Britain after the General Election of 1906, the poor grew less poor and the rich grew richer together. There was no set policy of correcting inequality of wealth, either by provision for the poor or by steeply graduated direct taxation. As late as 1913, it is estimated that those below the income tax level of £160 a year were contributing in indirect taxation more than the whole cost of the social services from which they were direct beneficiaries and were making a net contribution to general revenue.[1] Substantial

---

[1] This is stated as probable by Mr. R. Stone in a broadcast on Redistribution of Incomes made in September, 1947. Benefits under the National Insurance Act, 1911, had practically not begun in 1913.

change towards greater equality of incomes began only in the period between the two wars with the growth of direct taxation and of the social services. But there is nothing to suggest that in this period there was any substantial change in the distribution of the product of industry between wages and other factors. Apart from the action of the State in taxing and in providing services, the only definite change towards greater equality of income was a gain by the unskilled and less skilled wage-earners relatively to the skilled men. This resulted partly from action taken by the State in setting up trade boards in 1909, partly as the continuance of changes made in the war, partly from the growth of trade unionism among the less skilled workers. Reinforcing the rise of real wages generally, it led to a diminution of want in its traditional form. Between the two surveys of York made by Rowntree for 1899 and for 1936, and the surveys of London made by Charles Booth for the years about 1889 and through the London School of Economics for 1929, poverty of low wages was replaced largely by poverty through unemployment and other interruptions of earning power.

Social insurance and the allied services continued to develop during the period between the two wars, with unemployment insurance made general in 1920, contributory pensions and widows and orphans insurance in 1926, and unemployment assistance in 1934. By 1935 persons below the new income tax limit of £250 were paying in taxation of all kinds only about 80 per cent of what they were receiving as beneficiaries of the various social services. And direct taxation steeply graduated remained at levels much higher than those of 1913. In 1937 persons with gross incomes above £2,500 were paying 40 per cent and more of their incomes in taxation. The State was compressing the range of inequality of incomes from both ends, at the bottom and at the top.

The Second World War has carried this process a long stage further. From an interesting study in the *Bulletin of the Oxford University Institute of Statistics*,[1] Table 13 (page 220) is taken.

The total number of incomes was much the same in the two years, 20½ million in 1938–39 and 21½ million in 1945–46. The numbers at each end of the Table, below £150 and above £1,000 net, have been reduced, while the numbers in all the middle ranges have been increased. The reduction is most dramatic in the highest ranges.

[1] "The 1947 National Income White Paper," by D. Seers (printed in the *Bulletin* for July, 1947). The first line in the Table, for incomes below £150, is based on calculations made by Mr. Seers. The other lines represent tax assessments as given in the White Paper (Table 36).

TABLE 13
DISTRIBUTION OF POST-TAX INCOME

Range of Income after Tax	Number of Incomes	
	1938–39	1945–46
£		
Under 150	13,500,000	7,500,000
150–250	4,500,000	8,000,000
250–500	1,820,000	5,225,000
500–1,000	450,000	652,000
1,000–2,000	155,000	137,000
2,000–4,000	56,000	35,000
4,000–6,000	12,000	840
6,000 and over	7,000	45

In 1938–39 there were 7,000 people with £6,000 or more to spend after paying tax; in 1945–46 there were 45 persons only as rich as this. In 1938–39 there were 12,000 persons each commanding £4,000 to £6,000 a year net; in 1945–46 only 840 persons were as rich as this. Each £ of course would not buy as much after the war as before it. For obtaining consumers' goods and services the £ of 1938 had come to be 12s. 11d. in 1946.

Another interesting table of Mr. Seers', taking account both of taxation and of change in the value of money, gives the real incomes distributed along various channels as follows:

TABLE 14
MOVEMENTS OF REAL INCOME, 1938 TO 1946
(£000 millions at 1945 prices)

	1938	1945	1946
Net rent	0·48	0·20	0·21
Net profits and interest	1·94	1·58	1·57
Net salaries	1·60	1·33	1·41
Net wages	2·44	2·52	2·70
Net pay of H.M. Forces	0·11	1·23	0·50
Transfer incomes	0·39	0·46	0·72
Net aggregate private income	6·96	7·32	7·11
Net Government revenue	0·95	2·26	1·85
Net National Product	7·91	9·58	8·96

Those who live by rents have in eight years lost, in real terms, more than half their income. Those who depend on profits and interest have also lost substantially, a result calling for two comments. First, the post-war interest includes that on a greatly increased national debt. But, in spite of this increase of debt, the debt service seems likely to absorb no greater a proportion of the total national income than before the war; this is a consequence of the cheap money policy, combined with the large increase in money terms of the national output and income. Second, the net share of profits is smaller only because of high taxation. Out of the total product of industry, in spite of all that had been done to push up wage rates, a larger proportion went to profits and a smaller to wages in 1945 than in 1938; this presumably represents the normal consequence of rising prices, with wages lagging behind.

The decline in the share of "salaries" is due in the main, if not wholly, to the diminished numbers employed in distribution; shop assistants in the White Paper calculations are treated as salaried, and their number has fallen sharply since before the war.

As against these losses, wages show a substantial net increase. So do "transfer incomes" which include social security payments of all kinds—pensions, sick benefit, assistance, family allowances. These are in the main substitutes for wages.

REDISTRIBUTION OF LEISURE

Parallel to the movement towards more equal distribution of wealth, there has been a redistribution of leisure, giving more to those who had least, taking leisure from those who had most. In each case an impulse given in the First World War has been reinforced by the Second World War. But the redistribution of leisure owes less than does redistribution of incomes to direct action by the State, and more to social changes, whose origin in some cases lies well back in the nineteenth century.

Increase of the leisure of wage-earners comes through shortening of working hours. This was at all times one of the objectives of the trade unions. In the aftermath of the First World War something like an hour a day was taken off the normal working time of most people who worked for wages. In the aftermath of the Second World War there has been a move for another shortening of hours, taking the form in a good many cases of a proposal to knock Saturday off the working week. How far this can go and whether all the gains made can be held is at the moment uncertain. Increase of leisure of wage-earners has come in the last years in another form—the generalization of holidays with pay, usually a week at least.

The large class of those who do essential work not as wage-earners —the housewives without servants—have also had some increase of their leisure, as compared with their Victorian predecessors. To some extent this has come through improvement in their homes— light, water, sanitation, labour-saving equipment. To a larger extent it has come through decline in the size of families. To some extent it has come through opportunity to buy in shops things that they used to make at home. Under all three heads the gains have been distributed unequally; some housewives to-day have homes as bad as ever and families as large as their mothers or grandmothers had. To set against the gain through lightening of some old tasks, nearly all housewives, in the Second World War and since the war, have had thrown on them additional work of managing rations, of standing in queues, of fetching goods in place of having them sent. As Mr. Seers puts it, "housewives are now to a greater extent an auxiliary labour force for distribution" of consumer goods.[1]

While leisure has increased for those who before had least of it— even on balance probably for the servantless housewives taken as a whole—it has been cut down sharply for those who had most leisure, because they could get all their housework and much personal service done for them. In the Victorian age domestic servants could always be had; between the two wars they became scarce. Since the Second World War they often cannot be found even for helping those whose need is beyond question—mothers with young children beyond their strength, old people and invalids.

There is no doubt more leisure on an average of the whole people to-day than there was in Victorian times. But it is distributed more widely, in smaller parcels. This raises problems for Voluntary Action in two ways. There is, first, the problem of the good use of leisure —one of the general needs discussed in Chapter IX. There is, second, the problem of obtaining from the many the voluntary service which used to come before from some of the few, and without which a good society cannot be made.

THE COMING OF THE SOCIAL SERVICE STATE

There had been public action in many fields for the improvement of social conditions throughout the nineteenth century. There was a string of Factory and Mines Acts, largely associated in origin with Lord Shaftesbury, for regulating conditions of work. There were Acts to ensure the supply of public services of roads, bridges,

[1] *Op. cit.*, p. 234 n.

sanitation and water. There was a string of Housing Acts,[1] like the Factory Acts associated in origin with Lord Shaftesbury; beginning by the encouragement of voluntary action, these passed over largely to authorization and encouragement of action by local authorities. There were Education Acts, beginning by encouraging and helping voluntary agencies, proceeding in 1870 to the undertaking of elementary education for all as a responsibility of the State wherever voluntary provision was not adequate. There was the Workmen's Compensation Act of 1897, altering in selected dangerous occupations the terms of the contract between employers and employees.

Public action for social advance did not begin with the Government established in power by the General Election of 1905, but it took a new turn then. There began a new relation between the State and the citizen—the provision of income and services to individual adult citizens by use of the power of the State. The first measure of the new type was the Old Age Pensions Act of 1908, giving pensions at seventy, subject to a means test but without contributions, at the cost of the State. A greater change was made by the National Insurance Act of 1911 introducing social insurance; this meant the raising by compulsory contributions from wage-earners and their employers as well as by general taxation, of funds to be used to provide individual incomes in sickness and unemployment and the services of a doctor. In the major part of this scheme, covering employees generally for sickness, the State by the device of Approved Societies avoided responsibility for direct administration. The minor part, dealing with unemployment, was in several ways a greater innovation. In making insurance against sickness compulsory by Part I of the Act of 1911, Britain was following an example set thirty years before by Bismarck in Germany. But the scheme of compulsory insurance for unemployment benefit, applied by Part II of the Act to selected trades, was the first of its kind in the world. It was accompanied by a Labour Exchanges Act of 1909 by which the State undertook to perform directly for the citizen the service of guiding him in the search for employment, a service of a different degree of individuality and intimacy from anything that had been attempted before.

There had been Labour Exchanges before the Act of 1909. In this field, as everywhere, voluntary action did the pioneering—the first labour bureau being established by Mr. Nathaniel Cohen at

---

[1] Twenty-eight Housing and Health Acts between 1851 and 1903 are enumerated by Mr. E. R. Dewsnap in *The Housing Problem in England and Wales* (published in Manchester University Economic Series, 1907).

Egham in 1885. There followed experiments by local authorities, for which legal authority was given by a Labour Bureaux Act of 1902. When the Government was considering its policy for unemployment in 1908 the question was raised whether the projected Labour Exchanges should be administered directly by the State or should be entrusted to local authorities with Exchequer grants. The decision that they should be national, taken personally at the time by Mr. Winston Churchill as President of the Board of Trade, was more momentous than it seemed at the time. It involved making a new model of decentralized administration and a new type of public servant.

Social insurance, like all new things in Britain, roused widespread opposition when it was new. The battle to get it established was won by the driving force of its author, Lloyd George. In the next thirty years it gained general acceptance. The proposal made in my Report of 1942 to use the 1911 method of social insurance to secure a subsistence income for all at all times did not need to be argued, so far as the mass of the people were concerned. The British people are apt to dislike new things till they have tried them. It is not sensible, for example, to ask the housewives of Britain whether or not they would like some new way which they have never tried, of heating their homes, or cooking, or washing, or caring for the children. But the British people are open to argument and practical demonstration. It is vital to keep open the channels of practical experiment in such matters and in all other fields. Experiment has come in the past through Voluntary Action and is most certain to come that way.

DECLINE IN INFLUENCE OF THE CHURCHES

It is not remembered often that of the eighteen volumes in which Charles Booth published the result of his London Survey, eight were devoted to "Religious Influences." This reflected in part Charles Booth's personal interest; he was brought up as a Unitarian in a family for whom religious belief and practice were always important. It is difficult to believe that any present-day survey of social conditions in Britain would give proportionate space to the churches and their influence.

This is no place for attempting a reasoned estimate of the importance of organized religion in the life of modern Britain, as compared with its importance during the nineteenth century. Still less is it a place for looking forward and seeking to forecast the probabilities of a revival of influence for any particular church or for the churches generally in future.

That there has been loss of religious influence is certain. That this means a weakening of one of the springs of voluntary action for social advance is equally certain. The lives of the pioneers in Chapter V show how much of their inspiration for service to society most of them owed to their religious belief.

Diminished influence of the Churches must be taken as one of the changes in the environment of voluntary action.

SOCIAL SECURITY AND AFTER

The process begun by the National Insurance Act of 1911 is being completed in the aftermath of the Second World War. In the field covered by the Report on Social Insurance and Allied Services of 1942, five statutes have been passed already; the Family Allowances and Ministry of National Insurance Acts of 1945, the two National Insurance Acts and the National Health Service Act of 1946. Three more measures in the same field, dealing with national assistance, with claims for personal injury, and with the powers of industrial assurance companies and friendly societies, have been introduced in 1947 and will no doubt become law.

The speed and extent of this development owe something to the nature of the Government established after the General Election of 1945. But the development itself is not a party issue. The two National Insurance Acts represented a policy agreed by the Coalition Government of the war and the Family Allowances Act was passed before the election. It had been preceded in 1944 by the Education Act, immensely enlarging the scope of public responsibility in another field. That the State will seek to do more for the citizen in future than in the past, whatever the political colour of the Government, is certain. The future of Voluntary Action must be considered in the light of this conclusion.

The State has undertaken to see that, irrespective of the means of his parents, every child shall have education fitted to his abilities. The State has set out to ensure freedom from want by ensuring that at all times, of earning and not earning alike, the income of each family shall be enough for its basic needs. The State has set out to ensure freedom from avoidable disease, so far as this can be attained by providing that every sick person irrespective of means shall be able to get the treatment needed to make him well. What else remains to be done? This is considered in the two chapters that follow, one dealing with the needs that will remain in special classes of the community, the other dealing with two general needs of all classes.

VIII. SOME SPECIAL NEEDS THAT REMAIN

Needs of Age. Needs of Childhood; Children Outside their Parents' Homes; Children in their Parents' Homes. Needs of the Physically Handicapped: General Survey; the Blind; the Deaf and Deafened; Disabled Persons (Employment) Act; the Chronic Sick; Handicapped Children; Training Colleges for the Disabled. The Weakest Suffer. Other Classes with Special Needs: the Unmarried Mother and her Child; Discharged Prisoners; Parents. Conclusion as to Special Needs.

NEEDS OF AGE

In my Report on Social Insurance the problem of the provision to be made for old age was described as the most important and in some ways the most difficult of all the problems of social security. It presented itself as such for two reasons: the size of the problem and its variety. Owing to the large and rapidly growing proportion of old people in the population, the prospective cost of pensions was much the largest item in the social security budget. Owing to the variety in the economic and social consequences of old age in individual cases, the right line to take was not easy to determine. Very many of the old were desperately poor. Many were not in want at all; they did not need to apply for the old age pension of 10s. a week or they found themselves comfortable financially with that and what they had of their own from relatives.

The problem of making financial provision for old age is now in the main solved or in process of solution. But old age remains one of the main problems for this Report as for my former Report. It affords the simplest and perhaps largest illustration of needs which cannot be satisfied merely by providing a subsistence income. And it remains a problem of extremely unequal incidence in individual cases. For many people old age in future will present no problem beyond itself; in words once used by my father about his mother at eighty-eight, they will find themselves "as happy as so old a person can be," with a sufficient income, with family care, with occupation for their time. For many, however, old age wears a very different aspect, and, if we leave things as they are, will continue to wear it. Many old people will be desperately and needlessly unhappy, even on a subsistence income.

Fortunately, this problem has caught public attention. The administration of supplementary pensions by the Assistance Board has more

than once, in the admirable annual reports of the Board, been made
the occasion for showing how generally supplementary pensions need
themselves to be supplemented—by welfare; the discoveries, among
the clients of the Board, of 85,000 old age pensioners over eighty living
alone, and of 200,000 couples over seventy living alone are two only
of the Board's more dramatic contributions to showing the scale and
nature of the problem. Within the last two years the whole problem
of old people has been made the subject of survey by a committee
under the chairmanship of Mr. Seebohm Rowntree, whose work
was made possible by a grant from the Nuffield Foundation. Even
more recently the problem has been the subject of study by an
expert committee appointed by the British Medical Association,
which naturally gave particular attention to questions of medical
care. Both these reports should be widely read.[1] In the light of
them, the main needs to be met can be set out briefly, beginning
with a division of the aged into three main classes: those physically
capable of living independent lives, those needing help and care
but not regular medical attention or nursing, those needing doctoring
or nursing or both.

First, there is an unsatisfied need for suitable housing for old
people physically able to lead an independent life. The account of
the housing conditions of old people that is presented in the Nuffield
Committee Report, in the words of the report "makes a depressing
story"; the conditions are in many cases frankly intolerable. This
does not mean, as the Committee point out, that the old are generally
worse housed than the rest of the population; one of the interesting
facts established by the Committee is the length of time for which
most old people had been in their present homes. The houses are
the same as always, but what was merely an inconvenience in youth
—awkward steps in the house, or a difficult range, or no water tap
indoors, or having to go up or down many stairs or right out of
the house for coals or a lavatory—become intolerable and sometimes dangerous discomforts in old age. The bad housing of so many
old people who have nothing wrong with them except age is part

---

[1] *Old People, the Report of a Survey Committee under the Chairmanship of B. Seebohm
Rowntree*, is published for the trustees of the Nuffield Foundation by the Oxford
University Press (1947, 2s. 6d.); it is referred to below as *Old People. The Report
of the British Medical Association Committee on Care and Treatment of the Elderly and
Infirm* (referred to below as *B.M.A. Report* (1947)) is obtainable on request from
the offices of the Association. An excellent guide to practical treatment of the
problem, under the title *Old People's Welfare*, has been published for the National
Old People's Welfare Committee, by the National Council of Social Service,
26, Bedford Square, London, W.C.1.

of the general deficiency of good housing, and cannot be dealt with separately.

But the old do not need just the same houses as those with large families. Every new housing scheme should include a proportion of small houses adapted to the needs of the old, not isolated but built where the old people will want to live, among others, within reach of shops and bus routes. The Rowntree Committee rightly criticized the view which they found prevalent among individuals and local authorities that, in the present acute shortage of houses of all types, precedence in the use of labour and building materials should be given to family houses over dwellings for old people.

> Apart from the fact that it would scarcely be right entirely to deprive old people, who are a section of the community, of some share in the scarce commodities of building materials and labour, it is by no means certain, as is popularly supposed, that the interests of the old and of the young are at variance in this matter. On the contrary, there is evidence that with a little persuasion, quite a considerable proportion of old people, now occupying good houses that are too big for them, would be willing to move if a small house near to that which they are now occupying could be made available to them.

Town planning and housing policy should take account of the fact that a large and growing proportion of the people to be housed will be ageing couples, who, even if they have children and are on good terms with them, will want if they can to live in their own houses. The unwilling or undesired presence of old people in young homes is itself a handicap, inducing friction, undermining marriages, restricting geographical mobility.

Second, there is an unsatisfied need for homes with service and care at hand for emergencies, for old people who, though not in need of regular medical attention or nursing, cannot fend wholly for themselves. As is said in a description of a proposed new home for the aged, "a stage is reached by most old people sooner or later when they can no longer look after themselves in individual dwellings, but must be given accommodation in some kind of communal establishment with communal meals; they are still far from being bedridden, but they need help in such things as dressing and bathing and certainly need supervision."[1] The existing provision for this need, whether in public institutions like those of the Public Assis-

[1] Trustees of the London Parochial Charities, describing Isledon House, "a proposed building to accommodate Aged Poor and others." (December, 1946.)

tance Authorities, or in voluntary institutions such as almshouses and homes run as businesses, is insufficient in amount, largely antiquated in design, and sometimes deplorable in quality. Ninety-five per cent of all old people now live in private dwellings, but it is clear that a number of them do so unwillingly and that others should not do so; some, by their infirmities, throw intolerable burdens on their relatives and some live alone deplorably. The extent and nature of this unsatisfied need for old people's homes with service and care appear in the Nuffield Committee Report in many ways; in the long waiting lists for admission to well-managed voluntary homes; in the accounts of the existing out-of-date public institutions; in the shocking private homes run as businesses to which some old people are driven to have recourse.[1] These last are in some ways the most instructive of all. Many old people have money, many more will have money in future, but money will not buy them even a tolerable existence, as things stand to-day.

Third, there is need for a new approach in the medical treatment of the old. This is the gist of the British Medical Association Committee's Report.[2] Liability to sickness increases with age; the aged are a rapidly increasing proportion of the whole population. It follows that "in future, with an ageing population, there must be a rapid increase in the number of aged sick." It follows that a special determined attempt should be made to reduce preventable sickness among the old.

In the past, many of these elderly patients have found their way into institutions and hospitals for the chronic sick, where in some cases, with but few facilities for rehabilitation and in an atmosphere of defeatism, they have been treated by little more than recumbency. The results of this lack of treatment are all too well known to those who have had experience of such conditions. When confined to bed for long periods these patients soon drift into the "infirmary decubitus" with its avoidable contractures and deformities. In such positions they become fixed and immobile and often unable to feed themselves. . . .

Under such conditions the patient soon sinks into apathy and, having lost hope of recovery, grows fretful, irritable, and morose. This atmosphere of hopelessness is shared by staff and patients

[1] See particularly Appendix 14 to the *Nuffield Committee's Report*, with its specimen cases of unsuccessful applications for admission to a voluntary home, each telling a story of unhappiness; pp. 63–5 for the public institutions; pp. 69–70 for three private homes.

[2] *Report* (1947) *of the Committee on the Care and Treatment of the Elderly and Infirm.*

alike, for the latter are equally aware that life now offers them
no more than slow deterioration under regular nursing attention.

This preventable tragedy does not end here, for these unfortunate patients in their growing numbers must, if inadequately
treated, rapidly diminish the available hospital beds of all types.
Moreover, as a result of this slowing of the in-patient turnover,
out-patients awaiting admission to hospital will in future have
an even longer wait than at present. This state of affairs leads
to a wasteful use of nurses, and there can be no doubt that it
will tend to hamper recruitment to an already depleted profession. Without reform there is a grave likelihood that hospital
services throughout the country, already severely handicapped
by a shortage of beds due to insufficient nurses, will be still
further crippled.[1]

The Committee proposed accordingly the setting up in selected
general hospitals of "geriatric departments," that is to say wards
reserved exclusively for elderly patients "all of whom are under-
going investigation or active treatment and rehabilitation so that
in due course they may be discharged from such wards, either to
their own homes, or, after classification, to other appropriate accommodation." Some of those admitted would, of course, fail to recover,
they would die soon or they would become judged incurable, cases
for permanent nursing care in long term annexes of the hospitals.
But some who now go one or another of those roads would, by new
methods, that is to say by appropriate specialized treatment, be
given a new lease of happy independent life. The Committee suggest
from experience that some 40 per cent of all new admissions to a
geriatric department could recover in this way.

The three classes into which old people have been divided here
—those able to live independently, those needing service and care
without doctoring, those needing medical attention and nursing, are
not rigidly separate. Many people pass from one class to another,
and the provision made for age must provide for this. Very few of
the existing homes for the aged who are not infirm will keep them
when they become immobile; they have not, therefore, the quality
of a permanent refuge in which life can be ended peacefully. The
old people's homes of the Salvation Army appear to present an
exception, normally keeping the old people till death, unless they
become mentally incapable or in need of constant medical care.
And the Trustees of the London Parochial Charities in their imagi-

[1] *op. cit.*, paras. 26 and 27.

native planning of a new model home have faced this need. Isledon House, in addition to flats for old people and other accommodation in the same building for families, includes a sick bay for temporary treatment and a rest home for those who need continuous care.

> People who are hale and hearty when first selected for admission to homes eventually become infirm and require constant attention.
> There would therefore appear to be need (in any co-ordinated scheme for accommodation of old people) for a suitable rest home to which residents can be moved when they become ill; without such a home there is the risk that the character of the plan will be changed as the original residents become bedridden or that they will have to be moved to a home at a distance and be separated from their friends at a time when such a move is regarded with dread.

The needs of old people are not of course met simply by housing them. There are many for whom the possibility of a happy independent life depends on their getting help in one way or another with domestic tasks. This may take the form of meals cooked outside and sent round to them; there are interesting experiments in this being made by the Invalid Kitchens of London. It may take the form of home helps, people to do for the old some of the work of their homes. Local authorities are now empowered to extend their home helps schemes to cover persons sick or infirm whether through age or otherwise. The trouble is that the number of people willing to work as home helps is far less than the demand for them; in many cases hitherto local authorities have given preference to others than the old, confining their schemes to mothers with young children. This is another illustration of the tragic dilemma which results from shortage: are we to put first the building of the future or the saving of those who are weak through age? And it is another case in which Voluntary Action may provide the service which cannot be found by public authority.[1]

There remain two general needs of old people—for occupation and for companionship. Sooner or later the occupation of all old people must become recreation rather than paid work; retirement must come to all at last. But for many reasons the compulsory retirement at some fixed age, sixty-five, sixty, fifty-five, which is the rule in some occupations, and can be defended there, is bad as a universal rule. One of the most interesting chapters in the Nuffield Report is

[1] See *Old People's Welfare*, p. 11.

that on the old in employment, showing, when there is good demand
for men, how well in many occupations the older men can meet it.[1]
The State is now engaged on a new experiment in giving pensions
only on condition of retirement and at the same time seeking to
encourage men to postpone retirement by making the pension higher
for each year of postponement. The working out of this experiment
needs careful watching, and readiness to adjust the measures taken
in the light of experience.[2]

As to the need for companionship—the Nuffield Report emphasizes
loneliness as one of the distressing features of old age.

> All who have done welfare work among the old have found
> it the most common, if at the same time the most imponderable,
> of the ills from which the aged suffer, and its frequency was
> amply confirmed by our investigators.[3]

It illustrates this generalization by moving examples of loneliness,
particularly among old men and in cities. But although perhaps
loneliness is most striking in the big towns—in London and Wolver-
hampton rather than in Oldham and Mid-Rhondda—it certainly
is not always true that the more rural the area the less lonely the
old people.

> Village neighbourliness is sometimes a myth. Our Cambridge-
> shire investigator found a number of old people who had
> virtually no visitors at all.[4]

Nor, again, is loneliness confined to people living in their own
homes. It may afflict as distressingly old people in institutions, if
they cannot easily see their own young people, or if they find themselves with active minds cooped up day and night with others who
are senile. Companionship depends on fitting.

Provision of old people's clubs by the thousand was named to us
by Mr. Seebohm Rowntree as one of the things most required. Old
men, in his view, felt the need of continuing contacts outside their
homes even more than old women, to make up for the contacts lost
through retirement from work; they were less able to fill in their
time happily at home; the addiction of retired men in the higher

[1] See particularly para. 251 of the Report setting out the experience of a number
of individual firms.

[2] The occupations of old people have been the subject of an interesting study
made by the official Social Survey, relating to May, 1945. It would be of great
interest to repeat this survey for a date subsequent to the introduction of the new
pensions.

[3] *Op. cit.*, para. 144.

[4] *Op. cit.*, para. 147.

income brackets for "going round to the club" is sign of a need felt in every income bracket.

A great many clubs are now being started by agencies of many kinds. But a club which simply means the right to use a room in a public building one or two days a week, with someone else using it for the rest of the week, though better than nothing, does not meet the case. What is wanted is a room or rooms belonging to the old people, not shared with others, a place where each of them can go, or not go, as he feels inclined; where he can read and talk and play games and have some simple refreshment; where he will come to be missed if for some days he is not in his accustomed place, so that someone will go to look him up. Clubs afford perhaps the most natural centre from which visiting of old people in their homes can spring naturally.[1]

The vivid account given in one of the Mass Observation Reports printed in the Supplementary Volume of meetings of Old Age Pensioner Associations should be read to complete the picture of old age in Britain to-day. These associations exist primarily to advance the interest of their members in getting from the Government the largest possible pensions on the best possible terms. But from this common interest has sprung the habit of meeting, spreading to collaboration for social and other purposes. For many of their members these associations supply the spice of lively companionship.

The problem of the old people in the Britain of to-day and to-morrow is not one for uniform treatment. It is as varied as it is large and growing. The one thing certain about it is that it has not been solved by the pensions of the National Insurance Act, and that it cannot be solved by money payments of any kind. It makes a call for service of many kinds and for trying many differing plans. From this point of view a cordial welcome must be given to the action of the Nuffield Foundation in following up the report which they requested from Mr. Rowntree and his committee, by establishing, with a very substantial capital, a "National Corporation for the Care of Old People." This should be a material contribution towards making all old people as happy as old people can be.

NEEDS OF CHILDHOOD

Most children happily find all their needs, other than for education and similar technical help, met for them within their homes

[1] The *Nuffield Report*, paras. 231–36, gives an interesting description of the Sons of Rest Clubs initiated in the Midlands by Mr. W. H. Hackett and already more than fifty in number, as well as examples in other places.

or through their parents. There are some for whom this normal provision through the family fails. These children are to be found in two places, some outside their parents' homes, some in their homes.

(i) *Children Outside their Parents' Homes*

The children deprived of a normal home life who are outside their parents' homes have been the subject of a recent investigation by two Inter-Departmental Committees, for England and Wales and for Scotland respectively, and are the subject of a Children Bill introduced by the Government in the House of Lords in February, 1948. The appointment of these two Committees, as was explained by the Lord Chancellor in introducing the Bill in the House of Lords on February 10, 1948, is a good illustration of the influence of individual citizens in rousing public action. A letter from Lady Allen of Hurtwood, appearing in *The Times* of July 15, 1944, called attention to the unhappy conditions in which children deprived of their natural parents' care were being brought up in many institutions, both public and private, and urged an inquiry "with full government support . . . to explore this largely uncivilized territory." The letter brought to its writer many letters supporting her criticism and providing information which in due course became embodied in a pamphlet: *Whose Children?* Public feeling was roused and the Government, with commendable promptness, proceeded to the appointment of their two Committees. That for England and Wales, usually known by the name of its Chairman, Miss Myra Curtis, being appointed in March, 1945, reported in August, 1946. That for Scotland was under the chairmanship of Mr. J. A. Clyde, K.C. As it discovered much the same things and made broadly similar recommendations as did the Curtis Committee, it will be sufficient here to deal with the latter only. The problem in Scotland is much the same as in the southern part of Britain.

The Curtis Committee was known officially as the Care of Children Committee. The terms of reference required the Committee "to inquire into existing methods of providing for children who from loss of parents or from any cause whatever are deprived of normal home life with their own parents or relatives, and to consider what further measures should be taken to ensure that these children are brought up under conditions best calculated to compensate them for the lack of parental care." They confined their attention to children who were away from their parents, that is to say, in effect, to children in public institutions or in voluntary homes, whether the latter are maintained by philanthropic organizations or conducted as businesses. The total number of children thus coming under review was 125,000, of whom about 40,000 are in local authority institutions, about 40,000 in voluntary homes, and 45,000 in other places, including Approved schools, remand homes, and Approved probation homes and hostels for juvenile offenders, and a great variety of foster homes. Some, both of the Approved schools and of the foster homes, are maintained by public authorities and some by voluntary agencies. Altogether of the 125,000 children probably half are now in the care of a public authority and half in the care of a voluntary agency.

The report of the Curtis Committee leaves no doubt that the provision made for these children under public authorities is now unsatisfactory in many ways. In the first place, though under the regulations of the Ministry of Health no children over three ought to be in a workhouse at all (that is to say, in an institution dealing with adults also under the Poor Law) except as extremely temporary visitors, a substantial number are in fact still found there; the Ministry of Health, for whatever reason, has not felt able to enforce its regulations. The following extracts from the Committee's report are relevant:

> On the whole the standard of care of the older children in workhouses was much below the nursery standard. The provision for play and occupation for the older children, who in theory were there temporarily, was for the most part appallingly bad (para. 146).
>
> In a number of the institutions visited, defective children were associating with normal children (para. 149).
>
> The unsuitability of its staff and its inadequacy in numbers was even more serious in its effect on the children than the type of building. In very few institutions did the number and qualifications of the staff seem to be even fairly adequate (para. 151).
>
> We have no alternative but to paint this very gloomy picture of the conditions in which children are at present received and maintained by many authorities in adult institutions (para. 156).

When the Committee came to look at the public institutions kept specially for children under local authorities, that is to say the official children's homes, the picture was not quite so gloomy, but it was not cheerful.

> We saw very few examples of modern buildings in use as children's homes (para. 167).

We regard the whole of our report on these homes as to some extent illustrative of the effects of employment of staff without adequate qualifications (para. 177).

It was the exception rather than the rule to find children in the homes who were not unduly hungry for attention from visitors, or more constrained in their relation with adults than is usual for children of their age. We do not mean to imply by this that the children were seriously neglected or treated with deliberate personal harshness or rigidity. Our impression was rather that the lack of understanding of children's needs led with the best intentions to a dreary uninteresting life in many of the homes, and that this showed itself in a lack of liveliness and vigour in the children (para. 210).

Of course there were, by contrast to this, particular homes where a progressive authority or an inspired official was giving the children all that they could need for happiness, but it would be undue complacency to suggest that this was common.

When the Committee came on to the homes maintained by voluntary organizations they began by pointing out that "these organizations varied widely in size, funds and capacity." "At one end of the scale were the three large societies each caring for thousands of children in homes established all over the country; at the other, are the small villa homes managed by a local committee and financed as a local charity, for seven or ten local children."

Speaking generally the homes under the control of a central organization have the advantage of an enlightened general policy and the greater opportunities open to a large organization for making good staff appointments. . . . On the whole, therefore, a good average standard can more readily be attained than in the small independent homes. . . . In the independent homes there is a much greater variety of standard ranging from the good to the definitely bad.

These differences of standard from the good to the bad covered differences in the ratio of staff to children, in the training of staff, in the preparation of children for after careers and in many other matters.

The three large societies referred to by the Curtis Committee are presumably Dr. Barnardo's Homes, with some 7,500 children in their care, the Catholic Child Welfare Council with upwards of 14,000, and the Church of England Children's Society with more than 6,000.

There is also the National Children's Home with more than 3,000 in its direct care and over 1,000 adopted through it. And there are three smaller agencies—the Shaftesbury Homes and Arethusa Training Ship, the Jewish Board of Guardians and the Children's Aid Society, associated with the larger ones through the National Association of Children's Homes. Outside these are many small independent agencies.

The Curtis Committee summed up their general impression of the voluntary homes in the following terms.

> In the main homes run by the voluntary organizations expressed the sincere and general desire of their founders to do good to those in special need, and to make provision for the homeless child at a period in the nation's history when the statutory services were not as developed as they are to-day. Although often hampered by large buildings which made difficult the individual relationships so necessary to the full effectiveness of their work, there was no indication that as a group the voluntary homes fell below the general level of child care now obtaining throughout the country. In many instances they were well above it (para. 227).

The committee's principal recommendations include the following:

(1) That responsibility for the care of deprived children at the departmental level should be in one department. The Committee did not venture to suggest which of the three rival departments to which they owed their appointment (Home Office, Ministry of Health and Ministry of Education) should undertake this responsibility. Since their report, the Home Office has been designated for that purpose, though naturally the responsibilities of the Ministry of Health and the Ministry of Education in their special fields remain.

(2) That the central department should be empowered to make rules under which children may be boarded out or maintained in institutions, these rules being applied to voluntary organizations equally with local authorities.

(3) That all voluntary homes should be registered with and inspected by the central department, but that subject to general rules and to this inspection, voluntary organizations should be free to continue their present activities in the care of children.

The Report of the Curtis Committee, following on the revelations which led to its appointment, has had a marked effect on opinion and action. It has been accepted by the public and by the Government as convincing evidence of inadequacy in the provision now made for children deprived of normal home life. It has been followed within eighteen months by the introduction of a Bill in Parliament designed to give effect to its principal recommendations. The doubt is not whether such a Bill is necessary. The doubt is rather whether a Bill so designed goes far enough.[1]

Since the precise form in which this Bill will reach the Statute Book is uncertain, it would be unprofitable at this date to discuss its provisions in detail. But it may be worth while to name the two main problems that arise on the provisions of the Bill as introduced.

The first main problem is that of securing adequate care for deprived children wherever they are and at the same time avoiding segregation of them in any way from other children. Will both sides of this double object be achieved most readily by making the deprived children the subject of a special committee in every local authority area (as is proposed in the Bill), or by making them a new special responsibility of the committee which deals with children generally, that is to say the Education Committee (as is proposed by Lady Allen of Hurtwood in the article cited above)?

The second main problem is that of preserving the freedom, variety and interest of voluntary agencies, while taking steps to ensure that all of them are brought up to the standard of the best of them. It is possible for a voluntary agency, no less than a public agency, to be tied by bad traditions of the past and to acquire a vested interest in methods which should be discarded. The doubt may fairly be expressed whether the Bill, as first introduced, did not leave the voluntary agencies too much freedom to be antiquated and bureaucratic.

Behind these two problems in the drafting of the Children Bill looms a larger question. The care which parents give to their children is not given for money. When that care fails, it cannot be replaced by people who do what they do only for money. How are we going to find foster-parents and house-mothers who, under local authorities and voluntary agencies alike, will do their work for the sake of the children and not for the pay that they receive?

[1] See an article in the *Fortnightly Review* for March, 1947, by Lady Allen of Hurtwood, setting out "Some Criticisms of the Curtis Report." The gist of the criticisms is that the Report, "very favourably inclined to the voluntary organizations," did not apply to them the measures proposed for bringing all public authorities up to the right standard.

(ii) *Children in their Parents' Homes*

The Committees on the Care of Children did not concern themselves with children in their homes, but from one point of view their
reports have been described as "a revelation of the home life of this
country." This description, in the editorial of the first number of
a new periodical devoted to children,[1] is based on the fact that
relatively few of the children in voluntary homes are there because
they are orphans. "The majority of these children are deprived of
home life for other reasons, chiefly through the wreck of domestic
and marital relationships."[2] The editorial proceeded to infer that
the children outside their own homes were only a symptom of failure
of home life which sometimes left them still in their homes.

A Royal Commission on the home life of the children of this
country would produce evidence which would make the "black
spots" of the Curtis Report seem white as snow.

In much the same spirit the annual report of Dr. Barnardo's
Homes for the year 1946 points a contrast between the early days of
the homes and their present experience:

Material destitution of the type common when our founder
began his work is, of course, to-day practically non-existent.

[1] Editorial in Vol. 1, No. 1, of the *Child Care Quarterly* (March 1947).
[2] The reasons for admission to the Church of England Societies Homes in
two recent years are given as follows:—

				1936		1946	
				Number	Per cent	Number	Per cent
Orphans	..	..	..	40	3·6	95	5·0
Fatherless	..	..	..	65	5·8	57	3·0
Motherless	..	..	..	172	15·4	68	3·5
Broken Homes	..	..	..	302	27·1	383	20·0
Illegitimate	..	..	..	394	35·4	899	46·8
Unclassified	..	..	..	141	12·7	417	21·7
				1,114	100·0	1,919	100·0

The unclassified comprise cripples, Approved School cases and convalescent
cases.
These figures show no marked difference between the two years except perhaps
in the decline of those admitted because motherless. In each year something like
two-thirds of the cases represent broken homes or illegitimacy; no doubt a proportion of the unclassified comes indirectly through one or other of those causes.

Higher wages, abundant opportunities for employment and much social legislation have produced this very desirable result. Nevertheless the problem of the children deprived of normal home life still remains with us. Destitution as known in the Victorian era has been replaced by what might be termed a "moral destitution." To-day we find children suffering because of a widespread decline among a large section of the population of a sense of moral values.

In the early records of Dr. Barnardo's Homes may be found such grim phrases as "mother died of exhaustion"; "frequent exposure"; "grave lack of food." To-day the story is more often "father away on active service"; "mother neglecting children"; or "the father has deserted family. Mother of low mentality."

It is not necessary to accept literally these rather sweeping condemnations of popular morale. That there are more divorces and more broken families to-day than before the World Wars is undeniable. But the conditions are also different and more trying. With the housing shortage making normal family life impossible in so many cases, with the hasty marriages and the separations inseparable from war, it would be a wonder if there were not more broken homes.

We need not assert or admit that as a people we are of weaker moral fibre than our parents. What is certain is that, in the present as in the past, the children in public institutions and voluntary homes represent in the main a trouble originating in their own homes.

The other side of the work of the agencies which look after deprived children outside their homes is seen in the National Society for the Prevention of Cruelty to Children, which concerns itself with deprived children in their own homes. The Society began as a London Society in 1884. It became national five years later, and in 1895, eleven years after its founding in London, was incorporated by Royal Charter which assigned as its main purpose:

To prevent the public and private wrongs of children and the corruption of their morals.
To take action for enforcement of laws for their protection.

To-day the Society is established with Royal patronage with nearly three hundred paid inspectors, with many volunteers serving on its committees, and with an annual budget exceeding £120,000 a year. But it has had rough passages in its history; had once to bring a libel action and won the action; had once to invite a formal inquiry into its administration to clear its name from charges brought against it, and did so. At all times it has had to prove its case for interfering in the home, with the way in which parents treated their own children. It has done that also, by showing what happened in some homes in the way of brutality, neglect and other evils.

In the old days the Society had to prove the necessity for its existence. Time and again, when it proposed the formation of a new branch in some district till then without one, it would be met with the argument: your society may be needed in other towns, but there can be no need for it in our town; our people are different. Always when the branch had been established, the need for it was shown. The appalling cases of brutality which marked some of the early days of the Society have become happily rare,[1] but the continuance each year of 40,000 cases reported to the Society establish the need for its existence. This number is less than before the war, but represents probably no real fall, since for the moment the Society is less than full strength in inspectors. On the other hand, the 40,000 cases of to-day represent less evil than the same number would have done thirty years ago. The standard of what the public expects of parents has risen, and cases are reported to the Society to-day that would probably have passed unnoticed thirty or forty years ago. But they should be reported, for progress in civilization means a higher standard of morality, of regard for the weak. And there are still to-day cases of shocking neglect.

The *Child's Guardian*, a periodical published by the Society, in its last number issued in the summer of 1947, gives, under the heading of "The Day's Work," details of six or seven typical cases, such as come to any of its inspectors. The troubles recorded in these cases range from drink, gambling, indifference, filth, and brutality, to the suicide of a mentally affected father. In every case the inspector comes in, not to punish, but to effect a rescue of the children, and sometimes a reform of the parents. What the difference between neglect and care may mean to a child is shown again and again by the photographs of the same child when he first comes under the Society's notice in his own home, and a few weeks after, when he has been removed from his home. What careless cruelty there still may be is shown by the Society's explanation of some of the things that it includes under its heading of "Other Wrongs" to children. One of the commonest of these "Other Wrongs" is a

[1] See *The Life of Benjamin Waugh*, pp. 137–40, by Rosa Waugh (T. Fisher Unwin, 1913).

practice of parents, who want to go out for enjoyment, locking up
their child alone in a room in an empty house.[1]

The Society, of course, has taken a part both in extending the
law for protection of children and in enforcing the law, at need by
prosecution. Till 1889 there was no Act dealing generally with the
rights of children. The Society in that year secured the passing of
an Act, the first "Children's Charter" which laid it down that no
person having the custody, charge or care of a boy under fourteen
or of a girl under sixteen might neglect or ill-treat such child in
a manner likely to cause it unnecessary suffering. By removing the
requirement that a child must give evidence only on oath, the Act
got rid of one of the obstacles to successful prosecutions in the past;
there had been cases where the child had been clearly too young
to understand the nature of an oath, and had not been able to give
evidence which would have led to its rescue. The original "Children's Charter" has been developed in many ways, by Acts of 1894,
1904, 1908 and 1933. All these measures owe much to the existence
and determination of the Society.

Actual prosecutions are very rare. Before the war they were
running at about 500 a year, while about as many cases again were
dealt with in Juvenile Courts. Since the war the prosecutions have
been somewhat higher; 929 in 1945–6, with about 833 cases dealt
with in the Juvenile Court. But even these increased figures, no
doubt explicable by the demoralization of the war, are far less than
those of earlier years.[2] To be available always to rescue children
in distress in their homes is the function of the Society and its
inspectors. It enters now very largely on the initiative of others.
Of the 41,720 cases handled by it in 1945–46 9,800 came under the
head of "advice sought" by the parents themselves, in dealing with
their family problems, 14,391 were reported by other members of
the general public, 15,941 by the parents, school officials and other
officials, and only 1,588 had to be discovered originally by the
Society's own inspectors. These figures show how much the Society
and its inspectors have come to be a general agency to which others
turn to take up the case of unhappy children, whether their own or
known to them as neighbours or as officials.

The scope of public action in regard to children widens daily.

[1] The positive remedy for this lies in building towns so that neighbours can look
after one another's children. See also Chapter VIII on the Needs of Parents.
[2] The highest total of prosecutions was reached by the society in 1900–1
when 31,725 cases led to 2,884 prosecutions, of which all but 89 resulted in
conviction.

But the case for continuing Voluntary Action hardly needs to be argued. The service of and the necessity for the voluntary homes for children who cannot live in their parents' homes have been recognized emphatically by the Committees on the Care of Children. For the children in their homes the National Society for the Prevention of Cruelty to Children stands indispensable for curing evils of individual failure on which higher earnings, family allowances and social security will make no impression, and for raising continually the popular standard of responsibility in regard to childhood.

NEEDS OF THE PHYSICALLY HANDICAPPED

The physically handicapped people of Britain present a problem large in scale, distressing in the degree of suffering of individuals, and still more distressing in the deficiency of provision to prevent or alleviate suffering. One of the deficiencies is the lack of comprehensive systematized information. The accompanying table gives a general survey of the problem in the light of the most recent published information. But the figures represent either official records compiled for specific purposes and incomplete as a picture of the whole, or estimates of varying dates and degrees of accuracy. The figures, except where a different date is given, refer to a date since the end of World War II. The statements as to deficiency of provision as given briefly in the fourth column of the table are illustrated in the text following the table.

Some of the disabilities which are dealt with here—such as blindness and deafness—have long been familiar as subjects of remedial action. But there are crippling diseases of various kinds whose significance as creators of misery that is needless is only now coming to be appreciated. Quite often these sufferers, though physically helpless, have vigorous minds. Truly harrowing examples can be given of such persons landing in general Poor Law Institutions and left to rot there. Specialized care is the one thing needed and the thing that too often fails to-day.

Two of the principal classes of disability—tuberculosis and mental defect—are not considered at any length in this Report though shown for completeness at the end of the table. They have both for many years been the subjects of public and private remedial action, and of very large expenditure; on tuberculosis it is estimated that we are now spending £12 million a year, and on mental deficiency £5 million a year. The first of these figures is given in a paper on *The Problem of Phthisis*, read in April, 1947, at the Medical School

of Aberdeen University by R. R. Trail, Medical Director of th
Papworth and Enham–Alamein Village Settlements; from this pape
is taken also the estimate in column 2 of the table, of "at leas
150,000 men and women with positive sputum who are outside th
sheltered conditions which could provide for their own safety, an
for the safety of their contacts in the home and in the community
contacts to whom they can and do impart massive infection." Th
estimated expenditure on mental deficiency is given in a statemen
made by Mr. Glenvil Hall, M.P. (*Hansard*, December 19, 1947
pp. 452–4). The statement in the table as to shortage of beds i
mental hospitals comes from the Report of the Board of Control fo
1945. The fact that with so much legislation and so much expendi
ture the provision in both these fields should be unsatisfactory is ;
striking illustration of the need of something beyond legislation and
money for curing social ills, and of the way in which general shortag
of housing and other necessaries falls with special weight upon th
weaker members of the community.

Yet though any survey of the physically handicapped and of th
provision made for them to-day is depressing, there are encouraging
signs also. The Disabled Persons (Employment) Act of 1944 is ;
notable development of public action. Several of the organization
and institutions whose experience is called specially in aid in thi
section are new developments of private action. Such are the Surrey
Voluntary Association for Cripples established in 1935; the Queer
Elizabeth's Training College for the Disabled, opened at Leatherhead in 1935; the St. Loyes College for the Training and Rehabilitation of the Disabled, opened at Exeter in 1937; and the British
and Scottish Councils for the Welfare of Spastics established in 1946.
Thus new organizations are continually being thrown up by Voluntary Action to carry on and develop what has been done in the past,
beginning with the opening of the first orthopaedic hospital in
Birmingham in 1817.

The Blind

The blind stand in a special position in regard to help from public
sources, in virtue of Blind Persons Act, 1920, which

(1) Makes it the duty of every County and County Borough
Council to make arrangements to the satisfaction of the
Minister of Health for promoting the welfare of blind persons
ordinarily resident within their area and to submit to the
Minister a scheme for the exercise of their powers under the
Act.

TABLE 15

SURVEY OF THE PHYSICALLY HANDICAPPED

Type of Disability	Approximate Number Affected	Source of Figures	Evidence of Deficiency in Provision	Remarks
Blindness	76,000 England and Wales	Official Register under Blind Persons Act	Organization and money relatively more adequate than for other forms of disability, but deficiency of home teacher service and of employment	
Deafness	40,000 deaf; 150,000 seriously deafened	Estimates (see text below.)	No public provision for deafness as such. Deficient educational provision for children. Exploitation of deafened by businesses	Probably 1 in 6 of population, say 6¼ millions in England and Wales have some deficiency of hearing
Crippling	200,000 England and Wales, 1933	Estimated by Central Council for Care of Cripples	Waiting lists in practically all homes, training centres, etc.	Post-war figures increased by war 1933 Estimates probably too low. Register has 347,000 surgical cases, and 134,000 others, including blind, deaf, etc., presumably in other categories of this table
Other Disabling Diseases of Employable Persons	30,000 arthritis and rheumatism; 59,000 digestive; 40,000 cardiac; 64,000 lungs (not tuberculosis); 18,000 epilepsy, etc.; 44,000 neurosis and other nervous disorders; 16,000 skin and genito-urinary	Registered under Disabled Persons (Employment) Act, at May 1947	See text below for limitations of provision under the Act	
Other Chronic Sickness	No estimate of chronic sick, i.e. unemployable by disabilities not specified here and needing care, now possible. But number great and likely to grow with ageing population		Waiting periods for admissions to Homes for Incurables running to years. Beds in hospitals occupied wastefully by incurables. Infirm living wrongly alone or with relatives	
Tuberculosis	207,000 under observation; 150,000 not under observation	Official Register Estimate by R. R. Trail	6,512 patients on sanatorium waiting lists, December, 1945	Deaths 38,000 in 1922; 22,000 in 1938; 23,000 in 1945
Mental Defect	246,000 England and Wales	Board of Control Report, 1945	Shortage of beds in mental hospitals and other institutions so acute as to create "an unsatisfactory and at times dangerous situation"	Of total, 146,000 were in mental hospitals; 53,000 in institutions, certified houses or approved homes; 47,000 under care outside

(2) Provides non-contributory pensions on the same conditions
as to means as in the case of other persons, at age forty in
place of seventy. The rate of pension, originally 10s. a week,
has been raised to 26s. for a single person and 42s. for a
married couple, since October, 1946.

Congenital or early blindness, moreover, is now relatively rare.
Of the 75,897 persons registered as blind in England and Wales,
only 2,637 or $3\frac{1}{2}$ per cent were under twenty-one, while 58,950
or nearly 80 per cent were over fifty. This means that in future
most blind people who are unable to work will be qualified, by
contributions made before they became blind, for benefit or
pensions without Means Test under the National Insurance Acts
of 1946.

Public responsibility has thus been accepted for the blind more
comprehensively than for any other classes of handicapped persons.
The total expenditure from public funds on blind welfare is now
about £4½ million a year. But the problem has not been removed
from the scope of Voluntary Action.

There are about a hundred voluntary agencies concerned with
blind welfare and spending between them about £1½ million a year
of money from private sources. They include many endowed charities, many local societies, and national bodies for specific purposes
such as the National Library for the Blind, the National Association
of Workshops for the Blind, Servers of the Blind League, College
of Teachers of the Blind, or St. Dunstan's Organization for Blinded
Soldiers, Sailors and Airmen.

There is for general purposes the National Institute for the Blind,
a voluntary agency now governed by a council representative both
of public and of private bodies. The National Institute, begun in
1868 by Dr. Thomas Rhodes Armitage, a doctor who had become
blind himself, as the "British and Foreign Blind Association for
Promoting the Education of the Blind," and carried on after his
death in 1890 by his wife till her death in 1901, was incorporated
in 1902. After the passage of the Blind Persons Act, by agreements
between the Institute, the Ministry of Health, the Association of
County Councils and the Association of Municipal Corporations,
the National Institute in 1926 was placed under the government
of a council of ninety-seven persons representative, among others,
of these local authority associations and the London County Council,
of certain national agencies for the blind, of organizations of blind
persons, of "regional bodies" bringing together the local societies

in each region, and of "persons interested in national work for the blind," that is to say the original voluntary element.

The National Institute exists therefore as a means of promoting co-operation between the local authorities which have statutory responsibilities and the many voluntary agencies still in this field. Its specific function is the provision of those services which can most economically and effectively be provided on a national scale. It publishes in quantity and variety reading material for the blind in Braille and Moon type; it supplies apparatus of all kinds; it provides homes and educational establishments where they are needed and not otherwise provided; it conducts research into every aspect of blind welfare; it assists local societies financially and otherwise in a great variety of ways; and by "collecting agreements" it seeks to eliminate overlapping in public appeals and to promote the co-ordination of local and national work throughout the country. The operation of these collecting agreements is illustrated by the fact that in the year ending March 31, 1946, £182,002 was raised by unified voluntary collections; it was distributed as to £52,932 to the National Institute, as to £14,161 to another national body, the National Library for the Blind, and as to £114,909 to sixty-nine local societies.

The relatively large provision already made for the blind does not mean that nothing remains to be done. It is notable, for instance, that of the 74,308 registered blind persons of sixteen and upwards in 1946 only 9,010 were returned as employed and another 788 as being trained, while 64,510 were classed as unemployable; since this exceeds materially the number of blind people above fifty years of age, it must include substantial numbers of comparatively young persons who ought to be employable. The proportion of blind persons of working age who are returned as employed was actually lower in 1946 than in 1925, 28 per cent against 38 per cent; yet employment generally was much better in the later year.

The fact that money is available in relatively large amounts for the blind should not be allowed to stand in the way of making for them the much more important provision of work in which they can feel themselves useful. In Japan for many years the service of massage was reserved for blind persons, who because of their blindness had in many cases exceptional sensitiveness of touch. The possibility of giving to blind persons some kind of priority of training for this work appears to be well worth exploration. The blind are entitled to the dignity of being useful if they can.

But it must be recognized that many of the older people really are unemployable. For them home assistance and visiting are services of outstanding importance. To-day the number of persons engaged in this visiting, as a rule "home teachers" who have taken the certificate of the College of Teachers of the Blind, is manifestly too small in relation to the numbers to be visited.[1]

A great deal remains to be done for the blind, which will not be done simply by giving more money to them. But the machinery for doing it is in existence. The register compiled by the local authorities shows where every blind person is who needs and desires assistance; it is described as the envy of blind welfare organizations in other countries; there is no similar register of any other handicapped class in the community. The fervour of voluntary organizations continues. The National Institute for the Blind is there as a meeting-place of public action and Voluntary Action, and being voluntary itself is charged with the duty of continually trying new ways.

The Deaf and Deafened

There is no Deaf Persons Act comparable to the Blind Persons Act and, therefore, no means of giving precise figures of the numbers of persons handicapped to various degrees in their capacity for hearing. The number of those born deaf or losing all hearing before they learn to speak is generally estimated at about one in a thousand of the population, that is to say about 40,000 persons in Britain. It has been common in the past to describe these as the "deaf and dumb," but this is an unfortunate term, as suggesting that they cannot by special methods be taught to speak. Here they are described simply as "the deaf." Those who lose their hearing later, whether partly or wholly, are described as "the deafened." An estimate given by Mr. J. D. Evans[2] is to the effect that, in addition to the 40,000 deaf, there are between 130,000 and 180,000 deafened persons in England and Wales "so severely afflicted that they are in need of special legislation for their economic and social security." These figures appear to be adapted from a calculation made in 1937 by Mr. Arthur G. Wells of the number of persons who would qualify for assistance by a Deaf Persons Act if there were such an

---

[1] See *Report on Employment and Training of Social Workers,* by Eileen L. Younghusband, para. 379, "It is thought that a home visitor can adequately care for about 80 blind persons and should never be given a case load of more than 120. It is unfortunately not unknown to find workers with a case load of 200."

[2] In a chapter contributed to *Voluntary Social Services,* edited by A. F. C. Bourdillon (Methuen, 1945).

Act on the lines of the Blind Persons Act.[1] The figure of 150,000 printed in Table 15 is given as the most reasonable single figure that can be chosen to represent the probable size of the problem. The total number of persons with some deficiency of hearing is very great indeed; according to Mr. Wells's estimate roughly one in six of the whole population or about $6\frac{1}{2}$ millions in England and Wales.

The difference between those who have always been deaf so that they do not learn to speak naturally and those who become deafened later in life is profound in practice and in psychology. The former must have help. Most of the latter engage in an unending struggle to be as independent of help as they can; in Mr. Evans's phrase "they are normals threatened with the horror of abnormalcy. . . . They will not class themselves with the 'true deaf' nor will they readily approach the 'deaf organizations' for help."[2] The many missions which concern themselves with welfare in this field in practice concentrate on the deaf. Yet, as Mr. Evans says, many of the deafened are as completely helpless as the deaf. "Far more than the deaf they are to-day Britain's 'Forgotten Folk.' "[3] They need help which is personal if they need help at all.

For one particular class of those affected in their hearing, namely, the children, existing provision is manifestly inadequate. The Chief Medical Officer of the Department of Health for Scotland, Sir Andrew Davidson, in a recent address to the Scottish Council of Social Service stated that, while schools for deaf children in Scotland at present provide for about 660 children, the large number who were unable to obtain educational facilities was giving rise to concern. "The known waiting list numbers 122 and includes children over nine years of age who have never yet been to school." This is for Scotland. In England and Wales a recent survey carried out by the National Institute for the Deaf showed 305 deaf children between the ages of five and sixteen, and 137 under five who were receiving no special education. As is pointed out by the Institute, for the deaf "no special education" means "no education."

There is, on the other hand, one respect in which deafness, unduly neglected by public and philanthropic agencies, has attracted undesirable attention—from trading agencies vying with one another to exploit a widespread demand for hearing aids. The National Institute for the Deaf has thought it necessary to issue a pamphlet

---

[1] "An Attempt to Estimate the Incidence of Defective Hearing in England and Wales," by Arthur G. Wells, B.S., M.B., D.P.M., F.R.C.S., in *British Medical Journal*, July, 1937 (Reprinted by the National Institute for the Deaf).

[2] *op. cit.*, p. 76.

[3] *op. cit.*, p. 77.

dealing with "Exploitation of the Deaf in the sale of Aids to Hearing." This declares that "a large number of instruments and appliances, widely advertised and distributed, are practically useless in cases of serious deafness and should not be sold at all." Others, which might be useful for certain types of deafness but useless or harmful in others, are advocated and sold indiscriminately. Many are sold at prices out of all relation to their cost.

> The deaf naturally ask for inconspicuous aids and a large number of appliances have been produced to meet the demand. These cost a few shillings to produce, yet they are sold at varying prices up to £5 5s. od. . . . These inconspicuous aids, being less expensive than electrical instruments, are especially attractive to persons of small means. Poor people, old age pensioners and servant girls have been induced to throw away as much as £5 5s. od. on these useless appliances. A University Professor of Otology has demonstrated that by reducing the diameter of the ear-passage, these appliances may actually diminish hearing.

There are, of course, on the other hand, many hearing devices of great value if properly used. Provision of skilled independent advice as to whether a particular appliance is likely to be useful should be available and should be known to be available to all persons with defective hearing. It may be hoped that a solution of this problem will be one of the early results of the National Health Service Act. Under that Act, coming into operation in July, 1948, all persons in need of a hearing aid will be eligible to obtain one free of charge, and with free maintenance and repair service. An aid for this purpose has been designed by a Committee of the Medical Research Council, and is now in process of manufacture.

Deafness is in general an infliction far less severe than blindness; most even of those who have no hearing at all, if they have learned to speak, would regard themselves as employable, while most of the registered blind are regarded, rightly or wrongly, as unemployable. It is open to argument whether a Deaf Persons Act, at all closely on the lines of the Blind Persons Act, would be appropriate. It is not open to argument that the handicap of deafness should receive more consideration, from public and private agencies alike, than has been accorded hitherto.

Disabled Persons (Employment) Act

The Disabled Persons (Employment) Act of 1944 passed on the recommendation of a Committee on Rehabilitation under the chairmanship of Mr. Tomlinson, the present Minister of Education, marks a notable new departure. It provides, in the first place, for the registration of all physically handicapped persons seeking employment. It classifies them under four main heads relative to the special kind of treatment that they may need. As a preliminary to employment it provides courses of reconditioning treatment at eight centres. It provides vocational training courses in a number of the Ministry of Labour's own centres, and in technical colleges throughout the country. It includes three principal measures to secure employment, namely, a quota scheme, a designated employment scheme, and a sheltered workshop scheme for those whom there is no hope of placing in ordinary employment.

The numbers on the register in May, 1947, divided into four main categories, according to the type of disability, are summarized below:

Surgical	347,000	
Medical	260,000	(Tuberculosis, 32,000; other diseases of the lungs, 64,000; digestive, 59,000; heart and circulation, 40,000; arthritis and rheumatism, 30,000)
Psychiatric	44,000	
Others	134,000	(including 52,000 total or partial blindness and 37,000 total or partial deafness)
Total	785,000	

Of the total, 74,574 or 9½ per cent were unemployed, of whom 11,518 were described as needing sheltered employment. This register, being made in 1947, includes a large addition to the number of the physically handicapped as the results of war; 121,000 of the total are ex-service men of the First World War and 368,000 are ex-service men of the Second World War, making a total of 479,000 ex-service men. Not all of these owe their disability to their service, but it is estimated that just under half of all the registered persons do so, that is to say, owe disability either to war service or to air raids, civil defence service, and similar causes. The register of disabled persons, as made by the Ministry of Labour, is thus swollen by causes which it may be hoped will not return. On the other hand the register is far from complete in respect of causes which may be expected to persist. It is a register of those seeking employment and excludes, therefore, all those judged by themselves or their friends or the registering authority to be unfit for employment. This judgment may often be mistaken.

The quota scheme requires every employer with twenty or more workers to employ a basic percentage of registered disabled persons, now fixed at 3 per cent, which may be increased as necessary.

A number of employers in fact have many more than this percentage.

The designated employment scheme reserves future vacancies in selected employment for registered disabled persons. Up to the present two employments, that of passenger electric lift attendant and that of car park attendant, have been designated and reserved for registered disabled persons.

The sheltered employment scheme is described in an official pamphlet as "undoubtedly the most striking provision of the Act." These sheltered workshops may be established by local authorities or voluntary bodies, and the Ministry of Labour can contribute to the cost of such establishments, but the Ministry has also set up a Disabled Persons Employment Corporation wholly financed by the Government which is beginning to establish a network of "Remploy Factories" throughout Great Britain, with four factories already open and many more planned. In sheltered employment the disabled persons are to be paid full weekly wages based upon outside trade union rates irrespective of their individual output. The goods produced will be sold at market prices and the loss sustained by the workshop due to the lower productivity of the workers will be made good from the Exchequer.

The Disabled Persons (Employment) Act is a notable measure and one to be welcomed heartily. But it is far from meeting the whole case; it was never intended to do so. The Act is not concerned with those who are not seeking employment, in particular the chronic sick who are incapable of any work or the children too young for employment. It may fail to secure registration of some who should be registered but who wrongly judge themselves or are judged wrongly by the officers administering the Act to be beyond training; as will appear from the section below on Training Colleges for the Disabled, it is easy for handicapped persons to despair of themselves prematurely. The register may be incomplete as a record even of those who think themselves employable, because some of these, notably sufferers from tuberculosis and psychiatric afflictions, try to hide their disability from official notice. Finally, the measure is not concerned with the problem of finding residence for disabled persons though, as will appear, this is often the crux of the problem.

All these points represent not criticisms of the Disabled Persons Act itself, so much as points on which it needs supplementation. There is one criticism, or at least one doubt, to raise as to the sheltered employment scheme, guaranteeing trade union rates of wages, irrespective of how much work the handicapped persons can do, and particularly the official description of it as the most striking provision of the Act. Handicapped persons should have enough to live on, but it is as important that wherever possible they should get it by the work they do. The announced plans contemplate apparently that the four or five Remploy Factories already in existence should be multiplied ten or twenty times. If there are in fact enough disabled persons who can never work except under sheltered conditions those factories are needed. But it may be suggested that in the first instance it would be a better use of money to put more money into making more training colleges where physically handicapped persons can be made capable, not only of getting trade union wages, but of doing a satisfying amount of work. This rescue of the individual should come first.

The Chronic Sick

For those who are really incurable and unemployable, that is to say, the chronic sick, the accommodation at present available is unquestionably inadequate. The Institute of Hospital Almoners in November, 1946, set up a committee to consider the problem of the chronic sick and set out so far as possible to make an estimate of their numbers, but failed to obtain any estimate. The reason was given in the report from one of the main centres in the following words:

> Accommodation for the chronic sick of all ages is so entirely lacking, and is so generally known to be lacking, that the cases are not referred for help and are not recorded. In our region it is such a well-known fact that apart from the chronic wards of the municipal hospitals, accommodation does not exist, that only occasionally when the need is very obvious indeed would a case be sent to the almoner at all.
>
> Special homes for incurables, chronics or long-term cases are few, and in many districts non-existent. Waiting periods for vacancies often run into years, so that while much time and effort is wasted in trying home after home for some cases, in others it hardly seems worth while applying at all.

Not unnaturally the Institute of Almoners' Committee concluded that the whole subject of long term or chronic cases is ripe for an independent inquiry. Similar conditions are shown by many cases in the list of cripples reported on by the Surrey Voluntary Association and given in the Supplementary Volume.[1] Repeatedly in this list cases occur of chronic cripples now in hospitals, whom the hospitals are anxious to discharge in order to free their beds for acute cases. The passage of the National Health Service Act will set up authorities with a duty of making adequate provision for the chronic sick as for others. They will have the duty and they will control the money, but in the present acute shortage of building materials and the low output of building labour it will be many years before the present crying want can be overcome. This is another instance in which generally low output of useful things will continue to cause suffering to the most helpless.

Handicapped Children

There is no need to emphasize the importance of giving to every handicapped child the treatment and the training which may save it from growing up to a life of incapacity and unhappiness. The Central Council for the Care of Cripples estimated that in 1933 there were in England and Wales some 200,000 crippled persons, of whom 80 per cent had become so through preventable causes, that is to say through their not having had the right orthopaedic training as children; the numbers born with incurable deformities are almost negligible.

The Education Act of 1944 and the National Health Service Act of 1946 should between them put the treatment of handicapped children on an adequate basis. But they will do so only if they are administered to that end. And the requisite energy will be put into this reform only if it is realized how insufficient is the provision made to-day. The deficiency of special schooling for deaf children has been noted already. A few illustrations only can be given here as to other forms of handicap.

Thus the committee of the Institute of Almoners gave recently among other illustrations of inadequate provision of institutions for treatment the two following cases:

> Boy thirteen, pseudo-hypertrophic muscular dystrophy—on waiting list for Shaftesbury Society's Home. Is not likely to obtain a vacancy for one to two years, when he will be too old for the school. Meanwhile, another boy of nine also on waiting list remains in hospital, not requiring active treatment and blocking the beds.

[1] This association was formed in 1935 to give voluntary care to cripples in the county of Surrey. It had in September, 1946, 1,396 cripples on its register, so that the 57 cases shown in the annex are a small proportion of the whole.

Boy, aged nine, severe spastic paraplegia. No mother; father a wastrel. Admitted to hospital, 1943. Efforts by Education Authority to get vacancy in Cripples' School unsuccessful. Remains in Children's Ward, with no schooling.

The second of these cases refers to a form of handicap—cerebral palsy, more commonly called spastic paralysis—where the case for better remedial provision is particularly strong. It is estimated that there may be something like 10,000 spastic children in Britain under sixteen years of age; six out of seven of these may be expected to live through a full span of life; four or approximately 65 per cent are capable of education, and are therefore amenable to various degrees of physical, mental and consequently social rehabilitation; not a few can become entirely self-supporting. But as is pointed out in the memorandum of the two Councils just established for the Welfare of Spastics, from which these estimates are taken:

To attain these results, however, full recognition must be given to the complexity of the problem and comprehensive steps must be taken for its most effective solution. In particular, an adequate number of centres are urgently needed in which the requisite specialized treatment and education can be provided. At the moment only two such units are in existence with a total capacity for sixty children.

Even when the general education in a district is satisfactory, the handicapped child may be neglected. Thus in a southern county of England with a generally high reputation in educational matters, defective children aged four-and-a-half to sixteen years were found recently being taught in two classes only—an obviously inadequate provision. Even where special school arrangements are satisfactory the really difficult cases may be neglected. For example, an eleven-year-old boy in the West of England fell on the fire when he was two. As a result the shrinkage of skin on his face had drawn it so that he could not close his eyes or mouth, or use his hands. Considered by the Education Authorities to be mentally defective and a repellent sight, the boy received neither treatment nor schooling. Only through the *ultra vires* intervention of the secretary of a voluntary body has this boy now been admitted to a hospital specializing in plastic surgery for adults where he will, again unorthodoxly, receive both treatment and tuition. Somewhat similarly, a spastic boy with a very good brain (his IQ was put at 140) was found classified among mentally defective children because his multiple handicaps, unresolved, had impeded the expression of his intellectual powers. Recently, the Surrey Voluntary Association for the Care of Cripples found a totally uneducated cripple boy of fifteen; no official provision had been made for him. Eventually the association persuaded the head of a small private school to teach the lad at home, after school hours, and free of charge.

Failure to give special education to handicapped children means not uncommonly that they get no education at all. Those who have to deal with the handicapped later sometimes find youngsters wholly untaught, unable even to read and write. If they are to have any chance at all they must have special treatment. They cannot be taught with the rest. And they must be taught by people who believe that nothing is impossible.

Training Colleges for the Disabled

Rescue of the handicapped depends not simply upon there being sufficient institutions to undertake it, but on these institutions being kept up to the mark by individuals determined always to attempt what others may think impossible. How much can be done and therefore how much needs to be done may be illustrated by the experience of two training colleges for the disabled, both established within the past twelve years.

The Queen Elizabeth's Training College at Leatherhead and the St. Loyes College at Exeter, both take as their text: "The disabled can be made able." They have in the past ten years placed 2,000 persons in lucrative employment. They have done this for people of whom others had despaired completely. Here are some actual cases:

Spondylitis.—Aged 24. Regarded as unemployable. Trained as a watch repairer. Provided with specially designed portable seat (the disease, as usually happens, had involved fixation of both hips at an angle of 40 degrees). Now Branch Manager for his firm and married.

Arthritis.—Aged 35. Had been for some years in an institution and on admission to a training centre was almost entirely helpless, only feeding herself with difficulty. Gradually recovered mobility as a result of occupation and encouragement, became a skilled needlewoman. Now has a resident post as sempstress in a children's home.

Arthritis.—Ex-sailor, aged over 40. Was almost immobile. Trained in his home as weaver. Now self-supporting and relatively mobile.

Infantile Paralysis.—Middle-aged. Uses crutches. Was for

twenty-four years in a home for incurables and unoccupied. Then trained in precision instrument making, is now in good employment and married.

Infantile Paralysis.—Aged 22. Can walk a few yards only, with crutches. Trained as engineering inspector. Has now been in employment for four years, going from his home to factory in specially adapted chair. Earns £7 a week.

These are cases of success. In some ways even more instructive are cases where success has not yet been achieved because, though effective training has been given, it has not been possible to find suitable residential accommodation.

Spondylitis.—Aged 28. An educated, refined woman. Training with success in commercial designing and employment would be available, but as her only relative refuses to provide accommodation, and a good deal of help with toilet is necessary, a Public Assistance Institution is likely to be the only solution.

Disseminated Sclerosis.—Aged 31. Trained for the light leather industry and offered good employment in London. Educated woman with some private means. Own flat requisitioned and indefinitely unavailable. Application to ten voluntary agencies and persistent enquiry by Ministry of Labour failed to obtain suitable accommodation.

Still's Disease.—Aged 31. Was in Public Assistance Institution. Trained as a shorthand-typist and reached high standard of efficiency. Lack of residential accommodation where small amount of help required would be forthcoming is sole obstacle to employment.

Paralysis of the lower limbs.—Aged 36. A man trained as a leather worker proved to be exceptionally capable at that work. He was discharged from the training college in December, 1945. Willing to go anywhere; he needs no nursing. There would have been no difficulty in finding him employment, but it has proved impossible to find him the accommodation he needs on the ground floor. So for two years he has been in a Poor Law Institution, not allowed to work because he was there.

The general problem of the physically crippled is put by Dame Georgiana Buller, who has taken a leading part in the work of both these colleges, in the following terms:

Residential accommodation is therefore often the only real problem, but may be a very difficult one. Relatives may be unable or unwilling to provide it. A landlady is seldom prepared to give even the small amount of assistance needed. The ordinary type of home for incurables is unsuitable, because the idea still persists that incurable and unemployable are synonymous terms, and as a rule the only kind of occupation, if any, provided in such places is handicraft work of sub-commercial standard. The result is a devastating sense of frustration for the individual and a waste of valuable potential labour. Appeals from inmates of such homes have been received pointing out their potential economic capacity and the complete lack of opportunity for using it. Apart from this aspect, existing accommodation in homes for incurables is totally inadequate and admission to them is very difficult to secure.

Emphasis on the need for finding accommodation as well as training does not mean that more is not required in the way of training. In addition to the two colleges mentioned there is at the moment in the whole of England only one other. There is none at all in Scotland; cripples there who desire training may have to make for that the long journey to the south or south-west of England.

THE WEAKEST SUFFER

At every point the same difficulty occurs. Accommodation of all kinds for the physically handicapped of all ages is inadequate. Nearly all institutions of every kind that cater for this need—schools, adult training, residence, hospitals, homes, nursing—have long waiting-lists. Table 16 summarizes some of this information as to waiting-lists, at dates ranging from 1945 to 1947.

TABLE 16

HANDICAPPED PERSONS ON WAITING-LISTS OF INSTITUTIONS

Handicapped Persons	Facilities Sought	Known Waiting-List or Period
Deaf children in Scotland ..	Education	122 children
Severely crippled boys (10–19)	Hinwick Hall (residential home)	2–3 years
Tuberculosis patients ..	Sanatorium beds	6,500 persons
Incurables	Putney Home for Incurables	40 persons, 1 year for men, 2 years for women
Incurables	Midland Home	25 persons, 1–2 years
Children physically handicapped	Lord Mayor Treloar's Hospital	200 children, up to 6 months or more
Men and boys (16–25) ..	Searchlight Cripples' Workshops, Newhaven	18 persons (turnover, 2–3 per annum)

To Table 16 may be added a few typical reports from other institutions. Cripplecraft, a residential occupation centre for sixty physically handicapped men and women, aged 16 to 55, reports:

> "We have a waiting-list, and applications are received practically every day. Unfortunately a number of these applications are from folk who are too helpless to be embraced in our present scheme."

The Chailey Heritage Craft Schools, admitting children from birth to sixteen, write:

> "There is a long waiting-list, and it is impossible to say how long the children have to wait for admission."

At St. Margaret's, Croydon, taking spastic children four to ten years:

> "The waiting-list is very long. The children who were admitted this term had been waiting for a year, and it is quite likely that children for whom application is made at this juncture may have to wait even longer."

The waiting-lists mean hardship and unhappiness for adult applicants and their relatives. For the children they may mean preventable disasters, the loss of formative years for education and intensive treatment that might have saved them.

What the continuing shortage of suitable accommodation may mean, in terms of unnecessary misery, can be illustrated by the case of a particular patient, found recently by the Almoner of the National Hospital for Nervous Diseases in a Poor Law Institution. This was the middle-aged Daniel M., paralysed from the waist down, but an intelligent, even intellectual ex-commercial traveller. Awakened daily at 5.30 a.m., he used to read by the faint shaft of light until bed-time. His mates on either side were senile. Eventually Daniel M. stopped reading. "I am getting," he said, "so that I just lie and stare." This particular patient has been rescued, after months of effort, and placed unorthodoxly in a home which normally takes temporary cases only. Nobody knows where to put him ultimately, if he is not to return to the horror of the institution; application to one of the few homes for incurables has been met by the statement that already there is a waiting-list there.

In the general shortage of all good things, the dilemma arises constantly between inflicting exceptional suffering upon the weak, and on the other hand failing to ensure to those who are whole the means of healthy life and work. That is the dilemma in which too often we find ourselves to-day.

OTHER CLASSES WITH SPECIAL NEEDS

Three main types of special need—that of age, that of childhood, that of the physically handicapped—have now been described. They do not by any means exhaust the list of those who have special needs, either because they are handicapped otherwise than physically, or because they have special responsibilities, or because of their stage in life. It is impossible to do more than illustrate these needs, and three classes are chosen for illustration: the unmarried mother and her child, a type of the socially handicapped which does not receive enough popular consideration; the discharged prisoner, another type of the socially handicapped which is worth notice as an illustration of successful co-operation between the State and the voluntary agency; and finally, the class of parents, selected here because it is so large, and because it has special needs which are insufficiently recognized.

To these three types of which something is said here, many others would add a fourth type as even more important, the adolescents. Undoubtedly they have special needs and the meeting of those needs is one of the most vital tasks of the present, in order to ensure good citizens in the future. But this particular problem is well recognized to-day. It could not be dealt with adequately in anything less than a special volume. It is left here to what has been said in Chapter IV in dealing with youth organizations, in Chapter IX in dealing with leisure, and in the Memorandum on Youth included in the Supplementary Volume.

The Unmarried Mother and Her Child

It is evidence of confusion in the public mind that, of the causes to which the public is invited to subscribe, that of help to the illegitimate child and its mother is one of the least generously assisted. It appears to be forgotten that the greatest sufferer is the child, and the loss from avoidable mortality and physical and mental ill-health in the illegitimate child represents injury to the community as a whole.

That illegitimacy is a direct outcome of such social upheavals as war, the figures show clearly. The proportion of illegitimate to all live births in England and Wales fell gradually from 6·26 per cent to 4·19 per cent between 1918 and 1939. Thereafter it rose rapidly to 9·18 per cent in 1945. In that year 63,000 illegitimate children were born. The figures of deaths of infants under one year throw a shocking light upon the illegitimate child's prospects of survival. In 1944, out of 1,000 children legitimately born, 44 died under one year; the figure for illegitimate children was 69, over half as much again. It may be said that this represents a great improvement on previous years; in 1918 the figures were 91 for legitimate, and 186 for illegitimate children. There are no figures to measure the effect on the child's health of being often enough unwanted, and of suffering from his mother's inability to look after him properly, or the effect on his attitude to life when he comes to realize his position.

The importance of voluntary action in this sphere has been recognized by the State; an example of such recognition is the Ministry of Health Circular 2866 of 1943, in which the co-operation of local authorities with existing voluntary moral welfare organizations is urged. Only a few such organizations can here be mentioned. The Salvation Army, the Church Army, and the Church of England Moral Welfare Council are among those which manage homes where unmarried mothers can receive care before and after their confinement. The Salvation Army, as an example, maintains contact with them for up to three years after, endeavours to find work for them at which they can keep their baby with them, and states that a successful adjustment is arrived at in the majority of cases. At the present, accommodation of this kind is insufficient.

The National Council for the Unmarried Mother and her Child is a voluntary organization set up in 1918. It receives a grant from the Ministry of Health, donations from many local authorities and assistance from the London Parochial Charities; these together make up three-quarters of its income, the balance coming from subscriptions and affiliation fees. The work of the Council broadly covers three fields. First, it assists individual cases, through its case committee. From a monthly average of some 90 cases just before the war, the number of cases dealt with in 1946 averaged 450 a month: an indication of the pressing need for such work. Second, it gives much advice to both voluntary and statutory organizations in the management of homes. Third, it has been responsible for much activity in seeking to improve the law relating to illegitimacy and kindred matters, and in educating public opinion. When it was founded, "measures for the benefit of the unmarried mother were honestly regarded as a challenge to the accepted standards of morality, and the difficulty of getting workers or indeed subscribers to accept a constructive rather than a deterrent policy were considerable."[1] Since then it has seen some change in opinion, evidenced

---

[1] *Twenty-One Years and After*, by Mrs. H. A. L. Fisher (1946), p. 6. This is an account of the work of the National Council from its beginning.

by such measures as the Legitimacy Act of 1926, by the increase of maximum payments under affiliation orders, and by the introduction of abridged birth certificates, for all of which it had pressed.

A word should be said on the moral welfare work carried on under the Church of England Moral Welfare Council. This, carried on throughout England and Wales, includes in its scope help to unmarried mothers and their children; it seeks, for instance, to straighten out their relations with their families, to find them accommodation, both before and after childbirth, and later to settle themselves in work.

Among the administrative problems still remaining is the difficult one of the enforcement of affiliation orders. There is no machinery for the father to be traced; the police do not help as the father has not offended against the law; the Registrar-General's department does not reveal addresses for this purpose. On the whole this is right; but the financial position of the girls concerned is extremely hard.

It is hardly possible that the prospects of the illegitimate child can ever be as good as those of the child who is part of a normal family. There is all the more need for a wise public opinion combined with kindly and enlightened administrative machinery, both public and voluntary, to lessen the inequalities, so that the tens of thousands of children who even in normal times are born in this country out of wedlock should come to represent less of a loss to the community than they have done in the past.

Discharged Prisoners' Aid Societies

Another example of a handicapped group is the discharged prisoner. While much of the training of men and women when still incarcerated falls on the State, their general welfare (and that of their families) during their sentence, at the time of discharge, and often for some little time afterwards, is the concern of bodies which are mainly voluntary: the Discharged Prisoners' Aid Societies.

There were, in 1946, thirty-eight local Discharged Prisoners' Aid Societies in England, about half of them connected with particular prisons. They handled between them in that year 25,230 cases. The assistance given includes help in finding employment, cash grants, provision of tools or clothing, and such things as the writing of letters, visits to families, and so on. The societies work in close connection with the prison authorities, both local and national, yet they are voluntary bodies. Their personnel is composed of local citizens, serving unpaid (though they have usually full-time welfare officers working in the prisons); the State does not control them, otherwise than to concern itself with their efficiency; and the greater part of their income is from voluntary contributions. In 1945 rather more than a fifth of their income (£7,717 out of a total income of £36,030) was derived from Government grants; the remaining £28,313 was derived from voluntary sources.

To qualify for the grant, and also to gain access to a prison, a society must obtain a certificate of efficiency from the Home Secretary. The link between the local societies and the Home Office or the Prison Commission is the National Association of Discharged Prisoners' Aid Societies. This body was set up in 1936 by the local societies themselves to remedy the lack of co-ordination between them which had become apparent, and its committee is composed mainly of representatives of these societies, though it also includes representatives of the Prison Commission. This association is the normal channel of communication between the commission and a local society. In granting, cancelling or withholding a certificate of efficiency, regard is paid by the Home Office to the advice of the National Association. The Government grants to local societies are paid through the National Association which is responsible for collecting from them, for transmission to the Prison Commission, all necessary data concerning their expenditure and work. It has also carried out a good deal of reorganization of the area of operations of the local societies. Furthermore, it has direct responsibility for prisoners' aid work in special prisons, such as Wakefield. The National Association, like the local societies, obtains its income both from public and private sources. It receives a Treasury grant towards its administration expenditure; but what it spends directly on aid to prisoners is found from voluntary gifts or interest on legacies.

Prisoners' aid work is thus an example of social service largely carried on by voluntary zeal, regulated and assisted financially by the State through the medium of a co-ordinating body mainly representative of the voluntary agencies themselves.

The prisoner's punishment ought to stop at the moment of his discharge, but, as the National Association points out, this is frequently not the case. He is handicapped in seeking employment by the fact that the employment exchanges are obliged to communicate to prospective employers the fact that he has been in prison. Welfare Officers of Prisoners' Aid Societies, by tactful approaches to employers, do something to alleviate the hardship which this may cause. It may be added that the National Association initiated some ten years ago a system whereby a discharged prisoner, on first applying to an Employment Exchange, simply hands over a form in a sealed envelope, instead of having to state in the hearing of others that he has just come from prison. The convicted prisoner, and indeed even persons on remand, are handicapped in another way, in that they do not get their insurance cards stamped, either for the period of sentence, or while they are on remand, even if subsequently discharged. While there is an obvious reason for this, it nevertheless may involve not only financial loss but also, if the circumstances in which the cards were unstamped became known, a stigma may well attach to the person involved. The representations made by the National Association on these matters have so far had little result.

Needs of Parents

"The housewife is not human." This is the text from which Mr. Lawrence Wolfe expounds the Reilly Plan for a new departure in town-planning and housing, which is at the same time a return to the old plan of the village green.[1] The housewife's job, with a large family, is frankly impossible, and will remain so, unless some of what has now to be done separately in every home—washing all clothes, cooking every meal, being in charge of every child for every moment when it is not in school—can be done communally outside the home. This is part of the general change in the direction of reforming effort which is long overdue, from improving conditions and giving more leisure to the paid worker in the factory or home, to improving conditions and giving more leisure to the unpaid worker in the home. This was one of the ideas underlying the proposal of my Report on Social Insurance to recognize housewives as a special class of unpaid workers, members of a team rather than dependents on their husbands. The practical application of this idea requires for the most part public action—the strength of the State in a new planning of towns—rather than Voluntary Action. But there are at least two experiments in meeting needs of parents—chiefly, though not exclusively, the mother—which are appropriate for further Voluntary Action. And there is a special need of parents in relation to holidays.

One experiment already under trial is the establishing of means of helping women who, though not in need of actual hospital treatment, are for any reason in danger of breaking down, and failing to do their essential task as mothers and housewives. An institution

[1] See *The Reilly Plan—A New Way of Life*, by Lawrence Wolfe (Nicholson & Watson, 1945).

for this purpose is already in being—the Brentwood Recuperative Centre for Mothers and Children maintained by the Lancashire Council of Social Service. Ill-health, or having too many children too quickly, or a hopeless struggle with bad housing and queues, or domestic disagreement may lead to listlessness, and prepare the way for the family becoming a problem family, or breaking up altogether. Brentwood is a large house in a pleasant garden in Derbyshire where in such a case mothers with children can go for anything from a few weeks to a few months for a complete change, among fresh people able and willing to help them by advice and example. The idea underlying Brentwood is that a housewife and mother may at times be as much in need of rehabilitation to do her job as a crash-shocked airman or injured workman. That the idea is sound is shown by the demand; something like four hundred mothers with their children have come each year to Brentwood. And some almost miraculous restorations have been achieved. But the continuance of the experiment is threatened by financial difficulties and, as the experience of a recent wireless appeal shows, rehabilitation of mothers and families is not a cause for which up to the present it has proved easy to get much popular support.[1]

A second experiment worth trying is the establishing of communal night nurseries as well as day nurseries. The day nursery is designed to give the housewife freedom to do paid work, where this is necessary in the public interest or in her own. It has been suggested that there is a case for enabling a husband and wife every now and again to be free to enjoy themselves together for an evening or several evenings without worrying about their children. For most couples this need is happily met by calling one or other of the grandmothers or some other relative. But that is not always possible. Then sometimes it is met in a way calling down the attention of the National Society for Prevention of Cruelty to Children, by leaving a child locked up by itself in an empty house. Some voluntary agency might well experiment in offering a night nursery where the child could be left in good hands.

There is, related to the two points just named and also to what is said in the next chapter, a general question of holidays for housewives. The essence of a holiday is change. The great extension in the last ten years of holidays with pay has secured the possibility of change for millions of wage-earners. But for the millions of

---

[1] The appeal for Brentwood made by myself in July, 1947, appears in the account of "Week's Good Causes" in the Supplementary Volume as one of the least successful of the year.

mothers who with their children will accompany their husbands on holiday, there will be no change, unless steps are taken to bring it about. The holiday will merely mean looking after the children in unfamiliar and therefore less convenient surroundings away from home. A holiday place for the housewife must be one to which she can take the children, but not one in which she must look after them all the time. Some of the commercial holiday camps have realized this and have set out to meet the need. But they touch only a tiny fraction of all who need holidays.

CONCLUSION AS TO SPECIAL NEEDS

The picture presented in this chapter is a grim one. It is a picture of unhappiness of many different kinds, with relieving agencies working against odds. The unhappiness is not due primarily to want of money; it has not been and will not be remedied by redistribution of money. It is due to shortage of things which money should represent, but which are not being produced and of services of a kind which money often cannot buy. The unhappiness is of many kinds and of very different degrees of acuteness, from the boredom of a solitary healthy old man with an adequate pension to the physical suffering of the sick who cannot get into hospital, or the mental suffering of the intellectual man cooped up with seniles and treated as unemployable because incurable, or the wanton waste of the handicapped child deprived of teaching.

The grimness of the picture to-day is not made less by the fact that there were worse things in the past, which have been abolished by the crusading spirit of the Victorian pioneers. They were worse absolutely, but not perhaps relatively. The material standard of life for the average unhandicapped citizen—reckoned in wages and what they would buy, and now also in leisure and in security against total loss of income—has risen greatly. In a community with social conscience the standard of care for all the unfortunate should rise equally. At this moment there is danger that the provision made for the special needs of the handicapped will lag behind.

From the review in this chapter two practical conclusions emerge. First, there must be adequate diversion of physical resources, above all in the provision of suitable houses, homes, hospitals, training schools, to prevent needless suffering among the handicapped. Second, there must be full use of Voluntary Action, and for that purpose the voluntary agencies must have the material resources to enable them to do their work. How they are to obtain those resources in the changed economic and social conditions is one of the critical problems of the future.

Meeting special needs calls for special interest and sympathy. As it was put to us in relation to the blind:

> Voluntaryism must be an element in effective personal service. Many blind people need friendship and personal care such as cannot be rendered by any official however competent and kindhearted. In the nature of things a Local Authority Committee cannot be so successful in enrolling this kind of help for the blind as a society whose whole motive is voluntary. One of the irreplaceable values of voluntaryism is indeed its ability to select from the community at large the people who have time and are disposed to give themselves devotedly to helping people suffering from a handicap which engages their sympathy.

This was said of blindness, but is true of every form of special need. The Philanthropic Motive is like the scientific motive. It drives men to service by specialized interest. It must be free to experiment and it cannot live under orders. It needs material resources to make its service possible.

IX. SOME GENERAL NEEDS THAT REMAIN

Growing Leisure and its Use.   Growth of Entertainment and Gambling.
The new Holiday Problem.   Citizens' Advice Bureaux.   Conclusion as
to General Needs that remain.

THE preceding chapter has shown that many special classes in the
community are still without the means of happiness, in spite of the
rise in the standard of life and in spite of social security. The present
chapter is concerned with two needs of a general character, the
need for good use of growing leisure and the need for guidance in
the complexities of modern life.

LEISURE AND ITS GROWTH

A hundred years ago, in 1847, the Ten Hours' Act was passed,
limiting to ten the daily hours of work of women and young persons
in factories. Three years later the Factory Act of 1850 ordered the
stoppage of work of the same classes in textile factories at 2 p.m.
These measures, though formally applying only to women and young
persons would, it was realized, affect hours for all workers. They
represent the first statutory recognition of the claim of wage-earners
to leisure. Voluntary recognition of this had come a few years before
in the decision of the merchants of Manchester to make Saturday
a half-holiday for their employees. After the Act of 1850, statutory
limitation of Saturday hours was gradually extended to trades other
than textiles and the Saturday half-holiday became normal.

Seventy years ago, after the boom of the Franco-Prussian War,
the working week of industrial labour generally was reduced—to an
average of roughly fifty-four hours. It stayed there till the First World
War. To-day it is in most industries about forty-four hours, a gain
of ten hours altogether on seventy years ago. Spread over the five
full days, this means something like two hours of leisure more on
each of these days. About two-thirds of the gain, seven hours out
of the ten, followed the First World War; one-third has followed the
second. There is continuing pressure for further reduction of hours.

For some wage-earners leisure has grown in another way also.
Seventy years ago they walked to work; to-day there are many
public vehicles and the ubiquitous bicycle. As against this gain,
there has been loss through the unplanned growth of great cities;

the distances to be travelled have increased in very many cases and, even where the time taken is less, the method of travel may make a greater strain on nervous energy. Whether for the wage-earning population as a whole the gain outweighs the loss or the loss outweighs the gain would be hard to say.

A more certain gain is in holidays. Here there has been a marked advance of recent years, following the passage in 1938 of the Holidays with Pay Act. This encouraged voluntary agreements in each industry, while threatening compulsion if necessary. In fact holidays with pay have become all but universal by agreement. In 1937 it was estimated that four million employees were entitled to holidays with pay. In 1947 the figure is put at fifteen million, getting on for 90 per cent of all concerned. The holiday, in practically all cases, is for a week at least.

The special new problem of holidays will be dealt with separately later. The first question is as to how the additional time that most wage-earners and some housewives in Britain have at their disposal each week, as compared with their grandparents, is being used. No complete or detailed answer to that question can be given, because no comprehensive study of the use of leisure has been made. We know only how certain forms of commercially provided entertainment—notably the cinema and gambling—have grown. We can get figures of wireless licences, books bought and borrowed, evening class attendances, and so on. But we cannot yet paint a full and balanced picture of how those extra two hours a day to themselves enjoyed by most wage-earners are being spent. It is easiest and natural to begin with the two forms of commercial enterprise in entertainment which have grown of late to out-distance all rivals in the extent of their popular appeal.[1]

About two out of every five persons in Britain aged sixteen and upwards are regular patrons of the cinema, that is to say, go to it once a week or oftener; all but one in six go occasionally. In the adolescent population the frequency of attendance is much higher than among the general body. Three out of four young people from sixteen to

[1] The figures of cinema attendances as given here are based in part on a Government Social Survey relating to March and October, 1946, and in part on a survey by Research Services, Ltd., undertaken for Hulton Publications, Ltd., and relating to January–May, 1947. Further details as to the two surveys are given in the Supplementary Volume. The Research Services results, with other material, have been used in an interesting article on "Britain Off Duty," contributed by Mr. Mark Abrams (Director of Research Services) to *World Off Duty*, a "Contact Book," published in 1947 by Contact Publications, Manchester Square, London. Several references to this article are made below.

twenty-four go once a week or oftener; nearly two out of every four go twice a week or oftener; only two in every hundred do not go at all. The adolescent taste is prepared for at school; two out of every three boys and girls aged ten to sixteen go once a week or oftener. The total number of young people aged sixteen to twenty-four in Britain is about six million; four and a half million of them are regular cinemagoers in the sense of going once a week or more. The total number of boys and girls from ten to sixteen in Britain is about four million; two and a half million of these are regular cinemagoers. These figures are of a different order of magnitude from those of membership in youth organizations.

For the adult male population gambling is an equal competitor with the cinema as an occupation for the million. The most popular agency for this is the football pool. In a recent Research Services enquiry, practically half the men interviewed had filled in a football coupon in the preceding week; this means making a prediction or more probably a number of alternative predictions as to the results of several football matches due to occur shortly. The football coupon is a form of terrifying appearance ruled into innumerable small spaces, but the British public have been trained to form-filling by years of war and controls. The coupon-filling is not infrequently a family affair. Mr. Abrams estimates that "each week of the season 11,000,000 men and women fill up their coupons and each sends along a postal order for an average value of two shillings." The element of chance in the successful filling up of football coupons outweighs immensely any possible skill or judgment.

The cinema and the football coupon are comparable in the extent of their popular appeal to-day. But they are not comparable in any other respect.

The cinema, however foolish many of the films presented may appear to a highly educated taste, does not as such promote a wrong view of life. It may promote a right view of life and give entertainment which is recreation in the best sense of the word. It can be used for definitely educational purposes and is increasingly being used in that way. The football coupon at its best cannot be better than waste of time, like playing any other game of chance before going to bed. The trouble is that filling a coupon is not just waste of time; it is spending money and time to get mis-education. The sums won in individual cases are normally moderate, but every now and again a big prize comes out, is immensely advertised, and probably leads to withdrawing a citizen from useful work to unwise spending. The football pool prize stands as the shining disproof to all of the idea that prosperity depends upon production. When a party gathers for *chemin de fer* in a drawing-room its members may be caught by the police and punished; a plea that no one was making money by organizing the gamble as a trade goes unregarded.[1] When businesses are set on foot to exploit by football pools the same gambling desire among millions they obtain all the indispensable facilities from the State. They are businesses from which taking of risks by the promoter has been largely eliminated. The promoter retains his 20 per cent of what comes in one week and distributes the balance in the next week.

By contrast to the profits of the pool promoters and the glittering prizes of occasional patrons, the actual playing or organizing of football is a struggling concern. There has been threat of a strike of professional footballers for higher pay. According to Mr. Abrams, "most teams outside Division I in England and Division A in Scotland find it hard to make ends meet unless they enjoy a little luck in cup ties."

The football pools are the most popular form of gambling to-day. They do not involve as much money as several other forms. The dog tracks, for instance, represent much greater expenditure; there are some 160 such tracks in Britain to-day with about one and a quarter million admissions weekly, and handling five times as much money as the football pools.

Gambling expenditure in all its principal forms in 1938–39 and 1946–47 is set out in *The Economist* of March 29, 1947, in the following table.

TABLE 17

ESTIMATED GAMBLING RECEIPTS

(£ million)

	1938–39		1946–47	
	Gross	Net	Gross	Net
Football pools	22	4	45	9
Horse-racing	274	21	315	27
Greyhound racing	57	5	208	15
Sweepstakes	8	4	4	2
Gaming machines	10	2	10	2
	381	36	582	55

[1] "Spivs Caught at a Card Table" is the headline under which a case of this nature is reported in an evening paper of October 10, 1947.

On these figures[1] the gross amount of money used for gambling is now greater than that used for paying rent; the net amount that is left with the purveyors of gambling to cover their expenses and provide their profit is more than the total spent on books and magazines together.

It is not possible to look on the development of gambling businesses in modern Britain as anything but a serious misfortune. The Government of the day, regardless of its political complexion, should consider whether there is any principle of liberty which compels the State to give to private enterprise in this evil form legal sanction and the administrative facilities without which it could not proceed. But it is easy and wrong to exaggerate the evil.

Gambling in total does not use much money, in relation to the total national income. *The Economist*, putting the net cost of gambling in all forms at £55 million or slightly over ½ per cent of all personal incomes, observes that this proportion "seems almost startlingly small." The use of man-power is more serious. Mr. Abrams puts the number employed by the pools at 35,000 and those employed for other forms of gambling as the equivalent of 100,000 full-time workers. But even this is only about 1 per cent of the working population. The evil of gambling is qualitative rather than quantitative, moral rather than economic.

It is necessary also to preserve a sense of proportion in speaking of the British people's use of leisure. The football pools and the cinema are the two forms of commercial entertainment with the largest *clientèles*, but it would be absurd to suggest that filling coupons and watching films was all that our increased leisure had brought us.

There has, for instance, been a marked increase both in the buying of books and in the use of lending libraries in recent years. In London alone there were in 1937–38 more than 2,200,000 persons with borrowers' tickets at public libraries and more than 40,000,000 books were borrowed for home reading.

There is the wireless in nearly every home, bringing possibilities of music and poetry and knowledge of the world, as well as mere noise and entertainment everywhere.

[1] These figures are admittedly estimates only. Some of the critics of football pools put their gross receipts much higher; their defenders put them at £35 million a year. Mr. Abrams in the Contact Book article uses the *Economist* table with some minor adjustments, putting football pools down to £40 million gross and £8 million net, and putting up other items, to reach a gross total of £580 million and net of £58 million.

There is large and growing provision for part-time study. The figures for England and Wales, as given by the Ministry of Education for two recent years, are as follows:

TABLE 18

PART-TIME STUDENTS IN ENGLAND AND WALES

	1937–38	1945–46
Tutorial classes	14,953	11,803
One-year courses	18,515	21,316
Short courses	} 23,244	66,214*
Other courses		
Informal courses		
Evening classes in colleges	265,157	252,064
Evening institutes	913,706	791,301
Day continuation schools	19,629	29,796
Senior full-time courses in colleges	1,972	4,113
Technical day classes	29,675	97,732
Art colleges, etc.	61,652	82,048
Total	1,348,503	1,356,387

* The great increase in this figure is due to the development of week-end courses and weekly summer schools, etc., provided by the W.E.A., Ashridge and similar bodies which did not exist to the same degree before the war.

These figures show an increase of day students just more than compensating for declines at evening classes in colleges and at evening institutes. The period 1945–46 was abnormal in several ways. The falling-off of evening students as compared with 1937–38 is attributed to lack of accommodation, lack of staff and disturbance caused by demobilization.

Finally, a comprehensive balanced survey might well show the greater part of the new leisure being used as it should be used, in developing better and more understanding relations in the family at home.

This does not mean that we should be complacent about our use of leisure to-day. It is no ground for complacency that the commercial cinema and the football pools should reckon their "regulars" by the million, while evening classes struggle for hundreds of thousands and youth organizations compete for thousands. It is no ground for complacency that much leisure should be merely wasted, when leisure itself is so scarce, and so much needed for learning. The coming of political democracy has brought a new need. In the threatening world of to-day only a democracy educated to the political responsibilities at home and abroad can hope to survive, can choose its leaders wisely and make sure of preserving its freedom. Democracy if it wishes to survive cannot afford to be ignorant.

The people with most leisure to-day are the adolescents and the young adults before family responsibilities begin. They are the citizens of the future. Upon the kind of citizens that they become the future depends. To promote the right use of adolescent leisure is perhaps the greatest of all tasks for Voluntary Action to-day.

THE NEW HOLIDAY PROBLEM

Formally the Holidays with Pay Act of 1938 has been a great success. The great bulk of all employees can now get wages for at least one week in the year without working in that week. Practically this change has set the problem of holidays rather than solved it. When the question of holidays with pay was under consideration by a committee shortly before the war strong differences of opinion were expressed, as between those who thought that definite steps must be taken to organize holidays so that they should be really beneficial and enjoyable, and those who held that nothing was necessary except to give the holiday with pay. The most forcible exponent of the latter opinion was Mr. Ernest Bevin. "Holidays mean more to people than being organized in the mass. . . . Give them the money and the time and they know what to do with them." This may be cited as a good illustration of the inadequacy of the strict trade-union approach to social problems.

In the first place, it has now become abundantly clear that it is not enough greatly to increase the effective demand for holidays and to assume that a suitable supply will follow. As is shown in the first chapter of *Holidays*, a study made by the National Council of Social Service and published in 1945, the doubling or trebling of the demand for holidays raises extremely difficult problems of accommodation and of staggering of holidays. If everybody still insists upon trying to go away in August, or failing that July, the peak demand cannot be met except by an utterly wasteful amount of accommodation standing idle for the rest of the year. But staggering of holidays, particularly with children perhaps at different schools, remains extremely difficult. It may be added that the coming of holidays with pay for nearly all raises the question of a reconsideration of the Bank Holiday Act, which, by adding for all the August Bank Holiday, gives to all an additional reason for trying to take their weekly holiday then.

Second, to give the wage-earner a holiday does not in itself mean giving a holiday to the housewife and mother. As is pointed out in a Mass Observation Report on Holidays,[1] for the vast majority of Britons a holiday means "getting away not only from work, but from home and from familiar surroundings generally." But for the housewife with children a holiday still means in most cases going away with the children to seaside lodgings and continuing to do there, in unfamiliar surroundings and under irksome restrictions, what she was doing at home. This is one side of the defective appreciation of the housewife as an unpaid worker. Nothing short of a revolution in housing would give to the working housewife the equivalent of the two hours' additional leisure a day on five days of each week that has come to the wage-earners in the past seventy years, and nothing but a revolution in holiday accommodation can give to the housewife with children the essence of a holiday, that is to say change and release from normal duties.

The Holidays with Pay Act is in force, but there is little sign up to the present of the demand for holidays which it has mobilized being adequately met.

There has been a great development of commercial holiday camps. Some of the most successful and spectacular of these, such as the Butlin camps, undoubtedly owe their success in part to the fact that they do provide to some extent for children. They will not admit any child under two, but they do make it possible for parents of children of two and upwards to take the children to camp, and to find there nurseries and play places where the children can be left under supervision while the parents enjoy themselves elsewhere. They thoughtfully provide a night patrol of all the chalets in which children are sleeping, so that, if a child is found crying, this can be broadcast and the parent summoned back from the dance hall to look after the child.

But the commercial camps, and particularly the Butlin camps, do not cater for those of really limited means; the charge at the height of the season is seven guineas a week with half charges for a child between two and ten. The guest houses or camps run by non-profit-making associations such as the Co-operative Holidays Association, the Holiday Fellowship, and the Workers' Travel Association, while not as costly as the commercial camps, do not in fact largely cater for manual wage-earners, nor do most of them make special provision for children. Their *clientèle* are largely single persons or young married couples without children. In the opinion of Mr. Green, the General Secretary of the Workers' Educational Association, the proportion of

[1] See Supplementary Volume, Part I.

"genuine manual workers going to the holiday centres of the Workers' Travel Association does not amount to 10 per cent." For the wage-earner with a family the standard resort is the seaside lodging-house with a landlady, and the landlady is apt to insist on a rigid time table, even if she takes children at all. Mass Observation observes on the widely experienced "contrast between the dream of doing what you like when you like, and the rigid and inconvenient time tables and lists of rules and restrictions which exist in so many boarding houses and private hotels."

There is to-day an urgent need, both for a great increase in holiday accommodation at moderate prices, and for accommodation giving the mother and housewife a true holiday, relieving her from incessantly worrying about the children. With this should go a reconsideration of the times of holidays and of the Bank Holidays Act.

Solution of the holiday problem involves having regard to the different classes of people affected. There are the families with children; for these, camps with nurseries, or nurseries in the existing holiday resorts, are essential if the mother as well as the father is to have a holiday. There are the adults without children; these can largely be left to look after themselves, for they have relatively large resources. There are the old people, for whom occasional change of routine may mean prolongation of happiness in life. There are the adolescents; for these, encouragement of camping, hiking and travelling is important.[1]

For agencies seeking a new field of activity, as many friendly societies may be seeking it to-day, there are several possibilities for exploration here. Could not some friendly societies, when the present restrictions on capital development are relaxed, invest some of their funds in the provision of holiday camps and guest houses, of varying types to suit varying tastes, where holidays could be provided for members and their families on a non-profit-making basis? With the amendment of the law suggested in Chapter X of this Report, it would be open to them to set up specially authorized societies, with properly qualified staff, to manage such camps. Secondly, it is clear that holidays with pay schemes do not solve the financial problems

[1] The simplest form of organization for this is the Youth Hostel Association whose object is "to help all, especially young people of limited means, to a greater knowledge, love and care of the countryside, particularly by providing hostels and other simple accommodation for them in their travels." This association, started in 1931, has now 166,000 members and some 264 hostels with nearly 12,000 beds. The number of beds is unhappily quite insufficient for the demand and should be increased greatly.

of many families. Holiday savings schemes are at present in operation in a number of well-known firms; friendly societies might well consider the possibility of providing schemes whereby members could save for an annual holiday, obtaining some interest on their savings. This is one means to giving them a more restful and agreeable holiday than could be found in the ordinary cheap seaside lodging.

These are two possible lines of action; others might well suggest themselves whereby the friendly societies could extend the benevolent side of their activities and make a valuable contribution to the holiday problem.

The holiday problem arises at all stages of life in different forms. It arises to-day more seriously than ever before. It is a matter to which the friendly societies, as democratic organizations for people of all ages, might well turn their attention, as the State takes more of their original field.

CITIZENS' ADVICE BUREAUX

The growing complexity of modern life is a commonplace. The development of the institutions described here as Citizens' Advice Bureaux is a natural and necessary reaction.

A Citizens' Advice Bureau is an office to which any citizen can go in person to seek information and advice as to his rights and duties as a citizen, as to the bearing on him of laws and regulations, as to any problem of his relation to other citizens. The idea of setting up such offices was first mooted in the annual report of the National Council of Social Service for 1935–36. The project took definite form at a conference of voluntary organizations at the time of the Munich crisis in 1938. On the outbreak of war in September, 1939, 200 bureaux were opened. Their number expanded rapidly till in 1943 there were more than 1,000. Since the end of the war, a number have been closed, for a variety of reasons, but there are still about 600 working. It is estimated that during the war the bureaux dealt with ten million inquiries. In one of the busiest months, July, 1944, the number reached 240,000. To-day the seventeen bureaux maintained in London by the Family Welfare Association are still dealing with some 8,500 a month.

Each bureau is autonomous, dependent on local initiative and local service, with a local management committee. But all approved bureaux are linked through a central committee with a central office and secretariat provided by the National Council of Social Service. The central office produces regularly *Citizens' Advice Notes*, a printed résumé of recent laws and regulations, issued in loose leaf form so that each bureau can have a cumulative reference volume; the notes are issued free to all approved bureaux and on payment to local authorities, industrial undertakings and the public generally. Matters requiring fuller treatment are dealt with in special pamphlets and circulars. The central office is in close touch with the Government departments and is able thus to elucidate difficult questions referred to it by post or telephone from any part of the country.

The central office has travelling organizers, who advise on administrative difficulties, take part in training schemes and help to arouse local interest when a new bureau is being planned. The bureaux are autonomous but not isolated.

The work of the bureaux is done partly by paid workers and partly by unpaid ones. At one stage it was stated that more than 10,000 men and women worked in the bureaux and that 90 per cent of them were volunteers.[1] Since then the bureaux, taken as a whole, show an increase of paid staff; this is attributed not primarily to lack of voluntary helpers, "but to the need to open many bureaux for longer hours and on all normal working days now that many more are associated with the local authority; a condition which often cannot be met by volunteers alone." But the existence of voluntary workers is still a condition qualifying for approval by the central office. Most bureaux, apart from staff in regular attendance, have panels of experts giving their service on technical questions as they arise; some of the bureaux are staffed completely by the Women's Voluntary Services.

During the war and its immediate aftermath the bureaux received substantial public grants through the Ministry of Health, for central and for local work alike; averaging nearly £35,000 a year from 1941 to 1946. As from the end of March, 1946, grants from the Exchequer have been limited to £8,000 a year for headquarters and regional expenditure; but local authorities have been encouraged and empowered to spend money on advice bureaux, either undertaking the work themselves or making grants to local voluntary bureaux or assisting them in kind, as by the provision of an office. This was done by a Ministry of Health Circular issued to local authorities in November, 1945, and emphasizing the continuing need for advice to citizens. The circular itself followed on a National Conference of Citizens' Advice Bureaux workers convened by the National Council of Social Service in May, 1945, and opened by

[1] Citizens' Advice Bureaux leaflet issued by the National Council of Social Service, January, 1945.

the then Minister of Health, who in his own words paid "a very warm and indeed glowing tribute to the work of the Citizens' Advice Bureaux during the last five years." The Conference passed unanimously a resolution expressing their desire and intention of continuing.

The response of local authorities to the Ministry of Health Circular has varied. A few—as in Sheffield, Nottingham and Southampton—have declined any help to the existing voluntary agencies, and have set up their own bureaux. Some have undertaken part of the work, in particular the giving of information as to local authority activities themselves, while assisting the voluntary bureaux to continue for the many problems falling outside this range. Generally there has been recognition by local authorities, as by the central government, of the value of the work done by the bureaux and readiness to make its continuance possible. A report made in January, 1947, by the Standing Committee of Citizens' Advice Bureaux gives the number of bureaux at work in August, 1946, as 639. In 116 cases the local authorities were meeting the whole cost, and in another 334 they were meeting part of the cost; in 133 cases no help was being given and in 56 cases the decision was pending or unknown; 169 of the bureaux were attached to some permanent voluntary organization.

The inquiries coming to the bureaux have been and are extremely varied. They are classified under twenty-one heads ranging from rationing, social insurance, income tax and employment to housing, travel, and family and personal problems. In Table 19 below the enquiries made at the London Bureaux in three months of 1943 and of 1946 are shown, with some of the twenty-one heads combined, and with the subjects arranged in three main groups: of temporary war problems, aftermath problems and continuing problems. The numbers attached to the description of the problems are those of the heads of the classification to which they refer. In the first part of Appendix C on Citizens' Advice Bureaux, illustrative examples are given of the questions asked under each of the twenty-one heads.

The first group in Table 19 shows naturally a great decline from 1943 to 1946, most markedly under "Communications." This head was largely concerned with postal regulations during the war, helping to put people in touch with serving personnel, to send parcels, to search for missing friends. The second, or aftermath, group shows in total a decline, due to a reduction in the still very large head of "Rationing"; the other two heads in this group show an actual increase; the aftermath has still some time to go. The third group shows an increase, in spite of the much reduced

TABLE 19

CITIZENS' ADVICE BUREAUX INQUIRIES IN LONDON AND MANCHESTER*

	59 Bureaux 1943*		20 Bureaux 1946*		Manchester 1945–46	
	Number	Per cent	Number	Per cent	Number	Per cent
Temporary War Problems—						
1. Communications† and transferred workers ..	13,981		408		1,167	
4. Evacuation	1,743		38		54	
14. Service questions	3,225		647		4,324	
13. Prisoners of war and internees	413		15		34	
	19,362	43·0	1,108	4·1	5,579	33·7
Aftermath Problems—						
19. War damage to property ..	854		1,228		66	
20. War pensions (ex-service and civilian war injuries) ..	112		188		108	
16. Supplies and rationing ..	9,107		6,799		1,079	
	10,073	22·4	8,215	30·3	1,253	7·5
Continuing Problems—						
5. Family and personal problems (including 7 Health and Medical and 12 Matrimonial problems) ..	1,730		3,089		4,467	
8. Housing	3,625		5,328		980	
3. Employment	2,516		1,230		407	
17. Trading‡	363		559		—	
15. Social insurance	1,494		2,312		338	
2. Education and training; 11. local information§; 18. travel; 6. foreign‖; 9. income tax; 10. legal not covered by any other category; and 21. miscellaneous	5,831		5,203		3,542	
	15,559	34·6	17,721	65·6	9,734	58·8
	44,994	100·0	27,044	100·0	16,566	100·0

* The figures for London relate to three months—August, September, October—in each year 1943 and 1946, while those for Manchester cover twelve months ending in March, 1946.

† Postal regulations; S.E.A.C. parcels scheme; search for missing persons; etc.

‡ Hire purchase; money lending; business licences; trading with other countries.

§ Addresses; clubs; amenities.

‖ Problems of British subjects abroad or married to foreigners; position of refugees and other foreigners regarding employment, nationality, naturalization, repatriation, etc.

number of bureaux, and this increase is found in most of the heads where separate comparison can be made. The only considerable exception is in relation to employment. The falling off here may be due in part to the undertaking by the Ministry of Labour of its Resettlement Scheme, which is in effect an organization of official bureaux for giving advice on the major part of the problems of employment.

Figures for the central office of the Manchester City League of Help, which is a Citizens' Advice Bureau, covering twelve months, 1945–46, are given at the right of the table, arranged so far as possible in the same way. One or two of the heads cannot be compared exactly and Manchester has actually no head for rationing (such inquiries being presumably dealt with elsewhere). But the general picture is the same. As the period covered, 1945–46, is intermediate between the two periods of the London figures (1943 and 1946) the distribution as between temporary war problems, and continuing problems, is, as it should be, intermediate also.

The Citizens' Advice Bureaux help individual citizens. They are at the same time invaluable collectors of information about economic and social conditions. The enquiries put to them illustrate all the immense variety of perplexities in modern life, some trifling, many serious, some tragic. It has seemed worth while to print in Appendix C a substantial selection from these enquiries. They are a collection of stories from real life.

One class of story is sufficiently depressing in its repetition, to call for illustration here, in the body of the Report as well as in Appendix C, Section V. This consists of the problems rooted in bad housing.

I have lived all my life in London. My family consists of my wife and eight children. Our home was completely destroyed when we were bombed out in 1941. The family is now scattered, living in separate furnished lodgings, and I can't afford it. We need unfurnished accommodation to hold us all. Can you help?

I was a caretaker and have been turned out; where can I go?

We had to leave our furnished accommodation at Southampton yesterday and came to London for work. Can you tell us where we can go to-night?

I came out of hospital and found my furnished room let. Can you tell me of another room?

My father has gone into an L.C.C. Home and is very unhappy—he can pay £2 2s. od. per week. Can you get him else-where?

I live with my husband and three children in one room. Would we have a claim to be rehoused on account of over-crowding?

My husband and I are living apart because we cannot find accommodation. Can we get priority from the housing depart-ment on compassionate grounds?

My wife, self and two children are staying with my parents—the boy, aged seven, has a T.B. gland and we are advised by the doctor to give him a bedroom of his own. At present he shares with his grandparents who really resent us being there. Can you help?

My wife, baby and I are living with my parents, we have our own bedroom and share the rest of the house. My father has sold the house over my head, to my sister, who has given us notice to quit and has offered us her flat—but there are rats there. Must we go?

I married a Frenchman during the war and have only just returned to this country with him and our two babies. We are all living in one room in my sister's flat and have no con-veniences. The Local Authority cannot take our names for the housing list as we have only been here for a month. What can we do to find somewhere better to live?

I am living in one room with my wife and two children and most of our furniture is in the room too. The sanitary inspector has been to see us. What else can I do to get rehoused?

My wife is living with her parents and I with mine and we are drifting apart because we cannot get accommodation. Can you help us?

I have come out of a T.B. Convalescent Home and am living in Rowton House where I cannot get the proper food. My wife and children are with her parents and there is no room there for me. Can you do anything for me?

My husband, myself and our two children live in my mother-in-law's kitchen, and the strain of it, quite apart from the unhealthiness of it, is becoming more than we can stand. Can you help us get proper accommodation?

Can I get housed? The local council will not put my case as priority: there are seven living in three small rooms, five adults and two children. The room my husband and I occupy and the two children is so small that the girl, five and a half, has to sleep in a cot, and the baby, two months, with us; the local council say that they can do nothing.

My two brothers, aged over thirty, my husband and I live in three small rooms; we all have to feed in a very small room, and the washing has to be hung in this living-room, as the downstair tenant will not let us use the gardens and locks the place up during the daytime while at work. This is causing us to be bad friends with each other. The Borough Council who own the property will not rehouse us. What can be done?

I have one furnished room and the Rent Tribunal reduced the rent from 30s. to 5s. three months ago. The landlady now says that I must leave at the end of the week. Can she enforce this?

My husband is on night work and has to sleep during the day. The family above have their wireless on all day and the children run about on uncarpeted floors. What can I do?

My niece is occupying a flat in my house, which I let her have in an emergency during the war. I am now homeless as I can no longer live with my married daughter, who has moved away. Now can I claim possession of the flat?

My fireplace has fallen in so I cannot use it and the landlord will not repair it. Can you make him do so?

The Citizens' Advice Bureaux are discovering daily that the material cause of unhappiness, quarrelling and perplexity in Britain, which outweighs all others in importance, is lack of enough buildings in which to live, meet, teach, learn and do all else that is meant by civilized life. How can the meeting of this need as fully as possible and as quickly as possible be made into a crusade in which all concerned will join with all their strength?

The work of a Citizens' Advice Bureau is extremely varied in nature and in responsibility. Some of it is no more than handing out the correct information as to regulations of the social insurance scheme or war pensions or rationing. Some of it is smoothing the way through the tangles of these regulations for rather helpless citizens. Some of it—particularly under the growing heads of personal and family problems and matrimonial problems—involves handling human problems of extreme difficulty and delicacy. It may be questioned by some whether this work ought to be undertaken by any agency. But the need is there. In times past a citizen with that need might, as a member of a religious community, have found the help he wanted in some other member of his community. But he cannot so readily find help that way now. If there is no friend to give the hearing and advice and help required, it must be given by some such person as a bureau adviser.

The work of a Citizens' Advice Bureau cannot be done without training; the Family Welfare Association makes adequate training a condition for paid staff and for unpaid staff alike. But equally it cannot be done without a sense of mission. This was the theme of a striking address given recently by Miss Dorothy Keeling, chairman of the Councils of Social Service Committee of the Community Council of Lancashire, on "The Ethics of the C.A.B. Service."

> To-day there is much emphasis laid, and rightly laid, on the need for training in social service, and attention is being paid to the need for adequate salaries and for satisfactory conditions of service. But no training is of use on bad material, and without the background of a sense of vocation, social service will have no basic principles.

She went on to name as her basic principles: a real belief in brotherhood and in the equality of man; a reasoned and intelligent understanding of those for whom we work; a passionate sense of justice; a wider outlook beyond the palliative as to the constructive; a determination to do everything possible to fit us for the work which we have taken in hand.

The Citizens' Advice Bureaux, by the continuing demand for them, have proved their claim to survive. In the growing complexities of social relations and activities of public authorities, need for guidance is one of the general needs that will remain, however the level of money incomes may rise. The bureaux to-day make the difference between happiness and needless unhappiness to many a humble individual. They cannot solve all the problems brought to them, but they can do something to lighten every problem by bringing understanding of it. In all this they render much more than an individual service; they help to make a better, more united community. The bureaux are one answer to the questions posed in the Mass Observation Report on "Puzzled People," with its picture of a community of rudderless persons feeling discomforts and not knowing why. They render three general services:—

First, the bureaux explain the working of public authority to the citizen. In so far as the citizen comes to understand public authority, he comes to regard it as something not alien and hostile to himself but something for which he may be responsible.

Second, the bureaux help to protect the citizen against the public authority, when the latter through mistake or stupidity is acting wrongly. Every member of the House of Commons has the function of watching over the interests of all his individual constituents in their dealings with Government departments, of bringing errors and injustices to light, and of seeing that their cases are considered by persons of sufficient responsibility. By one of the best of our public traditions every Member of Parliament, though himself almost invariably belonging to a particular political party in the State, in this function has no party; he renders this service to all his constituents whether they have supported him or opposed him. The Citizens' Advice Bureaux have something of the same function for citizens in relation to local authorities, though not exclusively there. And by fundamental principle they are wholly unsectarian and non-political.

Third, the bureaux make the world appear to many citizens in distress to contain some element of reason and friendship. They are able to do this all the better, because they are not themselves the dispensers of any material assistance, because they are not themselves either makers or administrators of law. The adviser at a Citizens' Advice Bureau is only a fellow citizen with time and knowledge and, if worthy of his position, with infinite patience. The Southwark Bureau extracts with pardonable pride from its postbag a letter from a soldier:—

"I would willingly give you £4,000,000 if I had it, for your help, but as I haven't any amount of money, I can only thank you with all my heart."

Another bureau, having helped an old lady, who was unable to write letters herself, to obtain the Army gratuity due in respect of her soldier son killed in the Far East, finishes the story thus:—

"When the money—about £120—arrived the applicant was 'took bad' at the sight of so many £1 notes; and one was used for a day's convalescence at Herne Bay. On the advice of the Citizens' Advice Bureau the rest was safely deposited in the Post Office, but we hear that a small sum has been kept out for the purpose of buying a 'plant for the young ladies.' "

In all the three ways named above the Citizens' Advice Bureaux, in serving individuals, serve the community. But they can do this only if they are voluntary agencies independent of public authority. An official bureau maintained by the public authority itself cannot render either the first or the second of the three services named above, and is not likely to render the third service.

CONCLUSION AS TO GENERAL NEEDS

There is no need to argue at length the case for Voluntary Action in meeting the two general needs discussed in this chapter—the needs arising out of the growing leisure of wage-earners and the growing complexities of modern life.

The last stage in totalitarianism would be reached if the use of his leisure were being arranged for each citizen by the State. But to leave this field to the play of the business motive, to the extent to which it is so left to-day, produces results which are far from cheering. It is difficult to imagine any standard by which transfer of time from even the dullest form of earning by work to the filling in of a football coupon in hope of unearned wealth can be regarded as progress. The State should re-consider its attitude towards organized gambling and towards the facilities which it provides to-day for this particular form of private enterprise. But the main attack on wasteful or harmful use of leisure cannot, in a free society, be made by direct action of the State. It must depend on the development of alternative interests and free pursuits: it depends on education, in the widest sense of the term, at all stages of life, but above all in adolescence and after. The first call on the increased leisure of the democracy should be the fitting them for the responsibilities of democracy in choosing leaders and deciding on public issues. This is an interest of the State but should not be undertaken by the State. Here is a limitless field for Voluntary Action, assisted so far as is necessary but not controlled by the power of the State.

That citizens should find their way through the growing complexities of modern society is equally an interest of the State, but equally an interest which the State must seek to secure, not directly, but indirectly, through voluntary action. This point was put excellently by Mr. G. E. R. Bull, Town Clerk of Durham, at a conference held in May, 1945, on "Citizens' Advice Bureaux after the War."

The Citizens' Advice Bureaux, I feel, should be the allies of local authorities, not the employees or servants. A person who has a problem in which the local authority is concerned does not want to feel when he goes to the Citizens' Advice

Bureau that he is going to another department of the local authority; he wants to feel that he will get independent advice. And so I hope that when you continue your services after the war you will be the allies of the local authority; but I, as an officer of the local authority, do want you to keep your independence.

Advice to citizens must be given independently by other citizens. A public authority may provide the material means for Citizens' Advice Bureaux but should no more control them than it controls universities.

PART FOUR

CONCLUSION AND RECOMMENDATIONS

X. THE FUTURE OF VOLUNTARY ACTION

The Subject Limited.   The Future of Friendly Societies.   The Future
of Philanthropy.

THE SUBJECT LIMITED

No attempt is made in this chapter to discuss the future of voluntary
action in all the forms noticed in earlier chapters. The largest
numerically of the organizations based on Mutual Aid is that of the
co-operative stores, and the most powerful is that of the trade
unions. Each of these by itself would be a subject for inquiry at
least as lengthy as that which has led to the present volume. Here
a few words must suffice for each.

The co-operative movement has made a notable contribution to
the economic organization of Britain. Its founders thought of it
as doing more than that. There are great educational and social
purposes of which this association of nine million citizens might
well be made the instrument.

The trade unions, as organizations providing for sickness, unemployment, old age, and other contingencies, have the same
problems as the friendly societies in relation to the new developments
of State action. But this side of their work, important as it is in
itself, is by now for them a minor interest. The trade unions have
a continuing task of protecting individuals against injustice from
employers, and of securing for all their members fair remuneration
and conditions of work. But this side also of their activity, indispensable as it remains, is becoming overshadowed by larger problems. The industrial power of the trade unions is now so great
as to raise the issue of justice and freedom for the individual in a
new form. Their political power is so great as to make them a
tempting field for political adventure; it is as important to preserve
genuine educated democracy in the choice of trade-union leaders
as in the choice of Members of Parliament.

Of these and other great issues in the future of the co-operative
movement and the trade unions nothing more will be said here.
Very little will be said as to the other forms of Mutual Aid noticed
in Chapter III.

Building societies appear to have no particular problem, except
that of making clear to the public just what they are and what
services they can render. But they may well discover new forms of

service to their members in dealing with the tangled issues of house ownership to-day.

The housing societies represent a valuable harnessing of in-dividual effort for solution of the most serious problem of material need in this country to-day. In this work they are hampered by some inevitable difficulties. They are hampered by other diffi-culties that are not inevitable, but the results of Government action. These difficulties—relating to rent restriction, borrowing powers and rate of interest, priorities for material and other matters—have been noticed in Chapter III. The Government should make up its mind whether it wants voluntary housing societies or not. If it does, it must make their work possible.

The hospital contributory schemes, like the friendly societies, are profoundly affected by the effects of State action. Their amazing recent developments have shown the driving force that emerges when local feeling can be combined with Mutual Aid. It would be disastrous if the spirit that has gone to building up these associations should now be lost. They may continue for special medical treat-ment. What one would like to see would be that they should explore the possibilities of applying their methods to benevolent purposes generally.

The rest of this chapter will be concerned with the future of Mutual Aid in the form of the friendly societies, and with the future of philanthropy. In relation to each of these the future will be considered in the light of the present.

THE FRIENDLY SOCIETIES

The position of friendly societies to-day is in two important respects different from their position in the past.

First, their original function of enabling their members to escape from pauperism has gone. The State has set out through social insurance to ensure to each individual an income sufficient at all times for basic needs, an income provided as of right on condition of contributions. The execution of this design lags naturally behind the design itself. But it is undeniable that the original primary function of friendly societies has in principle been taken over by the State, as the function of other voluntary institutions—schools, hospitals and many more—has been taken over.

Second, the friendly societies have ceased to any appreciable extent to be societies whose members meet in person. On this the reports of Research Services and Mass Observation are decisive.

The sample investigation conducted by the Research Services shows that 5 or 6 per cent only of the members of the friendly societies attend meetings regularly, while another 12 per cent attend occasionally; seven out of eight never attend a meeting at all. Moreover, practically all attendances are drawn from older age groups. Of the younger people, sixteen to twenty-four, who belong to friendly societies, none attend meetings regularly, and only 1 per cent occasionally. The Mass Observation Report gives the same picture: "The membership of friendly societies to-day, judged in terms of attendance at meetings, lack of interest in the election of officials, and lack of desire to make contact with other members of the society, is very largely a passive one." The actual percentages given in this Mass Observation Report, are affected by the fact that in it no distinction is drawn between friendly societies proper and the collecting societies carrying on the business of industrial assurance, which are still entitled to call themselves friendly societies. The fact that the general public makes so little distinction between the friendly societies proper and the industrial assurance businesses is itself significant of weakness of popular appeal of the friendly society movement to-day.

The conclusion is inescapable that to the bulk of their eight million members, the friendly societies to-day represent not good fellowship but a means of insurance by contract. This conclusion represents a loss in comparison with the past. It does not mean that the friendly society movement has no future.

In the first place, a society may do excellent work even though most of its members never see one another. This is true, to name no others, of the Royal Economic Society, the Early Closing Association, the Mutual Aid organization known as the London Library, and the Royal Society for the Prevention of Cruelty to Animals. The friendly societies began as clubs as well as insurance institutions, at a time when there were few competing opportunities for social intercourse. Now there are thousands of clubs of many kinds, for wage-earners as for others. And since the early days of the friendly societies there has been a change in the character of family life affecting their position as clubs. The friendly society movement has always been predominantly a male movement; women, if they wanted insurance, were in the early days segregated in "societies of females"; the number of women who have held office of any kind in a society not confined to women is insignificant. The friendly society as a club was the man's occasional escape from a crowded home with few amenities. Now wives, with smaller

families, are more of social companions; the radio and the football
coupon at home and the cinema outside it compete with the club
as a way of passing a social evening, with the dice loaded in their
favour by family feeling. It is an interesting sign of the capacity
of voluntary associations, however long established, to adapt themselves to change, that the largest of the orders, the Manchester
Unity, which at first kept branches of men and women rigidly
separate, now favours the formation of branches open to both.

In the second place, while it is true that the friendly societies,
in proportion to their numbers, represent less of individual interest
and crusading spirit than they did in their early days, this is as
true of both the other great working-class movements of comparable
size—the trade unions and the co-operative stores. In the words of
the Mass Observation Report, "economic considerations and the
closed-shop system prevailing in some industries combine to make
belonging to a trade union meaningless from the point of view of
active and spontaneous membership of a social organization at least.
A high proportion of the members, both of political associations and
trade unions, are often more or less completely inactive; a parallel
of an extreme kind is provided by the co-operative stores statistics
which show that *only about 1 per cent of all members take any sort of
active part* in co-op. affairs." The trade unions in most of the
larger industries have become associations which men join, whether
they like it or not, in order to make a living. The co-op. for all
but a trifling proportion of its members is a shop with a dividend
and is nothing more.

In all three movements—trade unions, consumers' co-operation,
friendly societies—decline of the intensity of inner life is a natural
consequence of growth in size.

> It is not growing like a tree,
> In bulk, doth make men better be.

That is as true of human societies of all kinds as of men themselves.
As Aristotle said of Plato's Utopia, affection becomes watery when
it is spread over too many and too diverse people. In this respect
the friendly society movement has preserved an advantage over
most other movements. It has more units with a life of their own
than either the trade unions or consumers' co-operation. It has
resisted, not completely but better than these or other forms of
Mutual Aid, such as the building societies and the savings banks,
the tendency to concentrate in larger units. There were still in
1945 16,000 branches of orders with an average membership of

180 and there were 2,500 unitary friendly societies on the register, nearly two out of three of which had less than 200 members each; there are many unregistered societies. Good fellowship and coming together for Mutual Aid beyond the terms of any insurance contract exist in many of these branches and in small societies. The Mass Observation Report on "Mutual Aid and the Pub" shows the continuance of the forces of good fellowship which gave birth to the movement.

But while the friendly societies show more resistance to the weakness of growth than most other types of Mutual Aid association, they are as institutions in a more difficult position than any of the others. The State has occupied a large part of their field, as it has not occupied that of the trade unions or the co-operative stores. The friendly societies to-day are paying the price of their own achievement as pioneers of insurance against loss of earning power. This was inevitable and is not to be regretted. But it is just to regret some of the State's dealings with this movement from which it has learned so much. The State in the early nineteenth century encouraged the growth of friendly societies. The State has treated the friendly societies hardly on several occasions in their later history.

One such instance is the continued authorized use of the name "friendly society" by organizations of fundamentally different character, the societies undertaking the business of industrial insurance. These societies, using collectors and having special privileges in respect of the policies which they can issue, are known to the law and to the Chief Registrar as collecting societies. But they need not describe themselves so to the public, unless they were established or became collecting societies after 1895. To-day 56 out of 138 collecting societies describe themselves to the public simply as "friendly societies"; those so described include some of the largest. It is small wonder that the public does not realize any distinction between the two types of organization, and that in the Mass Observation report on friendly societies the distinction is ignored. The difference between them made by the Royal Commission of 1871–74, which praised the one and tried to put the other out of business, should have been reflected in a compulsory difference of names.

A second instance of unnecessary harm done by the State was when social insurance began in 1911. It was inevitable that the use of the friendly societies to establish Approved Societies, should turn them to some extent from good fellowship into being organs of State. But it was not necessary then either to bring in the industrial life offices, blurring the character of the friendly societies still more, or to make all insurance depend upon membership of an Approved Society. If the State had then introduced its own administration for those who could not or would not join a friendly society for State benefits, the position of the friendly society as a select body in the community qualified for self-government would have been clearly marked.

Finally, the raising of rates of benefit and their extension to so many new classes in 1946 made an inevitable further inroad on the sphere of the friendly societies. It has been accompanied unnecessarily by a rejection of the proposal to use the friendly societies as agents for their own members. The rejection was made in the teeth of an explicit electoral promise by the great majority of the members supporting the Government of the day.

As a result, first of their marriage to the State, then of the divorce pronounced by the State, the friendly societies are faced to-day by extremely critical problems, in reorganizing their work so as to meet both their contractual obligations to their members and their responsibilities to their staffs. Reorganization must be for several years to come the main preoccupation of all friendly societies which mean to survive, certainly of all the larger societies. It seems likely that some of the small societies will go out of business altogether. But it may be hoped that not many will decide upon this course. Many small societies, particularly if they are of a scale to use voluntary service in their organization, may do better in the future when they are free of the trammels of the State. So, too, may the orders, with their many small branches in federal union. Anything that can be done to encourage the friendly societies to be undefeated by their present troubles is well worth while. It would be a pity if the whole field of security against misfortune, once the domain of voluntary Mutual Aid, became divided between the State and private business conducted for gain.

Above all, the future of the friendly societies must not be painted too dark. They have a great past and a large continuing connection. And there are tasks of service to the community for them to accomplish as important as anything that they have done in the past. There are two main avenues for their exploration: provision in money and provision of service.

In spite of all that the State has done by social insurance to guarantee a minimum income for all at all times, there remains a large scope for insurance above the minimum. The British system of social insurance, unlike that of most other countries, is equalitarian, providing the same minimum for subsistence in sickness, unemployment and old age, without regard to differences in the income earned before, and the differing standards of life and expenditure to which that income has given rise. In giving to each one in social security according to his needs, Britain is nearer to the communist formula than is Soviet Russia, where pensions are related to previous earnings and may bear a higher proportion to those earnings for good service. The British system assumes a large measure of insurance to meet needs above the minimum. The making of provision above the minimum is left as the field of voluntary insurance.

There are many possibilities for exploration in this field: new forms of combining insurance and thrift; new endowment schemes, to keep for the children later, if not required at once, the additional resources made available by family allowances; new plans for special medical treatment beyond anything that is likely to be provided by the National Health Service. The proposal for a marriage grant, made in my Report, has not been accepted. Yet it is clear that insurance for a substantial sum to be drawn on marriage would solve many difficult problems and avoid recourse to the snares of hire purchase. Again, it is likely that the societies will find a strong demand for higher benefits in sickness, above what the State gives, particularly for a short period of incapacity.

In considering new developments of insurance, friendly societies should draw three lessons from the present study. The first lesson is the strong popular appeal of the combination of insurance and saving, which is shown by the persistence of dividing societies, by the growth of societies based on the deposit and Holloway principles, and by the adoption of these principles on the part of some societies, such as the Hearts of Oak and the Loyal Order of Shepherds, which had worked hitherto on conventional lines. The second lesson is that business interests have never found sickness insurance among wage-earners profitable. Here lies the outstanding advantage of the small local society, or branch of an affiliated order. The third lesson is that in voluntary insurance for everything except sickness the friendly societies must realize that they are competing with the industrial life offices for business. They must be prepared to use business methods, including propaganda and advertising. They can offer to the public in many ways a better service than the business concerns, free of liability to shareholders, free of the heavy expense of collectors. But they should not wait for these advantages to be discovered for themselves by the public.

Finally, still within the field of provision in money, it is possible and natural for a friendly society, as it is not natural for a business concern, to give help in emergencies beyond any contract—to have funds for benevolence as well as for strict insurance.

In making provision in money to meet inequalities of circumstances, over and above what is guaranteed by the State, there is a large and familiar field still open to friendly societies. But the main unsatisfied needs that remain, as they have been set out in Chapters VIII and IX, require provision, not of money, but of service. To meet those needs is a harder and therefore more important task. Some of the matters dealt with in those chapters, such as the care of cripples or the blind, or the development of education, fall perhaps unduly far from anything that friendly societies have done in the past. But there are four points which might well prove suitable for friendly society action.

There is, first, the provision of suitable housing for old persons who can live independent lives. Many friendly societies have funds seeking investment. Housing societies need capital. Investment by a friendly society in housing societies designed to secure homes particularly for the members of the friendly society itself, would stimulate interest both centrally and locally in friendly society work.[1]

There is, second, the urgent need for homes with service for old people who, while not in need of hospital treatment, cannot live independently. A number of the friendly societies now have convalescent homes. The need for such homes, for sick persons of working age, will presumably be diminished as the National Health Service Act comes into action. The need for old people's homes with service will grow, as the number of old people grows. It is true that the National Assistance Bill now before Parliament plans hotels for the old at public cost. But it is likely to be a long step from drafting and passing a Bill, to the building and staffing of homes. Friendly societies should make sure if they can of doing something for their members before it is too late.

There is, third, the provision of clubs. Many, perhaps most, friendly societies began as clubs. The need for clubs to give companionship for old people is greater to-day than ever it was. Young people with their families may not need clubs so much to-day as once they did; old people need them more than ever.

---

[1] This suggestion assumes that the Government decide to make the work of housing societies possible, instead of making it nearly impossible in the various ways described in Chapter III.

There is, fourth, the problem of making provision for the greatly increased demand for holidays. This is a need of the adolescent, of the young married couple, of the older married couple with children growing up, of the old as well; it runs through life. The commercial camps have shown the wisdom of making provision for holidays which give to the housewife and mother, as well as to the wage-earner, a relief from work, and not merely a change in the place of her work. But the commercial camps have a standard of expenditure and display which make them too expensive for the mass of the people. Some of the non-commercial holiday associations have recognized the same family need and have set out to meet it at less expense. But the scale of their operations is too small for the numbers. Why should not the friendly societies set out to meet this need? In providing for holidays, for clubs, for old people's needs, the friendly societies would show themselves as societies concerned with all stages of life.

These suggestions raise the question whether any amendment of the law is necessary in order that friendly societies may undertake new tasks of provision of service. Some of the proposals, such as provision of homes with service for the old might be held to come within the existing terms of Section 8 (1) of the Friendly Societies Act as a form of "relief or maintenance." Investment of funds in housing societies may also be within their present powers; provision for clubs and holidays almost certainly would not be so.

It is true that the Friendly Societies Act provides for registration of working men's clubs under Section 8 (4), but it seems clear that a society registered as a friendly society under Section 8 (1) could not also be registered as a club under Section 8 (4). It is true again that the provision of clubs or of holiday camps might be accepted as a specially authorized purpose under Section 8 (5), but at present no exemption is granted from income tax to a society undertaking a specially authorized purpose. This means either that a friendly society undertaking a specially authorized purpose would lose exemption from income tax on the whole of its investments for all purposes, or that the society would have to set up a subsidiary for the specially authorized purpose and incur all the inconveniences of a formally distinct government.

If friendly societies are to develop in new directions, they should receive express authority to do so, by a widening of the purposes under which they can be registered under Section 8 (1), so as to include the benevolent purposes of Section 8 (3), the social purposes of Section 8 (4), and the specially authorized purposes of Section 8 (5) without loss of any of the privileges of tax exemption, which now they enjoy.

There are other changes of friendly society law which should be considered at the same time.[1] One relates to the powers of investment. Here what is done for the friendly societies should be undertaken as a general revision of existing rules for trustees. The present list of trustee investments is clearly out of date. Second, if the existing law does not make it possible for the government to carry out explicitly and satisfactorily what it is completely pledged to, of allowing a single medical certificate to serve both for the State insurance and for voluntary insurance against sickness, this, too, should be dealt with by law. Third, the State should give to friendly societies in future the exclusive use of their name, requiring societies with collectors to describe themselves as collecting societies to the public as they are described in law. The real friendly societies should have the use of their trade name.

In relation to both the other great movements with which it has been compared above—trade unionism and consumers' co-operation—the friendly society movement has one distinctive advantage to-day. It stands outside party politics. Beyond what is needed to give it opportunities equal to its aims it has been and remains little concerned in getting action by the State. It can take as its function creation of channels for the spirit of voluntary service. The suggestions made in this chapter that friendly societies, not content with insurance for money, should widen their scope to include provision of service, is made both for its own sake and also because of its wider implications. The friendly society movement is a democratic movement of Mutual Aid sprung from the working classes. But Mutual Aid, in the more equal society of the future, must broaden into Philanthropy, into the promotion of social advancement, not simply each for himself, but for the whole of society. In commissioning the present report, to cover not its particular problems alone, but the whole field of Voluntary Action, one great friendly society has shown its breadth of view and social

[1] On one point which otherwise would have been discussed here, amending legislation has already been laid before Parliament. This is the statutory limitation on the maximum capital sum for which they can offer insurance to their members at death or as endowment. This limit has stood at £300 since 1908. The Industrial Assurance and Friendly Societies Bill, introduced in December, 1947, proposes to raise the figure to £500 and, also, by a subsequent amendment, to increase the maximum pension which friendly societies can offer from £52 to £104 a year.

interest. This might well be a precedent for similar action in many fields centrally and locally. The friendly societies centrally might become guardians and promoters of democratic voluntary action. Locally they might become leaders or active partners in every movement for social welfare or citizen service. That is the way to being more than organs for mutual insurance on business lines.

The suggestions made here leave untouched the question whether friendly societies should hope or seek ever again to be associated with the administration of State insurance. It may be that some future Government, faced with the difficulties of mass insurance for sickness, will wish to retrace some of the road on which the present Government has started, towards a centralized civil service administration. But that is a question which must be left to arise in the future. The essential business of friendly societies is Voluntary Action. Driven back on that once more, it rests with them to recapture for new ends the spirit of brotherly mutual service which made them the great pioneers of the past.

THE FUTURE OF PHILANTHROPY

The achievements of Voluntary Action inspired by the Philanthropic Motive represent one of the outstanding features of this Report. Time after time philanthropy is seen breaking in on official routine, unveiling evils, finding fresh channels for service, getting things done that would not be done for pay.

The field of philanthropic action, like the field of Mutual Aid, has been affected profoundly by economic, social and political changes. Ceaselessly the State has extended its activity in fields in which voluntary action had pioneered. There has been a cutting off of want. There has been, as the other side of this, the cutting off of wealth. That has meant a far greater equality, in the distribution both of incomes and of leisure.

In face of these changes philanthropy has shown its strength of being able perpetually to take new forms. The Charity Organisation Society has passed over to Family Welfare. Within this century entirely new organizations have arisen, such as the Boy Scouts and Girl Guides, Women's Institutes, the Workers' Educational Association, the National Council of Social Service, Training Colleges for the Disabled, Women's Voluntary Services, and Citizens' Advice Bureaux. The capacity of Voluntary Action inspired by philanthropy to do new things is beyond question. Voluntary

Action is needed to do things which the State should not do, in the giving of advice, or in organizing the use of leisure. It is needed to do things which the State is most unlikely to do. It is needed to pioneer ahead of the State and make experiments. It is needed to get services rendered which cannot be got by paying for them.

The Philanthropic Motive has been compared in an earlier chapter with the scientific motive. It is equally specialized, and pursuing its own course; equally it requires material sources, if it is to yield what it can yield of benefit to the community. With the changed distribution of income and of leisure, many philanthropic agencies are faced with difficult problems, of finance and of obtaining sufficient voluntary service. The possible contribution of the State on the side of finance will be considered in the following chapter. But Voluntary Action cannot depend wholly or mainly on help from the State and need not do so. There is no question that the mass of people in the country are prepared to give money. This is shown by the outstanding success of the Red Cross penny a week scheme. It is shown by many of the appeals made through the wireless for the week's good cause.[1] The democracy can and should learn to do what used to be done for public good by the wealthy.

The problem is that of getting the democracy to give for new things, and unfamiliar needs. An expert on such matters, asked to grade in order of attraction the causes for which it was easy to appeal to the mass of the people, put first sailors, then animals, then children. For all these money came easily. For cultural purposes, such as the National Trust, it hardly came at all. Nor is it easy now to get money for such bodies as the Marriage Guidance Council, institutions to care for the unmarried mother and her child, and other agencies designed to repair breakdowns in family life. The general public are apt to regard family misfortunes as the fault of the people who suffer them, and not a case for charitable giving. There are other limitations of popular view which unduly hamper valuable causes. It is much easier, for instance, to get money for crippled children than to get money for crippled adults. It is particularly difficult to get money for administrative expenditure. Yet without some administrative expenditure voluntary agencies cannot be well managed.

Fortunately the age that came to an end with the Second World

[1] By the courtesy of the British Broadcasting Corporation it has been possible to include a note on the results of Week's Good Cause Appeals in the Supplementary Volume.

War has left behind a group of large charitable foundations, money in living responsible hands other than those of the State and its rulers, but devoted to public purposes. A brief account of the largest of these has been given in Chapter VI. Some represent funds raised to commemorate an historic event, others are the foundations of wealthy individuals. One of the largest of them represents the gathering together of many small charitable trusts, which in isolation were doing little good; application of a similar review to other existing endowments might yield results as notable.

But Voluntary Action should not depend on endowments from the past any more than it should depend on favours from the State. The exploring of new channels for the impulse of giving among the mass of the people is one of its main tasks to-day. The experience of the hospital contributory schemes suggests that success will come most readily when local feeling can be combined with some element of self-help. Can the principle upon which the hospital schemes have been built up be applied to wider purposes of welfare? Could there not in all places with strong local feeling be a local welfare fund meeting a great variety of needs—care of the old, or of children, for clubs, for holiday camps, and so on and so on? This is a possibility worth exploration.

Voluntary Action needs not only money but service. There are not so many people to-day with leisure for full-time service as there were in the Victorian age. There are many more people with some leisure; the voluntary services must adapt themselves to use such help. There should, it is suggested, be in every locality some means of registering offers of neighbourly service. This would be the natural other side of the Citizens' Advice Bureaux. The same organization which invites citizens to put their problems to it might invite other citizens to offer personal help in dealing with problems.

Voluntary Action, as it is specialized, is also essentially local. There should be in every locality some organization to which people can join, who wish by Voluntary Action to improve the conditions in their locality. There should be everywhere a local organization of citizens for Voluntary Action.

What shall it call itself? This raises a question of name which arose also at the outset of this Inquiry. As a short title Voluntary Social Service Inquiry was chosen then. At the end the Report comes simply as a Report on Voluntary Action. The State has become a Social Service State. It might be well in future to leave the term "Social Service" to the State, to mean something done by the State or under its authority, as Social Insurance was used in my first Report to mean insurance organized by the State. The theme of this Report is that the State cannot see to the rendering of all the services that are needed to make a good society. One way of making this point would be to describe simply as Voluntary Services what is done by individual citizens, to supplement what is done as Social Service by the State.

XI. THE STATE AND VOLUNTARY ACTION

Promotion of Voluntary Action a cardinal Public Policy. An Eight-Point Programme for the State: Co-operation of Public Authorities and Voluntary Agencies; a Friendly Societies Act; Royal Commission on Charitable Trusts; Re-examination of Taxation of Voluntary Agencies; Enquiry as to Physically Handicapped; Minister-Guardian of Voluntary Action; Specialized Staff Training; Continuance and Extension of Public Grants to Voluntary Agencies. Conclusion as to the State and Voluntary Agencies.

Throughout the period covered by this review, encouragement of Voluntary Action for improvement of social conditions has been a principle of public policy, reflected in legislation, in administration, and in judicial decisions. The policy began in the time of Elizabeth by the favouring of gifts for charitable purposes; this favour was shown first by judicial decisions, later by the establishment of the Charity Commission to facilitate the adjustment of charitable gifts to changing conditions without excessive legal cost, and finally by exemption from income tax, an advantage of growing significance.

In the present day, State encouragement of Voluntary Action has taken an even more direct form. Grants of public money have been made to voluntary agencies on conditions, leaving them a large measure of independence. Some idea of the scale and diversity of these grants is given by the statement printed in Part III of the Supplementary Volume. This statement is based on information specially supplied for the purpose of this Inquiry by the Treasury. It includes far more than appears as grants to voluntary agencies in the annual estimates. Where a Government department, in order to get work done for which it feels responsible, provides the funds to a voluntary agency, the expenditure appears in the estimates of the department, but may not appear as a grant to a voluntary agency. The total provided from the Exchequer in grants of this nature during the financial year 1946–47 was about £6 million for Universities and about £10 million for other voluntary agencies, having some funds from private sources. This is exclusive of large sums paid to bodies like the Medical Research Council and the British Council which are financed wholly by the Government though having some independence of action.

The statement in the Supplementary Volume shows for each grant the basis on which it was made and the degree of departmental control involved. In general, though the department concerned takes steps to see that the money is spent for the broad purposes for which it is given, there is neither detailed public control nor official audit such as applies to the expenditure of the department itself.

The statement covers only grants made directly from the Exchequer. Many voluntary agencies receive public money also in another way, from local authorities. In some cases these grants are made in pursuance of a general policy advocated by the Government; the Citizens' Advice Bureaux are a leading recent example of this. In all cases, in so far as the expenses of local authorities are now met to a substantial extent by central grants, the ultimate source of the money is to that extent the Exchequer.

Encouragement of Voluntary Action for the improvement of society and use of voluntary agencies by public authorities for public purposes is no less desirable for the future than it has been in the past. The reasons for it have not been diminished and will not be destroyed by the growing activities of the State. On this it is appropriate to quote a pronouncement made nearly forty years ago in the Minority Report of the Poor Law Commission of 1906–9[1]:

> "We think that it should be a cardinal principle of public administration that the utmost use should, under proper conditions, be made of voluntary agencies and of the personal service of both men and women of good will. But it is, in our opinion, essential that the proper sphere of this voluntary effort should be clearly understood. In the delimitation of this sphere, a great distinction is to be drawn between the use of voluntary agencies in the visitation of the homes of the poor, and the use of these agencies in the establishment of institutions. In the one case there should be absolutely no finding of money. In the other case, the more private money, the better.
>
> With regard to the whole range of charitable work in connection with the home life of the poor, there is, in our judgment, nothing more disastrous, alike to the character of the poor and to the efficiency of the public assistance which is at their disposal, than the alms dispensed by well-meaning persons in the mere relief of distress. . . . Even when such gifts are discreetly dispensed by the most careful visitor, they have the drawback of being given without knowledge of what the other resources of the family may be, without communication to

[1] Cd. 4499, ch. XII of Minority Report.

other agencies which may be simultaneously at work, and without power to insist on proper conditions.[1] We are definitely of opinion that no encouragement whatever should be given to any distribution of money, food, or clothing, in the homes of the poor by any private persons or charitable societies whatever. . . . It is not that we undervalue the utility of the personal visits of sympathetic men and women. . . . The utility of such a service of specialized visitation has already been demonstrated in many directions.[2] . . . It is, however, we repeat, essential that such domiciliary visitors should not have the distribution of money or relief in the homes, whether this be from public or private funds, their own or other people's.

On the other hand, there is still enormous scope for beneficent gifts of money, to be administered under voluntary management. There are many kinds of institutional treatment which the various public authorities are not likely themselves to initiate; and there are others that they are almost debarred from conducting. . . . The whole tendency of modern applied science is the sub-division and the breaking up of old categories into newer specializations. We cannot expect our County and County Borough Councillors to launch out into experiments of this kind . . . In this field of initiating and developing new institutional treatment, whether it be the provision of perfect almshouses for the aged, or the establishment of vacation schools or open-air schools for the children, whether it be the enveloping of the morally infirm, or of those who have fallen in a regenerating atmosphere of religion and love, or some subtle combination of physical regimen and mental stimulus for the town-bred 'hooligan'—very large sums of money can be advantageously used, and are, in fact, urgently needed. And not the financing alone, but also the management of such institutions affords a sphere for unofficial work. Just as no public authority can hazard the ratepayer's money in those experimental institutions, so no public authority can

---

[1] This is the case for Charity Organisation. At about the time of this Report, I used to say that C.O.S. and SOC(ialist) were only different ways of spelling the same thing. Both parties wanted adequate action and held that inadequate action might cause more harm than doing nothing at all.

[2] This is illustrated in the Minority Report by reference to health visitors under the Medical Officer of Health, and to Children's Care Committees. Similar voluntary assistance is suggested in connection with pensions and the mentally defective.

assume responsibility for the desirable unconventionality of their daily administration."[1]

These are the words of Sidney and Beatrice Webb, two of the most effective advocates in history of the extension of the activities of the State. They are as emphatic here in stressing the need of Voluntary Action for public purposes and in urging continued co-operation between public authorities and voluntary agencies. The special point which they make, that voluntary agencies should not undertake the distribution of relief, is in accord with all that has happened since these words were written. Voluntary agencies have in fact largely ceased to be concerned with meeting basic needs for food, clothing, or fuel, and will be concerned with such things even less in future, through the extension of social security. In accord with the argument of the Webbs, they will be needed even more than in the past, for exploring as specialists the new avenues of social service which will open when want is abolished.

AN EIGHT-POINT PROGRAMME FOR THE STATE

The proposals made or implied in earlier chapters can be summed up in an eight-point programme for the State in relation to Voluntary Action.

1. Co-operation of Public Authorities and Voluntary Agencies.
2. A Friendly Societies Act.
3. A Royal Commission on Charitable Trusts.
4. Re-examination of Taxation of Voluntary Agencies.
5. An Enquiry as to the Physically Handicapped.
6. A Minister-Guardian of Voluntary Action.
7. Specialized Staff Training.
8. Continuance and Extension of Public Grants to Voluntary Agencies.

The first of these eight points and the last two represent policies already accepted. The remaining five points represent new departures though on established lines.

1. *Co-operation of Public Authorities and Voluntary Agencies*

The practice of public bodies, whether they are central Government departments or local authorities, using voluntary institutions

[1] The Minority Report proceeds to suggest that local authorities should send cases for treatment to voluntary institutions, subject to the latter being open to inspection and ready to receive representatives of the local authority on their governing bodies.

and individual volunteers as responsible agents is well-established. Some observers rank this practice as a contribution of British political sense to world affairs comparable to the inventions of representative government and of the British Commonwealth of free and independent nations. It is hardly that, perhaps, yet it is undoubtedly a valuable practice and a sensible one. In a free society public power should be exercised only by or under the direct orders of persons elected by the citizens to represent them in the use of power. But it is not sensible to limit public service in the same way. There are many people able and willing to serve the public, who are neither suited nor ready to submit to democratic election themselves or to become the paid officers of an elected authority. To reject their help is to delay social advance, experiment, invention, self-criticism.

There is no need to labour this point, implicit in all that has been said in earlier chapters. It is necessary only to make the point that such public service can be obtained either directly from individuals or through voluntary institutions which they create. These institutions in turn can be inspired mainly by the motive of Mutual Aid, or by the motive of Philanthropy, or by a combination of the two.

2. *A Friendly Societies Act*

The reasons for proposing new legislation in regard to friendly societies and the points to be covered have been set out in the previous chapter. The main requirement is a re-defining of the purposes for which a friendly society may be formed, so as to include, without loss of existing privileges of tax exemption, the benevolent purposes of Section 8 (3) of the Act of 1896, the social purposes of Section 8 (4) and the specially authorized purposes of Section 8 (5). The other points for consideration in any new measure dealing with these societies are their powers of investment, their claim to medical certificates without charge, and the exclusive use of their trade name. One hundred and fifty years ago these democratic non-political organizations for Mutual Aid were encouraged by the State and enabled to do what then seemed most important, of providing financial security against misfortune. Now they should be enabled and encouraged, by a suitable widening of powers, to lift their sights and enlarge their scope beyond monetary insurance to provision of services and neighbourly mutual aid.

3. *A Royal Commission on Charitable Trusts*

The case for a complete overhaul of the law and of the administrative machinery for dealing with charitable trusts has been set

out in Chapter VI. There are some things which should clearly be
done in any case. There are some problems on which formation of
policy must wait upon full authoritative enquiry and discussion.
There is a general need for exhaustive survey of the charitable
trusts already established and of the means of making them most
beneficial to the community.

For survey and for authoritative discussion of issues of policy,
the first and essential step is the appointment of a Royal Commission
with adequate powers and wide terms of reference, covering the
whole of Britain. The Commission should be asked :—

1.   To make a survey of the existing charitable trusts, and of
     the law and the administrative machinery concerned with
     such trusts.
2.   To make recommendations for making charitable trusts at
     all times most beneficial to the community and adjusting
     their application to changing circumstances.

On these terms of reference, the first business of the Commission
would be survey of existing trusts. It would do for the whole of
Britain what the Royal Commission of 1878–80 did for the City of
London. There can be little doubt that, like that earlier Commission,
it would discover a mass of small endowed charities which, by
appropriate legislation, might be turned to better use, as has been
done in the City of London.

There is included, in the suggested terms of reference, survey of
two other fields—of the law of charitable trusts and the administrative machinery, for dealing with them. As to the administrative
machinery, the weaknesses of this have been illustrated sufficiently
in Chapter VI. As to law, the question of whether a purpose is
legally charitable is of greater practical importance to-day than it
ever was, for upon this depends exemption from taxation. But,
apart from educational endowments, the definition of what is a
charitable purpose has been untouched by legislation, that is to
say by Parliament, for close on three hundred and fifty years. It is
reasonable that some expert independent body should consider
whether the law of charitable trusts, as it is being developed by
legal judgments referring back ultimately to the Statute of Elizabeth,
is in accord with modern needs.

Survey is only the first step. The reason for proposing a Royal
Commission is not research but to get practical reforms after the
consideration. A programme of reforms which might be submitted
to the commission is set out as the New Deal for Charitable Trusts

in Section IV of Appendix B. This programme is designed to secure, first, that there is continuous effective information for Parliament and the public; second, that there is power to adjust the use of charitable endowments to changing needs and circumstances.

But the programme in Appendix B, though drafted as definitely as possible, is put forward only as a basis for discussion. And some important issues are left open expressly, because judgment on them should wait upon the facts. It is certain, for instance, that neither of the beneficent reforms described in Chapter VI—the dealing with endowed schools and the setting up of the City Parochial Foundation—could have been carried through without giving power to some public authority to over-ride the views of the trustees of individual charities; the trouble with many of the endowments dealt with by those measures was that they had come into the hands of small-minded or selfish persons. It is possible that a review of existing charities would show the same thing to-day, and the same need for power to over-ride trustees. But it is not certain. Decision on this, as on many other issues of policy, should wait upon the results of authoritative investigation and informed discussion.

For that a Royal Commission is the suitable instrument. It remains only to repeat that the proposal of a Royal Commission on Charitable Trusts does not imply that such trusts are undesirable or should be abolished. On the contrary, the view taken here is that the power of individuals to devote endowments to public purposes is one that should be retained, and that its exercise should be encouraged. Voluntary Action needs the support of money in private hands. The object of having a Royal Commission on Charitable Trusts is to make such trusts even more beneficial in future than they have been in the past.

4. *Re-examination of Taxation of Voluntary Agencies*

With the present and prospective levels of direct taxation, exemption from tax is a potent means of influencing action. All charities are granted exemption from income tax and surtax on their income from investments. More than that, till recently it has been possible for those who wished to give money to charitable purposes to do so by making seven-year covenants, under which sums that the State would otherwise have received from the donor as income tax and surtax to spend on public purposes, were in fact handed over to a charity to be spent by it. This arrangement doubled many small gifts by persons of moderate means, becoming the corner-stone of finance for a number of voluntary institutions.

It made possible very large gifts by wealthy persons, giving them power to direct to a public use chosen by themselves money most of which would otherwise have been paid by them to the State as taxation. When a man rich enough to pay 17s. 6d. in the £ as income tax and surtax made a covenant to pay, say, one million pounds over a period of seven years, in effect he was only poorer by a million half-crowns, not by a million pounds, but the charity to which he gave money was richer by a million pounds. This arrangement led to some extremely beneficial gifts which would not have been made without it. But it has now been changed. Since the Finance Act of 1946, seven-year covenants give the charity the benefit of the income tax alone. The surtax is still levied and retained by the State. This change, made suddenly in the Finance Act, has produced a serious situation for many voluntary agencies, which find covenants being cancelled and new covenants not being made.

There is, of course, some justification for the change. With income tax in the neighbourhood of 10s. in the £, the State and the donor remain roughly equal partners in every charitable gift made under covenant. It can be argued that that is enough for the State to do. Whether or not it is enough, depends upon the importance which the State attaches to independent experiment for social advance. What seems clear is that changes of policy as fundamental as this should not be made without fuller discussion of all the issues than is possible in the preparation and debating of a Budget.

With the present and the prospective levels of direct taxation, the conditions of exemption from taxation assume an importance unimagined in former times. The possibility of financing independent Voluntary Action may come to depend upon taxation policy in regard to covenants. A decision that a particular purpose is or is not legally charitable may affect vitally the prospects of an agency set up to serve it. Problems of taxation or tax exemption arise in relation not only to charitable endowments and philanthropic agencies but also in relation to Mutual Aid agencies of many kinds: friendly societies, trade unions, building societies, housing associations, and others.

The whole question of taxation policy in relation to charitable gifts and philanthropic and Mutual Aid agencies should stand referred to some impartial organ of inquiry. It might be included as a third point in the terms of reference to the Royal Commission on Charitable Trusts. Or it might go to a committee constituted for this special purpose.

5. Inquiry as to the Physically Handicapped

A great deal is being done for some classes of the physically handicapped, in particular the blind and those of the disabled who regard themselves as fit for employment. But even for these classes action too often takes the easy way of providing incomes, rather than the hard way of restoration to independence and usefulness. For many other classes of the physically handicapped the financial provision now made is meagre. For all of them, practically without exception, provision of more buildings in which they can be trained and can work is desperately needed. There are long miserable waiting-lists at practically every institution for the physically handicapped. Behind this lack of accommodation for training and work lies the difficulty of places to live in. In total, the physically handicapped represent to-day a volume and variety of unhappinesses which once appreciated cannot be dismissed from the mind.

The Disabled Persons (Employment) Act, the last great measure of the State in this field, was passed in pursuance of recommendations made by a committee mainly of officials whose time for making inquiry outside was limited. There was a compelling reason for rapid action. The State wished to be ready to deal with a large mass of casualties of the war. The Disabled Persons (Employment) Act was a necessary measure. But as has been pointed out in Chapter VIII it does not cover the ground. There is a proved case for sympathetic inquiry as to all classes of the physically handicapped, to discover how the measures already undertaken, including the Disabled Persons (Employment) Act are working and how they could be improved, to discover what further measures are needed.

6. A Minister-Guardian of Voluntary Action

If Voluntary Action for social advance is to be part of public policy, it is important that the voluntary agencies should have a recognized voice and protector in the Government itself. This does not mean that there should be a new Minister for Voluntary Action, or a department for that purpose. That would be a contradiction in terms.

The suggestion made here is that the Lord President of the Council, who is now Minister-Guardian of Voluntary Action in the academic and scientific fields, should extend his interests to the field surveyed in this Report. There should in future be attached to him, rather than to the Treasury, those public agencies which are needed to encourage and assist voluntary agencies, in particular the Registrar of Friendly Societies and the Charity Commissioners. Any Advisory Committee on Public Grants for Voluntary Service,

or new corporation to administer general grants, such as are discussed below, would also be appointed by the Lord President.

7. *Specialized Staff Training*

When the State established the Labour Exchanges in 1909, a
new era of more intimate relations between the State and the
citizen began. It is one thing to sell stamps to the citizen or transmit
his telegrams; it is another thing to try to get him into a job suited
to his powers; when fitting involves special training or physical
and mental rehabilitation, the task becomes still more individual
and more intimate. There has been a similar development in the
character of Voluntary Action. When charity meant giving money
or food or coals it needed little training. When voluntary service
means running a Citizens' Advice Bureau or a Training College for
the Disabled, the best intentions are not enough without skill. Here
public and private authorities have complementary weaknesses.
Public authorities, able to draw on an inexhaustible purse, are not
prevented by lack of means from paying adequately to get staff
of sufficient quality and skill but may fail for other reasons to do so;
they are apt to be slow in recognizing the need for specialized training. Voluntary agencies, being specialist by nature, more easily
recognize the need of special qualifications and training in their work.
But even they do not always recognize the need. And when they do,
they are apt to be hampered by financial difficulties. These difficulties
are particularly acute in the present era of rising costs, lower interest
on endowments, heavier taxation and greater equality of incomes.

The need for specialized training for the new and more difficult
tasks of service to the public to-day is happily being recognized in
authoritative quarters. There is at the Treasury an official known
as the Director of Training. There are in most of the modern
universities departments for training in various branches of social
service. Within the past year the problems of employment and
training of social workers have been dealt with in two valuable and
interesting reports, one commissioned by the Carnegie United
Kingdom Trust, the other issued by the National Council of Social
Service. The first of these reports by Miss Eileen Younghusband,
while showing that the need for training is recognized in principle,
shows also how much remains to be done among public and among
voluntary agencies alike to extend it in practice.[1] The other report,

[1] *Report on the Employment and Training of Social Workers*, by Eileen L. Younghusband. (Dated January, 1946. Published 1947 by the Carnegie United Kingdom
Trust.)

by a Joint Committee of the British Federation of Social Workers and of the National Council of Social Service, under the chairmanship of Professor T. S. Simey,[1] is concerned primarily with the question of salaries and conditions of service of social workers under statutory or voluntary bodies, but has much to say also as to the qualifications and training required. This report leads naturally to the last point in the eight-point programme, the question of finance for voluntary agencies.

8. *Continuance and Extension of Public Grants to Voluntary Agencies*

The practice of making public grants to voluntary agencies without destroying their voluntary character is well established. Should it be pushed still further? A plausible analogy at once presents itself. The philanthropic motive, more than once in this Report, has been compared to the motive which finds its home in institutions of learning and teaching. Universities are nothing, if they are not autonomous. The universities of Britain, until the present century, remained practically independent of public grants and were autonomous without question. To-day they are largely dependent on public grants, and the largest proportion of these come centrally, through the University Grants Committee appointed in 1919 by the Chancellor of the Exchequer of that time, to distribute among the universities and university colleges of Britain the grant from the Exchequer which he was making available for them. The end of the First World War saw the beginning of Exchequer grants to universities; the end of the Second World War has seen a large increase in the scale of grants made. The total disbursed through the University Grants Committee in 1946–47 was more than £6 million and represents about half the total income of the Universities. Yet these public grants are given without destroying self-government. The University Grants Committee, established without any formality by the Chancellor of the Exchequer, seems to have solved the problem of paying away public money without demanding public control.

It can be argued that, if desirable Voluntary Action now needs material help from the State, this should take the form of direct considered grants by the State rather than of continuance or development of the system of covenants whereby rich men, by giving up something of their own, are able to direct to charitable

---

[1] *Salaries and Conditions of Work of Social Workers* (Published September 1947, by the National Council of Social Service).

purposes comparable or greater sums that otherwise would have flowed into the coffers of the State through taxation.

It is tempting to suggest that, as a parallel to the University Grants Committee, there should be a Voluntary Service Grants Committee, allotting resources to voluntary agencies without destroying their freedom. But the analogy of the University Grants Committee is not, in practice, as close as at first sight it may appear. There are some twenty universities in Britain differing from one another in details, but pursuing the same general aim by similar methods. They are all of established position, similar constitution, and high sense of responsibility. They differ from one another only as individuals of the same species and race differ from one another. To divide a total grant between these twenty institutions from time to time, after reviewing their needs and aims of the moment, is not a simple but is a quite possible task.

The task of allotting a single public grant among all philanthropic agencies would be quite different. They are numbered not by tens but by thousands. They are infinitely various in scale, methods, form of government, and degree of responsibility. And unlike the universities, they have widely differing aims. All the universities are trying to do the same thing, to a degree which makes the questions that arise on distribution of a grant voted for all of them questions of means, not of ends, and questions therefore that a Minister can rightly leave to an expert body like the University Grants Committee. But the diversity of aims of philanthropic agencies is so great as to make the question of how to distribute a grant voted for all of them a question of ends rather than means. It would mean deciding, say, between unmarried mothers and lifeboats, between spastic children and the preservation of rights of way. Such decisions are different in character from anything undertaken by the University Grants Committee.

This argument does not mean that public money should not be made available for spending by voluntary agencies of social service. It is being made available to-day. It should be made available in increasing amount in future. But it should in the main follow the same channels as at present—of departmental grants for purposes in which the department is interested and which its Minister is prepared to defend in Parliament. These grants might be made not simply to cover the bare cost of services but to help with the overheads as well. But, large or small, they should always be the expression of joint specialist interest, in the department and in the voluntary agency. It would be wrong to break the direct contact between public authorities and voluntary agencies in the same field. The philanthropic agencies are alike only in their independence of one another, and their demand to be treated individually. No one voluntary agency and no committee representative of such agencies could be used to allocate a central public grant among the rest.

This argument does not exclude the possibility of placing in the hands of some responsible central committee a grant, not to replace, but to supplement help given by the departments. There may be purposes of too general or too novel a character to attract the interest of any particular department. The National Council of Social Service is perhaps of this type; it has done invaluable work in the past in helping to promote new agencies, and something of the sort may always be needed. But this service may not be forth-coming without help from public sources. The general public, up to the present, have shown themselves more ready to give for familiar humanitarian purposes than for new social experiments, typified by the Citizens' Advice Bureaux or the Marriage Guidance Council. In the unequal society of the past the promoters of ex-periments could interest wealthy individual patrons. They may find it hard to secure enough private givers in future. The State on be-half of the democracy may have to do what the aristocracy did before.

There may therefore be a case for placing alongside of the great charitable foundations—London Parochial, Carnegie, Pilgrim, Nuffield, and the rest—an independent corporation endowed by the State for social advance by Voluntary Action, where departmental interest is unlikely. There is a special ground for suggesting this, as a temporary measure at least, at the present juncture.

The sudden change made by the Finance Act of 1946 in the con-ditions affecting charitable covenants has added seriously to the difficulties of voluntary agencies in a time already difficult. It has been suggested earlier in this chapter that there should be a re-examination of taxation policy in relation to Mutual Aid and charit-able gifts alike. It has been suggested that there should be a Royal Commission to report on existing charitable trusts everywhere as the Commission of 1878–80 surveyed the City of London charities. Each of these measures may help the voluntary agencies to new resources: the first of them may on further consideration lead to a more generous treatment of covenants to give money for charitable purposes and a wider definition of those purposes; the second may, and almost certainly will, uncover old endowments which can be used to better purpose than at present. But each of these measures will take time; neither can bring immediate relief. There is a case for ensuring interim support, both by an increase of departmental grants and through an independent corporation of general powers.

CONCLUSION AS TO THE STATE AND VOLUNTARY ACTION

The State should encourage Voluntary Action of all kinds for social advance. In respect of that form of Voluntary Action for Mutual Aid which is the starting-point of this Report—the friendly societies—the State should make amends for damage to them in the past by a generous agreed measure of legislation opening the road to new service in the future. It should remove difficulties in the way of the other forms of Mutual Aid discussed in this Report. It should in every field of its growing activity use where it can, without destroying their freedom and their spirit, the voluntary agencies for social advance, born of social conscience and of philanthropy. This is one of the marks of a free society.

XII. FIRST THINGS FIRST

THE *Report on Social Insurance and Allied Services*, submitted by me to the Government in November, 1942, set out a practical programme for putting first things first. There was to be bread and health for all at all times before cake and circuses for anybody at any time, so far as this order of priority could be enforced by redistribution of money. The plan for social security put forward in my first Report was in essence a plan for redistributing money, as between times of earning and not earning, as between richer and poorer. It took money from people when they had money, took money in the form of social insurance contributions and general taxation, in order to hand back to people, when they could not earn, enough money to buy the necessaries of healthy life, and in order to pay for medical treatment of all kinds when they needed treatment.

This first Report was not put forward as anything but a first step. Bread and health are not all that a citizen needs. Idleness even with bread demoralizes. I followed the first Report as soon as possible by a second Report in October, 1944, suggesting how Full Employment in a Free Society could be achieved. The second Report was unlike the first Report in being unofficial, not made at the request of the Government. It was like the first Report in being largely, though not wholly, concerned with the management of money. It emphasized the fact that the State is or can be master of money, while in a money economy all individuals are controlled by money. The State alone can ensure that at all times unsatisfied needs are clothed with purchasing power, so as to turn them into effective demand for goods and services. The State alone, by its management of money, can prevent there being at one and the same time in a community unsatisfied needs, and idle men and machinery by whose employment those needs could be met. The programme for full employment in a free society was expressed as in essence a programme for socializing demand rather than socializing production. The State was to do that which the State alone can do: manage money so as to maintain spending. Subject to that, the State should leave as much as possible to the initiative and enterprise of the citizens.

The sting of this third Report, on Voluntary Action, lies in showing that the aim of the first Report, of putting first things first, cannot be accomplished simply by redistribution of purchasing power.

Money, however well distributed, will not buy the material necessaries of healthy life for all, if they are not being produced in sufficient quantities for all. There are some things—not goods but services—which often cannot be bought with money, but may be rendered from sense of duty. Clearly in Britain to-day first things are not in practice being put first. It is not putting first things first to rank an idle Saturday before decent homes for all; to let scarce man-power go to build cinemas or holiday camps while old people struggle in solitude with discomforts beyond their strength, while sick men suffer needlessly for want of hospitals, while handicapped adults who have learned a trade cannot use it because they find no place to live, while handicapped children miss the training that might make them useful citizens, while for many thousands of married pairs life in their own homes remains impossible and unnatural living makes unhappy families.

If we ask why, with complete democratic control of our Government, with social security established by law and full employment established in practice, life in Britain is not better than we find it to-day, the answer is twofold.

First, the State is or can be master of money, but in a free society it is master of very little else. The making of a good society depends not on the State but on the citizens, acting individually or in free association with one another, acting on motives of various kinds, some selfish others unselfish, some narrow and material others inspired by love of man and love of God. The happiness or unhappiness of the society in which we live depends upon ourselves as citizens, not on the instrument of political power which we call the State.

Second, we citizens of Britain have been slow to recognize how in fifty years with two world wars the world around us has changed, and calls for a change in our behaviour. We have not realized sufficiently how much of our easy prosperity in the nineteenth century we owed to the accident of being the first nation to become industrial. We were able once to exchange our scarce manufactures on very favourable terms for the food and the raw materials of other nations. To-day we have lost that priority in the market. The other nations, some more some less, have followed us down the same industrial path. They do not depend upon us for manufactures at our price in terms of food and raw materials. We can no longer exploit something like a monopoly; we meet more and more of competition.

This general economic development of the world, while depriving us of one early advantage, would have brought compensating advantages if our nineteenth-century dream of growing international co-operation had come true. But the dream has been shattered by two world wars. In the aftermath of these wars Britain, as the most international of all the larger nations, finds her material prosperity and her standard of living threatened.

That does not make the plan for social security in my first Report inappropriate. The poorer a country is, the greater is the urgency of using rightly its material resources, putting bread and health for all before comforts for any. Nor does it mean that the full employment which was the object of my second Report is less important than it seemed before. Full employment is more important than ever before; we cannot afford to waste man-power in any form. Our present difficulties are not a ground for retracing the steps that we have just taken towards greater social justice. But our difficulties are something that we must take very seriously indeed. They are not insurmountable, but they will not be surmounted by trusting to luck—or to any Government. The loss of our position of industrial priority does not mean that we cannot maintain and even raise our standard of living. It does mean that prosperity will no longer come to us as easily as in the past. If we want to live as well as our fathers, we must either work harder or work more effectively, not rejecting or limiting any machine that will make work easier, not rejecting or obstructing the utmost use of man-power in any form. We cannot expect in future that all of us will go on living better and better by each of us doing less and less. We shall come to see that in time, for we are sensible people, and not the less sensible because we are slow to change our line. We are changing already. The crisis of to-day will pass. The tasks of the future await us.

This third Report is not concerned with the immediate task of making our people prosperous again, able to help themselves and to help others. But it is designed to show some of the tasks that must be undertaken if prosperity when it comes is to mean the chance of happiness for all. This Report shows in Chapters VIII and IX how much unhappiness remains in Britain, untouched by social security and full employment. That is the negative side of the Report. The positive side is more important.

The positive side of this third Report is in the earlier chapters, I to VI, which show how much the making of better conditions of life has owed to Voluntary Action. The world at large is engaged in debating, sometimes by reason and voting, sometimes in other ways, the advantages and disadvantages of private enterprise in business. This third Report is concerned with private enterprise, not in business but in the service of mankind, not for gain but under the driving power of social conscience. The need for private enterprise in that form is beyond debate.

If we are really to put first things first, bread and health for all at all times before cake and circuses for anybody, we must go beyond the simple redistribution of money to the much harder task of ensuring production of goods and services, to provision not in money but in kind. We must continue to use to the full the spirit that made our great organizations for full Mutual Aid and that fired the philanthropists of the past. It is necessary to face two new difficulties in the way of doing this.

First, it involves making and keeping something other than pursuit of gain as the dominant force in society. The business motive, in the field covered by this Report, is seen in continual or repeated conflict with the Philanthropic Motive, and has too often been successful. The industrial assurance offices exploited successfully for gain a universal desire to avoid a pauper burial. They have been succeeded by the businesses of football pools, dog tracks and cinemas, all exploiting in different ways for personal gain the increased leisure of the people. The business motive is a good servant but a bad master, and a society which gives itself up to the dominance of the business motive is a bad society. We do not put first things first in putting ourselves first. In former days there was a great alternative to the pursuit of gain, as the guiding force in society; there was force for good inspired by religious belief and based on membership of a Christian community. Now this religious force for good is less widely influential than it was in the nineteenth century. It must either be revived or be replaced by some equally good alternative, if that can be found. Perhaps it must be both in part revived and in part replaced.

Second, with the passage from class rule to representative democracy, little can be done except by influencing directly, not a few leaders, but the mass of the people. We shall not take the difficult steps of going beyond redistribution of money to provision in kind, unless we really want to do this, and "we" for this purpose means in Britain now the whole people—the democracy. In the unequal society of the past there were always dynamic individuals with social conscience, and, in giving their personal service, they could usually get the necessary help for their purposes from the superfluities of money and leisure among their friends. In the society of the future there will still be dynamic individuals with consciences, but they may not so easily find the material means of doing their work, and they will not find it in the same way. Democracy to-day has to show that in discarding the inequalities it can learn the virtues of aristocracy.

Just half-way through the nineteenth century, Wordsworth, the poet of its beginnings, died, and Matthew Arnold wrote his "Memorial Verses."

> Goethe in Weimar sleeps, and Greece
> Long since saw Byron's struggle cease.
> But one such death remained to come,
> The last poetic voice is dumb—
> We stand to-day by Wordsworth's tomb.
>
> Ah! since dark days still bring to light
> Man's prudence and man's fiery might,
> Time may restore us in his course
> Goethe's sage mind and Byron's force;
> But where will Europe's later hour
> Again find Wordsworth's healing power?
> Others will teach us how to dare
> And against fear our breast to steel;
> Others will strengthen us to bear—
> But who, ah! who, will make us feel?

Time in his course will bring to us endless successors in spirit of the Victorian pioneers of social advance—men and women with the conscience and industry of Shaftesbury, the strength of purpose of Elizabeth Fry, the courage and inventiveness of the Barnetts, the untutored fervour of William Booth, the passion to understand of Charles Booth, the exuberant humanity of Quintin Hogg, the pity and the anger of Benjamin Waugh. But who will restore the conditions in which these men and women did their work? When and how shall we replace the lost power of widespread religious belief, the material resources which must support the Philanthropic Motive as the body clothes the soul, and the sense of brotherhood in the human race? None of the Victorian pioneers dreamed of a world with dangers such as ours. None of them doubted that man could and would be master of his fate.

To restore the conditions in which these pioneers did their work will not be the work of any one man. But restoration may come through one spirit breathing again through many men, as it did in the special field from which this study began. So at last human society may become a friendly society—an Affiliated Order of branches, some large and many small, each with its own life in freedom, each linked to all the rest by common purpose and by bonds to serve that purpose. So the night's insane dream of power over other men, without limit and without mercy, shall fade. So mankind in brotherhood shall bring back the day.

APPENDICES

APPENDIX A

STATISTICAL AND OTHER DATA AS TO FRIENDLY SOCIETIES

I. Statistics of Registered Friendly Societies;
II. Affiliated Orders in 1945;
III. Specimen Contributions and Benefits;
IV. Section 8 of the Friendly Societies Act, 1896;
V. The Chief Friendly Societies Acts;
VI. Industrial Assurance and Friendly Societies Bill, 1947;
VII. The Registrar's Field: Notes to Tables 6 and 7.

I. STATISTICS OF REGISTERED FRIENDLY SOCIETIES

THE Chief Registrar of Friendly Societies has furnished statistics as to each of the main types of societies registered as friendly societies, at various dates from 1899 to 1946, and the tables in this Appendix are based on these statistics, with a few adjustments.

Table 20 covers all registered friendly societies, general and specialized, other than the collecting societies. It shows in the eleven years from 1899 to 1910 just before the coming of National Insurance little change in the number of societies and branches, substantial increases in membership and funds, and a slightly smaller increase of benefit expenditure, so that per head this expenditure fell from 20s. to 18s. 11d. in the later year. This is connected probably with the rapid growth in those years of the National Deposit Friendly Society. The "other" expenditure includes all payments from benefit funds, and thus includes sums paid as dividend in the dividing societies and withdrawals by members of sums allocated to them in the deposit and Holloway societies.

The next twenty-five years, 1910 to 1935, show a reduction by a third in the number of societies and branches, combined with an increase in total membership of nearly a quarter, a trebling of the funds, and an increase of benefit expenditure per head from 18s. 11d. to 28s. 6d. The concentrating influence of National Insurance is obvious. But in total, voluntary mutual aid and thrift are increased instead of being discouraged. The influence of the further spread of the deposit and Holloway systems is shown in the "other" expenditure, which is nearly trebled. But expenditure on sickness benefit also rises by nearly 50 per cent.

In the last ten years to 1945 the decline in the number of societies
and branches has continued, with rising total membership and funds,
and benefit expenditure per head higher in 1945 than in 1935.
The expenditure on other benefits by 1939 exceeded in total the
sick benefit, and has continued to grow more rapidly.

Table 21 shows over the same period 1899 to 1946 the general
friendly societies, i.e. those giving sick benefit, in their main classes
as set out in Table 1 in Chapter I. In preparing this table, it has
been necessary to make a special calculation as to the deposit and

TABLE 20

ALL REGISTERED FRIENDLY SOCIETIES

Numbers, Membership, Funds and Benefit Expenditure: 1899–1946

Year	Number of Societies or Branches	Member-ship (000)	Funds (£000)	Benefit Expenditure (£000)				Benefit, Shillings per Head
				Sickness	Death	Other	Total	
								s. d.
1899	27,592	5,466	32,654	—	—	—	5,455	20 0
1905	26,795	6,164	41,795	4,056	859	779	5,694	18 6
1910	26,877	6,623	49,802	3,649	890	1,738	6,277	18 11
1935	20,241	8,166	135,312	5,241	1,466	4,949	11,656	28 6
1939	19,429	8,307	155,596	5,549	1,623	5,893	13,074	31 6
1945	18,535	8,720	192,829	5,575	1,801	6,617	13,993	32 1
1946	18,293	8,670	197,975	5,631	1,781	7,635	15,047	34 9

Holloway societies before 1910. The Registrar classifies as deposit
societies both those which operate on the principles of the National
Deposit Friendly Society and those which follow the somewhat
different Holloway principles, marking both of them by the letter
"P." It has not been possible to distinguish between the two types
in the tables given here.

Nor did the Registrar before 1910 prepare statistics for the "P"
societies, as distinct from the accumulating societies giving sick
benefit. Having regard to the importance of comparing tendencies
for different types of society before and after the introduction of
National Health Insurance in 1911, figures of numbers and membership for individual societies classified by the Registrar as belonging
to the deposit and Holloway types have been obtained from the
Registrar's reports from 1899 and 1905. Figures for societies classified by the Registrar as "accumulating with some deposit members"
have been obtained by direct reference to the societies. As a result

it has been possible to present the figures shown for 1905 and 1910 as the number and membership of deposit and Holloway societies in combination in Tables 21 and 23. The basis of the figures is explained below in the Notes to Tables 21–25.

From 1899 to 1910 as shown in Table 21, the number of branches

TABLE 21

GENERAL FRIENDLY SOCIETIES

(*Numbers and Membership:* 1899–1946)

	Number of Branches or Societies	Total Membership	Members per Branch or Society
ORDERS AND BRANCHES (A.1 OF TABLE 1)			
1899	20,578	2,397,618	117
1905	20,077	2,654,955	132
1910	20,580	2,782,953	135
1935	17,213	2,904,365	169
1939	16,625	2,813,595	169
1945	16,017	2,686,836	180
1946	15,868	2,641,502	166
UNITARY ACCUMULATING SOCIETIES (A.2)			
1899	4,367	1,604,104	367
1905	3,736	1,700,673	455
1910	3,117	1,277,185	410
1935	977	1,140,365	1,167
1939	893	1,145,694	1,283
1945	826	1,079,365	1,307
1946	794	1,058,958	1,334
DIVIDING SOCIETIES (A.3 (a))			
1899	916	114,786	125
1905	1,302	227,102	174
1910	1,335	292,909	219
1935	680	416,829	613
1939	610	379,487	622
1945	556	311,499	560
1946	530	310,494	586
DEPOSIT AND HOLLOWAY SOCIETIES (A.3, (b) AND (c))			
1899	66	100,703	1,526
1905	70	240,728	3,439
1910	81	381,491	4,710
1935	97	2,008,087	20,702
1939	92	2,174,500	23,636
1945	92	2,480,278	26,959
1946	90	2,459,840	27,332

of affiliated orders remained the same, but the total membership and so the average size of each branch increased by about 15 per cent. The dividing societies increased in numbers and membership; the membership of the deposit and Holloway societies almost quadrupled. The unitary accumulating societies—the original type of friendly society—were losing ground to all these rival forms, falling in number by nearly 30 per cent and in total membership by 20 per cent, from 1899 to 1910.

The later part of Table 21, from 1910 onwards, emphasizes the concentrating effect of National Insurance. Between 1910 and 1945 nearly three out of four of the unitary accumulating societies and three out of five of the dividing societies disappeared; the total membership of the former has fallen slightly, that of the latter actually rose from 1910 to 1935, and in 1945 is still higher than in 1910. The orders with their branches show much greater resisting power to the tendency to replace small units by large ones, with the number of branches in 1945 still four-fifths of what it was in 1910. The total deposit and Holloway membership is now little short of that of the orders. The total of 2,480,278 includes 268,766 in ten societies classified by the Registrar as accumulating with some deposit members.

Table 22 shows the main types of specialized friendly society (B.1 of Table 1). Points calling for comment are the decline of the death and burial societies (no doubt due to competition by the collecting societies and industrial assurance companies); decline of the widows' and orphans' societies between 1910 and 1935 (no doubt due to contributory insurance in 1926); fall in the numbers of separate juvenile societies, probably due to their absorption in adult branches or societies. The medical societies, after a decline from 1910, show recovery of membership of late. The societies for institutional treatment (not covered by the National Insurance Act of 1911) show notable progress.

Table 23 shows in greater detail the benefit expenditure of the principal types of general friendly society. The fall in the proportion of sick benefit in the total benefit expenditure of the orders between 1905 and 1910 is apparent only, being due to the transference of medical benefit from being treated as sick benefit to being reckoned among "other benefits." From 1910 the distribution of expenditure in the orders shows great steadiness, with sick benefit about 70 per cent of the total, and with death benefit rising (at the cost of "other benefits") from 15 per cent to 19 per cent. After 1910 the expenditure of accumulating societies changes greatly in character.

TABLE 22

SPECIALIZED FRIENDLY SOCIETIES

Numbers and Membership: 1899–1946

Type	1899		1910		1935		1945		1946	
	Number	Membership	Number	Membership	Number	Membership	Number	Membership	Number	Membership
Death and Burial*	402	766,939	401	855,962	318	320,924	283	302,382	278	307,869
Widows and Orphans†	117	53,100	102	108,002	39	22,963	45	24,469	44	24,220
Annuities and Pensions‡	No information		No information		76	108,792	72	98,497	70	95,370
Endowments§	No information		No information		16	116,554	13	130,165	13	132,899
Medical‖	75	296,127	85	329,450	63	143,930	55	166,650	53	164,504
Institutional¶	No information		6	36,651	10	435,877	12	1,020,662	12	1,053,694
Accident	No information				20	193,950	19	178,352	19	178,996
Shipwreck and Miscellaneous	13	2,564	95	403,190	87	175,571	79	149,158	79	158,245
Juvenile**	1,058	135,995	971	154,923	656	214,128	476	141,193	453	133,556

* These are death and burial societies without collectors. They are declining in numbers and even more in membership. Among the largest are the Coventry Church General Burial Society and the Provident Benefit Fund of the United Kingdom Commercial Travellers' Association.

† This includes old service funds such as that for the Royal Regiment of Artillery, dating from 1752; and that for the Royal Marine Forces dating from 1766.

‡ This includes several Railway Pension Funds, the Glasgow Corporation Superannuation Fund, etc.

§ This includes the Post Office Insurance Society.

‖ These, after declining since National Insurance, show increased membership from 1935 to 1945.

¶ This includes Civil Service Sanatorium Society, Industrial Orthopaedic Society, and L.M.S. Railway Hospital Fund (the last accounting for much of the recent increase).

** Juvenile societies are formed largely for the purpose of recruiting members for branches of orders and by their rules provide for the admission to membership being confined to juveniles. Membership normally ends at the age of twenty-one and there is usually an incentive to join the branch in connection with which the society is run. Both the numbers and the membership of such societies had shown a very considerable falling off in the past fifty years, partly a reflection of the diminishing number of juveniles, partly from other causes.

TABLE 23

GENERAL FRIENDLY SOCIETIES' BENEFIT EXPENDITURE ANALYSED,* 1899–1946

Type of Society	1899 £000	1905‡ £000	1905‡ Per cent	1910 £000	1910 Per cent	1935 £000	1935 Per cent	1939 £000	1939 Per cent	1945 £000	1945 Per cent	1946 £000	1946 Per cent
Orders S		2,428	80·6	2,197	69·2	2,665	72·0	2,667	71·5	2,306	70·4	2,304	70·0
D		478	15·8	487	15·3	635	17·2	668	17·9	618	18·9	589	17·9
O		109	3·6	492	15·5	400	10·8	295	10·6	350	10·7	399	12·1
Total	3,266	3,015	100·0	3,176	100·0	3,701	100·0	3,780	100·0	3,273	100·0	3,291	100·0
Unitary Accumulating† S		1,512	68·7	1,178	70·2	1,255	45·6	1,311	42·8	1,286	38·9	1,286	36·8
D		248	11·3	215	12·8	362	13·2	401	13·1	428	13·0	427	12·2
O		440	20·0	285	17·0	1,133	41·2	1,351	44·1	1,591	48·1	1,779	51·0
Total	1,825	2,200	100·0	1,679	100·0	2,750	100·0	3,063	100·0	3,305	100·0	3,492	100·0
Deposit and Holloway† S				164	39·9	1,040	40·2	1,271	39·8	1,587	46·1	1,649	39·9
D				16	3·9	164	6·3	208	6·5	349	10·2	378	9·1
O				230	56·2	1,386	53·5	1,710	53·5	1,501	43·7	2,107	51·0
Total				410	100·0	2,590	100·0	3,190	100·0	3,436	100·0	4,134	100·0
Dividing S		87	30·6	91	25·1	268	29·8	289	30·0	270	33·2	268	35·1
D		24	8·5	31	8·6	101	11·2	116	12·0	121	14·9	121	15·8
O		173	60·9	239	66·3	530	59·0	561	58·0	423	51·9	375	49·1
Total	167	284	100·0	360	100·0	899	100·0	966	100·0	815	100·0	764	100·0
All General Friendly Societies S		4,027	73·3	3,629	64·5	5,228	52·6	5,539	50·6	5,448	50·3	5,506	47·1
D		750	13·6	749	13·3	1,262	12·7	1,393	12·7	1,516	14·0	1,515	13·1
O		722	13·1	1,247	22·2	3,449	34·7	4,017	36·7	3,864	35·7	4,660	39·9
Total	5,258	5,499	100·0	5,625	100·0	9,940	100·0	10,949	100·0	10,829	100·0	11,681	100·0

* S = Sick Benefit; D = Death Benefit; O = Other Expenditure from Benefit Funds.

† Deposit and Holloway Societies are not shown separately before 1910, their expenditure being included with that of Unitary Accumulating Societies.

‡ Medical Benefit is included as part of Sick Benefit in 1905; thereafter among Other Benefits.

Sick benefit, from representing 70·2 per cent of their benefit expenditure in 1910 (the same proportion as in the orders), by 1945 represents only 38·9 per cent. Death benefit in these societies represents much the same proportion throughout, about 13 per cent; "other benefits," which include payments of all kinds to members, increase. While some local sick clubs failed, those accumulating sick societies which went in for other benefits (endowment and so forth) held their own. The growth in expenditure of deposit and Holloway societies, like that of their membership, is an outstanding feature of all the tables. It is interesting that in 1945 sickness and death benefits together in this group account for 56·3 per cent as compared with 43·8 per cent in 1910; and the proportion returned to members as deposit has fallen. The expenditure of dividing societies is more than twice as great in 1945 as in 1910 (£814,566 as against £360,445). The expenditure at the later date includes a larger proportion for sickness and less as dividend—a trend similar to that seen in deposit and Holloway societies.

Table 24, taking all the registered sick benefit societies together,

TABLE 24

MEMBERSHIP AND BENEFIT EXPENDITURE PER HEAD OF GENERAL FRIENDLY SOCIETIES: 1899–1946

Year	Membership	Benefit Expenditure	Expenditure per Head
		£	£
1899	4,217,211	5,258,324	1·247 = 24s. 11d.
1905	4,823,458	5,498,536	1·140 = 22s. 10d.
1910	4,734,538	5,625,355	1·188 = 23s. 9d.
1935	6,469,642	9,940,156	1·536 = 30s. 8d.
1939	6,513,276	10,948,697	1·681 = 33s. 7d.
1945	6,557,978	10,828,690	1·651 = 33s. 0d.
1946	6,470,794	11,680,719	1·805 = 36s. 1d.

shows from 1899 to 1939 membership rising about 50 per cent, and total benefit expenditure about 100 per cent, i.e. the expenditure per head has risen substantially from under 25s. a year to nearly 34s. a year. From 1910 to 1939 benefit expenditure, as shown at the foot of Table 23, has risen for these societies as a whole from £3,629,000 or about 15s. per head to £5,539,000 or about 17s. per head.

TABLE 25

ACCUMULATING SOCIETIES WITH DEPOSIT MEMBERS IN 1945

Registration No. of Society	Name of Society	Accumulative Section		Deposit Section		Duplicate Membership of both Sections
		Members	Funds	Members	Funds	
			£		£	
86 Berks	Compton Pilgrims B.S.	2,394	69,176	2,328	19,687	—
299 Berks	Royal Berkshire F.S.	2,355	26,081	5,261	59,050	—
48 Hants	Hampshire and General F.S.	26,245	590,515	21,443	306,273	—
1899 Lancs	Rational Assoc.	68,816	1,632,792	183	3,026	—
43 London	Royal Oak B.S.	8,632	192,746	329	6,936	—
62 London	Hearts of Oak	322,246	14,939,162	124,581	1,746,042	17,616
68 London	United Patriots Nat. B.S.	11,865	172,209	1,963	30,403	—
296 London	Teachers' Provident	42,176	4,506,774	104,051	4,661,414	31,918
580 Warwick	Birmingham General P. and Ben. Inst.	3,024	103,273	287	8,216	—
192 Wilts	Wiltshire F.S.	393	14,063	8,340	190,108	—
		488,146	22,246,791	268,766	7,031,155	49,534

B.S. = Benefit Society.   F.S. = Friendly Society.

Notes to Tables 21–25

1. The numbers and membership of deposit and Holloway societies in 1899 and 1905 have been calculated as follows:—

(a) All societies classified by the Registrar as deposit in 1945 and known to exist in the earlier years have been treated as deposit or Holloway societies in those years. There were 39 such societies in 1899 with a membership of 85,746, and 41 in 1905, with a membership of 214,516. These societies would not necessarily have been deposit or Holloway societies in the earlier years but were probably such and have been treated as such.

(b) Societies classified by the Registrar as Deposit in 1905, but ceasing to exist before 1945, have been included in the figures of deposit or Holloway Societies for 1905. There were 26 such Societies with 5,722 members. In the Registrar's report for 1899 there is no mark to show whether a society is of the deposit or Holloway type, or one working on another principle;

in this case, wherever one of the 26 Societies classed as deposit in 1905 was found in the 1899 report, it was again classed as deposit for that year. There were 24 such societies with 5,126 members.

(c) In addition to 82 societies classified as wholly deposit in 1945, the Registrar describes ten societies as having both accumulating and deposit sections, thus making the total of 92 shown in Table 21. He distributes the membership between "accumulating" and "deposit" (including Holloway), according to the section to which they belong. These ten societies and the distribution of their membership are shown in Table 25. Some of these societies are large (Hearts of Oak, Teachers' Provident, Rational Association, and Hampshire and General). The ten between them have 488,146 members in the accumulating sections and 268,766 in the deposit section, or deducting 49,534 who are in both sections, a total membership of 707,378. From information supplied direct by the societies it is known that three of them (Hants and General Friendly Society, Teachers' Provident, and Wilts Friendly Society) had between them 9,831 deposit members in 1899 (out of a total membership of 24,959) and 20,490 deposit members in 1905 (out of a total membership of 35,789). Five of the others are known to have had no deposit members in those years. From two societies no information has been received, but both of these (Royal Berks and Birmingham General) are small with total membership in 1899 of 4,541 and 1905 of 4,424; it has been assumed that these had no deposit members in either year. On this assumption, the ten societies had in 1899 158,474 accumulative, and 9,831 deposit members; in 1905 183,818 accumulative and 20,490 deposit members.

The 66 societies shown in Table 21 as "Deposit and Holloway" in 1899 represent therefore 39 which were classified "P" in 1845, 24 so classified in 1899 but no longer in existence, and 3 classified as accumulating with same and deposit members. These three (as is explained below) appear also in the number of unitary accumulating societies, with membership divided between the two groups. The 70 societies shown as "Deposit and Holloway" in 1905 represent a similar calculation.

2. The sum of the various classes of society produces a figure slightly larger, both for numbers of societies and for membership,

than the correct total of individual societies and individual members. The reasons for this are:—

(a) As stated above, a number of societies (ten in 1945) did both accumulating and deposit business. These are counted by the Registrar in both the accumulating and the deposit classes, but are only counted once each in his summary total of societies.

(b) As stated above, in a few of these societies (two in 1945), some individuals are members *both* of the accumulating and the deposit sections. Such individuals are similarly included both in accumulating and in deposit membership; but again only counted once in the summary total of membership. There were 49,534 such people in 1945.

3. The total number of societies for 1910 is shown as 26,773. This figure is actually that of the number of returns furnished to the Registrar by societies in that year. The total number of societies was corrected in a later report to 26,948. As, however, the membership total of 6,622,716 refers to these 26,773 societies, and no other membership figure is available for 1910, it is less misleading to use the figure of 26,773.

4. Accident, annuity, and pension and endowment societies were not separately classified in 1899, 1905, and 1910. Such as there were of them were probably classified under accumulating sick benefit societies. On the other hand, the rise in numbers of the "Shipwreck and Miscellaneous" class represents largely a real increase of registrations, rather than a reclassification.

II. AFFILIATED ORDERS

Table 26 below, supplied by the Registrar of Friendly Societies, shows all the orders on the register in 1945 with numbers of branches and members.

TABLE 26

AFFILIATED ORDERS IN 1945: BRANCHES AND MEMBERSHIP

Name of Society	Number of Branches	Number of Members
Amalgamated Order of Comical Fellows	3	39
Ancient Independent Order of Oddfellows	24	3,309
Ancient Noble Order of United Oddfellows, Bolton Unity, Friendly Society	107	12,457

TABLE 26—*continued*

AFFILIATED ORDERS IN 1945: BRANCHES AND MEMBERSHIP

Name of Society	Number of Branches	Number of Members
Ancient Order of Foresters Friendly Society	3,111	518,043
Ancient Order of Hibernians (Board of Erin) Friendly Society of Northern Ireland and Great Britain	108	6,929
Ancient Order of Odd Fellows, Leeds Unity Friendly Society	21	1,006
Ancient Order of Romans Friendly Society	48	4,767
Ancient Order of Shepherds Friendly Society	55	1,887
British Order of Ancient Free Gardeners Friendly Society ..	257	42,629
British United Order of Oddfellows Friendly Society ..	84	7,934
Caledonian Order of United Oddfellows Friendly Society ..	37	2,428
Craven Unity Golden Fleece Friendly Society	6	786
Derby Midland United Order of Oddfellows Friendly Society	36	4,438
Derby United Order of Goodfellows Friendly Society ..	6	203
Drapers' and Warehousemen's Friendly Society	—	*
Eastern Star Provident Association Friendly Society ..	7	1,363
Free and Independent United Order of Mechanics Friendly Society	7	744
Friendly Benevolent United Order of Mechanics Friendly Society	3	55
Grand Independent Order of Loyal Caledonian Corks Friendly Sick and Dividend Society	191	18,503
Grand Order of Israel and Shield of David Friendly Society	73	4,493
Grand Order of Sons of Jacob..	38	2,813
Grand United Order of Oddfellows Friendly Society ..	463	63,074
Halifax and District Friendly Societies Association	36	*
Halifax United Order of the Peaceful Dove Friendly Society	5	631
Ilkeston and Erewash Valley United Order of Oddfellows Friendly Society	8	369
Ilkeston and Erewash Valley United Order of Oddfellows Juvenile Society	—	440
Imperial United Order of Mechanics Friendly Society ..	6	295
Improved Independent Order of Oddfellows London Unity	19	2,278
Improved Order of Total Abstinent Sons of the Phoenix Sick and Burial Friendly Society	—	104
Independent Order of Bnei Brith Friendly Society	14	903
Independent Order of Comical Fellows Tunbridge Wells Unity	4	161
Independent Order of the Golden Fleece, Bradford Unity, Friendly Society	2	450
Independent Order of Odd Fellows, East Anglian Unity, Friendly Society	24	2,646
Independent Order of Oddfellows, Kingston Unity, Friendly Society	106	31,397
Independent Order of Odd Fellows, Manchester Unity, Friendly Society	4,240	770,654
Independent Order of Rechabites, Salford Unity, Friendly Society	2,667	499,723
Independent Order of Shepherds (Poynton Unity) Friendly Society	1	58

* No voluntary members; State Insurance only.

TABLE 26—*continued*

AFFILIATED ORDERS IN 1945: BRANCHES AND MEMBERSHIP

Name of Society	Number of Branches	Number of Members
Independent Order of United Brothers, Loughborough Unity, Friendly Society	3	551
Independent Order of United Brothers, Midland Unity	12	687
Independent United Order of Mechanics Friendly Society	2	7
Independent United Order of Scottish Mechanics Friendly Society	12	1,588
Irish National Foresters (England and Wales) Benefit Society	42	3,033
Irish National Foresters (Scotland) Benefit Society	69	8,460
Kent United District of the Ancient Order of Britons Friendly Society	16	471
Knutsford District of Foresters	4	490
Leicestershire Seraphic Order of Oddfellows Friendly Society	5	430
London Caledonian Friendly Society	1	111
London and Provincial Yearly Dividing Friendly Society	208	13,596
Loyal and Independent Modern Order of Foresters, Guildford Unity, Friendly Society	4	722
Loyal Order of Alfreds Friendly Society	41	626
Loyal Order of Ancient Shepherds, Ashton Unity, Friendly Society	838	238,119
Loyal United Order of Anglo-Saxons Friendly Society	24	3,594
National Independent Order of Oddfellows Friendly Society	383	43,482
National United Order of Free Gardeners Friendly Society	334	34,354
Northern Counties Brewers', Wine and Spirit Merchants' Assistants' Provident Society	3	83
Nottingham Imperial Order of Oddfellows Friendly Society	250	25,154
Order Achei Ameth Brethren of Truth Friendly Society	20	1,744
Order Achei Brith and Shield of Abraham	56	5,221
Order of Ancient Maccabeans	21	893
Order of Druids Friendly Society	98	41,128
Order of the Sons of Temperance Friendly Society	975	178,250
Original Grand Order of the Total Abstinent Sons of the Phoenix	5	182
Pure Order of United Britons Friendly Society	8	424
Royal Navy Seamen, Signalmen and Telegraphists Benefit Society	2	477
St. Andrew Order of Ancient Free Gardeners Friendly Society	57	10,437
St. David's Unity of Ivorites	108	2,434
Scottish Domestic Servants Association Friendly Society	—	*
Scottish Order of Oddfellows Friendly Society	4	3,099
Sons of the Empire Friendly Society	2	143
Sons of Rechab, Glasgow Unity, Temperance Friendly Society	15	1,923
Sons of Scotland Temperance Friendly Society	94	10,698
United Ancient Order of Druids Friendly Society	359	44,817
United Order of the Total Abstinent Sons of the Phoenix Friendly Society	36	881
Wales Unity of Oddfellows Friendly Society	10	430
Women's Friendly Society of Scotland	5	*

* No voluntary members; State Insurance only.

III. SPECIMEN CONTRIBUTIONS AND BENEFITS

Tables of contributions and benefits vary from society to society, according to its aims and its experience, and societies often have more than one table open at a time.

Following are a few examples of tables from societies of various kinds. The first four are fairly simple tables from branches of two different orders, the Ancient Order of Foresters and the Loyal Order of Ancient Shepherds (Ashton Unity).

Branches of orders are usually given the option either of using their own special tables or of adopting some of the tables drawn up by the order. In a few orders, however, notably the Manchester Unity of Oddfellows, branches are required to adopt order tables. The fifth example here represents one of the Manchester Unity's tables in present use.

The sixth and seventh examples, described as the prospectuses of the National Deposit Friendly Society and of the Ideal Benefit Society, are the statements of contributions, benefits, etc., which these two societies issue to the public. These are the largest societies based on deposit and on Holloway principles respectively.

1. ANCIENT ORDER OF FORESTERS, COURT "PROVIDENCE"

(289 *members*, 1945)

TABLE 2 (from Court Special Rules)
(Applicable to members admitted on or after January 1, 1905)

Age last Birthday			Contributions per lunar month
			s. d.
16 and under 19 ..	..	..	1 9
19 and under 21 ..	..	..	1 10
21 and under 24 ..	..	..	1 11
24 and under 26 ..	..	..	2 0
26 and under 28 ..	..	..	2 1
28 and under 29 ..	..	..	2 2
29 and under 31 ..	..	..	2 3
31 and under 32 ..	..	..	2 4
32 and under 34 ..	..	..	2 5
34 and under 35 ..	..	..	2 6
35 and under 36 ..	..	..	2 7
36 and under 38 ..	..	..	2 8
38 and under 40 ..	..	..	2 9

Sickness Benefits
10s. weekly for first 20 weeks.
5s. weekly for next 20 weeks.
2s. 6d. weekly for remainder of illness.

Funeral Benefits
£8 at death of member.
£8 at death of member's wife (one wife only).

2. ANCIENT ORDER OF FORESTERS, COURT "PERSEVERANCE"

(128 *members*, 1945)

TABLE 2 (from Court Special Rules)

(Applicable to members admitted on or after January 1, 1906)

Sickness Benefits

14s. per week for first 26 weeks of sickness.
7s. per week for next 26 weeks of sickness.
3s. 6d. per week for remainder of sickness.

Death Benefits

£12 on death of member.
£6 on death of such member's wife, if she should predecease the member.

CONTRIBUTIONS

Age at Entry last Birthday	Contributions per Quarter		Age at Entry last Birthday	Contributions per Quarter	
	s.	d.		s.	d.
14 to 18	5	4½	29	6	11
19	5	5	30	7	0½
20	5	7	31	7	3½
21	5	8	32	7	5½
22	5	9½	33	7	8½
23	5	11½	34	7	11½
24	6	1	35	8	2
25	6	2	36	8	4½
26	6	4½	37	8	8½
27	6	6	38	9	0
28	6	8½	39	9	3

3. LOYAL ORDER OF ANCIENT SHEPHERDS, ASHTON UNITY. LODGE "JAMES ALBERT SMITH"

(56 *members*, 1945)

Table

"Members shall pay contributions and receive benefits in accordance with the following Table, or such other as may be adopted by the Lodge, subject to the Approval of the District Executive and the Executive of the Order, and duly registered."

Contributions per Fortnight			Benefits		
			Relief in Sickness		
Age on Admission	Sick and Funeral Fund	Management and Distress Fund	First 26 Weeks	Second 26 Weeks	Next 52 Weeks
	s. d.				
16 and under 21	0 9¼	2¾d. per fortnight	10s. per week	7s. 6d. per week	5s. per week
21 and under 24	0 10¼	2¾d. per fortnight	10s. per week	7s. 6d. per week	5s. per week
24 and under 27	0 11¼	2¾d. per fortnight	10s. per week	7s. 6d. per week	5s. per week
27 and under 31	1 0¼	2¾d. per fortnight	10s. per week	7s. 6d. per week	5s. per week
31 and under 34	1 1¼	2¾d. per fortnight	10s. per week	7s. 6d. per week	5s. per week
34 and under 37	1 3¼	2¾d. per fortnight	10s. per week	7s. 6d. per week	5s. per week
37 and under 40	1 6¼	2¾d. per fortnight	10s. per week	7s. 6d. per week	5s. per week

Sums Payable at Death

Member	£12
Member's wife (first wife)	£10
Member's wife (second wife)	£5
Member's widow	£5

No member shall be allowed to draw more than £40 from the Sick and Funeral Fund in Sick Pay.

4. LOYAL ORDER OF ANCIENT SHEPHERDS, ASHTON UNITY.
LODGE "SHEPHERDS IN THE VALLEY"
(203 *members*, 1945)

TABLE I (from Lodge Special Rules)
SCALE OF CONTRIBUTIONS PER LUNAR MONTH

Age at Entry	Sick and Funeral Fund	Management Fund	Distress Fund	Total
	s. d.	s. d.	s. d.	s. d.
16 and under 21	1 10	0 5	0 1	2 4
21 and under 23	1 11	0 5	0 1	2 5
23 and under 25	2 0	0 5	0 1	2 6
25 and under 28	2 1	0 5	0 1	2 7
28 and under 30	2 2	0 5	0 1	2 8
30 and under 32	2 3	0 5	0 1	2 9
32 and under 34	2 4	0 5	0 1	2 10
34 and under 37	2 5	0 5	0 1	2 11

Sickness Benefits
9s. per week for first 26 weeks.
4s. per week for next 26 weeks.
1s. 6d. per week for remainder of illness.

Death Benefits
£10 for member.
£8 for wife.
£8 for widows or second wives.

5. INDEPENDENT ORDER OF ODDFELLOWS, MANCHESTER UNITY

Twentieth Century Table AA (Men)

(Applicable to members admitted on or after January 1, 1935. Combined Sickness, Funeral and Endowment Benefits)

CONTRIBUTIONS payable every four weeks:—

1. The amount stated in the Table below, according to age at entry, for sickness and funeral benefit purposes; and
2. The sum of 6d., or any multiple thereof, for Increasing Cash Benefit (I.C.B.) purposes, subject to the limitation that the total amount assured for payment in the 65th year of age shall not exceed £300.

The former of these contributions ceases at age 70 and the latter in the 65th year of age.

BENEFITS.—The contributions will provide the following benefits:—

(a) Sickness benefit (ceasing at age 70); 10s. per week for the first 26 weeks; 5s. per week thereafter.
(b) Funeral benefit of £5 payable on the death of the member.
(c) Funeral benefit of £5 payable on the death of the member's first wife or widow.
(d) Increasing Cash Benefit payable on the anniversary of the date of I.C.B. membership following the attainment of age 64, or on previous death, in accordance with the I.C.B. Table.

Age last Birthday at Entry	Contributions Payable every Four Weeks for Benefits (a), (b) and (c) above		Age last Birthday at Entry	Contributions Payable every Four Weeks for Benefits (a), (b) and (c) above	
	s.	d.		s.	d.
16	1	3	34	1	11
17	1	4	35	2	0
18	1	4	36	2	1
19	1	4	37	2	2
20	1	4	38	2	2
21	1	5	39	2	3
22	1	5	40	2	4
23	1	5	41	2	5
24	1	6	42	2	6
25	1	6	43	2	7
26	1	7	44	2	8
27	1	7	45	2	9
28	1	8	46	2	11
29	1	8	47	3	0
30	1	9	48	3	2
31	1	9	49	3	3
32	1	10	50	3	5
33	1	11			

The contributions in the above Table include no provision for expenses of management.

A member may insure for one-half, or one and one-half, of the benefits (a), (b) and (c) specified above, or any multiple thereof permitted by the District or Lodge rules, by the payment of a proportionate contribution. In addition he shall contribute for I.C.B. purposes the sum of 6d. or any multiple thereof every four weeks as stated in (2) above.

No contribution is payable by the widow of a member for the funeral benefit payable at her death.

6. NATIONAL DEPOSIT FRIENDLY SOCIETY—PROSPECTUS

THE SOCIETY WITH A DIFFERENCE—because when you have paid your Contributions they are not lost to you for ever, a proportion being given back to your Deposit (or Bank) account at the end of the year. In 1945 the members paid £1,418,358 in Contributions and were given back £418,179.

ADMISSION—subject to good health and accepted occupation you are classified into one of the following classes :—

Males, between 16 and 30—Class A.
Males, between 5 and 16 and between 30 and 40—Class B.
Males, between 40 and 50—Class C.
Females, between 5 and 30—Class B.
Females, between 30 and 45—Class C.

YOU PAY

a fixed Monthly Contribution and an optional amount to Deposit.

CONTRIBUTIONS.—You fix your own monthly rate, which may be from —

2s. to 20s. Males; 1s. 6d. to 10s. Females (with lower rates under 21 years of age).

Your daily sickness benefit is the amount of your monthly contribution.

DEPOSITS.—From 3d. to £30 yearly according to age. This Deposit or Savings Bank is of special value, because on it depends the duration of benefits. Your Deposit finds a portion of each shilling received as Sick or Medical Pay :—

Class A finds 3d. in the 1s.   the Society finds the balance of 9d.
Class B finds 4d. in the 1s.   the Society finds the balance of 8d.
Class C finds 6d. in the 1s.   the Society finds the balance of 6d.

The length of time that you can draw Sick Pay is limited only by the amount in your Deposit. There is no "full benefits for six months with half benefits for the following six months." You can have daily Sick Pay for six years or more if your Deposit can bear its portion. The Society helps you in this because at the end of each year it pays back into your Deposit some of the contributions which you have paid. This Deposit account is better than the ordinary Savings Bank account because it not only receives interest at 2½ per cent, but regulates your benefits.

JUVENILES—are admitted from birth to age 5 on Class B scale for Medical Benefit. Death Benefit is also paid in addition to any balance in the Deposit (or Bank) with full interest. The contribution is 1s. a month plus not more than £1 in any Calendar year to Deposit. Medical Benefit is also subject to Deposit as explained above.

YOU GET

SICK PAY.—You are entitled to benefit as soon as you have paid six months' contributions and have an equal amount in Deposit. This amount can be paid at once to ensure immediate benefit.

Subject to Deposit as already explained:—

A CONTRIBUTION OF—

1s. a calendar month (or less than 3d. p.w.) entitles a member to 6s. a week Sick Pay.
1s. 6d. a calendar month (or less than 4½d. p.w.) entitles a member to 9s. a week Sick Pay.
2s. a calendar month (or less than 6d. p.w.) entitles a member to 12s. a week Sick Pay.
2s. 6d. a calendar month (or less than 7½d. p.w.) entitles a member to 15s. a week Sick Pay.
4s. a calendar month (or less than 1s. p.w.) entitles a member to 24s. a week Sick Pay.
And so on to £1 a calendar month for Males and 10s. for Females, which provides £6 and £3 a week Sick Pay respectively.

GRACE PAY.—If you exhaust your Deposit by Sick Pay and continue ill you are entitled to a free benefit called "Grace Pay" for the same length of time that you received Sick Pay continuously and immediately before the exhaustion of Deposit.

A Class A member receiving 2s. a day Sick Pay for 12 months would receive a free benefit of 1s. 6d. a day for a further 12 months.

A Class B member receiving 2s. a day Sick Pay for 12 months would receive a free benefit of 1s. 4d. a day for a further 12 months.

A Class C member receiving 2s. a day Sick Pay for 12 months would receive a free benefit of 1s. a day for a further 12 months.

This free benefit is given once in every 5 years.

MATERNITY BENEFIT—is paid to women members and is equal to 24 times the monthly rate of contribution on Class C scale.

OLD AGE.—When you become 70 you are not cast adrift. Sick and Medical Pay continue to be paid on Class C Scale.

MEDICAL BENEFIT WHEREVER YOU GO.—You may be attended by any doctor wherever you may be within the United Kingdom, and allowances are made for attendances according to a fixed scale.

OPERATIONS.—A grant is made in operation cases, including an allowance for the administration of anaesthetic.

SPECIALISTS.—If your doctor advises you to see a Specialist a grant of £1 1s. is made towards the Specialist's consultation fee.

ELECTRICAL AND RAY TREATMENT, X-RAY AND INJECTIONS.—Allowances are made for these treatments.

CONVALESCENT HOME TREATMENT.—Two weeks' free residence in one of the many Convalescent Homes. In addition railway fares are paid both ways and Sick Pay continues.

WITHDRAWALS.—It is your money in the Deposit Account and you may draw from it as you would from any Savings Bank, but you must not reduce the balance below an amount equal to your last twelve months' contributions.

FUNERAL BENEFIT.—On death the balance in Deposit is paid out in full at interest with an additional allowance of £6.

ASSURANCE BRANCH.—If you require extra insurance cover the Society provides policies for sums not exceeding £300 at low premiums.

MORTGAGES.—The Society helps you to buy your house. The low rate of mortgage interest is 4 per cent.

NATIONAL MEMBERSHIP.—Wherever you go you will find a District of the Society. You need never lose touch. This is the largest centralized Society with more than a million and a half Deposit Members and it admits more new members than all the rest of the Friendly Societies in the country put together. It is approved for National Health Insurance business and has over 960,000 State members.

YOUR SECURITY.—Assets exceed £22,800,000. Reserve and Benefit Funds exceed £7,700,000. All Rules and Amendments are approved by the Registrar of Friendly Societies. Accounts are passed by independent Auditors, and the funds are valued by a public Actuary. The Society is governed by its members.

IN ITS 78 YEARS' EXISTENCE THERE HAVE BEEN NO LEVIES

7. IDEAL BENEFIT SOCIETY—PROSPECTUS

This Society is established to enable its members to make substantial provision for
SICKNESS, OLD AGE AND DEATH

These objects are accomplished upon strict principles of equity, by the payment of

ONE PENNY PER DAY

per share, from members not over 30 years of age, and a halfpenny per month extra for each year beyond 30, to cover the increased cost of sickness risk, thus placing old and young upon an exact equality.

THE NEW PRINCIPLE

which commends the Society above all others is the division of the Surplus Fund (after paying for the Sickness and management) amongst the members, and the appropriation of this surplus as

A SAVINGS BANK INVESTMENT IN EACH MEMBER'S OWN RIGHT, AT 5 PER CENT INTEREST

The Surpluses are estimated to realize at least 25s. per annum to each share, so that members paying a Penny per day may look forward, in addition to pay during sickness, to the accumulation of wealth, as follows:—

> In 10 years, a One Share Member will have £15 14s. 5d.
> In 20 years, a One Share Member will have £41 6s. 6d.
> In 30 years, a One Share Member will have £83 0s. 9d.
> In 40 years, a One Share Member will have £150 19s. 8d.
> In 50 years, a One Share Member will have £261 13s. 2d.

That the foregoing statement is not an exaggeration is shown by the following table, calculated on the above basis, and compared with the actual results realized:—

	Estimated Results			Actual Realization		
	£	s.	d.	£	s.	d.
End of 10th year	15	14	5	16	14	9
End of 20th year	41	6	6	44	6	5
End of 30th year	83	0	9	87	13	8
End of 37th year	127	0	3	133	17	1

According to the estimated calculation (which is shown by the foregoing to be under-stated), the account of a person joining at 15 years of age, and remaining a member till 65, will, for that period, stand as follows —

	£	s.	d.
The total Contributions during the term named would amount to	91	18	11
Whilst the amount standing to the credit of the member would be	261	13	2
Showing a net profit of	£169	14	3

and in addition to this, the member would have received Sick Pay as required during the whole period.

All the preceding calculations relate to one share (Class III) or One Penny per Day.

Members may subscribe for as little as half a share (½d. per day) or for as many as Ten Shares (10d. per day), with Sick Pay from 5s. to 100s. per week, and corresponding shares of the surplus. Thus Professional Men, Merchants, Manufacturers, Tradesmen and others may subscribe for as much as 10d. per day, may secure 100s. per week in Sickness, and if they are members for 50 years, would accumulate no less than £2,616 0s. 0d.

By giving three months' notice in September,

MEMBERS CAN LEAVE THE SOCIETY AND WITHDRAW THEIR FUNDS

by forfeiting the amount placed to their credit in the last two years, as compensation to the Society.

AT DEATH

the representatives of the deceased member will receive the entire amount standing to his credit in the books of the Society, without deduction.

AT SIXTY-FIVE YEARS OF AGE

members may draw out the whole of their money without deduction, or they may receive in lieu thereof.

A Life-long Annuity

The property of the Society is vested in the Trustees, and lent chiefly upon Freehold and Leasehold security, on terms not equalled elsewhere, preference being given to members who will be encouraged to buy or build

Their Dwelling Houses

Management

The Rules empower the Executive Committee to appropriate 10 per cent of the contributions for this, but any surplus arising therefrom may be returned to the General Fund for division.

The Officers and Executive are elected by the Council

Members are Admitted from 12 to 50 Years of Age

IV. SECTION 8 OF FRIENDLY SOCIETIES ACT, 1896

8. The following societies may be registered under this Act:—

(1). Societies (in this Act called friendly societies) for the purpose of providing by voluntary subscriptions of the members thereof, with or without the aid of donations, for:—

(a) the relief or maintenance of the members, their husbands, wives, children, fathers, mothers, brothers, or sisters, nephews or nieces, or wards being orphans, during sickness or other infirmity, whether bodily or mental, in old age (which shall mean any age after fifty) or in widowhood, or for the relief or maintenance of the orphan children of members during minority; or

(b) insuring money to be paid on the birth of a member's child, or on the death of a member, or for the funeral expenses of the husband, wife, or child of a member, or of the widow of a deceased member, or, as respects persons of the Jewish persuasion, for the payment of a sum of money during the period of confined mourning; or

(c) the relief or maintenance of the members when on travel in search of employment, or when in distressed circumstances, or in case of shipwreck, or loss or damage of or to boats or nets; or

(d) the endowment of members or nominees of members at any age; or

(e) the insurance against fire, to any amount not exceeding fifteen pounds, of the tools or implements of the trade or calling of the members; or

(f) guaranteeing the performance of their duties by officers and servants of the society or any branch thereof;

Provided that a friendly society which contracts with any person for the assurance of an annuity exceeding fifty pounds per annum, or of a gross sum exceeding two hundred pounds, shall not be registered under this Act;

(2). Societies (in this Act called cattle insurance societies) for the purpose of insurance to any amount against loss of neat cattle, sheep, lambs, swine, horses, and other animals by death from disease or otherwise:

(3). Societies (in this Act called benevolent societies) for any benevolent or charitable purpose:

(4). Societies (in this Act called working men's clubs) for purposes of social intercourse, mutual helpfulness, mental and moral improvement, and rational recreation:

(5). Societies (in this Act called specially authorized societies) for any purpose which the Treasury may authorize as a purpose to which the provisions of this Act, or such of them as are specified in the authority, ought to be extended. Provided that where any provisions of this Act are so specified, those provisions only shall be extended.

V. THE CHIEF FRIENDLY SOCIETIES ACTS

1793   33 GEO. III, C. 54 ("ROSE'S ACT").

"Any number of persons may form a society of good fellowship for the purpose of raising among themselves a fund for their mutual benefit, etc."

1819   59 GEO. III, C. 128.

Tables of payments and benefits of friendly societies are to be approved by the Justices, after they have been "approved by two persons at the least known to be professional actuaries or persons skilled in calculation."

1829   10 GEO. IV, C. 56.

Friendly societies defined as societies for raising a stock or fund "for the mutual relief and maintenance of all and every the members thereof, their wives or children, or other relations, in sickness, infancy, advanced age, widowhood, or any other natural state or contingency whereof the occurrence is susceptible of calculation by way of average."

Rules of societies to be approved by a barrister.

Tables of contributions and benefits to be approved by the Justices,

1834 4 & 5 WIL. IV, C. 40.
>   Provision in the previous Act requiring approval of tables by the Justices now done away with.

1846 9 & 10 VIC., C. 27
1. The barrister certifying the rules is to be called the Registrar of Friendly Societies and paid by salary in place of fee.
2. No society allowed to be registered unless its tables have been certified by an actuary.
3. Re-defines friendly society purposes, and expressly authorizes insurance for burial expenses of members, husbands, wives or children, "provided that no insurance shall be effected on the life of any child under six years of age." Purposes include "frugal investment" of savings, opening way to co-operative stores.
4. Exempts from Acts of 1799 and 1817 against sedition, on conditions.

1850 13 & 14 VIC., C. 115
1. Division of societies into two kinds—(a) those whose rules had been "*certified*" by an actuary; (b) all others.
2. The affiliated orders first recognized by law. Societies with branches now enabled to register them as such.
3. Purposes re-defined, to include burial expenses of member, husband, wife, child or kindred, subject to restrictions in case of a child under ten to actual expenses not exceeding £3 to be paid to the undertaker.

1855 18 & 19 VIC., C. 63.
>   Abolishes distinction between certified and registered societies. Consolidates the law repealing in whole or in part 18 previous measures.

1875 38 & 39 VIC., C. 60.
>   Repeals previous Acts and consolidates the law.
>   Sets up a Registry of Friendly Societies.
>   Provides for yearly audits, five yearly valuations, etc. etc.

1896 FRIENDLY SOCIETIES' ACT, 1896 (59 & 60 VIC., C. 25).
>   Now the main Act. It did not, however, embody any substantial change in the law.

1908 FRIENDLY SOCIETIES' ACT (8 EDW. VII, C. 32).
>   Increases the limits of assurance to £300 by way of gross sum, and £52 per annum by way of annuity, and makes other minor amendments.

1911 NATIONAL INSURANCE ACT (1 & 2 GEO. V, C. 55).
      The friendly societies made the agencies for the scheme of
      State Insurance.

1924 FRIENDLY SOCIETIES' ACT (14 & 15 GEO. V, C. 11).
      Limits the amounts for which children might be insured, and
      makes other minor amendments.

1946 THE NATIONAL INSURANCE ACT (9 & 10 GEO. VI, C. 67).
      A centralized scheme of State Insurance, in which the friendly
      societies no longer participate, substituted for the previous
      scheme.

VI. INDUSTRIAL ASSURANCE AND FRIENDLY SOCIETIES BILL, 1947

In view of the inclusion of a death grant in the National Insurance
Act of 1946, it has become necessary to revise the powers of insurance
on the life of another given to companies and collecting societies
undertaking industrial assurance, and the powers of friendly societies.
For this purpose an Industrial Assurance and Friendly Societies Bill
was introduced in December, 1947. The Bill proposes also a number
of changes in the law for which an opportunity was awaited.

The general effect of the Bill is to bring to an end the original
purpose for which the industrial life offices were established, namely,
insurance for funeral expenses. It gives instead a limited power of
insuring the lives of older generations (parent, step-parent or grandparent) without reference to funeral expenses; it gives to friendly
societies the same power of insuring lives of spouses as applies to
ordinary life insurance; and it abolishes the power of insuring lives
of others. Funeral expenses insurance as such comes to an end.
The industrial life offices are left to develop insurance in general by
use of collectors.

The following notes are based on an explanatory memorandum
issued by the Government. Reference is made in the Memorandum
to Appendix D of the *Report on Social Insurance and Allied Services*,
and to the *Report of the Cohen Committee in Industrial Assurance* (1933
Cmd. 4376).

Life-of-Another Insurance

In ordinary life insurance a person is not normally regarded as
having an insurable interest in the life of anyone except himself and
his spouse. To insure anyone else's life would ordinarily be unlawful.

It is, however, lawful in industrial assurance (which means life insurance on which premiums are payable at intervals of less than two months, and are received by collectors) to insure money to be paid for the funeral expenses of one's parent, child, grandparent, grandchild, brother or sister.

The National Insurance Act, 1946, provides for payment of a death grant to a person who incurs expenses in connection with the death of another person, provided that certain contribution conditions are satisfied. Where the person on whose death the grant is payable is over age eighteen at death, the amount of the grant is to be £20. The position as to the death of children is dealt with below. The forthcoming introduction of this grant, which will first become payable on July 5, 1949, has made it necessary to reconsider the law as to voluntary insurance for funeral expenses.

Clause 1 of the Bill proposes to terminate, without prejudice to existing insurances, the existing powers to insure the life of another "for funeral expenses," and Clause 2 proposes to substitute for these powers a power to insure the life of one's parent, step-parent, or grandparent for £15 exclusive of any bonus other than guaranteed bonus. The life of one's child, grandchild, brother or sister is to cease to be insurable.

Insurances on the Lives of Spouses

Under the existing law a friendly society may insure the life of a member's spouse "for funeral expenses." This power is one of those to be repealed by Clause 1. In its place is to be substituted, by Clause 3, a power to insure the life of a member's spouse, subject to no limit other than that applying to all friendly society insurance. The reason for treating the insurance of a spouse's life differently from other life-of-another insurance is that in ordinary life insurance a person is regarded as having an unlimited insurable interest in his spouse's life.

Limits of Friendly Society Benefits

Clause 5 proposes to raise the gross sum for which a friendly society may insure to £500. The limit was last raised, to £300, in 1908, and the change proposed is to be made on account of the change in the value of money since that date. It is also proposed, by a subsequent amendment on the Committee stage, to increase the maximum pension from £52 to £104 a year.

Insurances on the Lives of Children

The sums payable by industrial assurance offices, friendly societies

and trade unions on the death of children under age ten are now
limited by law as follows:—

Children dying under age 3	..	..	..	£6
Children dying under age 6	..	..	..	£10
Children dying under age 10	..	..	..	£15

Under the National Insurance Act, 1946, death grant up to the
above amounts will be payable from July 5, 1949, on the death
after that date of children born on and after July 5, 1948. Consequently there will be no longer room for voluntary insurance in
these cases.

Accordingly, Clause 1 of the Bill proposes to make illegal insurance of one's child in life-of-another form, and Clause 6 proposes
to prohibit insurances in own-life form under which anything more
than a return of premiums would be payable on the death of a
child under age ten. The proviso excepts from this prohibition
certain classes of case in which no death grant will be payable
under the National Insurance Act, 1946.

Other Changes

The other changes proposed cover details of administration,
in regard to premium receipt books, warranties, delivery of policies
and rules, and audit. They include also termination of the power
of friendly societies to invest money with the National Debt Commissioners at 2¾ per cent and repayment of money so invested. This
is explained as due to the fall in the rate of interest on investments.

VII. THE REGISTRAR'S FIELD IN 1935 AND 1945—NOTES TO
TABLES 6 AND 7

1. The *General Friendly Societies* are Group A of Table 1, societies
giving sick benefit. The *Specialized Friendly Societies* are Group B.1
of Table 1; further information about them is given in Table 22 of
Appendix A. The collecting societies (Group B.2 of Table 1) though
formally registered as friendly societies under Section 8 (1) of the
Friendly Societies Act, 1896, are included not here but at the foot
of the tables with the industrial assurance companies.

2. *Cattle Insurance Societies* may be "established for the insurance
to any amount against loss by death from disease or otherwise of neat
cattle, sheep, lambs, swine, horses and other animals." They date
from 1850 and received a stimulus during a cattle plague in 1866
but are now of diminishing importance, with small and falling
membership.

3. *Benevolent Societies* are those registered under Section 8 (3) of the Friendly Societies' Act, 1896, "for any benevolent or charitable purpose." The Registrar interprets this as meaning that the society should be substantially established for the purpose of providing benefits for persons other than the members, their wives or their relatives. This type of society therefore represents not Mutual Aid but association for a philanthropic motive and is exempt from valuation.

The fact of registration as a benevolent society does not exempt the society from income tax, though in most cases it could presumably apply for exemption on the grounds of its charitable aims. It is exempt from the provisions of the Charitable Trusts Act, 1853, if it is wholly maintained by voluntary contributions, but if it is endowed it is not so exempt as regards such endowment. It cannot hold more than one acre of land, nor divide its funds. The main advantage of registration to a society is that it is an easy method of gaining legal recognition for purposes of holding property and the like.

The number of registered benevolent societies, which was rising from 1935 to 1945, fell in the next two years. In November of 1947 there were ninety-five societies registered. They served a variety of purposes. In terms of the figures of "benefits" distributed, by far the largest was the National Council of Social Service Benevolent Society, with "benefits" distributed of £512,953 in 1945. This is an organization set up for dealing, on behalf of other charities, with the refund of income tax and surtax in connection with charitable covenants. The "benefits" in this case will mainly be tax refunds handed over to the charities for whom they were destined. There is a similar institution connected with the Manchester and Salford Council of Social Service.

A few of these societies are general medical or surgical institutions: these include St. Paul's Hospital, the City Dispensary, the North Western Child Guidance Clinic. A few are homes, such as the Post Office Orphan Homes, the Metropolitan Benefit Asylum, the Yorkshire Foresters' Orphanage. The National Adoption Society is also registered. The majority (some seventy-five), however, appear to be charitable funds. These are mostly connected with some trade or calling; examples are the Licensed Victuallers' Benevolent Society, the Essex Special Constabulary Benefit Fund, the Ashford and District Fire Services Old Comrades Association, the Royal Engineers Benefit Fund, the Lowestoft Fishermen's Widows and Orphans Society. Some of these funds appear to be restricted by locality rather than by calling, such as the Stepney District Distressed Members Benevolent Society, the Bromley Philanthropic Society.

The societies are not in general large. Figures of 1945 expenditure are the latest available. The ninety-three societies on the registers at the end of 1947 (the two connected with councils of social service ignored) include twenty-four societies who returned no expenditure in benefits for 1945; no doubt some of these gave benefits in kind or service. The average of benefits expended in 1945 by the remaining sixty-nine was about £1,700. The average of funds of these ninety-three societies (the two above named again ignored) was £15,665.

4. The class of *Shop Clubs* is exceptional in that a shop club must be registered and has not the option, as most other associations of British citizens have, of remaining unregistered. Shop clubs are clubs or societies for providing benefits to workmen in connection with a factory, dock, ship, or other place of employment. If such a society is certified under the Shop Clubs Act of 1902 the employer may make membership of it a condition of employment, but he must not require the workman to cease to be a member or refrain from becoming a member of any other friendly society. Before certifying such a club with compulsory membership the Registrar must be satisfied that it affords benefits of a substantial form at the cost of the employer in addition to anything paid for by the workmen, that it is of a permanent character not periodically dividing its funds, and that at least 75 per cent of the workmen concerned desire the establishment of such a club. There are only eight such clubs in existence but they have a large membership, accounted for almost wholly by two large clubs, one with Pilkington Brothers, and one in Imperial Chemical Industries. The compulsory registration of shop clubs springs from the fact that membership in them is compulsory for the individual.

5. *Certified Loan Societies* under the Act of 1840 (passed as another measure of aid to the "industrious classes") are exempt from stamp duty and the Money Lenders Act, with interest limited. Since loans made by them may not exceed £15, new societies are seldom registered and the existing societies are of diminishing importance.

6. Under the *Scientific Societies Act* of 1843 societies established exclusively for the purposes of literature, science or the fine arts can obtain exemption from local rates, if the Registrar certifies that their rules comply with the requirements of the Act. Besides being established exclusively for the purposes mentioned the society must

be supported wholly or in part by annual voluntary contributions, and must be debarred by its constitution from making any gift, dividend or bonus in money to its members. The Act was passed on the initiative of the Prince Consort for the encouragement of learning. Under it libraries can and do obtain exemption from local rates, if they are libraries and nothing more. To obtain this advantage the Library of the London School of Economics and Political Science was established in 1895 as the "British Library of Political and Economic Science," and exemption from rates was obtained for a good many years, till the school, growing in the interstices of the library, became too large to be concealed. About 1,000 certificates in total have been granted under this Act, but the societies are not themselves registered and no information is available as to membership and funds; it is not known even how many of the certificates remain in force.

7. The *Superannuation and Other Trust Funds (Validation) Act* of 1927 was passed to remove the disabilities of the rule of law against perpetuities under which such funds were placed by reason of the rule. Registration is a condition of obtaining this relief.

APPENDIX B—CHARITABLE TRUSTS

I. A Charities' Chamber of Horrors;
II. Anti-Vivisection and Founder's Kin as Subjects of Charity;
III. Note on Charitable Trusts in Scotland;
IV. A New Deal for Charitable Trusts.

I. A CHARITIES' CHAMBER OF HORRORS

THE first thirteen charitable foundations described below are all taken from *The Dead Hand* by Sir Arthur Hobhouse, Q.C., K.C.S.I. (Chatto & Windus, 1880), a collection of addresses given by the author at various dates from 1868 to 1879.

The first part of what is said about each foundation gives the facts as stated by Hobhouse, closely following his language, with page references to his book and with exact quotations from him marked as such. The second part, separated by a line, shows briefly what has happened to the foundation since Hobhouse's day, so far as it has been possible to discover this. The cases are arranged in no particular order except in so far as they proceed from misguided pedantry, through foolish almsgiving or gifts which became inappropriate through new conditions, to gifts illustrating chiefly vanity or malice.

To Hobhouse's exhibits I have added three cases, numbered 14 to 16, from the Royal Commission on the City of London Parochial Charities which reported in 1880, after the last of Hobhouse's addresses. These charities are now being turned to good purpose in the living hands of the Trustees of the London Parochial Charities, but it took a Royal Commission and an Act of Parliament to get them into such hands.

Many of Hobhouse's cases have been cured. But two at least of them (Jarvis and Tancred) needed special Acts of Parliament. One of them (Burnett) was dealt with under a Scottish Act of Parliament of a strictly temporary nature and no longer in force. Others, also with the help of legislation, have come under the strong hand of the Ministry of Education. In others the cure is far from complete. In some cases legislation promoted to make the best use of the money has been rejected.

And the law which made these cases possible is in substance the law to-day.

. *Burnett's Foundation for Treatises on the Goodness of the Creator* (1783),
pp. 230–3.

John Burnett, merchant in Aberdeen, dying in 1784, bequeathed
property which he had already been accumulating since 1774 to
trustees, partly for the general support of the sick and poor with
a gift over for a lunatic asylum, and partly for the awarding in 1814
and at intervals of forty years thereafter of prizes to reward the
composition of treatises relating to the goodness of the Creator of
his world. Three judges were to be chosen by the trustees, in combination with the university professors of Aberdeen, bound to give
their opinions on comparative merit of every treatise rendered;
300 copies of the winning treatise were to be printed and distributed,
at the cost of the trust. In the year 1814 fifty-three treatises were
presented and the first prizeman, Mr. Brown, afterwards Principal
of Aberdeen University, received £1,200, while the second, Mr.
Sumner, afterwards Archbishop of Canterbury, received £400. In
the year 1854 the three judges had to peruse 208 treatises, many
said to be of great bulk. The first prizeman was Mr. Robert Archer
Thompson, an English clergyman, who received £1,800; the second
was Mr. Tulloch, afterwards principal of St. Andrews University,
who received £600. The expenses of advertising amounted to £400.
The judges received £615, which "seems a small amount for their
dreary work." "It is said, alas! that none of the treatises have done
any good, either to its author's reputation or to anyone else."

This, being a Scottish trust, did not come within the scope of the
Charity Commissioners or the Endowed Schools Act of 1869, but
has been diverted from its original purpose by a Provisional Order
made in June, 1881, under the Endowed Institutions (Scotland) Act
of 1878. This Act gave extremely wide powers to the Home Secretary, on the application of the governing body of any school, hospital,
or other institution maintained wholly or partly by an endowment,
to change the government of the institution or the use of the
endowments. The procedure included advertisement, enquiry by
commissioners, and the making of a Provisional Order which had
to lie for forty days before both Houses of Parliament. The Act
was given a life of only two or three years, expiring on December 31,
1880, subject to a power of the Home Secretary to extend it, on
special cause shown in relation to any particular institution, for
another six months. The Home Secretary had to use this power of
extension in relation to the Burnett Literary Fund and a few other

Scottish trusts, making six Provisional Orders in June, 1881. The Burnett Fund was diverted in the first instance to founding a lectureship at the University of Aberdeen and thereafter to establishing a Chair of History and Archaeology; for this purpose it has now been combined with another bequest.

The Provisional Order of June, 1881, gives several details of John Burnett's will not mentioned by Hobhouse. There were elaborate provisions as to advertising the competition seven years in advance and a definition "for all time coming" of the essay subject: "That there is a Being all-powerful, wise and good, by whom everything exists, and particularly to obviate difficulties regarding the wisdom and goodness of the Deity; and this in the first place from considerations independent of written revelation, and, in the second place, from the revelation of the Lord Jesus; and from the whole to point out the inferences most necessary for, and most useful to, mankind."

The third competition anticipated by Hobhouse for 1894, when the fund for prizes and printing would have been about £4,800, was forestalled by the Provisional Order; but the powers under which this was done were strictly temporary. There is no existing law which would make it possible to divert a similar bequest if made to-day.

2. *Brown Animal Sanatory Institution* (1852), pp. 58–63.

Thomas Brown, dying in 1852, bequeathed property amounting to over £20,000 in Consols to the University of London to found an institution for investigating, studying and, without charge, endeavouring to cure the maladies of quadrupeds or birds useful to man. Unfortunately he also proceeded to details as to where the institution should be—"within a mile of Westminster, Southwark or Dublin"—and just how it should be conducted. If the University of London should refuse the gift or omit to found the institution within nineteen years or it should not continue to be conducted *bona fide* for the said purpose agreeably to the condition aforesaid, the property was to go to the University of Dublin for the exclusive purpose of establishing professorships in three or more of the following languages: Welsh, Slavonic, Russian, Persian, Chinese, Coptic and Sanskrit. The validity of the gift was disputed by Thomas Brown's family, but was affirmed by the Court of Chancery in 1857. The University of London, trying to carry out the trust, found that the detailed conditions made this extremely difficult, and the Charity Commissioners agreeing with them, propounded a scheme for attaining the object of treating and curing the diseases of animals useful to man in a more effective way, and promoted a Bill for that purpose in 1867. The House of Lords, largely moved by the Opposition by Lord Cairns, rejected the commissioners' scheme and the Bill by 46 votes to 18. Lord Cairns said:

> "The question was not whether Mr. Brown made the wisest will, nor whether their Lordships could not have made a better. . . . The question now was whether the Charity Commissioners had a right to make a new will for the testator."

This bequest led first to spirited three-cornered litigation between the University of London wanting the money for veterinary science, the next of kin arguing that the whole bequest was invalid, and the University of Dublin arguing that the bequest for an animal institution in London offended against the Statute of Mortmain and that the money should come to them for languages. The University of London, having won a resounding victory over both opponents in the Court of Appeal, was in no hurry to give effect to the testator's precise desires. It first, as stated above, tried to get the will altered by legislation. Unsuccessful in that, it allowed the money to accumulate with interest for the maximum period of nineteen years possible under the founder's will, and at last established the institution in accord with the will in 1871. Since that date there have been considerable changes in general circumstances, making it increasingly difficult to carry out the purpose of the trust. On the one hand, there has been wide extension of facilities for healing the domestic animals of the poor, and on the other hand the number of animals kept in the centre of London has decreased considerably. Whereas forty years ago a wide range of material from the research point of view passed through the institution each year, by 1939 the place had become mainly a cat and dog out-patients' hospital, and the research work of the superintendent had ceased to have much direct connection with the curative work of the institution. The hospital was closed at the outbreak of the Second World War and its buildings have been destroyed in an air raid. The University of London has once more to reconsider the whole problem of the future of this charity, and in particular the possibility of obtaining an alteration of the terms of the trust, in order to secure greater freedom of action.

3. *Pursglove School* (1560), pp. 80–1.

Robert Pursglove, Bishop of Hull, founded a school to embrace in four forms scholars ranging from those who had not yet learned to speak plainly to those who could write Latin verses. Nearly the whole teaching for all four forms was to be given by the master in person; the curriculum and mode of teaching were prescribed in detail. The master must be in the school ten hours a day during the lighter half of the year and eight during the darker half. The governing body was so devised that either there was no control over the schoolmaster or there was constant collision between him and the governors, who were bound either to break the oath which they took religiously to abide by every ordinance and statute of the founder or compel the schoolmaster to carry out an impossible and ridiculous system of teaching.

Bishop Pursglove's pedantic provisions were cited by Hobhouse to destroy a suggestion that what was chiefly wrong with the use of endowments was departure from the intentions of the founders. Mr. Forster had expressed a desire that the founders were now present. "The wish is very easily gratified. They are present. Being dead they yet speak. I will take the liberty of introducing Mr. Forster to Bishop Pursglove."

———

The Pursglove School is now regulated under a scheme made under the Endowed Schools Act, not at all in accord with the instructions of the founder.

4. *Etwall Hospital* (1556), pp. 63–5.

Sir John Port, dying in 1556, settled property for the purpose of founding a school and also an almshouse for six of the poorest of Etwall parish who were to have weekly for ever 1s. 8d. apiece. Etwall in 1869 had just fifty-eight labourers living in it, while the income of the charity approached £3,000 per annum. Careful enquiries showed that the chance of being elected into the almshouse attracted into Etwall the class of persons who like to live at other people's expense, and that the poor rates of Etwall were much higher than the average rates of neighbouring parishes with the same class of population. Nevertheless a proposal to make any but Etwall men eligible for the almshouse excited keen opposition, and was rejected by a committee of the House of Commons. So Etwall retained the peculiar boon of an almshouse whose effect at best was to relieve the poor rate and which indirectly made the poor rate higher there than elsewhere, because Sir John Port more than three centuries ago had willed this.

———

A scheme was made in 1874 under the Endowed Schools Act, allocating most of the income to maintenance of Sir John Port's School in Repton, and fixing the income of the Etwall Hospital at £900 a year payable by the governors of the school. The hospital itself is now regulated by a scheme of the Charity Commissioners of September 22, 1908, as varied by a scheme of 1923. In addition to the sixteen almspeople there are a number of out-pensioners. Almspeople and pensioners have to be poor men or women who (except in special cases to be approved by the Charity Commissioners) have resided, in the case of almspeople, in the parish of Etwall, and, in the case of pensioners, in the county of Derby for not less than ten years next preceding their appointment. The difficulty recently has been to find qualified applicants for the almshouses.

5. *Fulbourn Bread and Sixpences* (1474 and 1712), pp. 200–1.

Fulbourn is a place very curiously situated, being divided into two parishes, the boundaries of which appear only to be known so far as houses have been built in one or the other. One of the parishes, called All Saints, is entitled to an endowment producing £215 a year distributable in bread and sixpences; the other, St. Vigor's, does not have this boon. Higher rents are asked for cottages in the bread and sixpences parish than in the other. When a cottage in St. Vigor's falls down or becomes untenantable the owner does not rebuild it on the same site if he has land elsewhere, but builds it somewhere else so that it can claim to be in All Saints. The bread and sixpences used to be distributed every Sunday at the church, but are now distributed ten times a year, not on Sundays. The whole labouring population come for it and tradesmen too.

This relates to the charities of Geoffrey Bishop founded in 1474 and William Farmer founded in 1712. This is a good example of the effect of sect. 4 of the Charitable Trusts Act, 1860, which precludes the Commissioners from making a scheme in the matter of a charity the income of which exceeds £50 per annum except upon an application by a majority of the trustees. The Commissioners have tried at various times to obtain from the trustees applications for schemes improving the administration of the charities, but without success. The last occasion was in 1926. Then the trustees referred the Commissioners' suggestions to a parish meeting which was attended by some 300 to 400 parishioners, and at which the following resolution was passed unanimously: "That this meeting objects to the scheme put forward by the Charity Commissioners and that under no circumstances will this meeting consider any alterations of the present system of administration." As a result the suggestions made no further progress.

6. *Henry Smith's Charity* (1627), pp. 201–3.

Henry Smith's Charity possesses a large estate applicable to several purposes. About £8,000 a year is devoted to direct gifts among the poor of 209 different parishes. In the year 1869 the Charity Commissioners made an elaborate report upon it, in which they set forth the unsatisfactory work it was doing.

In Fetcham:

> The churchwardens, in reply to a printed circular, state—
> That several of the recipients are on the parish; that the charity is often taken as a right; that improper persons ask for it; that much dissatisfaction is expressed by those who are unsuccessful; that the moral effect is unsatisfactory and that it is an inducement for people to take up their residence in the parish whose daily work is at a distance, and that it tends to raise the rent of cottages.

In Kingston:

> Half the town apply for the gifts. They ask for them as a right, and abuse you if they do not get them. Mr. Martin adds: "It seems that people are attracted to Kingston because there is so much to be given away."

Of Lichfield this is said:

> At Lichfield the charity is given away by the church wardens of the parish of St. Mary in flannel petticoats and shoes. There are a great many applicants; no name is put down two years running. In St. Mary's many of the recipients are on the parish. The gifts are received as a right, in a spirit of grumbling. Many improper persons apply. Those who are successful are dissatisfied. *A fortiori* those who are not. The gifts (it would seem the *general* gifts are intended) have turned half the inhabitants of Lichfield into beggars, hence idleness, drunkenness, poaching, and thieving. "It is impossible to exaggerate the evils they produce."

An incumbent of one parish says:

> I consider that a charity was never worse applied. I think its effects are demoralizing, and as the parish becomes larger

the difficulty of dispensing the charity becomes every day greater. It is practically almost impossible for a church warden to give it to suitable objects. At present there is not even an attempt.

And another writes thus:

That I have no particular suggestion to offer, but would express an earnest hope that the commissioners will deal thoroughly with Smith's Charity throughout the country, and utilize it for purposes tending to raise and not (as at present) to degrade the moral tone of our labouring class.

A third wrote to the Charity Commissioners as follows:

With all my heart I wish that [Smith's Charity] were either reformed or annihilated. . . . Of all the pauperizing influences brought to bear upon the poor population of this and other parishes, I do not see any more patent than Smith's Charity.

This charity owes its existence to a will made by Henry Smith in 1627, bequeathing £1,000 to be laid out in the purchase of lands of the value of £60 per annum at the least for the use and relief of the poorest of his kindred, i.e. the poorest of his sister's children and their children successively. About 84 acres in Kensington were purchased.

The gross income of the charity is now £60,000 per annum, and is administered under a scheme made by the Charity Commissioners and approved by the court in 1889. According to a statement in the *Annual Charities Register and Digest* for 1947, the income is applicable to (a) Relief of kindred of the founder, under a scheme approved by the Court of Chancery; (b) Relief of poor of about 200 parishes and donations to provincial hospitals and convalescent homes; (c) Relief of clergy in regular duty in certain counties. Large sums go also to London Hospitals. There are still kindred receiving benefits.

7. *Woodbridge Almshouses* (1587), pp. 54 *et seq.*

Thomas Seckford in 1587 gave land in Clerkenwell to found an almshouse at Woodbridge in Suffolk. At the date of the foundation the rent of the land was £113. By 1860 the income was £3,600 made by the development of Clerkenwell. It was held 300 years afterwards that nevertheless Woodbridge people should have a preference, which in effect meant that the whole of this large income went to them.

Seckford's Charity, at the time when Hobhouse wrote, had already, under a scheme approved by the Court of Chancery in 1861, been amalgamated with the Free Grammar School at Woodbridge, which at that time had an income of only £38 per annum. The endowments of the almshouses, described as Seckford Hospital, and the school are now separate.

The original almshouses were rebuilt in 1869, a large additional building having been erected in 1840. The two buildings provide accommodation for forty-three persons or fifty-nine if married couples are appointed. Inmates are to be poor persons not less than fifty years of age who have resided in the ancient Parish of Woodbridge for not less than three years before appointment. If at any time there are not sufficient qualified persons to fill vacancies, persons being inhabitants of any of the parishes adjacent to Woodbridge but otherwise qualified may be appointed.

This case illustrates successful diversion of part of a large surplus, from almshouses to education, with the money still flowing from Clerkenwell to Woodbridge.

8. *Abbott Foundation for Manufactures in Guildford* (1633), pp. 100–2.

George Abbott, Archbishop of Canterbury, was a native of Guildford and desired to benefit the town he loved. At an earlier date certain manufactures had been carried on in Guildford but had ebbed away from it. Abbott's intention was to restore the trade and also to build an almshouse. Dying in 1633 he left one property for the purpose of setting up manufactures of stockings and other things, that the place might flourish as theretofore, and other property to endow the almshouses which he had built in his lifetime. In about twenty years' time the Guildford people demanded relief, arguing that manufactures of different kinds had been tried, had failed, and had been found to be even prejudicial to the town A decree in 1656 put a stop to the manufactures but provided instead for distributing funds among poor, honest tradespeople and shopkeepers of the town who might want schools. This led to a practice of money doles which, according to information filed in 1785, used often to operate as an inducement to idleness and drunkenness. Ultimately, after various intervening stages, the Court in 1855 transferred the whole fund for the manufactures to the maintenance of a middle-class school.

The endowment of the hospital and school are now separated,

two-thirds going to the hospital under a scheme approved by the Charity Commissioners, while the remaining third goes to the school.

9. *Norwich Foundation for a Sermon in Low Dutch* (seventeenth century), p. 106.

The minister is required to preach annually a sermon in Low Dutch which nobody understands. He now learns a sermon by heart and preaches it.

There was a Dutch congregation in Norwich which in 1619 obtained the right to occupy the choir of one of the churches and there were various endowments for the minister and poor of the congregation, dating from the seventeenth and eighteenth centuries. When an assistant charity commissioner held an enquiry into the charities of Norwich in 1906–7, £30 a year was being paid to the minister of the Dutch Church in the City of London who once a year conducted a service and preached a sermon in the church in Norwich. The service was usually attended by twelve to sixteen persons of Dutch extraction. After a few words in Dutch the minister conducted the rest of the sermon in English as those present did not understand Dutch. After consideration of the assistant commissioner's report the Commissioners invited the trustees to apply for a scheme. This they were unwilling to do. But the payment to the minister was reduced to £20 per annum. In 1921 a scheme was at last established, the gist of which is that if and when the trustees of the charity find a congregation of Dutch-speaking persons of the Dutch Church in need of the ministrations of a Dutch-speaking minister they can pay his stipend, but failing that can use the money in support of the Netherlands Christian Sailors' Union in London, or any other society in the United Kingdom concerned with the spiritual welfare of Dutchmen.

The point of this case is the length of time taken to divest a charity from a manifestly useless purpose.

10. *Joanna Southcote*, pp. 7–8.

A lady dying about 1860 left property for the purpose of "printing, publishing and propagating the sacred writings of Joanna Southcote" who, among other things, had announced that she was to give birth to the Messiah and whose sect by 1860 had only a nominal existence. Yet the Court in the case of *Thornton* v. *Howe*, 31 Beav., p. 14 (1862), felt bound to uphold the gift. "If the tendency were not immoral and though the Court might consider the opinions sought to be propagated foolish or even devoid of foundation, it would not on that account take it out of the class of legacies which are included in the general term 'charitable bequests' " (Romilly M. R.). Most fortunately, apart from land which could not be willed to charity, the property of the testator had shrunk to zero. But for this happy accident, as Hobhouse observes, "here was a machinery established for teaching, it might be for ever, absurdities in which no human being even at the date of the foundation believed."

11. *Jarvis Foundation for Doles in Herefordshire* (1793), pp. 40–1.

George Jarvis was a man of property in Herefordshire. The neighbours say that no charitable intentions entered his mind until he was displeased at the marriage of his only daughter or at some incident connected therewith. He lived to see her become a mother and a grandmother but nursed his resentment to the end. He gave his property, about £100,000, away from his family to trustees, bidding them to apply the income to the poor of three specified parishes in money, provisions, physic or clothes. A scheme for the trust was settled by Lord Eldon as Chancellor in 1802. The whole population of all classes in the three parishes by the census of 1801 was under 900, and the distribution of £2,300 a year in alms brought into the parishes not labourers seeking employment where it was likely to be found, but persons naturally desirous of participating in gifts which could be obtained without labour. Jarvis, among other things, prohibited his trustees from using any of the money for building houses, so that the parishes became over-crowded as well as idle and immoral. This charity, after fifty years of doing harm, was reformed by special Act of Parliament in 1852.

The Jarvis's Charity Act, 1852, and a scheme made by the court in the same year, provided for erection and maintenance of boarding schools, an infants' school and almshouses, and for the sum of not more than £500 per annum to be distributed in specified proportions between the three parishes of Staunton, Bredwardine, and Letton, in provisions, clothing, and fuel, among such deserving poor of the parishes as were aged or infirm or widows. The trustees were given further powers of subscribing not more than £50 per annum to a local hospital, and of spending limited amounts in apprenticing scholars or advancing in life persons under twenty-one. The educational part of the endowment is now under the jurisdiction of the Minister of Education. The non-educational part, with an income of about £1,100 a year, is still regulated by the Act of 1852 and the court scheme which has only been slightly supplemented and varied. Following disputes among the trustees and between the three parishes, and allegations that persons who were not poor were sharing in the benefits of the yearly sum distributable, the Charity Commissioners sent an assistant commissioner to hold a public enquiry in Staunton in 1946, and are still corresponding with the trustees in an endeavour to get from them an application for a new scheme.

12. *Tancred's Hospital for Decayed Gentlemen* (1754), pp. 65–8.

Christopher Tancred was a Yorkshire squire without issue whose natural heirs were his five sisters, but, as he stated in his deed of foundation, he did not choose that his landed property, which was large, should be divided or become disconnected with his name, so he gave it on his death to charity. The usual litigation took place on his will with the usual ill success on the part of the natural heirs. The judge could only lament that he was not able to decide in their favour. Christopher Tancred's plan was to keep up his mansion-house and park as a residence for twelve decayed gentlemen, natives of Great Britain, and of the religion of the Church of England. The local curate was to read prayers to Tancred's pensioners every day and preach a sermon on the anniversary of Tancred's death every year. He founded also twelve studentships for Divinity, Physic, and Law, directing that the four students of Divinity should graduate at Christ's College, the four of Physic at Caius College, and the four of Law should be called to the Bar at Lincoln's Inn, in the halls of which three institutions public orations were to be delivered on the anniversary of his death in perpetual remembrance of the said charity. By 1809 it had become clear that the mode of life forced on the pensioners was so wretched and resulted in such scandals that the hospital must be broken up. But the scheme framed for breaking it up was rejected in Parliament.

At last in 1872 the commissioners in pursuance of an Act of Parliament were able to direct that Whixley Manor House should cease to be occupied as a place of residence for pensioners. As the result of a further scheme made by the commissioners, confirmed by a special Act of Parliament in 1923, the income of the pension branch of Tancred's charities, amounting to about £1,500 a year, is applied in payment of annuities to out-pensioners who must be decayed and necessitous gentlemen, clergymen, commissioned land or sea officers of fifty years of age or more, natives of Great Britain and of the religion of the Church of England, that is to say, possessing the original qualifications required for admission to the Manor House. There are at present thirteen such out-pensioners receiving £100 each.

13. *Nash Bequest for Bellringing* (1813), p. 102.

Thomas Nash bequeathed to the mayor, senior alderman, and town clerk of Bath for the time being the sum of £50 per annum, for the use, benefit and enjoyment of the set of ringers belonging to the Abbey Church, Bath, "on condition of their ringing on the whole peal of bells with clappers muffled various solemn and doleful changes, allowing proper intervals for rest and refreshment, from eight o'clock in the morning until eight o'clock in the evening, on the fourteenth May in every year, being the anniversary of my wedding day; and also on every anniversary of the day of my decease to ring a grand bob major and merry mirthful peals, unmuffled, during the same space of time, and allowing the same intervals as before mentioned, in joyful commemoration of my happy release from domestic tyranny and wretchedness."

Thomas Nash went on to make it plain that it was not only his wife that he hated:

And now that dear divine man, the Rev. P. B., may resume his amatory labours without enveloping himself in a sedan-chair for fear of detection.

"This outrage on decency," comments Hobhouse, "constituted a perfectly good 'charity.' "

In relation to Thomas Nash, Hobhouse over-played his good hand. Nash may have made a good charity but he does not seem ever to have had his peals. The Charity Commission know nothing of him and the only other reference to his bequest which I have found is in a book published in 1847, *Rambles About Bath and Its Neighbourhood*, by James Tunstall. This, while describing the bequest, states that "the terms of this extraordinary will have not been complied with."

Such a bequest would not be a good charity to-day. In the

case *re Benjamin Arber* reported in *The Times* of December 12, 1919, the court decided that a gift by will to make a yearly payment to the ringers of the bells in a certain church, in consideration of their ringing the bells half muffled upon the anniversary of the testator's death in every year for ever, was not charitable, on the ground that it was simply an endeavour on the part of the testator to commemorate his own memory.

A bequest made within the past few months by a Cambridge merchant tailor for a trumpeter to sound Reveille and Last Post at his graveside on each anniversary of his death and say, "Do your best for England" has had even shorter shrift. The cemetery authorities said: "We have had to decline. It just isn't possible." (*Daily Mirror*, October 10, 1947.)

14. *St. Christopher-le-Stock in the Bank of England.*

The parish of St. Christopher-le-Stock was wholly absorbed in the Bank of England (whose building dates from 1788). But it was reported in 1860 that four persons "who live in various parts of the suburbs of London and are said to belong to this parish . . . have for many years received" gifts from charities assigned for the parishioners.

15. *Cemetery without any Dead in St. Michael's, Crooked Lane* (1346).

Just before the Black Death, Edward III gave to the inhabitants of the parish of St. Michael's, Crooked Lane, a piece of land for the enlargement of their burial ground. In 1878, under a scheme sanctioned by the Master of the Rolls some twenty years before, part of the income of the trust was still being accumulated for a cemetery. "If ever the cemetery is purchased, however, it will remain almost unoccupied, for there are hardly any residents in the parish of St. Michael, and there is certainly no need of a cemetery for them." (Report of Royal Commission on City of London Parochial Charities, p. 8.) As the Commissioners were told by the vestry clerk: "We have not buried anybody for some years."

16. *Love Feast in St. Clement's, Eastcheap* (1491).

Halliday, dying in 1491, left lands from which 5s. was to be spent each year on a "love feast," to be arranged by the churchwardens, for bringing together on Maundy Thursday parishioners who had fallen out with one another during the preceding twelve months. By 1870 the income of the trust had been multiplied many times and the 5s. love feast had become a dinner at Richmond costing £60 to £70 a year, given to some eighty rate-payers of the parish, secretaries of companies and the like, whether resident in the parish or not and whether they had quarrelled with one another or not. As the vestry clerk of St. Clement's explained to the Royal Commission, the churchwardens found it embarrassing to make these enquiries "and therefore we invite everybody." But "the poor of the parish are not invited; they have their gifts weekly." "Perhaps they never quarrel," suggested one of the Commissioners and received from the witness the answer: "Probably not."

In this same parish there was a charity founded in 1585, one of whose purposes included payment of "£1 6s. 8d. yearly . . . for the maintenance of some godly, virtuous and well-disposed scholar resident in the University of Cambridge or Oxford." By 1860 the total income of this particular charity had multiplied some thirty times, but the churchwardens continued to pay exactly £1 6s. 8d. a year as before to keep a scholar at the university, only saving it up for four years at a time to make the gift look handsomer as £5 6s. 8d. The Commissioners commented acidly on the contrast between 5s. for a love feast in 1491 becoming £70 for a dinner at Richmond in 1860, while £1 6s. 8d. for education remained £1 6s. 8d. exactly, for ever.

II. ANTI-VIVISECTION AND FOUNDER'S KIN AS SUBJECTS OF CHARITY

Two decisions of considerable importance have been given recently narrowing the scope of charitable trusts. One is the decision of the House of Lords in July, 1947, that abolition of vivisection is not a charitable purpose (*The National Anti-Vivisection Society* v. *the Commissioners of Inland Revenue*). The other is the decision of the Court of Appeal that bequests to provide education for descendants of named individuals are not charitable. (*In re Compton*, 1945, Ch. 123.) Each of these decisions raises difficult issues for the future.

Anti-Vivisection

For more than fifty years, under a decision given by Mr. Justice Chitty in 1895, in the case *in re Foveaux*,[1] Anti-Vivisection Societies, that is to say societies for securing prohibition of all experiments on living animals, had been treated as societies for charitable purposes, entitled to exemption from income tax. The Inland Revenue Commissioners, while feeling bound by this decision of

---

[1] 1895, 2 Ch., 501.

1895, did not like it and recently took steps to challenge it in the Courts. The question was carried to the House of Lords, which in July, 1947, overruled the decision *in re Foveaux*, and decided that the National Anti-Vivisection Society was not a charity within the legal definition of that term. The decision was given by a majority of four Law Lords to one. There had been dissent also in the Court of Appeal, where the decision against the society was given by two to one. The decision rests on two distinct grounds accepted with differing degrees of emphasis by all the Law Lords of the majority.

The first ground is that the main purpose of the National Anti-Vivisection Society is "political," in the sense of its being directed to bring about a change of the law and to prohibit by law all experiments on living animals. Such experiments are now permitted, subject to elaborately devised conditions, under an Act passed in 1876 for Prevention of Cruelty to Animals; the main object of the National Anti-Vivisection Society could in practice be accomplished only by a radical amendment of this Act. In holding that this made the society "political" and therefore not a charity, the Lords followed a judgment given in 1917, in which it had been held that the Secular Society was not a charity because practically all its main objects could be accomplished only by a change of the existing law; these objects were the abolition of all religious tests, disestablishment of the Church, secularization of education, alteration of the law as to religion, marriage, and Sabbath observances.[1]

In basing themselves on this "political" ground, two of the Law Lords quoted with approval a saying from a legal text-book: "The law could not stultify itself by holding that it was for the public benefit that the law itself should be changed." This sounds rather formal, but, apart from the formality of the reasoning, it may be suggested that the present decision, as it is now good law, is also good sense. It is desirable that Britons should be free to associate themselves for the purpose of bringing about changes of law, but there is no reason why in doing so they should have the advantages attached to charities, of exemption from tax and of perpetuity. There is indeed something incongruous in endowing in perpetuity an organization for bringing about a specified change of law; the law is a subject for the minds of living man.

It is true that the present decision means that objects for purposes now regarded as admirable, such as abolition of slavery or securing the Factory Acts, would not be charities. But if a society for extending the Factory Acts is a charity, then a society opposing extension

[1] *Bowman* v. *Secular Society*, 1917, A.C., 408.

has equally a claim to be a charity. If the Courts distinguish between one as beneficial and the other as harmful, they usurp the function of Parliament. The present decision of the Law Lords rejects explicitly the suggestion that the term "political" for ruling a society out of a class of charities means "party political." That, too, is good sense. The border between reforms which are and those which are not "party political" is not a fixed or firm line.

In saying that a society is not charitable if its main object is "political," i.e. a change of law, the word "main" must be stressed. A society like the National Society for the Prevention of Cruelty to Children, which is an undoubted charity and mainly engaged in enforcing the law and making public opinion, does not cease to be charitable, because from time to time it takes steps to secure an improvement of the law for its general purposes of preventing cruelty to children.

The second ground of the new decision, and the one to which most attention was devoted in the judgments, is that, if the National Anti-Vivisection Society accomplished its purpose, this, so far from benefiting the community, would do more harm than good by hindering the progress of science and medicine. The majority of the Lords asserted the right and duty of the Courts to form a judgment in each case as to whether an organization claiming to be a charity would yield on the whole a public benefit. The decision of 1895, which they overruled, had gone on the line that the intention of the testator to confer a benefit was decisive; it was not for the Court to decide whether benefit would in fact result. The new decision is thus a forward step in the assertion of public interest as against the dead hand of the testator. It is possible that the decision goes far enough to make unnecessary measures to give effect to the first of the two fundamental principles laid down by Hobhouse (p. 197 above), namely, that the public should not be compelled to take whatever is offered, but should here as in other countries have the right of considering whether that particular use which the founder has fancied should take effect. But the question may still be raised whether Courts of Law are the right people to decide such questions of public policy and on what grounds they can decide them. Two further comments may be made:—

1. One of the Law Lords of the majority, Lord Simmonds, stressed the fact that views of what was good public policy altered in time. Things accepted as beneficial charities in one century would not be accepted in another century. This, no doubt, is true,

but it is most unlikely that any law court would reject a new charity now which came directly within the named purposes of the still living preamble of the Statute of Elizabeth.

2. However far the new decision is carried, it gives no means of revising established charities or even of discovering that revision is desirable. Revision depends upon the agreement of the trustees of each individual charity. As the Royal Commission on the City of London Parochial Charities showed, one of the evils of charitable trusts is that after centuries they may fall into the hands of small-minded people who use them for no good purpose and see no reason for changing them.

Founder's Kin

For hundreds of years provision for relief in poverty and for education, both appearing in the preamble to the Statute of Elizabeth, have been treated as charitable purposes, even when the benefits were confined to members of a particular family, normally kindred of the founder. By a recent decision in the Court of Appeal a distinction has been drawn between relief of poverty and provision of education in relation to Founder's Kin.

In the case reported as *in re Compton*, 1945, Ch., 123, it was held that a gift to provide scholarships for ever for the descendants of three named persons was not a valid charitable trust; the testatrix did not save her bequest by providing that the money was to be "used to fit the children to be servants of God serving the nation, not as students of research of any kind." The Master of the Rolls laid it down that a gift for the education of the descendants of named individuals must be regarded as a family trust and not as one for the benefit of a section of the community. At the same time he accepted as still correct old decisions that gifts for the relief of such descendants in poverty are charities: "Many trusts of this description have been carried on for generations on the faith that they were charitable, and many testators have no doubt been guided by such decisions. The cases must at this date be regarded as good law, though they are perhaps anomalous." The Master of the Rolls felt bound here by the reported decisions establishing as charitable the relief of poor Founder's Kin. The reported decisions for Founder's Kin scholarships as charities were fewer and less clear and the Court of Appeal felt able to disregard them. The Master of the Rolls observed, in defence of this distinction between doles and scholarships in the case of Founder's Kin, that relieving individuals in poverty might be regarded as more of a benefit to the community which would otherwise have to support them, than merely ensuring that they received education.

It is difficult to follow the reasoning underlying this distinction between doles and education for Founder's Kin, or to regard the resulting legal position as satisfactory. First, the suggestion made in the judgment that relief of poverty by doles is somehow a more public purpose than education, runs counter to the course both of legislation (such as the Endowed Schools Act of 1869) and of judicial decisions (such as Ashton's case noted above on p. 192) which have combined to transfer endowments from doles to education. Second, while there are not so many or so strong recorded decisions of the Courts for Founder's Kin scholarships as for Founder's Kin doles as being charitable, this appears to be due to little more than the accident that the scholarships have less often been challenged. They equally have been carried on as charities for generations, and the view of the Courts of Equity in their favour is equally clear. For instance, the William Akroyd Founder's Kin Scholarships (referred to in Chapter VI) were put on a formal basis by a Chancery Decree of 1699.

The tendency shown by the judges, both in the Anti-Vivisection case and in *in re Compton*, to narrow the definition of charitable purposes is clearly related in each case to the fact that with modern levels of taxation, the advantage given to any institution by regarding it as charitable and entitled to tax exemption is greater than in the past. But it seems likely that both the Anti-Vivisection decision and *in re Compton* will raise more problems for the Courts than they can solve satisfactorily by continuing to interpret past decisions and referring to the Statute of Elizabeth. The same may be said of decisions such as *in re Macduff* (1896) and *Keren Kayemeth Le Jisroel Ltd.* (1931) declaring that a philanthropic purpose is not necessarily charitable, compared with *in re Dupree's Deed Trusts* (1945) deciding that endowment of prizes for chess is charitable. The law as well as the administration of charitable trusts calls for examination, with the possibility of suggesting a revision of the famous preamble.

III. NOTE ON CHARITABLE TRUSTS IN SCOTLAND

The Scottish law knows nothing of the Statute of Elizabeth and the Scottish Courts talk Latin more often than Norman French. But the legal treatment of charitable trusts has come to be much the same in both parts of Britain. This is stated in so many words in Lord Macnaghten's famous judgment in *Pemsel's Case*, 1891, A.C., 531. In Scottish Acts and decisions, "the words 'charity' and 'charitable' are used sometimes in the sense which they bear in English law, sometimes in a sense hardly distinguishable from it" (p. 582). *Pemsel's Case* was English, not Scottish, but as the point at issue was one of exemption from income tax, on which it would be awkward to have differences of law in the two parts of Britain, the question of Scottish law arose and was discussed. There do not appear, in fact, to be any substantial differences in the law of the two countries, in respect of charities.

Thus, according to the Encyclopaedia of the Laws of Scotland, the Scottish Courts, like the English, construe trust deeds "with benignance towards the charitable purposes." "When the general intention is indicated, the Court will find the means of carrying the details into operation."

The Scottish Courts again apply the *cy près* principle in much the same way as the English, and even have been known to use the term *cy près* though it is completely outlandish to them. They apply it also with the same limitations. It is not sufficient ground for varying the use of charitable funds to show "that changing circumstances have made the duties of trustees much more arduous to perform and discouraging in their results."[1]

The Scottish Courts finally, even without the help of Elizabeth's Statute, construe "charitable purpose" as "public purpose." But the purpose must be genuinely public, not self-advertisement. This was shown when the Court of Session had before them the will of John Stuart McCaig of Muckairn, Soroba and Oban, Argyllshire, leaving more than £2,000 a year to be used for all time in erecting on his estate statues of himself, five brothers, two sisters, and his parents, varied by "artistic towers." The testator, writing his own will, knew enough about the law to give a colour of public benefit to his project by saying that he wished to encourage young and rising artists and that for this purpose prizes were to be given for the best designs of statues and towers. He tried also to make the Court of Session themselves into his trustees as his first choice, but they declined. The University of Glasgow, whom he named second, were ready to accept the trust. But by the time that John Stuart

---

[1] *Glasgow Domestic Training School*, 1923, S.C., p. 92. While issuing this warning the Court of Session in the particular case before them felt it just permissible to divert to another purpose money which had been left for training girls as domestic servants; hardly any girls were presenting themselves for training.

McCaig died none of his brothers and one only of his sisters was left alive. She preferred the £2,000 a year to having a statue and fought and managed to upset the will. The Court of Session held that such a trust was not charitable at all, and could not defeat the claim of the sister as next-of-kin. But it took five years to settle this.[1]

Though the law of charitable trusts in both parts of Britain is now much the same, the administrative machinery for non-educational trusts is different. There is an Endowed Schools Act of 1882 for Scotland, broadly parallel to the Endowed Schools Act of 1869 in England. But there are no Charity Commissioners in Scotland. The only way of getting a change made in the purposes or use of a non-educational charitable trust in Scotland is by a judicial decision, as in England before 1853.

There was for two years only under the Endowed Institutions (Scotland) Act, power, by order of the Home Secretary with the consent of the trustees, to make almost any desired change in the administration or use of a trust, regardless of *cy près* or the instructions of the founder. The use of this power is illustrated by Burnett's case in the "Charities' Chamber of Horrors." But the power came to an end finally in 1880.

IV. A NEW DEAL FOR CHARITABLE TRUSTS

The following paragraphs set out in as definite a form as now seems possible a programme of reforms in regard to charitable trusts, such as might be submitted to a Royal Commission if one were appointed.

> Exemption of charitable foundations from income tax or other taxation shall be conditional upon their being registered with the appropriate authority, that is to say, the Minister of Education in respect of educational foundations and the Charity Commissioners in respect of all other foundations. If any question arises and cannot be settled by agreement between the Minister of Education and the Charity Commissioners as to which is the appropriate authority in respect of any particular foundation, the question shall be determined by the Lord Chancellor.
>
> Every foundation applying for registration shall furnish to

---

[1] The testator died in 1902. The case is reported as *McCaig v. University of Glasgow*, 1907, S.C., p. 231.

the appropriate authority the prescribed particulars as to its governing body, funds, purposes, rules and other relevant matters as a condition of remaining registered and shall comply with any requirements of the appropriate authority under the Charitable Trusts Acts, giving power to the authority to require accounts and written statements and the attendance of trustees, managers, etc., for examination.

The appropriate authority shall have power, either on their own motion or on that of the governing body of a foundation, with the consent of the governing body or a majority thereof:—

(a) At any time to make a scheme for the administration of the funds of the foundation, applying the *cy près* principle.

(b) At any time fifty years or more after a bequest or other gift has been made, to make a scheme for the use and administration of the gift in the manner that may seem to them most expedient for serving the general charitable purpose of the giver, whether relief in old age; relief in sickness or infirmity; relief in poverty; assistance of young persons or children; promotion of science, art or learning; promotion of religion; education or some other public purpose. But they shall not be bound, otherwise than they think expedient, by any specific directions of the giver as to general mode of giving effect to this purpose or by limitations as to locality, race, kindred, or classes of persons to be benefited.

(c) At any time one hundred years or more after a bequest or other gift has been made to make such scheme for the administration of the gift for any charitable purpose as may appear to them most expedient.

Provided that unless a contrary desire of the giver appears from the terms of his gift every scheme shall provide

(i) for keeping intact so far as possible the capital of the gift;

(ii) for keeping the name and memory of the giver, or any person named by him in that connection, associated with the use of the gift.

The appropriate authority, after an enquiry in which persons interested in a proposed gift have an opportunity of expressing their views, shall have power to declare that the purposes of a gift or the mode prescribed for its application by the giver are

mischievous or foolish. Any such declaration shall be laid
before both Houses of Parliament and, unless annulled by
resolution of either House within a prescribed time, shall come
into effect to give to the appropriate authority the power of
making a scheme forthwith as if the gift had been made a
hundred years before.

Except in so far as they are inconsistent with the above,
the existing powers and functions of the Charity Commissioners and Minister of Education under the Charitable Trusts
Acts shall continue, and the staffs of these authorities will be
enlarged so as to make possible

(*a*) a compilation of annual statistical reports on charitable
foundations comparable to those of the Registrar of Friendly
Societies; and

(*b*) personal examination of foundations by inspectors.

These proposals, referring to the Minister of Education and the
Charity Commissioners, are set out in language appropriate only
to England. In Scotland, the Department of Education has powers
in respect of educational endowments similar to those of the English
Minister of Education. There is no authority in Scotland corresponding to the Charity Commissioners for dealing with trusts other
than educational. The setting up of such an authority would, it is
hoped, be one of the results of the Royal Commission.

The proposals, it will be seen, would make it possible fifty years after
a testator's death to disregard his detailed instructions as to method
while continuing to serve the general purpose preferred by him,
e.g. old age or education, and a hundred years after his death to
divert the money to some different charitable purpose. But his
name would continue to be associated with the charity.

The proposals affect in the main endowments which are not
educational. For those which are held to be educational, the Ministry
of Education in England and Wales and the Department of Education in Scotland have within the limits of the Endowed Schools
Acts sufficient powers to secure use according to modern views of
education. But the Royal Commission might well be asked to
consider :—

(i) A re-definition of what endowments are to be treated as
educational, as well as the proposition made in the first paragraph above, that the final decision on this should rest neither
with the Charity Commission nor with the education depart-

ments but with some impartial body. The treatment of libraries is a good case in point.

(ii) A widening of the purposes for which endowments can be used under the Endowed Schools Acts, to cover all the activities, including adolescent and adult education, which are the aim of the Education Act of 1944.

The proposals set out above leave three important issues for further enquiry.

First, should the appropriate authority have power in any circumstances, and, if so, by what procedure, to override the trustees of a foundation and make a scheme against their will? As drafted the proposals do not give this power, requiring the consent of the trustees in every case. Argument for giving this power is provided by cases such as those of Fulbourn and Jarvis in Section I of Appendix B, where reform is still blocked, and by the Dutch sermon in Norwich where it took till 1921 to make a change whose need had been obvious for generations. The argument against giving this power is that the community has more to fear from the dead hand of a central bureaucracy, or the unjust hand of a political party, than from the dead hand of the founder exercised through living trustees. As Mill said, variety is more important than uniformity in this field. There are thus strong arguments each way, and it should be left to the Royal Commission to say which way the balance of advantage tips. If any power is given of overriding the trustees of a charity in making a new scheme, the procedure should clearly include laying the scheme before both Houses of Parliament for approval.

Second, should the administrative expenses of the appropriate authority, which will be greater than at present, be met in whole or in part by a levy on the charitable foundations themselves? This question, too, can be left to the Royal Commission, but it may be hoped that they would answer the question in the negative. The object of the new deal is to continue to encourage charitable gifts. It would pay the State to provide adequate administrative expenses as part of its encouragement to charitable donors.

A third open question relates to the constitution and the constitutional position of the Charity Commissioners, and their proposed counterpart in Scotland, who will be the appropriate authority for non-educational trusts. At present the scope of the Charity Commissioners in making schemes is purely judicial. They take the place of the Courts, they are tied by the *cy près* principle, and they are controlled by the possibility of a judicial decision against them, as in the Weir Hospital case. If they are to have a discretion, as proposed above, to depart from the *cy près* principle, they become administrative. Should they become subject to Ministerial control? The suggestion made here is that so far as possible the Charity Commissioners should be left free of direct Ministerial control. This would be facilitated by placing alongside of them an independent advisory committee. The final answer on this constitutional point may well be left to the Royal Commission. On the choice of the Minister to whom in future the Charity Commissioners for England and their counterpart in Scotland should be attached, a suggestion is made as point 6 in Chapter XI.

APPENDIX C—CITIZENS' ADVICE BUREAUX—
SPECIMEN PROBLEMS

   I.   Examples of Questions illustrating each Head (London—supplied by Family Welfare Association);

   II.   An afternoon and a morning in a C.A.B. (London Area);

   III. C.A.B. Quiz (Southwark);

   IV. Some Harder Problems (Family Welfare Association);

   V.   Problems Rooted in Bad Housing.

I. EXAMPLES OF QUESTIONS ILLUSTRATING EACH HEAD

THE following are brief examples supplied from London Bureaux of the kind of question that is asked under each of the twenty-one heads under which questions are normally classified (*see* p. 279).

1. *Communications.*

Must a mother pay duty on a wool rug made by her son in hospital in India, the materials having been given to him by the Red Cross?

2. *Education and Training.*

Refugee girl aged 16½ called to ask for advice on careers. Had passed school certificate but failed to get matric. and did not know whether she should take exam. again before starting training. Was interested in medicine and wanted information on openings, training, etc.

3. *Employment.*

Employed in publishers' office. Are employers entitled to deduct one day's salary from week's wages because she was absent without a doctor's certificate?

4. *Evacuation and Transferred Workers.*

Is man who works in London, but has to support a home in the country, entitled to Ministry of Labour Lodging Allowance if he cannot find accommodation for his family in London?

5. *Family and Personal Problems.*

Typist called to ask how she could help friend, aged 19, who had run away from home and was expecting illegitimate baby. The landlady was turning her out of her lodgings and nothing had been done in preparation for the arrival of the baby.

Married woman called to say she is expecting a second child and wants to get it adopted as neither she nor her husband "are struck on the idea of a bigger family." What is procedure for adoption? (This shows the necessity for having a trained worker in a bureau, who knows when reference to a case work agency is needed.)

6. *Foreign.*

Demobilized soldier is expecting to marry the Italian girl he left behind in Italy. She writes to him in Italian and he has five letters he cannot read—can C.A.B. translate for him? He has completed necessary papers to marry her two months before but she is unable to get permission to come to England. She is expecting his baby next month and now her mother says she cannot travel alone. Can he get permission to go back himself to marry and bring her home?

7. *Health and Medical.*

Must man with tuberculosis accept accommodation offered for himself and family in damp basement, which Borough Sanitary Inspector admits is unsuitable for tubercular patient?

8. *Housing.*

An old lady called to ask if she should accept estimate she had obtained for repairing and painting her house. Nothing had been done to it since her husband died sixteen years ago. On enquiry it was found that she was only a weekly tenant and that the landlord was responsible for all repairs. The sanitary inspector contacted the landlord and necessary repairs were carried out.

After applying to the Furnished Rents Tribunal for a decrease in his rent (which should give three months' protection), man found on return from work that his door was locked and possessions removed to a station left luggage office. What action could he take? Tribunal told him local authority should take action, local authority told him County Court should be approached, County Court referred him to the C.A.B.

9. *Income Tax.*

Young woman, after domestic upheaval, walked out of job without paying income tax. After six months she wanted to put matters straight, but was afraid to go to income tax office in case she got into trouble. What could she do?

10. *Legal.*

Man paid deposit of £25 to solicitor to start divorce proceedings. Nothing seemed to be done, so he consulted C.A.B. as to whether delay was unusual. C.A.B. discovered solicitor had been "struck off" and was working for another firm, who eventually agreed to continue with case without further deposit.

11. *Local Information.*

Where can a man get accommodation for his dog, to whom he is very attached? No landlady will take them both.

12. *Matrimonial Problems.*

Woman called to ask if her marriage was invalid because her single name on marriage certificate is not the same as that on her birth certificate. Her mother had remarried and she had always taken her step-father's name. Now husband says they have never been married, he wishes to marry someone else, and he is going to take his child from her.

13. *Prisoners of War and Internees.*

Returned prisoner of war called for help in completing war damage claim, which wife had never made. His wife suffered from nerves and had been unfaithful while he was away, but he had forgiven her. He needed help to get better accommodation and advice as to procedure for starting in business again as decorator—how to get materials and resettlement grant?

14. *Service Questions.*

Conscript, aged 19, married with one child, called to ask how his wife was to live while he was in the army, as she was not entitled to a Dependants' Allowance until he was 21.

The mother of a man who had been killed in action had applied five months previously for his gratuity and had heard nothing. As C.A.B. discovered that the right documents had not been sent with the application, the matter was taken up with the R.N. Accounts Dept. on her behalf.

15. *Social Insurance.*

Woman called to ask how she can claim Widow's Pension Husband committed bigamy and then went to live with the other woman, who had her name put on his death certificate as the widow.

Widow with three children wanted help in completing Family Allowance form. Two of the children are in Dr. Barnardo's Homes: she also has two children by another father, to whom she is not married. His wife does not know about these children, but caller had changed her name to that of the father of the children.

16. *Supplies and Rationing.*

His utility furniture has furniture beetle in it. Can he make firm replace it and will he have to produce more dockets?

How can old lady of 86 get a new mattress? Sanitary inspector has removed her old one and she may not be entitled to dockets for a new one.

17. *Trading Questions.*

As a hobby, a man is making cigarette cases out of odd pieces of glass. He has been selling to friends; and wants to know whether he must have a licence to sell to shops and whether he will have to pay purchase tax?

18. *Travel.*

A widow, whose husband had "always dealt with these things," was thinking of leaving England and wanted information on how to get a visa, what income tax relief she would get if she were domiciled abroad, how long she could stay in the South of France and how many clothes coupons were given to people leaving the country.

19. *War Damage to Property.*

Man's house was requisitioned by local authority in 1940 and he was not notified when it was damaged by bombs. It has not been properly repaired and he wanted to know whether he could now send in claim to War Damage Commission.

20. *War Pensions.*

Working woman not well educated whose son had got a commission in the Royal Engineers before he had been killed, called for help in settling his affairs and applying for pension for herself. He had been her main support and she could not deal with the correspondence with the War Office and Ministry of Pensions.

II. AN AFTERNOON AND A MORNING IN A C.A.B.

Extract from day book of a Citizens' Advice Bureau in London
Area during April, 1947

Tuesday, April 22nd.

Name	*Request*	*Advice Given*
Mrs. M.	Clothing burnt while airing. Not insured. Can she get coupons?	If she will bring in what remains we will give covering letter to send with form CRSC/1A.
Mrs. H.	Further trouble with husband and thinks it useless to live with him any longer. If she goes (a) will she have custody of child? (b) Will she forfeit right to maintenance?	In view of all facts did not try to deter her from leaving. (a) Most unlikely she will lose custody of child in view of his age. (b) She may be able to make out case of "constructive desertion." To consult solicitor about this.
Mrs. F.	Shirt and sheet lost by laundry.	Given forms CRSC/1A and UFD/1A.
Mrs. J.	Wants bed and bedding for child aged 5, now too big for cot.	Given form UFD/1A and help given to complete it.
Mrs. E.	She and baby staying with sister in council house after being turned out of furnished room. Housing manager is threatening to evict sister because of breach of tenancy agreement with Council.	Council could do this but it is unlikely they will. Advised to go and talk matter over fully with housing manager and to let us know if there are any further developments.
Miss W.	Age and conditions for non-contributory pension.	Explained: advised to apply.
Miss I.	Getting married: how to get units for furniture?	UFD/1A.
Mrs. L.	Delay in issue of increased pension after husband's death. Getting into financial difficulties.	Advised to go to Assistance Board for help in hastening matters.

Name	*Request*	*Advice Given*
Mr. J.	(1) Has now as we advised seen sanitary inspector, who will deal with matter of boiler.	
	(2) Is rent increase in respect of rates correct?	Yes.
Mr. R.	Have we heard yet of suitable accommodation?	Nothing yet.
Mrs. McM.	Wants to be a blood donor.	Given address of local branch and times.
Mrs. E.	Application for sheet dockets rejected by Board of Trade.	She appears to be priority so we will restate case to Board of Trade.
Mr. J.	Immigrant from West Africa.	Given form RH/591.
Mrs. C.	To say Adoption Society agree to let her adopt Mrs. H's baby. Will we let her know when it is born and whether it is boy or girl?	Yes, we have asked Mrs. H. to keep in touch with us.
Mrs. A.	(1) Boy aged 12 sharing bed with sister aged 10 because of shortage of sheets.	(1) Not strictly priority, but form completed on grounds of special hardship.
	(2) Holiday on farm for Tony.	(2) Too young for camps —put in touch with Youth Service Volunteers.
Mrs. P.	Wants someone to sit with children occasionally in evening so she and husband can go out.	Referred Miss R.
Mrs. A.	Man lodger is being very difficult. How to get rid of him?	Give him written notice and then take no money and stop meals. To come back if this doesn't work.

Wednesday, April 23rd: 10–12.30.

Name	Request	Advice Given
Mrs. W.	Has adopted child: Can she get extra clothing coupons?	Yes—given form CRSC/1.
Mrs. P.	Regulations about parcels to New Zealand.	Advised about regulations.
Miss S.	Still worried about poor quality of war damage repairs—house damp and lodger is leaving on this account. (Poor Man's Valuer says house very shoddily built originally.)	Explained that Poor Man's Valuer can't help any further. Referred to Poor Man's Lawyer to see if any action possible against builder.
Mrs. R.	(1) Where to get vaccinated and inoculated against yellow fever?	Dr. P. For inoculation, advised Bureau of Scientific Disease.
	(2) Light job wanted while waiting passage.	Will go on our list of child-minders.
Mrs. P.	Having difficult time with daughter-in-law who is waiting for council house. Thinks daughter-in-law is not making sufficient effort.	As daughter-in-law has been repeatedly to us and we have approached council on her behalf, advised that everything possible had been done.
Mr. M.	Wife has had twins. Home help wanted—two other children.	Will ask Mrs. H. how soon she will be free and notify him.
Mr. D.	Returning to rebuilt house. Electricity Department are treating him as new consumer and ask 12s. 6d. which he was paying when bombed.	Would like to discuss this with rehousing officer before taking any action. He will call back.
Mrs. W.	Has now had notice to quit from father. Does this affect advice given her earlier by Poor Man's Lawyer on getting possession of their own house (post 1939 purchase).	It makes no difference. To ask for further appointment with lawyer when summons issued.

Name	Request	Advice Given
Mrs. O.	Husband in Forces and insured herself until August. Do they get two maternity benefits?	Yes.
Mrs. McR.	Situation with husband deteriorating. He now says baby she is expecting is not his and is refusing to maintain her.	Referred Poor Man's Lawyer. Monday next.
Mrs. O'L.	Can she get licence for leaded lights?	Council at present not granting licences for this but advised to apply as licences are deferred, not refused.
Mrs. B.	Living with daughter and very unhappy. Furniture in store and firm say she must remove it by end of week as they are giving up depository.	Possible candidate for old people's hostel. She will consider this. Arranged with another firm to store furniture meanwhile.
Gunner M.	To hear what arrangements we have made for confinement of wife and subsequent adoption of baby (not his). Has got extension of leave.	Told him of suggestions made by moral welfare worker. He will discuss them with wife and come in again.
Mrs. L.	Has son of 18 who is 6 ft. 4 ins. and she can't keep him clothed.	She has had all the coupons to which he is entitled.
Mrs. S.	Still no reply from County about help with home help expenses.	Rang County again who assure us action being taken. They are waiting for report of health visitor.
Mrs. T.	To say can find no correspondence to help in dispute with Ministry of Pensions about arrears of rent allowance.	We will refer case to L.C.S.S. for advice as to further action.

III. C.A.B. QUIZ (SOUTHWARK)

Some of the questions the citizens asked us to answer.

HOW   to get legal aid while in prison.
           to make a will.
           to get an ambulance to take a patient to hospital.
           to get passage money to South Africa.
           to be married by proxy.
           to get Dutch fiancé home from Germany.
           to get cat collected and destroyed.
           to disclaim debts of wife.
           to change name of adopted baby.
           to get a special marriage licence.
           to get coaching in bookkeeping.
           to get clothes coupons for an adopted child.
           to get Letters of Administration.
           to obtain possession of his own house from war-time
               tenant.
           to register under Disabled Persons Act.
           to get rent allowance while on convalescence.
           to get married outside your parish church.
           to get marriage annulled.
           to determine paternity of a child.
           to trace wife who has left him with three children.
           to get a baptismal certificate.
           to get exemption from jury service.
           to get rid of a noisy tenant.
           to find out if husband is alive.
           to get a funeral grant.
           to dispose of a large picture of Gladstone's Parliament.
           to translate letters in Italian, Dutch, and Greek.
           to adopt a child.
           to manage a difficult child.
           to claim Post Office savings of deceased husband.
           to register as a foster-mother.
           to marry a girl in Italy.
           to adopt two children by his wife's former marriage.
           to get rid of woodworm and beetle in furniture.
           to get legal representation at an inquest after motor
               accident?

WHERE   to find the nearest Turkish bath.
         to borrow a wedding dress.
         to board a dog.
         to get lip-reading classes.
         to get birth control information.
         to find a child to entertain at Christmas.
         to send National Insurance cards.
         to join a social club.
         to report that a child of five is left alone in a house.
         to get equipment for a public-house.
         to get a licence—
             to buy and sell fish;
             to buy paint;
             to open a café;
             to buy and sell plants;
             to start a decorating business?

CAN   she be forced to pay her husband's debts?
         she withdraw piano for sale on which prospective pur-
             chaser has paid a deposit?
         family claim income paid by American Consul to de-
             ceased parent?
         he remarry after his wife has left him seventeen years?
         she claim back payments of insurance if policy is for-
             feited?
         she get wages in lieu of notice on summary dismissal?
         an employer give him notice because he is a suspected
             tuberculosis patient?
         a doctor's wife join him in Germany and can she get
             welfare work there?
         an expectant mother claim Sickness Benefit?
         a sub-tenant remain in the house if the tenant gives it
             up?

IV. SOME HARDER PROBLEMS (FAMILY WELFARE ASSOCIATION)

Some of the harder or less usual problems that may present
themselves are illustrated below; most, but by no means all of them,
come under the head of Family and Personal Problems.

Widow from France.—Mrs. D. had been living in France prior
to the war; she and her husband were British but he had been

working there. Both were interned during the German occupation and her husband subsequently died. After the war Mrs. D.
was repatriated to Britain. She came to stay with her sister in
a London borough but had no adequate accommodation and
slept on a sofa. Furthermore, she had no income. She called at
the bureau about recovering her husband's assets (£72) held
in a London bank.

Action taken: (1) Mrs. D. was referred to the Assistance
Board, who made her an allowance (P.R.D.) until she found
work. She later took a good canteen job, which she still
holds.

(2) An introduction was given to the L.C.C. Welfare Officer,
who placed her in an emergency hostel, where she was able
to stay for six months. She has now moved to another hostel
of a more permanent character.

(3) The question of her husband's assets was then taken up
with Lloyds and National Provincial Foreign Bank. This
matter is still not solved; it has been necessary to see Mrs. D.
a number of times in order to complete forms and answer
enquiries, to ascertain names of French references, and to trace
relatives of her late husband, so that the French legal position
may be determined and her claim to the money at the bank
established.

Meanwhile, Mrs. D. continues at her work and is reasonably
comfortable. Advice about insurance, and the selection of a
panel doctor, etc., has been given; and it was possible to arrange
a week's holiday for her last autumn through the women's
holiday fund, which she greatly appreciated.

Deserted Wife.—Mrs. M. came to the bureau saying that her
daughter had seen an advertisement for the next-of-kin of a
William M. whom she took to be her husband who had left
her and her three children twenty-seven years ago for no
apparent reason. She had never heard of him since. At first
she could not establish her claim to be the lawful wife as another
Mrs. M. was said to be living; also she herself could not believe
that after their early happy married life her husband could
leave her for another woman. C.A.B. took the matter up with
the Treasury and eventually the claim was established and
Mrs. M. was left to tackle the other woman who was living in
Surrey. The local C.A.B. visited her one evening and found
that the woman had lived very happily with Mr. M. for
twenty-seven years. He had always been reticent about his

past, but he had made it clear that he could not marry her as he was not free to do so. He had been a full-time warden during the war and had had very good health but died suddenly after a heart attack. She realized she had no claim to the money and bore no resentment. C.A.B. helped Mrs. M. to get her husband's balance of pay and post-war credit.

Later she called in for advice about her widow's pension, having no record of her husband's insurance. The local council, for whom he had worked, could not produce this evidence, but fortunately they had a note that Mr. M. had taken out an insurance policy with the Pearl, so it seemed likely that he might have been insured with that society for National Health Insurance purposes. This proved to be the case and his membership number was obtained. The application for the widow's pension could then go forward and four months from her call for advice, Mrs. M.'s pension came through with arrears and she came in to share the good news with C.A.B.

Birth Certificate.—A young man of twenty-three was sent to us by the Welfare Officer of a Government department for help in obtaining a birth certificate without which it was difficult to obtain permanent employment in the Civil Service or to procure a passport. A few years previously he had discovered that he was illegitimate and that the foster parents with whom he had been left at the age of two had given their name to him but had not adopted him legally. The young man knew his mother's name, but Somerset House had not been able to find record of his birth and so furnish a birth certificate, and the Legal Aid Department of the Army had told him that nothing further could be done. The only clue he had was a baptismal certificate from a Holborn church giving the name of his parents and the date of birth and the christian name as Anthony. Somerset House told us that they could probably accept this certificate as evidence of date of birth and of parents' names but they must have proof of place of birth.

The Bureau wrote to the moral welfare agencies in Holborn and to all the hospitals in Holborn and St. Pancras asking them to look up their records to see if they could produce the evidence we needed. All replied that there was no trace, but one L.C.C. hospital offered to send the letter to County Hall. From there we received the news that they had records from the old St. Pancras Workhouse showing that the child had been born in the Thavies Inn Infirmary, which is now closed. The birth had been registered at Somerset House but the child's name was James Anthony and not Anthony.

With this information the birth certificate was easily obtained, and the applicant was referred to a lawyer for advice about change of name.

Tubercular Man and Housing.—Mr. R.—ex-service, invalided out with tuberculosis—had been advised to leave London. He owned cottage in Wales, but it was let; tenant refused to go. C.A.B. referred applicant to Free Legal Advice Centre who advised that a local solicitor would be necessary. C.A.B. got in touch with Tuberculosis Care Committee Worker and asked her if statement could be provided by dispensary or tuberculosis officer to support case. This was done. Applicant then went to Wales and saw solicitor who thought if he got employment locally he would get possession of cottage. Applicant reported he had been offered employment in the district. In six weeks case was heard and applicant was successful.

Dishoused Widow. Mrs. C. was a widow of 72, suffering from heart trouble and very frail, who came to the bureau in July, 1946, in urgent need of alternative accommodation. She had lived for forty years in the same house, in a superior district of Stepney, when her home was destroyed by bombing in 1940. Since then, she had occupied two rooms as a sub-tenant in the same locality. Now her landlord was anxious to get rid of her and use her rooms for his growing family and had applied to Bow County Court for possession. Mrs. C. was quite incapable of conducting her own case, apart from the fact that her statements would have been inaudible and that she was extremely deaf.

Action taken: (1) The C.A.B. arranged for legal representation in court. The landlord was granted possession, but the court allowed stay of execution for two months in order that the C.A.B. might assist Mrs. C. to find other rooms.

(2) The C.A.B. approached Stepney Rehousing Department who, after some discussion, finally agreed to rehouse in requisitioned property; a medical certificate was obtained which enabled them to offer ground-floor rooms. Eventually, two offers were made, one in a distant part of the Borough, the other in Bow but of a very different standard from that of her old home. Visits to the properties with Mrs. C., and renewed negotiations with the rehousing department, at last reconciled her to the change, and she accepted the second offer.

(3) At the request of the C.A.B., the local Pacifist Service Unit undertook to clean the rooms and get them ready for the removal.

(4) After removal, countless other problems, such as fresh registration, permits for linoleum and curtains and difficulty in getting fuel, were dealt with by the C.A.B.

All this necessitated sustained contact with the client, over a period of several months, and demanded considerable effort on the part of the bureau, both to bring her position to the notice of the authorities concerned and also to help Mrs. C. to meet a very distressing situation and to adjust herself to its consequences.

Social Insurance and Income Tax.—This citizen looks many years older than her age and is easily agitated. She is an old friend of the C.A.B. having brought a variety of problems in the last six months. First she lost her post office savings book and her identity card and needed help to get them replaced. Her frequent changes of address did not make this any easier. Then she asked C.A.B. to contact an employer by telephone, but this employment fell through. She was accustomed to domestic work in hotels.

Later the police needed her as a witness in connection with the lost post office savings book and she was afraid to give her employer's address an interview was arranged with the police by C.A.B.

The Income Tax authorities required a list of places where she had been working for the last year and this was patiently obtained from her somewhat fragmentary memory.

A change of job brought her back to C.A.B. to ask if we would take care of her £10 savings as she did not like to carry it about with her. In a fortnight a post in the Isle of Wight was found and the £10 reclaimed from C.A.B. This post, however, fell through owing to her age and she now had a misunderstanding with the Employment Exchange so that she was suspended from benefit. C.A.B. took the opportunity to point out that it was important for her to keep her insurance cards stamped during the next three years in order to get her contributory Old Age Pension. As she was uncertain of her age she applied to Dublin for her birth certificate and found that she was already 61. Hurriedly she sent the certificate back and asked the authorities to alter it so that her age would show as 60. The next day she appeared panic-stricken at C.A.B. lest she should get into trouble and she was advised to cancel the last letter explaining that she was upset and suffering from nerves. She did indeed suffer with her health and C.A.B. advised her to see her doctor—who prescribed tablets for her. A few days later she returned, much calmer, with the certificate and application form for contributory Old Age Pension. This was filled up and sent to the Ministry of National Insurance with a covering letter from C.A.B. explaining why she had not applied earlier and asking if arrears could be considered.

Matrimonial.—A young wife called in great distress to ask if she could divorce her husband, who, a week after their marriage, had returned to his job in Rhodesia and had stopped writing or sending money. The C.A.B. wrote to a probation officer in Rhodesia, who was asked to see the man. He reported that he found that misunderstandings had arisen and because of the distance the breach had widened; and statements had been made in writing that rankled in a way that would not have occurred had they been made in conversation. The husband promised to write to the wife; and the C.A.B. is hoping that the couple will make things up.

Trade.—An American called to say that he had come to England to buy steel water-pipes of a certain size. Could we tell him where to go? The Ministry of Supply were able to give us the name of the only possible firm and we were asked to phone and make an appointment as the American could not make "head or tail" of the dialling system.

War Pension.—Mrs. T. called on us after her son, who had got a commission, had been killed in the Middle East. He had been her main support and she needed assistance in settling up his affairs, applying for a pension, etc. She is a working woman, not well educated, and she could not deal with these matters herself. We got in touch with the Officers' Families Fund, which was willing to give her a small allowance temporarily. Then followed a spate of correspondence with the War Office and Ministry of Pensions; and finally a War Pension was granted. Even more correspondence ensued with the Effects Board of the War Office and Messrs. Cox & Kings about the dead officer's emoluments, personal effects, gratuities, etc. We helped her over obtaining Letters of Administration and exemption from Estate Duty. It took over a year to get all these matters settled, but the result was satisfactory.

Mrs. T. continues to count on our help when she needs it over filling up forms connected with her War Pension or Old Age Pension.

V. PROBLEMS ROOTED IN BAD HOUSING

Case. Man whose wife is returning from convalescence to-day with baby. No accommodation. Self sharing a room with four men. Housing Department unable to help. Relieving Officer can only offer Institution, which is not acceptable. Becoming too worried to work. Seven years in Services, plus five years previous residence in borough. Originally from Northern Ireland. Relatives in locality already over-crowded.

Reply. Under circumstances, Institution would be better for wife than being in street. Made telephone call for any possible recommendations and obtained three addresses. Client to advise us of result following day.

Case. Woman becoming desperate over housing situation. Fears separation will be inevitable. Self, husband, and baby have only enough room for single mattress on floor. No room for bedstead. Baby recently very ill, measles and pneumonia, now again ill with digestive trouble. Husband alternate weeks night work, and unable to rest. Enquiries at housing department where they have registered, received reply that nothing can be done, and no investigation has been made. Both are Acton residents. Recently gave up flat to go to aged parents requiring care in north, but had to return as no work for the husband was available. Could have had old flat back if had written one week earlier, but flat now requisitioned and occupied.

Reply. Telephoned housing department and confirmed that flat had been requisitioned. Informed that a very simply-worded application form had been lodged a month earlier, and no details had been given. C.A.B. outlined case to department and sent client to see them.

Case. Man married prior to 1939, but owing to nature of profession has always been provided with furnished house. Now has to furnish for self. Requires furnishing units. No children.

Reply.   Outside all priority classes, but advised to make "Special Circumstances" claim.

Case.   Woman bought house two years ago with tenant (family of three) in small upper flat. Later allowed tenant to accommodate temporarily a friend in distress. He has now been there twelve months and tenant, annoyed at recent rates increase, says she intends taking in more lodgers, and that landlady can do nothing about it. Landlady had had increases properly assessed by Rents Department.

Reply.   Tenant has no right to take in lodgers in this way. Is already over-crowded. If persist, owner can apply to court, or see solicitor.

Case.   Client had taken in sister, and her husband and child, as members of the family, asking no rent, while they found business premises with living accommodation. Landlady objects and says they must leave. Can this be forced? In addition, client has complaint over water supply being cut owing to damage to pipes, and landlady says they must see to this themselves. Electricity wiring unsafe as further result of the broken water pipes. In view of all this, can they be expected to pay the recent increase in rent due to rates increase?

Reply.   Landlady has right to object to permanent extension of family in this way, but suggest a friendly discussion. If landlady refuses to attend to repairs, matter should be referred to sanitary department. Increase of rent owing to rates increase is correct, but amount can be checked.

APPENDIX D—THE EVIDENCE FOR VOLUNTARY ACTION

(Contents of Supplementary Volume)

INDEX

*